*To:*

*From:*

*Date:*

# ONE YEAR® WITH JESUS

### THE LIVING BIBLE

Selected and Edited by

James C. Galvin, Ed.D.

Linda Chaffee Taylor

David R. Veerman, M.Div.

 Tyndale House Publishers, Inc.
Wheaton, Illinois

---

**Library of Congress Cataloging-in-Publication Data**

One year with Jesus : the Living Bible / selected and edited by James
C. Galvin, Linda Chaffee Taylor, David R. Veerman.
    p.    cm.
  ISBN 0-8423-4597-3 (pbk.)
  1. Jesus Christ—Biography—Sources, Biblical. 2. Jesus Christ—
Biography—Meditations. 3. Bible N.T. Gospels—Meditations.
4. Bible N.T. Gospels—Harmonies, English. 5. Devotional
calendars. I. Galvin, James C. II. Taylor, Linda Chaffee, date–.
III. Veerman, David R. IV. Bible. N.T. Gospels. English. New
International. 1995.
BT299..054  1995
232.9'01—dc20                  95-8010

---

Printed in the United States of America

00  99
7

# Introduction

*One Year with Jesus* has been prepared especially for those who want to learn more about Jesus and grow closer to him through the year. Each day contains a selection from the four Gospels, a Life Application note, and an information note.

The readings for each day are arranged according to the Harmony of the Gospels found in the back of this book. A harmony is a useful tool for studying the life of Christ. It simply arranges the events in the four Gospels in chronological order and makes it easier for you to compare parallel accounts. Each day's reading includes a number that guides you to the correct location in the harmony. Referring to the harmony helps you see what happened before and after any particular event. You can deepen your study by looking up any parallel passages noted for a particular reading. The Life Application notes provide insight and encouragement to take action. The information notes provide interesting background and helpful explanations.

Although these daily readings begin January 1, you can easily begin with today's date. Alternatively, you can use a bookmark to begin on the first reading no matter what date you begin. Either way, you will finish in one year and meet your goal of learning more about Jesus and growing closer to him.

## Luke's purpose in writing

### LUKE 1:1-4 *(Harmony 1)*

*D*ear friend who loves God: Several biographies of Christ have already been written using as their source material the reports circulating among us from the early disciples and other eyewitnesses. However, it occurred to me that it would be well to recheck all these accounts from first to last and after thorough investigation to pass this summary on to you, to reassure you of the truth of all you were taught.

*The Gospel of Luke tells Jesus' story from Luke's unique perspective as a Gentile, a physician, and the first historian of the early church. Though not an eyewitness of Jesus' ministry, Luke nevertheless was concerned that eyewitness accounts be preserved accurately.*

**GOD'S TRUTH**

As a medical doctor Luke knew the importance of being thorough. He used his skills in observation and analysis to thoroughly investigate the stories about Jesus. His diagnosis? The gospel of Jesus Christ is true! You can read the accounts of Jesus' life with confidence that they are true and reliable. Because the gospel is founded on historical truth, our spiritual growth must involve careful, disciplined, and thorough investigation of the truth of God's Word so that we can understand how God has acted in history. Christianity doesn't say, "Close your eyes and believe," but rather, "Check it out for yourself." The Bible encourages you to investigate its claims thoroughly (John 1:46; 21:24; Acts 17:11-12) because your conclusion about Jesus is a life-and-death matter. Check out the evidence.

## God became a human being

### JOHN 1:1-5 *(Harmony 2a)*

*B*efore anything else existed, there was Christ, with God. He has always been alive and is himself God. He created everything there is—nothing exists that he didn't make.

Eternal life is in him, and this life gives light to all mankind. His life is the light that shines through the darkness—and the darkness can never extinguish it.

*Christ created the world, but the people he created didn't recognize him (1:10). Even the Jews rejected him although they had been chosen by God to prepare the rest of the world for the Messiah (1:11) and although the entire Old Testament pointed to his coming.*

**READ AND BELIEVE**

What Jesus taught and what he did are tied inseparably to who he is. John shows Jesus as fully human and fully God. Although Jesus took upon himself full humanity and lived as a man, he never ceased to be the eternal God who has always existed, the Creator and Sustainer of all things, and the source of eternal life. This is the truth about Jesus and the foundation of all truth. If we cannot or do not believe this basic truth, we will not have enough faith to trust our eternal destiny to him. That is why John wrote this Gospel—to build faith and confidence in Jesus Christ so that we may believe that he truly was and is the Son of God (20:30-31). You can trust John, an eyewitness to what Jesus said and did. You can believe in Christ, God's Son.

*January 3*

## God became a human being

*JOHN 1:6-13 (Harmony 2b)*

God sent John the Baptist as a witness to the fact that Jesus Christ is the true Light. John himself was not the Light; he was only a witness to identify it. Later on, the one who is the true Light arrived to shine on everyone coming into the world. But although he made the world, the world didn't recognize him when he came. Even in his own land and among his own people, the Jews, he was not accepted. Only a few would welcome and receive him. But to all who received him, he gave the right to become children of God. All they needed to do was to trust him to save them. All those who believe this are reborn!—not a physical rebirth resulting from human passion or plan—but from the will of God.

*John wrote to believers everywhere, both Jews and non-Jews (Gentiles). As one of Jesus' twelve disciples, John was an eyewitness to Jesus' ministry. His book is not a biography (like the book of Luke); it is a thematic presentation of Jesus' life.*

All who welcome Jesus Christ as Lord of their lives are reborn spiritually, receiving new life from God. Through faith in Christ, this new birth changes us from the inside out—rearranging our attitudes, desires, and motives. Being born makes you physically alive and places you in your parents' family (1:13). Being born of God makes you spiritually alive and puts you in God's family (1:12). Have you asked Christ to make you a new person? This fresh start in life is available to all who believe in Christ.

*January 4*

## God became a human being

### *JOHN 1:14-18 (Harmony 2c)*

And Christ became a human being and lived here on earth among us and was full of loving forgiveness and truth. And some of us have seen his glory—the glory of the only Son of the heavenly Father!

John pointed him out to the people, telling the crowds, "This is the one I was talking about when I said, 'Someone is coming who is greater by far than I am—for he existed long before I did!'" We have all benefited from the rich blessings he brought to us—blessing upon blessing heaped upon us! For Moses gave us only the Law with its rigid demands and merciless justice, while Jesus Christ brought us loving forgiveness as well. No one has ever actually seen God, but, of course, his only Son has, for he is the companion of the Father and has told us all about him.

*When Christ was conceived and born, God became a man. He was not part man and part God; he was completely human and completely divine. Christ is the perfect expression of God in human form. The two most common errors people make about Jesus are to minimize his humanity or to minimize his divinity. Jesus is both God and man.*

### GOD AND MAN

When "Christ became a human being and lived here on earth among us," he became (1) *the perfect teacher*—in Jesus' life we see how God thinks and therefore how we should think (Philippians 2:5-11); (2) *the perfect example*—as a model of what we are to become, he shows us how to live and gives us the power to live that way (1 Peter 2:21); (3) *the perfect sacrifice*—Jesus came as a sacrifice for all sins, and his death satisfied God's requirements for the removal of sin (Colossians 1:15-23). Keep your focus on Christ.

# The ancestors of Jesus

*LUKE 3:23-38 (also in MATTHEW 1:1-17) (Harmony 3)*
Jesus was about thirty years old when he began his public ministry.

Jesus was known as the son of Joseph. Joseph's father was Heli; Heli's father was Matthat; Matthat's father was Levi; Levi's father was Melchi; Melchi's father was Jannai; Jannai's father was Joseph; Joseph's father was Mattathias; Mattathias's father was Amos; Amos's father was Nahum; Nahum's father was Esli; Esli's father was Naggai; Naggai's father was Maath; Maath's father was Mattathias; Mattathias's father was Semein; Semein's father was Josech; Josech's father was Joda; Joda's father was Joanan; Joanan's father was Rhesa; Rhesa's father was Zerubbabel; Zerubbabel's father was Shealtiel; Shealtiel's father was Neri; Neri's father was Melchi; Melchi's father was Addi; Addi's father was Cosam; Cosam's father was Elmadam; Elmadam's father was Er; Er's father was Joshua; Joshua's father was Eliezer; Eliezer's father was Jorim; Jorim's father was Matthat; Matthat's father was Levi; Levi's father was Simeon; Simeon's father was Judah; Judah's father was Joseph; Joseph's father was Jonam; Jonam's father was Eliakim; Eliakim's father was Melea; Melea's father was Menna; Menna's father was Mattatha; Mattatha's father was Nathan; Nathan's father was David; David's father was Jesse; Jesse's father was Obed; Obed's father was Boaz; Boaz's father was Salmon; Salmon's father was Nahshon; Nahshon's father was Amminadab; Amminadab's father was Admin; Admin's father was Arni; Arni's father was Hezron; Hezron's father was Perez; Perez's father was Judah; Judah's father was Jacob; Jacob's father was Isaac; Isaac's father was Abraham; Abraham's father was Terah; Terah's father was Nahor; Nahor's father was Serug; Serug's father was Reu; Reu's father was Peleg; Peleg's father was Eber; Eber's father was Shelah; Shelah's father was Cainan; Cainan's father was Arphaxad; Arphaxad's father was Shem; Shem's father was Noah; Noah's father was Lamech; Lamech's father was Methuselah; Methuselah's father was Enoch; Enoch's father was Jared; Jared's father was Mahalaleel; Mahalaleel's father was Cainan; Cainan's father was Enos; Enos's father was Seth; Seth's father was Adam; Adam's father was God.

*Matthew's genealogy goes back to Abraham and shows that Jesus was related to all Jews. Luke's genealogy goes back to Adam, showing that Jesus is related to all human beings. This is consistent with Luke's picture of Jesus as the Savior of the whole world.*

## GOD'S TIMING

Imagine the Savior of the world working in a small-town carpenter's shop until he was thirty years old! It seems incredible that Jesus would have been content to remain in Nazareth all that time, but he patiently trusted the Father's timing for his life and ministry. Priests began their ministry at thirty (Numbers 4:3). Joseph began serving the king of Egypt at thirty (Genesis 41:46), and David was thirty years old when he began to reign over Judah (2 Samuel 5:4). Age thirty, then, was a good time to begin an important task in the Jewish culture. Like Jesus, we need to resist the temptation to jump ahead before receiving the Spirit's direction. Are you waiting and wondering what your next step should be? Don't jump ahead—trust God's timing.

# January 6

## An angel promises the birth of John to Zacharias

### LUKE 1:5-20 *(Harmony 4a)*

*M*y story begins with a Jewish priest, Zacharias, who lived when Herod was king of Judea. Zacharias was a member of the Abijah division of the Temple service corps. (His wife, Elizabeth, was, like himself, a member of the priest tribe of the Jews, a descendant of Aaron.) Zacharias and Elizabeth were godly folk, careful to obey all of God's laws in spirit as well as in letter. But they had no children, for Elizabeth was barren; and now they were both very old.

One day as Zacharias was going about his work in the Temple—for his division was on duty that week—the honor fell to him by lot to enter the inner sanctuary and burn incense before the Lord. Meanwhile, a great crowd stood outside in the Temple court, praying as they always did during that part of the service when the incense was being burned.

Zacharias was in the sanctuary when suddenly an angel appeared, standing to the right of the altar of incense! Zacharias was startled and terrified.

*A Jewish priest was a minister of God who worked at the Temple. The priests were divided into twenty-four separate groups of about one thousand men each, according to David's directions (as described in 1 Chronicles 24:3-19). Zacharias was a member of the Abijah division, on duty this particular week. Each morning a priest was to enter the Holy Place in the Temple and burn incense. Lots were cast to decide who would enter the sacred room. One day the lot fell to Zacharias.*

But the angel said, "Don't be afraid, Zacharias! For I have come to tell you that God has heard your prayer, and your wife, Elizabeth, will bear you a son! And you are to name him John. You will both have great joy and gladness at his birth, and many will rejoice with you. For he will be one of the Lord's great men. He must never touch wine or hard liquor—and he will be filled with the Holy Spirit, even from before his birth! And he will persuade many a Jew to turn to the Lord his God. He will be a man of rugged spirit and power like Elijah, the prophet of old; and he will precede the coming of the Messiah, preparing the people for his arrival. He will soften adult hearts to become like little children's, and will change disobedient minds to the wisdom of faith."

Zacharias said to the angel, "But this is impossible! I'm an old man now, and my wife is also well along in years."

Then the angel said, "I am Gabriel! I stand in the very presence of God. It was he who sent me to you with this good news! And now, because you haven't believed me, you are to be stricken silent, unable to speak until the child is born. For my words will certainly come true at the proper time."

### LET GOD DO THE IMPOSSIBLE

While Zacharias was burning incense on the altar, he was also praying, perhaps for a son or for the coming of the Messiah. In either case, God answered his prayer. He would soon have a son, who would prepare the way for the Messiah. God answers prayer in his own way and in his own time. He worked in an "impossible" situation—Zacharias's wife was barren—to bring about the fulfillment of all the prophecies concerning the Messiah. If you want to have your prayers answered, you must be open to what God can do in impossible situations. And you must wait for God to work in his way, in his time.

*January 7*

## An angel promises the birth of John to Zacharias

### LUKE 1:21-25 (Harmony 4b)

Meanwhile the crowds outside were waiting for Zacharias to appear and wondered why he was taking so long. When he finally came out, he couldn't speak to them, and they realized from his gestures that he must have seen a vision in the Temple. He stayed on at the Temple for the remaining days of his

*The people were waiting outside for Zacharias to come out and pronounce the customary blessing upon them as found in Numbers 6:24-26.*

Temple duties and then returned home. Soon afterwards Elizabeth his wife became pregnant and went into seclusion for five months.

"How kind the Lord is," she exclaimed, "to take away my disgrace of having no children!"

### FAITHFULNESS

Zacharias and Elizabeth were faithful people, yet they were suffering. At that time some Jews did not believe in a bodily resurrection, so their hope of immortality rested on their children. In addition, children would care for their elderly parents, and they added to the family's financial security and social status. Children were considered a blessing, and childlessness was seen as a curse. Zacharias and Elizabeth had been childless for many years, and at this time they were too old to expect any change in their situation. They felt humiliated and hopeless. But God was waiting for the right time to encourage them and take away their disgrace. If you are facing difficult times, remain faithful to God. One day, in this world or in the world to come, God will take away your pain and replace it with his glory and peace!

## *January 8*

## An angel promises the birth of Jesus to Mary

### *LUKE 1:26-33 (Harmony 5a)*

he following month God sent the angel Gabriel to Nazareth, a village in Galilee, to a virgin, Mary, engaged to be married to a man named Joseph, a descendant of King David.

Gabriel appeared to her and said, "Congratulations, favored lady! The Lord is with you!"

Confused and disturbed, Mary tried to think what the angel could mean.

"Don't be frightened, Mary," the angel told her, "for God has decided to wonderfully bless you! Very soon now, you will become pregnant and have a baby boy, and you are to name him 'Jesus.' He shall be very great and shall be called the Son of God. And the Lord God shall give him the throne of his ancestor David. And he shall reign over Israel forever; his Kingdom shall never end!"

*Nazareth, Joseph's and Mary's hometown, was a long way from Jerusalem, the center of Jewish life and worship. Located on a major trade route, Nazareth was frequently visited by Gentile merchants and Roman soldiers. Jesus was born in Bethlehem but grew up in Nazareth. Nevertheless, the people of Nazareth would reject him as the Messiah (Luke 4:22-30).*

Mary was young, poor, female—all characteristics that, to the people of her day, would make her seem unusable by God for any major task. But God chose Mary for one of the most important acts of obedience he has ever demanded of anyone. You may feel that your ability, experience, or education make you an unlikely candidate for God's service. Don't limit God's choices. He can use you if you trust him.

## January 9

# An angel promises the birth of Jesus to Mary

### LUKE 1:34-38 (Harmony 5b)

*M*ary asked the angel, "But how can I have a baby? I am a virgin."

The angel replied, "The Holy Spirit shall come upon you, and the power of God shall overshadow you; so the baby born to you will be utterly holy—the Son of God. Furthermore, six months ago your Aunt Elizabeth—'the barren one,' they called her—became pregnant in her old age! For every promise from God shall surely come true."

Mary said, "I am the Lord's servant, and I am willing to do whatever he wants. May everything you said come true." And then the angel disappeared.

*Jesus was born without the sin that entered the world through Adam. He was born holy, just as Adam was created sinless. In contrast to Adam, who disobeyed God, Jesus obeyed God and was thus able to face sin's consequences in our place and make us acceptable to God (Romans 5:14-19).*

#### WILLING OBEDIENCE

A young unmarried girl who became pregnant risked disaster. Unless the father of the child agreed to marry her, she would probably remain unmarried for life. If her own father rejected her, she could be forced into begging or prostitution in order to earn her living. Mary, with her story about being made pregnant by the Holy Spirit, also risked being considered crazy. Still Mary said, despite the possible risks, "May everything you said come true." When Mary made that statement, she didn't know about the tremendous opportunity she would have. She only knew that God was asking her to serve him, and she willingly obeyed. Don't wait to see the bottom line before offering your life to God. Offer yourself willingly, even when the outcome seems difficult.

## Mary visits Elizabeth

*LUKE 1:39-45 (Harmony 6a)*

A few days later Mary hurried to the highlands of Judea to the town where Zacharias lived, to visit Elizabeth.

At the sound of Mary's greeting, Elizabeth's child leaped within her and she was filled with the Holy Spirit.

She gave a glad cry and exclaimed to Mary, "You are favored by God above all other women, and your child is destined for God's mightiest praise. What an honor this is, that the mother of my Lord should visit me! When you came in and greeted me, the instant I heard your voice, my baby moved in me for joy! You believed that God would do what he said; that is why he has given you this wonderful blessing."

*Apparently the Holy Spirit told Elizabeth that Mary's child was the Messiah because Elizabeth called her young relative "the mother of my Lord" as she greeted her. Elizabeth's greeting must have strengthened Mary's faith. Mary's pregnancy may have seemed impossible, but her wise relative believed in the Lord's faithfulness and rejoiced in Mary's blessed condition.*

**GOD DELIVERS**

When told he would have a son, Zacharias had doubted the angel's word. From his human perspective, his doubt had been understandable—but with God, anything is possible. Although Zacharias and Elizabeth seemed long past the age of childbearing, God gave them a child! It is easy to doubt or misunderstand what God wants to do in our life. Even God's people sometimes make the mistake of trusting their intellect or experience rather than God. When tempted to think that one of God's promises is impossible, remember his work throughout history. God's power is not confined by narrow perspective or bound by human limitations. Trust him completely.

## Mary visits Elizabeth

### *LUKE 1:46-56 (Harmony 6b)*

Mary responded, "Oh, how I praise the Lord. How I rejoice in God my Savior! For he took notice of his lowly servant girl, and now generation after generation forever shall call me blest of God. For he, the mighty Holy One, has done great things to me. His mercy goes on from generation to generation, to all who reverence him.

"How powerful is his mighty arm! How he scatters the proud and haughty ones! He has torn princes from their thrones and exalted the lowly. He has satisfied the hungry hearts and sent the rich away with empty hands. And how he has helped his servant Israel! He has not forgotten his promise to be merciful. For he promised our fathers—Abraham and his children—to be merciful to them forever."

*This song is often called the Magnificat, the first word in the Latin translation of this passage. Mary's song has often been used as the basis for choral music and hymns. Like Hannah, the mother of Samuel (1 Samuel 2:1-10), Mary praised God in song for what he was going to do for the world through her.*

Mary stayed with Elizabeth about three months and then went back to her own home.

#### GOD'S GOOD GIFTS

When Mary said, "Now generation after generation forever shall call me blest of God," was she being proud? No, she was recognizing and accepting the gift God had given her. If Mary had denied her incredible position, she would have been throwing God's blessing back at him. Pride is refusing to accept God's gifts or taking credit for what God has done; humility is accepting the gifts and using them to praise and serve God. Don't deny, belittle, or ignore your gifts. Thank God for them and use them to his glory.

## John the Baptist is born

### *LUKE 1:57-66* *(Harmony 7a)*

*B*y now Elizabeth's waiting was over, for the time had come for the baby to be born—and it was a boy. The word spread quickly to her neighbors and relatives of how kind the Lord had been to her, and everyone rejoiced.

When the baby was eight days old, all the relatives and friends came for the circumcision ceremony. They all assumed the baby's name would be Zacharias, after his father.

But Elizabeth said, "No! He must be named John!"

"What?" they exclaimed. "There is no one in all your family by that name." So they asked the baby's father, talking to him by gestures.

*Family lines and family names were important to the Jews. The people naturally assumed that the child would receive Zacharias's name, or at least a family name. Thus they were surprised that both Elizabeth and Zacharias wanted to name the boy John, as the angel had told them to do (see Luke 1:13).*

He motioned for a piece of paper and to everyone's surprise wrote, "His name is *John!*" Instantly Zacharias could speak again, and he began praising God.

Wonder fell upon the whole neighborhood, and the news of what had happened spread through the Judean hills. And everyone who heard about it thought long thoughts and asked, "I wonder what this child will turn out to be? For the hand of the Lord is surely upon him in some special way."

#### GOD'S FAMILY

The circumcision ceremony was an important event in the family of a Jewish baby boy. God commanded circumcision when he was beginning to form his holy nation (Genesis 17:4-14), and he reaffirmed it through Moses (Leviticus 12:1-3). This ceremony was a time of joy when friends and family members celebrated the baby's becoming part of God's covenant nation. Today there is also great joy when a baby is born, and some churches have special ceremonies to commemorate the blessed event. You were born into a human family, but to become a part of God's family, you must accept Jesus as your Savior. Are you a part of God's family?

## John the Baptist is born

*LUKE 1:67-80 (Harmony 7b)*

hen his father, Zacharias, was filled with the Holy Spirit and gave this prophecy:

"Praise the Lord, the God of Israel, for he has come to visit his people and has redeemed them. He is sending us a Mighty Savior from the royal line of his servant David, just as he promised through his holy prophets long ago—someone to save us from our enemies, from all who hate us.

"He has been merciful to our ancestors, yes, to Abraham himself, by remembering his sacred promise to him, and by granting us the privilege of serving God fearlessly, freed from our enemies, and by making us holy and acceptable, ready to stand in his presence forever.

"And you, my little son, shall be called the prophet of the glorious God, for you will prepare the way for the Messiah. You will tell his people how to find salvation through forgiveness of their sins. All this will be because the mercy of our God is very tender, and heaven's dawn is about to break upon us, to give light to those who sit in darkness and death's shadow, and to guide us to the path of peace."

*Zacharias prophesied the coming of a Savior who would redeem his people, and he predicted that his son, John, would prepare the Messiah's way. All the Old Testament prophecies were coming true. The Jews were eagerly awaiting the Messiah, but they thought he would come to save them from the powerful Roman Empire. They were ready for a military Savior, but not for a peaceful Messiah who would conquer sin.*

The little boy greatly loved God, and when he grew up he lived out in the lonely wilderness until he began his public ministry to Israel.

### GOD'S POWER AND FAITHFUL PEOPLE

Zacharias had just recalled hundreds of years of God's sovereign work in history, beginning with Abraham and going on into eternity. Then, in tender contrast, he personalized the story. His son had been chosen for a key role in the drama of the ages. Although God has unlimited power, he chooses to work through frail humans who begin as helpless babies. Don't minimize what God can do through those who are faithful to him. You may not feel as though you can do much for God, but all he requires is faith and a willing spirit. Let God do his work in and through you!

## An angel appears to Joseph

### MATTHEW 1:18-19 *(Harmony 8a)*

 hese are the facts concerning the birth of Jesus Christ: His mother, Mary, was engaged to be married to Joseph. But while she was still a virgin she became pregnant by the Holy Spirit. Then Joseph, her fiancé, being a man of stern principle, decided to break the engagement but to do it quietly, as he didn't want to publicly disgrace her.

**BORN OF A VIRGIN**

Why is the Virgin Birth important to the Christian faith? Jesus Christ, God's Son, had to be free from the sinful nature passed on to all other human beings by Adam. Because Jesus was born of a woman, he was a human being; but as the Son of God, Jesus was born without any trace of human sin. Jesus is both fully human and fully divine.

Because Jesus lived as a man, we know that he fully understands our experiences and struggles (Hebrews 4:15-16). Because he is God, he has the power and authority to deliver us from sin (Colossians 2:13-15). We can tell Jesus all our thoughts, feelings, and needs. He has been where we are now, and he has the ability to help.

*An engaged couple in our culture may call off a wedding at any time. But for the Jews, engagement was more permanent and could be broken only through death or divorce (even though sexual relations were not yet permitted). Because Mary and Joseph were engaged, Mary's apparent unfaithfulness carried a severe social stigma. According to Jewish civil law, Joseph had a right to divorce her, and the Jewish authorities could have had her stoned to death (Deuteronomy 22:23-24).*

## An angel appears to Joseph

### MATTHEW 1:20-25 *(Harmony 8b)*

As he lay awake considering this, he fell into a dream, and saw an angel standing beside him. "Joseph, son of David," the angel said, "don't hesitate to take Mary as your wife! For the child within her has been conceived by the Holy Spirit. And she will have a Son, and you shall name him Jesus (meaning 'Savior'), for he will save his people from their sins. This will fulfill God's message through his prophets—

*'Listen! The virgin shall conceive a child!* She shall give birth to a Son, and he shall be called "Emmanuel" (meaning "God is with us").' "

When Joseph awoke, he did as the angel commanded and brought Mary home to be his wife, but she remained a virgin until her Son was born; and Joseph named him "Jesus."

*The angel declared to Joseph that Mary's child was conceived by the Holy Spirit and would be a son. This reveals an important truth about Jesus—he is both God and human. The infinite, unlimited God took on the limitations of humanity so he could live and die for the salvation of all who would believe in him.*

### A CHANGE OF PLANS

Perhaps Joseph thought he had only two options: divorce Mary quietly, or have her stoned. But God had a third option—marry her. In view of the circumstances, this had not occurred to Joseph. But God often shows us that there are more options available than we think. Joseph changed his plans quickly after learning that Mary had not been unfaithful to him. He obeyed God and proceeded with the marriage plans. Although others may have disapproved of his decision, Joseph went ahead with what he knew was right. Sometimes we avoid doing what is right because of what others might think. Like Joseph, we must choose to obey God rather than seek the approval of others.

*January 16*

## Jesus is born in Bethlehem

### LUKE 2:1-5 *(Harmony 9a)*

About this time Caesar Augustus, the Roman emperor, decreed that a census should be taken throughout the nation. (This census was taken when Quirinius was governor of Syria.)

Everyone was required to return to his ancestral home for this registration. And because Joseph was a member of the royal line, he had to go to Bethlehem in Judea, King David's ancient home—journeying there from the Galilean village of Nazareth. He took with him Mary, his fiancée, who was obviously pregnant by this time.

*Augustus's decree went out in God's perfect timing and according to God's perfect plan to bring his Son into the world. God controls all history. By the decree of Emperor Augustus, Jesus was born in the very town prophesied for his birth (Micah 5:2), even though his parents did not live there.*

**GOD'S PLAN**

The government forced Joseph to make a long trip just to pay his taxes. His fiancée, who had to go with him, was about to have a baby. Joseph and Mary were both descendants of David. (The Old Testament is filled with prophecies that the Messiah would be born in David's royal line [see, for example, Isaiah 11:1; Jeremiah 33:15; Ezekiel 37:24; Hosea 3:5]). But when they arrived in Bethlehem, they couldn't even find a place to stay. When we do God's will, we are not guaranteed a comfortable life. But we are promised that everything, even our discomfort, has meaning in God's plan.

*January 17*

## Jesus is born in Bethlehem

*LUKE 2:6-7 (Harmony 9b)*

*A*nd while they were there, the time came for her baby to be born; and she gave birth to her first child, a son. She wrapped him in a blanket and laid him in a manger, because there was no room for them in the village inn.

**MORE THAN A BABY**

This mention of the manger is the basis for the traditional belief that Jesus was born in a stable. Stables were often caves with feeding troughs (mangers) carved into the rock walls. Although our first picture of Jesus is as a baby in a manger, it must not be our last. The Christ-child in the manger has been made into a beautiful Christmas scene, but we cannot leave him there. This tiny, helpless baby lived an amazing life, died for us, rose from the dead, ascended to heaven, and will come back to this earth as King of kings. Christ will rule the world and judge all people according to their decisions about him. Do you still picture Jesus as a baby in a manger—or is he your Lord? Make sure you don't underestimate Jesus. Let him grow up in your life.

*The blanket that Mary wrapped Jesus in actually was strips of cloth. These were used to keep a baby warm and give the baby a sense of security. The cloths were believed to protect the internal organs. The custom of wrapping infants this way continues to be practiced in many Mid-eastern countries.*

# Shepherds visit Jesus

### LUKE 2:8-14 *(Harmony 10a)*

*T*hat night some shepherds were in the fields outside the village, guarding their flocks of sheep. Suddenly an angel appeared among them, and the landscape shone bright with the glory of the Lord. They were badly frightened, but the angel reassured them.

"Don't be afraid!" he said. "I bring you the most joyful news ever announced, and it is for everyone! The Savior—yes, the Messiah, the Lord—has been born tonight in Bethlehem! How will you recognize him? You will find a baby wrapped in a blanket, lying in a manger!"

Suddenly, the angel was joined by a vast host of others—the armies of heaven—praising God:

"Glory to God in the highest heaven," they sang, "and peace on earth for all those pleasing him."

*Some of the Jews were waiting for a savior to deliver them from Roman rule; others hoped the Christ (Messiah) would deliver them from physical ailments. But Jesus, while healing their illnesses and establishing a spiritual kingdom, delivered them from sin. His work is more far-reaching than anyone could imagine. Christ paid the price for sin and opened the way to peace with God.*

#### GREAT NEWS!

What a birth announcement! The shepherds were terrified, but their fear turned to joy as the angels announced the Messiah's birth. First the shepherds ran to see the baby; then they spread the word. The good news about Jesus is that he comes to all, including the plain and the ordinary. He comes to anyone with a heart humble enough to accept him. Whoever you are, whatever you do, you can have Jesus in your life. Don't think you need extraordinary qualifications—he accepts you as you are. Jesus is *your* Messiah, *your* Savior. Do you look forward to meeting him in prayer and in his Word each day? Discover a Lord so wonderful that you can't help sharing your joy with your friends!

## Shepherds visit Jesus

*LUKE 2:15-20 (Harmony 10b)*

*W*hen this great army of angels had returned again to heaven, the shepherds said to each other, "Come on! Let's go to Bethlehem! Let's see this wonderful thing that has happened, which the Lord has told us about."

They ran to the village and found their way to Mary and Joseph. And there was the baby, lying in the manger. The shepherds told everyone what had happened and what the angel had said to them about this child. All who heard the shepherds' story expressed astonishment, but Mary quietly treasured these things in her heart and often thought about them.

Then the shepherds went back again to their fields and flocks, praising God for the visit of the angels, and because they had seen the child, just as the angel had told them.

*The conception and birth of Jesus Christ are supernatural events beyond human logic or reasoning. Thus God sent angels to help certain people understand the significance of what was happening (see Luke 1:11, 26; 2:9, 13, 19). Angels are spiritual beings created by God who live in God's presence and help carry out his work on earth.*

### SHEPHERDS AND THE LAMB OF GOD

God continued to reveal his Son, but not to those we might expect. Luke wrote that Jesus' birth was announced to shepherds in the fields. These may have been the shepherds who supplied many of the lambs that were sacrificed in the Temple for the forgiveness of sin. Here the angels invited these shepherds to greet the Lamb of God (John 1:36) who would take away the sins of the whole world forever. Christ paid the price for sin and opened the way to peace with God. He offers us more than temporary political or physical changes—he offers us new hearts that will last for eternity. God continues to invite men and women to discover the Savior. Have you found him?

## Mary and Joseph bring Jesus to the Temple

*LUKE 2:21-24 (Harmony 11a)*

ight days later, at the baby's circumcision ceremony, he was named Jesus, the name given him by the angel before he was even conceived.

When the time came for Mary's purification offering at the Temple, as required by the laws of Moses after the birth of a child, his parents took him to Jerusalem to present him to the Lord; for in these laws God had said, "If a woman's first child is a boy, he shall be dedicated to the Lord."

At that time Jesus' parents also offered their sacrifice for purification— "either a pair of turtledoves or two young pigeons" was the legal requirement.

*Jewish families went through several ceremonies soon after a baby's birth: (1) Circumcision. Every boy was circumcised and named on the eighth day after birth (Leviticus 12:3; Luke 1:59-60). (2) Redemption of the firstborn. A firstborn son was presented to God one month after birth (Exodus 13:2, 11-16; Numbers 18:15-16). (3) Purification of the mother (Leviticus 12:4-8).*

#### A BABY'S BIRTH

Why did Joseph and Mary have to return to the Temple? For forty days after the birth of a son and eighty days after the birth of a daughter, the mother was ceremonially unclean and could not enter the Temple. At the end of her time of separation, the parents were to bring a lamb for a burnt offering and a dove or pigeon for a sin offering. The priest would sacrifice these animals and declare her to be clean. If a lamb was too expensive, the parents could bring a second dove or pigeon instead. This is what Mary and Joseph did. Jesus was God's Son, but his family carried out all the specified ceremonies according to God's Law. Jesus was not born above the Law; instead, he fulfilled it perfectly. Mary and Joseph forthrightly obeyed God, fulfilling the requirements in the Law. What has God told you to do? Be obedient, be faithful.

## Mary and Joseph bring Jesus to the Temple

*LUKE 2:25-35 (Harmony 11b)*

That day a man named Simeon, a Jerusalem resident, was in the Temple. He was a good man, very devout, filled with the Holy Spirit and constantly expecting the Messiah to come soon. For the Holy Spirit had revealed to him that he would not die until he had seen him—God's anointed King. The Holy Spirit had impelled him to go to the Temple that day; and so, when Mary and Joseph arrived to present the baby Jesus to the Lord in obedience to the Law, Simeon was there and took the child in his arms, praising God.

"Lord," he said, "now I can die content! For I have seen him as you promised me I would. I have seen the Savior you have given to the world. He is the Light that will shine upon the nations, and he will be the glory of your people Israel!"

Joseph and Mary just stood there, marveling at what was being said about Jesus.

Simeon blessed them but then said to Mary, "A sword shall pierce your soul, for this child shall be rejected by many in Israel, and this to their undoing. But he will be the greatest joy of many others. And the deepest thoughts of many hearts shall be revealed."

*When Mary and Joseph brought Jesus to the Temple to be consecrated to God, they met an old man who told them what their child would become. Simeon's song is often called the Nunc Dimittis because these are the first words of its Latin translation. Simeon could die in peace because he had seen the Messiah.*

### ALL WHO BELIEVE

The Jews were well acquainted with the Old Testament prophecies that spoke of the Messiah's blessings to their nation. They did not always give equal attention to the prophecies saying that he would bring salvation to the entire world, not just the Jews (see, for example, Isaiah 49:6). In the days following the Ascension, many thought that Christ had come to save only his own people. Luke made sure his Greek audience understood that Christ had come to save *all* who believe, Gentiles as well as Jews. Simeon prophesied that Jesus would have a paradoxical effect on Israel. Some would fall because of him (see Isaiah 8:14-15), while others would rise (see Malachi 4:2). With Jesus there would be no neutral ground: People would either joyfully accept him or totally reject him. What have you done with Jesus?

## Mary and Joseph bring Jesus to the Temple

### LUKE 2:36-40 *(Harmony 11c)*

*A*nna, a prophetess, was also there in the Temple that day. She was the daughter of Phanuel, of the Jewish tribe of Asher, and was very old, for she had been a widow for eighty-four years following seven years of marriage. She never left the Temple but stayed there night and day, worshiping God by praying and often fasting.

She came along just as Simeon was talking with Mary and Joseph, and she also began thanking God and telling everyone in Jerusalem who had been awaiting the coming of the Savior that the Messiah had finally arrived.

When Jesus' parents had fulfilled all the requirements of the Law of God, they returned home to Nazareth in Galilee. There the child became a strong, robust lad, and was known for wisdom beyond his years; and God poured out his blessings on him.

*Did Mary and Joseph return immediately to Nazareth, or did they remain in Bethlehem for a time (as implied in Matthew 2)? Apparently there is a gap of several years between verses 38 and 39—ample time for them to find a place to live in Bethlehem, flee to Egypt to escape Herod's wrath, and return to Nazareth when it was safe to do so.*

#### NEVER TOO OLD

Although Simeon and Anna were very old, they had never lost their hope that they would see the Messiah. Led by the Holy Spirit, they were among the first to bear witness to Jesus. In the Jewish culture, elders were respected, so because of Simeon's and Anna's age, their prophecies carried extra weight. Our society, however, values youthfulness over wisdom, and potential contributions by the elderly are often ignored. As Christians, we should reverse those values whenever we can. Encourage older people to share their wisdom and experience. Listen carefully when they speak. Offer them your friendship and help them find ways to continue to serve God.

## Visitors arrive from eastern lands

***MATTHEW 2:1-8** (Harmony 12a)*

Jesus was born in the town of Bethlehem, in Judea, during the reign of King Herod.

At about that time some astrologers from eastern lands arrived in Jerusalem, asking, "Where is the newborn King of the Jews? for we have seen his star in far-off eastern lands and have come to worship him."

*Most Jews expected the Messiah to be a great military and political deliverer like Alexander the Great. Herod's counselors undoubtedly told this to Herod. No wonder this ruthless man took no chances and ordered all the baby boys in Bethlehem killed (Matthew 2:16)!*

King Herod was deeply disturbed by their question, and all Jerusalem was filled with rumors. He called a meeting of the Jewish religious leaders.

"Did the prophets tell us where the Messiah would be born?" he asked.

"Yes, in Bethlehem," they said, "for this is what the prophet Micah wrote:

'O little town of Bethlehem, you are not just an unimportant Judean village, for a Governor shall rise from you to rule my people Israel.'"

Then Herod sent a private message to the astrologers, asking them to come to see him; at this meeting he found out from them the exact time when they first saw the star. Then he told them, "Go to Bethlehem and search for the child. And when you find him, come back and tell me so that I can go and worship him too!"

**WISE MEN**

Not much is known about these astrologers (also known as wise men). We don't know where they came from or how many there were. Tradition says they were men of high position from Parthia, near the site of ancient Babylon. How did they know that the star represented the Messiah? (1) They could have been Jews who had remained in Babylon after the Exile and knew the Old Testament predictions of the Messiah's coming. (2) They may have been eastern astrologers who studied ancient manuscripts from around the world. Because of the Jewish exile centuries earlier, they would have had copies of the Old Testament in their land. (3) They may have had a special message from God directing them to the Messiah. Some scholars say that each of these astrologers was from a different nation, representing the entire world bowing before Jesus. These men from faraway lands recognized

Jesus as the Messiah when most of God's chosen people in Israel did not. Matthew pictures Jesus as King over the whole world, not just Judea. These men traveled thousands of miles to see the King of the Jews. When they finally found him, they responded with joy, worship, and gifts. This is quite different from the approach people often take today. We expect God to come looking for us, to explain himself, prove who he is, and give *us* gifts. But those who are wise still seek and worship Jesus, not for what they can get, but for who he is.

## January 24

### Visitors arrive from eastern lands

**MATTHEW 2:9-12** *(Harmony 12b)*

After this interview the astrologers started out again. And look! The star appeared to them again, standing over Bethlehem. Their joy knew no bounds!

Entering the house where the baby and Mary, his mother, were, they threw themselves down before him, worshiping. Then they opened their presents and gave him gold, frankincense, and myrrh. But when they returned to their own land, they didn't go through Jerusalem to report to Herod, for God had warned them in a dream to go home another way.

*Jesus was probably one or two years old when the astrologers found him. By this time Mary and Joseph were married, living in a house, and intending to stay in Bethlehem for a while.*

#### TRUE WORSHIP

The astrologers gave these expensive gifts because they were worthy presents for a future king. Bible students have seen in the gifts symbols of Christ's identity and what he would accomplish. Gold was a gift for a king; frankincense, a gift for deity; myrrh was a medicine and was also used as a burial spice. The astrologers brought gifts and worshiped Jesus for who he was. This is the essence of true worship—honoring Christ for who he is and being willing to give him what is valuable to you. Worship God because he is the perfect, just, and almighty Creator of the universe, worthy of the best you have to give.

## The escape to Egypt

### MATTHEW 2:13-15 *(Harmony 13a)*

*A*fter they were gone, an angel of the Lord appeared to Joseph in a dream. "Get up and flee to Egypt with the baby and his mother," the angel said, "and stay there until I tell you to return, for King Herod is going to try to kill the child." That same night he left for Egypt with Mary and the baby, and stayed there until King Herod's death. This fulfilled the prophet's prediction,

"I have called my Son from Egypt."

*Going to Egypt was not unusual because there were colonies of Jews in several major Egyptian cities. These colonies had developed during the time of the great captivity (see Jeremiah 43–44).*

**FOLLOWING HIS LEAD**

This was the second dream or vision that Joseph received from God. Joseph's first dream had revealed that Mary's child would be the Messiah (1:20-21). His second dream told him how to protect the child's life. Although Joseph was not Jesus' natural father, he was Jesus' legal father and was responsible for his safety and well-being. Divine guidance comes only to prepared hearts. Joseph remained receptive to God's guidance. How willing are you to listen to God? When you know what God wants, are you willing to follow his instructions?

## The escape to Egypt

### MATTHEW 2:16-18 *(Harmony 13b)*

*H*erod was furious when he learned that the astrologers had disobeyed him. Sending soldiers to Bethlehem, he ordered them to kill every baby boy two years old and under, both in the town and on the nearby farms, for the astrologers had told him the star first appeared to them two years before. This brutal action of Herod's fulfilled the prophecy of Jeremiah:

Screams of anguish come from Ramah,
Weeping unrestrained;
Rachel weeping for her children,

Uncomforted—
For they are dead.

**WHO'S ON THE THRONE?**

Herod was afraid that this newborn king would one day take his throne. He completely misunderstood the reason for Christ's coming. Jesus didn't want Herod's throne; he wanted to be king of Herod's life. Jesus wanted to give Herod eternal life, not take away his present life. Today people are often afraid that Christ wants to take things away when, in reality, he wants to give them real freedom, peace, and joy. Don't fear Christ—give him the throne of your life.

*Herod, the king of the Jews, killed all the boys under two years of age in an obsessive attempt to kill Jesus, the newborn King. He stained his hands with blood, but he did not harm Jesus. Herod was king by a human appointment; Jesus was King by a divine appointment. No one can thwart God's plans.*

---

*January 27*

---

## The return to Nazareth

*MATTHEW 2:19-23 (Harmony 14)*

When Herod died, an angel of the Lord appeared in a dream to Joseph in Egypt and told him, "Get up and take the baby and his mother back to Israel, for those who were trying to kill the child are dead."

So he returned immediately to Israel with Jesus and his mother. But on the way he was frightened to learn that the new king was Herod's son, Archelaus. Then, in another dream, he was warned not to go to Judea, so they went to Galilee instead and lived in Nazareth. This fulfilled the prediction of the prophets concerning the Messiah,

"He shall be called a Nazarene."

*Herod the Great died in 4 B.C. of an incurable disease. Rome trusted him but didn't trust his sons. Herod knew that Rome wouldn't give his successor as much power, so he divided his kingdom into three parts, one for each son. Archelaus received Judea, Samaria, and Idumea; Herod Antipas received Galilee and Perea; Herod Philip II received Trachonitis.*

**ANYTHING GOOD?**

Nazareth sat in the hilly area of southern Galilee near the crossroads of great caravan trade routes. The Roman garrison in charge of Galilee was housed in this small town. The people of Nazareth had constant contact with people from all over the world, so world news reached them quickly. These people had an attitude of independence that many of the Jews despised. This may have been why Nathanael commented, "Nazareth! . . . Can anything good come from there?"(1:46). Obviously it was not wise for Nathanael to be prejudiced against the entire town, for someone truly good did live there: Jesus the Messiah. Be careful not to make quick or prejudicial judgments because of where people live or originate.

## *January 28*

### Jesus speaks to the religious teachers

#### *LUKE 2:41-50 (Harmony 15a)*

*W*hen Jesus was twelve years old, he accompanied his parents to Jerusalem for the annual Passover Festival, which they attended each year. After the celebration was over they started home to Nazareth, but Jesus stayed behind in Jerusalem. His parents didn't miss him the first day, for they assumed he was with friends among the other travelers. But when he didn't show up that evening, they started to look for him among their relatives and friends; and when they couldn't find him, they went back to Jerusalem to search for him there.

Three days later they finally discovered him. He was in the Temple, sitting among the teachers of Law, discussing deep questions with them and amazing everyone with his understanding and answers.

His parents didn't know what to think. "Son!" his mother said to him. "Why have you done this to us? Your father and I have been frantic, searching for you everywhere."

*According to God's Law, every male was required to go to Jerusalem three times a year for the great festivals (Deuteronomy 16:16). In the spring the Passover was celebrated, followed immediately by the weeklong Festival of Unleavened Bread. Passover commemorated the night of the Jews' escape from Egypt when God had killed the Egyptian firstborn but had passed over Israelite homes (see Exodus 12:21-36). Passover was the most important of the three annual festivals.*

"But why did you need to search?" he asked. "Didn't you realize that I would be here at the Temple, in my Father's House?" But they didn't understand what he meant.

#### LETTING GO

Mary had to let go of her child and let him become a man. Fearful that she hadn't been careful enough with this God-given child, she searched frantically for him. But she was looking for a boy, not the young man who was in the Temple astounding the religious leaders with his questions. It is difficult to let go of people or projects that we have nurtured. It is both sweet and painful to see our children as adults, our students as teachers, our subordinates as managers, and our inspirations as institutions. But when the time comes to step back and let go, we must do so in spite of the hurt. Then our protégés can exercise their wings, take flight, and soar to the heights God intended for them.

*January 29*

## Jesus speaks with the religious teachers

*LUKE 2:51-52 (Harmony 15b)*

 hen he returned to Nazareth with them and was obedient to them; and his mother stored away all these things in her heart. So Jesus grew both tall and wise, and was loved by God and man.

**KEEPING IN BALANCE**

The second chapter of Luke shows us that, although Jesus was unique, he had a normal childhood and adolescence. In terms of development, he went through the same progression that we do. He grew physically and mentally, he related to other people, and he was loved by God. A full human life is not unbalanced. It was important to Jesus—and it should be important to all believers—to develop fully and harmoniously in each of these key areas: physical, mental, social, and spiritual. Think about each area of your life. Work hard to stay physically fit, mentally sharp, socially adept, and spiritually in tune with God.

*The Bible does not record any events of the next eighteen years of Jesus' life, but he undoubtedly was learning and maturing. As the oldest in a large family, he assisted Joseph in his carpentry work. Joseph may have died during this time, leaving Jesus to provide for the family. The normal routines of daily life gave Jesus a solid understanding of the Jewish people.*

# John the Baptist prepares the way for Jesus

### MARK 1:1-6 *(also in MATTHEW 3:1-6;*
### LUKE 3:1-6) *(Harmony 16a)*

*H*ere begins the wonderful story of Jesus the Messiah, the Son of God.

In the book written by the prophet Isaiah, God announced that he would send his Son to earth, and that a special messenger would arrive first to prepare the world for his coming.

"This messenger will live out in the barren wilderness," Isaiah said, "and will proclaim that everyone must straighten out his life to be ready for the Lord's arrival."

This messenger was John the Baptist. He lived in the wilderness and taught that all should be baptized as a public announcement of their decision to turn their backs on sin, so that God could forgive them. People from Jerusalem and from all over Judea traveled out into the Judean wastelands to see and hear John, and when they confessed their sins, he baptized them in the Jordan River. His clothes were woven from camel's hair and he wore a leather belt; locusts and wild honey were his food.

*John's clothes were not the latest style of his day. He dressed much like the prophet Elijah (2 Kings 1:8) in order to distinguish himself from the religious leaders, whose longflowing robes reflected their great pride in their position. John's striking appearance reinforced his striking message.*

#### TIME FOR A CHANGE

John chose to live in the desert (1) to get away from distractions so he could hear God's instructions; (2) to capture the undivided attention of the people; (3) to symbolize a sharp break with the hypocrisy of the religious leaders who preferred their luxurious homes and positions of authority over doing God's work; (4) to fulfill Old Testament prophecies that said John would be a voice calling in the wilderness to prepare the way for the Lord (Isaiah 40:3). The purpose of John's preaching was to prepare people to accept Jesus as God's Son. When John challenged the people to confess sin individually, he signaled the start of a new way to relate to God. Is change needed in your life before you can hear and understand Jesus' message? You have to admit that you need forgiveness before you can accept it. To prepare to receive Christ, repent. Denounce the world's dead-end attractions, sinful temptations, and harmful attitudes.

## John the Baptist prepares the way for Jesus

*LUKE 3:7-14 (also in MATTHEW 3:7-10)* *(Harmony 16b)*

*H*ere is a sample of John's preaching to the crowds that came for baptism: "You brood of snakes! You are trying to escape hell without truly turning to God! That is why you want to be baptized! First go and prove by the way you live that you really have repented. And don't think you are safe because you are descendants of Abraham. That isn't enough. God can produce children of Abraham from these desert stones! The ax of his judgment is poised over you, ready to sever your roots and cut you down. Yes, every tree that does not produce good fruit will be chopped down and thrown into the fire."

The crowd replied, "What do you want us to do?"

"If you have two coats," he replied, "give one to the poor. If you have extra food, give it away to those who are hungry."

*Many of John's hearers were shocked when he said that being Abraham's descendants was not enough for God. The religious leaders relied more on their family lines than on their faith for their standing with God. For them, religion was inherited. But a personal relationship with God is not handed down from parents to children. Everyone has to commit to it on his or her own.*

Even tax collectors—notorious for their corruption—came to be baptized and asked, "How shall we prove to you that we have abandoned our sins?"

"By your honesty," he replied. "Make sure you collect no more taxes than the Roman government requires you to."

"And us," asked some soldiers, "what about us?"

John replied, "Don't extort money by threats and violence; don't accuse anyone of what you know he didn't do; and be content with your pay!"

#### BEYOND WORDS

John's message demanded at least three specific responses: (1) Share what you have with those who need it; (2) whatever your job is, do it well and with fairness; and (3) be content with what you're earning. John had no time to address comforting messages to those who lived careless or selfish lives—he was calling the people to right living. Just as a fruit tree is expected to bear fruit, God's people should produce a crop of good works. God has no use for people who call themselves Christians but do nothing about it. Like many people in John's day who were God's people in name only, we are of no value if we are Christians in name only. If others can't see our faith in the way we treat them, we may not be God's people at all.

## John baptizes Jesus

### MATTHEW 3:13-17 (also in MARK 1:9-11; LUKE 3:21-22) (Harmony 17)

hen Jesus went from Galilee to the Jordan River to be baptized there by John. John didn't want to do it.

"This isn't proper," he said. "I am the one who needs to be baptized by you."

But Jesus said, "Please do it, for I must do all that is right." So then John baptized him. After his baptism, as soon as Jesus came up out of the water, the heavens were opened to him and he saw the Spirit of God coming down in the form of a dove. And a voice from heaven said, "This is my beloved Son, and I am wonderfully pleased with him."

*Why did Jesus ask to be baptized? It was not for repentance for sin because Jesus never sinned. He was baptized because (1) he was confessing sin on behalf of the nation, as Nehemiah, Ezra, Moses, and Daniel had done; (2) he was showing support for what John was doing; (3) he was inaugurating his public ministry; and (4) he was identifying with the penitent people of God, not with the critical Pharisees who were only watching.*

#### LET GO OF EGO

Put yourself in John's situation. Your work is going well, people are taking notice, everything is growing. But you know that the purpose of your work is to prepare the people for Jesus (John 1:35-37). Then Jesus arrives, and his coming tests your integrity. Will you be able to turn your followers over to him? John passed the test by publicly baptizing Jesus. Soon he would say, "He must become greater and greater, and I must become less and less" (John 3:30). Can you, like John, put your ego and profitable work aside in order to point others to Jesus? Are you willing to lose some of your status so that everyone will benefit?

## Satan tempts Jesus in the wilderness

*MATTHEW 4:1-4 (also in MARK 1:12-13; LUKE 4:1-4)*
*(Harmony 18a)*

hen Jesus was led out into the wilderness by the Holy Spirit, to be tempted there by Satan. For forty days and forty nights he ate nothing and became very hungry. Then Satan tempted him to get food by changing stones into loaves of bread. "It will prove you are the Son of God," he said. But Jesus told him, "No! For the Scriptures tell us that bread won't feed men's souls: Obedience to every word of God is what we need."

*Jesus was tempted by the devil, but he never sinned! Although we may feel dirty after being tempted, we should remember that temptation itself is not sin. We sin when we give in and disobey God. Remembering this will help us turn away from the temptation.*

**TEMPTATION**

The devil, also called Satan, tempted Eve in the Garden of Eden; here he tempted Jesus in the wilderness. Satan is a fallen angel. He is *real,* not symbolic, and is constantly fighting against those who follow and obey God. Satan's temptations are strong, and he is always trying to get us to live his way or our way rather than God's way. One day Jesus will reign over all creation, but Satan tried to force his hand and get him to declare his kingship prematurely. The devil's temptations focused on three crucial areas: (1) physical needs and desires, (2) possessions and power, and (3) pride. If Jesus had given in, his mission on earth—to die for our sins and give us the opportunity to have eternal life—would have been lost. But Jesus did *not* give in! When temptations seem especially strong, or when you think you can rationalize giving in, consider whether Satan may be trying to block God's purposes for your life or for someone else's life.

## Satan tempts Jesus in the wilderness

*MATTHEW 4:5-7 (also in LUKE 4:9-13)* (Harmony 18b)

hen Satan took him to Jerusalem to the roof of the Temple. "Jump off," he said, "and prove you are the Son of God; for the Scriptures declare, 'God will send his angels to keep you from harm,' . . . they will prevent you from smashing on the rocks below." Jesus retorted, "It also says not to put the Lord your God to a foolish test!"

**THE WHOLE TRUTH**

Satan used Scripture to try to convince Jesus to sin! Sometimes friends or associates will present attractive and convincing reasons why you should do something you know is wrong. They may even find Bible verses that *seem* to support their viewpoint. Study the Bible carefully, especially the broader contexts of specific verses, so that you understand God's principles for living and what he wants for your life. Only if you really understand what the *whole* Bible says will you be able to recognize errors of interpretation when people take verses out of context and twist them to say what they want them to say. Jesus was able to resist all of the devil's temptations because he not only knew Scripture, he also obeyed it. Ephesians 6:17 says that God's Word is a sword to use in spiritual combat. Knowing Bible verses is an important step in helping us resist the devil's attacks, but we must also obey the Bible. Satan had memorized Scripture, but he failed to submit to it. Knowing and obeying the Bible helps us follow God's desires rather than the devil's.

*The Temple was the religious center of the Jewish nation and the place where the people expected the Messiah to arrive (Malachi 3:1). The Temple was the tallest building in the area, and this "roof" was actually a pinnacle on the corner wall that jutted out of the hillside, overlooking the valley below. From this spot, Jesus could see all of Jerusalem behind him and the country for miles in front of him.*

*February 4*

## Satan tempts Jesus in the wilderness

### MATTHEW 4:8-11 (also in LUKE 4:5-8)
### (Harmony 18c)

*N*ext Satan took him to the peak of a very high mountain and showed him the nations of the world and all their glory. "I'll give it all to you," he said, "if you will only kneel and worship me." "Get out of here, Satan," Jesus told him. "The Scriptures say, 'Worship only the Lord God. Obey only him.'" Then Satan went away, and angels came and cared for Jesus.

*Did the devil have the power to give Jesus the kingdoms of the world? Satan may have been lying about his implied power, or he may have based his offer on his temporary control and free rein over the earth because of humanity's sinfulness.*

### THE TEST

This time of testing showed that Jesus really was the Son of God, able to overcome the devil and his temptations. A person has not shown true obedience if he or she has never had an opportunity to disobey. We read in Deuteronomy 8:2 that God led Israel into the wilderness to humble and test them. God wanted to see whether or not his people would really obey him. We too will be tested. Because we know that testing will come, we should be alert and ready for it. Remember, your convictions are only strong if they hold up under pressure!

## February 5

# John the Baptist declares his mission

**JOHN 1:19-23** *(Harmony 19a)*

he Jewish leaders sent priests and assistant priests from Jerusalem to ask John whether he claimed to be the Messiah.

He denied it flatly. "I am not the Christ," he said. "Well then, who are you?" they asked.

"Are you Elijah?"

"No," he replied.

"Are you the Prophet?"

"No."

### WHO WAS JOHN THE BAPTIST?

In the Pharisees' minds, there were four options regarding John the Baptist's identity: He was (1) the prophet foretold by Moses (Deuteronomy 18:15), (2) Elijah (Malachi 4:5), (3) the Prophet (the Messiah), or (4) a false prophet. John denied being any of the first three personages. Instead he called himself, in the words of the Old Testament prophet Isaiah, "A voice from the barren wilderness, shouting, 'Get ready for the coming of the Lord!' " (Isaiah 40:3). The leaders kept pressing John to say who he was because people were expecting the Messiah to come (Luke 3:15). But John emphasized only *why* he had come—to prepare the way for the Messiah. The Pharisees missed the point. They wanted to know who John was, but John wanted to point them to Jesus. Believers need to be like John, preparing the way for the Savior. What can you do to point people to Christ?

*The priests and assistant priests were respected religious leaders in Jerusalem. Priests served in the Temple. These leaders that came to see John were Pharisees. Many of them outwardly obeyed God's Laws to look pious, while inwardly their hearts were filled with pride and greed. They believed that their own oral traditions were just as important as God's inspired Word.*

# February 6

## John the Baptist declares his mission

### JOHN 1:24-28 (Harmony 19b)

**W**hen those who were sent by the Pharisees asked him, "If you aren't the Messiah or Elijah or the Prophet, what right do you have to baptize?"

John told them, "I merely baptize with water, but right here in the crowd is someone you have never met, who will soon begin his ministry among you, and I am not even fit to be his slave." This incident took place at Bethany, a village on the other side of the Jordan River where John was baptizing.

*John the Baptist said he was not even worthy to be Christ's slave. But according to Luke 7:28, Jesus said that John was the greatest of all prophets. If such a great person felt inadequate even to be Christ's slave, how much more should we lay aside our pride to serve Christ!*

**TO FORGIVE SINS**

John was baptizing Jews. The Essenes (a strict, monastic sect of Judaism) practiced baptism for purification, but normally only non-Jews (Gentiles) were baptized when they converted to Judaism. When the Pharisees questioned John's authority to baptize, they were asking who gave John the right to treat God's chosen people like Gentiles. John said, "I merely baptize with water"—he was helping the people perform a symbolic act of repentance. But soon one would come who would truly *forgive* sins, something only the Son of God—the Messiah—could do. Jesus can forgive your sins, no matter how big or small they may be. Have you accepted his forgiveness? Confess to Christ.

# February 7

## John the Baptist proclaims Jesus as the Messiah

### JOHN 1:29-34 (Harmony 20)

**T**he next day John saw Jesus coming toward him and said, "Look! There is the Lamb of God who takes away the world's sin! He is the one I was talking about when I said, 'Soon a man far greater than I am is coming, who existed long before me!' I didn't know he was the one, but I am here baptizing with water in order to point him out to the nation of Israel." Then John told about seeing the Holy Spirit in the form of a dove descending from heaven and resting upon Jesus. "I didn't know he was the one," John said again, "but at the time God sent me to baptize he told me, 'When you see the Holy Spirit descending and resting upon someone—he is the one you are looking for. He is the one who baptizes with the Holy Spirit.' I saw it happen to this man, and I therefore testify that he is the Son of God."

*John the Baptist's baptism with water was preparatory, because it was for repentance and symbolized the washing away of sins. Jesus, by contrast, would baptize with the Holy Spirit. He would send the Holy Spirit upon all believers, empowering them to live and to teach the message of salvation. This outpouring of the Spirit came after Jesus had risen from the dead and ascended into heaven (see 20:22; Acts 2).*

**THE LAMB OF GOD**

Every morning and evening, a lamb was sacrificed in the Temple for the sins of the people (Exodus 29:38-42). Isaiah 53:7 prophesied that the Messiah, God's servant, would be led to the slaughter like a lamb. To pay the penalty for sin, a life had to be given—and God chose to provide the sacrifice himself. The sins of the world were removed when Jesus died as the perfect sacrifice. This is the way our sins are forgiven (1 Corinthians 5:7). The "world's sin" means everyone's sin, the sin of each individual. Jesus paid the price of *your* sin by his death. You can receive forgiveness by confessing your sin to him and asking for his forgiveness.

*February 8*

## The first disciples follow Jesus

### JOHN 1:35-42 *(Harmony 21a)*

he following day as John was standing with two of his disciples, Jesus walked by. John looked at him intently and then declared, "See! There is the Lamb of God!" Then John's two disciples turned and followed Jesus. Jesus looked around and saw them following. "What do you want?" he asked them. "Sir," they replied, "where do you live?"

"Come and see," he said. So they went with him to the place where he was staying and were with him from about four o'clock that afternoon until the evening. (One of these men was Andrew, Simon Peter's brother.)

*One of the two disciples was Andrew (1:40). The other was probably John, the writer of this book. These were Jesus' first disciples, along with Peter (1:42) and Nathanael (1:45).*

Andrew then went to find his brother Peter and told him, "We have found the Messiah!" And he brought Peter to meet Jesus.

Jesus looked intently at Peter for a moment and then said, "You are Simon, John's son—but you shall be called Peter, the rock!"

**NAMES OF JESUS**

These new disciples used several names for Jesus: Lamb of God (1:36), Messiah (1:41), Son of God (1:49), and King of Israel (1:49). As they got to know Jesus, their appreciation for him grew. The more time we spend getting to know Christ, the more we will understand and appreciate who he is. We may be drawn to him for his teaching, but we will come to know him as the Son of God. Although these disciples made this verbal shift in a few days, they would not fully understand Jesus until three years later (Acts 2). What they so easily professed had to be worked out in experience. We may find that words of faith come easily, but deep appreciation for Christ comes with living by faith.

*February 9*

## The first disciples follow Jesus

***JOHN 1:43-51*** *(Harmony 21b)*

he next day Jesus decided to go to Galilee. He found Philip and told him, "Come with me." (Philip was from Bethsaida, Andrew and Peter's hometown.) Philip now went off to look for Nathanael and told him, "We have found the Messiah!—the very person Moses and the prophets told about! His name is Jesus, the son of Joseph from Nazareth!"

"Nazareth!" exclaimed Nathanael. "Can anything good come from there?"

"Just come and see for yourself," Philip declared. As they approached, Jesus said, "Here comes an honest man—a true son of Israel."

"How do you know what I am like?" Nathanael demanded.

And Jesus replied, "I could see you under the fig tree before Philip found you."

Nathanael replied, "Sir, you are the Son of God—the King of Israel!"

*Nazareth was despised by the Jews because a Roman army garrison was located there. Some have speculated that an aloof attitude or a poor reputation in morals and religion on the part of the people of Nazareth led to Nathanael's harsh comment. Nathanael's hometown was Cana, about four miles from Nazareth.*

Jesus asked him, "Do you believe all this just because I told you I had seen you under the fig tree? You will see greater proofs than this. You will even see heaven open and the angels of God coming back and forth to me, the Messiah."

### DON'T MISS JESUS

When Nathanael heard that the Messiah was from Nazareth, he was surprised. Philip responded, "Come and see for yourself." Fortunately for Nathanael, he went to meet Jesus and became a disciple. If he had stuck to his prejudice without investigating further, he would have missed the Messiah! Don't let people's stereotypes about Christ keep them from his power and love. Invite them to come and see the real Jesus.

## February 10

## Jesus turns water into wine

### JOHN 2:1-12 (Harmony 22)

Two days later Jesus' mother was a guest at a wedding in the village of Cana in Galilee, and Jesus and his disciples were invited too. The wine supply ran out during the festivities, and Jesus' mother came to him with the problem.

"I can't help you now," he said. "It isn't yet my time for miracles."

But his mother told the servants, "Do whatever he tells you to."

Six stone waterpots were standing there; they were used for Jewish ceremonial purposes and held perhaps twenty to thirty gallons each. Then Jesus told the servants to fill them to the brim with water. When this was done he said, "Dip some out and take it to the master of ceremonies."

When the master of ceremonies tasted the water that was now wine, not knowing where it had come from (though, of course, the servants did), he called the bridegroom over.

"This is wonderful stuff!" he said. "You're different from most. Usu-

*Beyond mere superhuman events, miracles demonstrate God's power. Almost every miracle Jesus did was a renewal of fallen creation—restoring sight, making the lame walk, even bringing the dead back to life. When the disciples saw Jesus' miracle, they believed. The miracle showed his power over nature and revealed the way he would go about his ministry—helping others, speaking with authority, and being in personal touch with people.*

ally a host uses the best wine first, and afterwards, when everyone is full and doesn't care, then he brings out the less expensive brands. But you have kept the best for the last!"

This miracle at Cana in Galilee was Jesus' first public demonstration of his heaven-sent power. And his disciples believed that he really was the Messiah.

After the wedding he left for Capernaum for a few days with his mother, brothers, and disciples.

### GOD'S WAY

Mary was probably not asking Jesus to do a miracle; she was simply hoping that her son would help solve this major problem and find some wine. Tradition says that Joseph, Mary's husband, was dead, so she probably was used to asking for her eldest son's help in certain situations. Jesus' answer to Mary is difficult to understand, but maybe that is the point. Although Mary did not understand what Jesus was going to do, she trusted him to do what was right. Those who believe in Jesus but encounter situations they cannot understand must continue to trust that he will work in the best way. Mary submitted to Jesus' way of doing things. She recognized that he was more than her human son—he was the Son of God. When we bring our problems to Christ, we may think we know how he should take care of them. But he may have a completely different plan. Like Mary, we should submit and allow Christ to deal with the problem as he sees fit.

*February 11*

## Jesus clears the Temple

### *JOHN 2:13-17 (Harmony 23a)*

hen it was time for the annual Jewish Passover celebration, and Jesus went to Jerusalem. In the Temple area he saw merchants selling cattle, sheep, and doves for sacrifices, and money changers behind their counters. Jesus made a whip from some ropes and chased them all out, and drove out the sheep and oxen, scattering the money changers' coins over the floor and turning over their tables! Then, going over to the men selling doves, he told them, "Get these things out of here. Don't turn my Father's House into a market!" Then his disciples remembered this

*The Passover celebration took place yearly at the Temple in Jerusalem. Every Jewish male was expected to make a pilgrimage to Jerusalem during this time (Deuteronomy 16:16).*

prophecy from the Scriptures: "Concern for God's House will be my undoing."

### RIGHTEOUS ANGER

The Temple area was always crowded with thousands of out-of-town visitors during Passover. The religious leaders crowded it even further by allowing money changers and merchants to set up booths in the Court of the Gentiles. They rationalized this practice as a convenience for the worshipers and as a way to make money for Temple upkeep. But the religious leaders did not seem to care that the Court of the Gentiles was so full of merchants that foreigners found it difficult to worship. Yet worship was the main purpose for visiting the Temple. No wonder Jesus was angry at the merchants who exploited those worshipers. There is a difference between uncontrolled rage and righteous indignation—yet both are called anger. We must be very careful how we use the powerful emotion of anger. It is right to be angry about injustice and sin; it is wrong to be angry over trivial personal offenses.

# February 12

## Jesus clears the Temple

### JOHN 2:18-25 *(Harmony 23b)*

*W*hat right have you to order them out?" the Jewish leaders demanded. "If you have this authority from God, show us a miracle to prove it."

"All right," Jesus replied, "this is the miracle I will do for you: Destroy this sanctuary and in three days I will raise it up!"

"What!" they exclaimed. "It took forty-six years to build this Temple, and you can do it in three days?" But by "this sanctuary" he meant his body. After he came back to life again, the disciples remembered his saying this and realized that what he had quoted from the Scriptures really did refer to him, and had all come true!

Because of the miracles he did in Jerusalem at the Passover celebration, many people were convinced that he was indeed

*The Son of God knows all about human nature. Jesus was well aware of the truth of Jeremiah 17:9, which states, "The heart is the most deceitful thing there is, and desperately wicked. No one can really know how bad it is!" Jesus was discerning, and he knew that the faith of some followers was superficial. Some of the same people claiming to believe in Jesus at this time would later yell "Crucify him!"*

the Messiah. But Jesus didn't trust them, for he knew mankind to the core. No one needed to tell him how changeable human nature is!

### STRONG PROOF

The Jews understood Jesus to mean the Temple out of which he had just driven the merchants and money changers. This was the Temple Zerubbabel had built more than five hundred years earlier, but Herod the Great had begun remodeling it, making it much larger and far more beautiful. It had been forty-six years since this remodeling had started (20 B.C.), and it still was not completely finished. They understood Jesus' words to mean that this imposing building could be torn down and rebuilt in three days, and they were startled. However, Jesus was not talking about the Temple made of stones, but about his body. His listeners didn't realize it, but Jesus was greater than the Temple (Matthew 12:6). His words would take on meaning for his disciples after his resurrection. That Christ so perfectly fulfilled this prediction became the strongest proof for his claims to be God. If you ever have doubts about Jesus' divinity, remember that he fulfilled his promise to rise from the dead. You worship a *living* Savior.

*February 13*

## Nicodemus visits Jesus at night

### JOHN 3:1-8 (Harmony 24a)

After dark one night a Jewish religious leader named Nicodemus, a member of the sect of the Pharisees, came for an interview with Jesus. "Sir," he said, "we all know that God has sent you to teach us. Your miracles are proof enough of this."

Jesus replied, "With all the earnestness I possess I tell you this: Unless you are born again, you can never get into the Kingdom of God."

"Born again!" exclaimed Nicodemus. "What do you mean? How can an old man go back into his mother's womb and be born again?"

Jesus replied, "What I am telling you so earnestly is this: Unless one is born of water and the Spirit, he cannot enter the Kingdom of God. Men can only reproduce human life, but the Holy Spirit gives new

*What did Nicodemus know about the Kingdom? From the Bible he knew it would be ruled by God, it would be restored on earth, and it would incorporate God's people. Jesus revealed to this devout Pharisee that the Kingdom would come to the whole world (3:16), not just the Jews, and that Nicodemus wouldn't be a part of it unless he was personally born again (3:5).*

life from heaven; so don't be surprised at my statement that you must be born again! Just as you can hear the wind but can't tell where it comes from or where it will go next, so it is with the Spirit. We do not know on whom he will next bestow this life from heaven.

### A NIGHT MEETING

Nicodemus was a Pharisee and a member of the ruling council called the Sanhedrin. The Pharisees were a group of religious leaders whom Jesus and John the Baptist often criticized for being hypocrites. Most Pharisees were intensely jealous of Jesus because he undermined their authority and challenged their views. But Nicodemus was searching, and he believed that Jesus had some answers. A learned teacher himself, he came to Jesus to be taught. Nicodemus came to Jesus personally, although he could have sent one of his assistants. He wanted to examine Jesus for himself in order to separate fact from rumor. Perhaps Nicodemus was afraid of what his peers, the Pharisees, would say about his visit, so he came after dark. Later, when he understood that Jesus was truly the Messiah, he spoke up boldly in his defense (7:50-51). Like Nicodemus, we must examine Jesus for ourselves—others cannot do it for us. If we believe he is who he says, we will want to speak up for him.

*February 14*

---

## Nicodemus visits Jesus at night

*JOHN 3:9-17 (Harmony 24b)*

 hat do you mean?" Nicodemus asked.

Jesus replied, "You, a respected Jewish teacher, and yet you don't understand these things? I am telling you what I know and have seen—and yet you won't believe me. But if you don't even believe me when I tell you about such things as these that happen here among men, how can you possibly believe if I tell you what is going on in heaven? For only I, the Messiah, have come to earth and will return to heaven again. And as Moses in the wilderness lifted up the bronze image of a serpent on a pole, even so I must be lifted up upon a pole, so that anyone who believes in me will have eternal life. For God loved the world so much

*When the Israelites were wandering in the wilderness, God sent a plague of serpents to punish the people for their rebellious attitude. Those doomed to die from snakebite could be healed by obeying God's command to look up at the elevated bronze serpent and by believing that God would heal them if they did.*

that he gave his only Son so that anyone who believes in him shall not perish but have eternal life. God did not send his Son into the world to condemn it, but to save it."

### THE GOSPEL

The entire gospel comes to a focus in John 3:16. God's love is not static or self-centered; it reaches out and draws others in. Here God sets the pattern of true love, the basis for all love relationships—when you love someone dearly, you are willing to give freely to the point of self-sacrifice. God paid dearly with the life of his Son, the highest price he could pay. Jesus accepted our punishment, paid the price for our sins, and then offered us the new life that he had bought for us. When we share the gospel with others, our love must be like Jesus'—willingly giving up our own comfort and security so that others might join us in receiving God's love. To "believe" is more than intellectual agreement that Jesus is God. It means to put our trust and confidence in him that he alone can save us. It is to put Christ in charge of our present plans and eternal destiny. Believing is both trusting his words as reliable and relying on him for the power to change. If you have never trusted Christ, let this promise of everlasting life be yours . . . and believe.

## February 15

---

## Nicodemus visits Jesus at night

### JOHN 3:18-21 (Harmony 24c)

There is no eternal doom awaiting those who trust him to save them. But those who don't trust him have already been tried and condemned for not believing in the only Son of God. Their sentence is based on this fact: that the Light from heaven came into the world, but they loved the darkness more than the Light, for their deeds were evil. They hated the heavenly Light because they wanted to sin in the darkness. They stayed away from that Light for fear their sins would be exposed and they would be punished. But those doing right come gladly to the Light to let everyone see that they are doing what God wants them to.

*People often try to protect themselves from their fears by putting their faith in something they do or have: good works, skill or intelligence, money or possessions. But only God can save us from the one thing that we really need to fear—eternal condemnation.*

Many people don't want their lives exposed to God's light because they are afraid of what will be revealed. They don't want to be changed. Don't be surprised when these same people are threatened by your desire to obey God and do what is right, because they are afraid that the light in you may expose some of the darkness in their lives. Rather than giving in to discouragement, keep praying that they will come to see how much better it is to live in light than in darkness.

## *February 16*

# John the Baptist tells more about Jesus

### *JOHN 3:22-30 (Harmony 25a)*

Afterwards Jesus and his disciples left Jerusalem and stayed for a while in Judea and baptized there.

At this time John the Baptist was not yet in prison. He was baptizing at Aenon, near Salim, because there was plenty of water there. One day someone began an argument with John's disciples, telling them that Jesus' baptism was best. So they came to John and said, "Master, the man you met on the other side of the Jordan River—the one you said was the Messiah—he is baptizing too, and everybody is going over there instead of coming here to us."

John replied, "God in heaven appoints each man's work. My work is to prepare the way for that man so that everyone will go to him. You yourselves know how plainly I told you that I am not the Messiah. I am here to prepare the way for him—that is all. The crowds will naturally go to the main attraction—the bride will go where the bridegroom is! A bridegroom's friends rejoice with him. I am the Bridegroom's friend, and I am filled with joy at his success. He must become greater and greater, and I must become less and less."

*John's willingness to decrease in importance shows unusual humility. Pastors and other Christian leaders can be tempted to focus more on the success of their ministries than on Christ. Beware of those who put more emphasis on their own achievements than on God's Kingdom.*

### FOLLOWING GOD'S CALL

Why did John the Baptist continue to baptize after Jesus came onto the scene? Why didn't he become a disciple too? John explained that because God had given him his work, he had to continue it until God called him to do something else. John's main purpose was to point people to Christ. Even with Jesus beginning his own ministry, John could still turn people to Jesus. Although John was the first genuine prophet in four hundred years, Jesus the Messiah would be infinitely greater than he. What John began, Jesus finished. What John prepared, Jesus fulfilled. Yet John willingly did the task to which he had been called. We must do the same, serving where we are called, doing to the best of our ability the tasks set before us. While others may get the glory, while we may feel jealous of others or wish we had their gifts or positions, we must remember that our goal is to glorify Christ and complete his work on earth.

## February 17

## John the Baptist tells more about Jesus

### JOHN 3:31-36 *(Harmony 25b)*

He has come from heaven and is greater than anyone else. I am of the earth, and my understanding is limited to the things of earth. He tells what he has seen and heard, but how few believe what he tells them! Those who believe him discover that God is a fountain of truth. For this one—sent by God—speaks God's words, for God's Spirit is upon him without measure or limit. The Father loves this man because he is his Son, and God has given him everything there is. And all who trust him—God's Son—to save them have eternal life; those who don't believe and obey him shall never see heaven, but the wrath of God remains upon them."

*Jesus says that those who believe in him have (not will have) everlasting life. To receive eternal life is to join in God's life, which by nature is eternal. Thus, eternal life begins at the moment of spiritual rebirth.*

#### THE CHOICE

Jesus' testimony was trustworthy because he had come from heaven and was speaking of what he had seen there. His words were the very words of God. Your whole spiritual life depends on your answer to one question: "Who is Jesus Christ?" If you accept Jesus as only a prophet or teacher, you have to reject his teaching, for he claimed to be God's Son, even God himself. The heartbeat of John's Gospel is the dynamic truth that Jesus Christ is God's Son, the Messiah, the Savior, who was from the beginning and will continue to live forever. This same Jesus has invited us to accept him and live with him eternally. When we understand who Jesus is, we are compelled to believe what he said. We are responsible to decide today whom we will obey (Joshua 24:15), and God wants us to choose him and life (Deuteronomy 30:15-20). The wrath of God is his final judgment and rejection of the sinner. To put off the choice is to choose not to follow Christ. Indecision is a fatal decision.

## February 18

## Herod puts John in prison

### LUKE 3:19-20 (Harmony 26)

But after John had publicly criticized Herod, governor of Galilee, for marrying Herodias, his brother's wife, and for many other wrongs he had done, Herod put John in prison, thus adding this sin to all his many others.

#### THROWING AWAY THE KEY

John the Baptist publicly spoke out against Herod's adultery. This was Herod Antipas, tetrarch of Galilee and Perea, and he had married Herodias, who was previously married to his brother, Herod Philip I. Besides being his brother's wife, Herodias was also his niece. Rather than accept John's rebuke, Herod moved to silence John. People hate to be confronted with their sin. We should not be surprised when the world tries to silence Christians today. Yet we should have the courage of John the Baptist and speak the truth in love, regardless of the consequences.

*The Herods were a murderous and deceitful family. Rebuking a tyrannical Roman official who could imprison and execute him was extremely dangerous, yet that is what John did. He fearlessly risked his life to speak out against sin.*

## February 19

## Jesus talks to a woman at the well

### JOHN 4:1-15 (Harmony 27a)

When the Lord knew that the Pharisees had heard about the greater crowds coming to him than to John to be baptized and to become his disciples—(though Jesus himself didn't baptize them, but his disciples did)—he left Judea and returned to the province of Galilee.

He had to go through Samaria on the way, and around noon as he approached the village of Sychar, he came to Jacob's Well, located on the parcel of ground Jacob gave to his son Joseph. Jesus was tired from the long walk in the hot sun and sat wearily beside the well.

Soon a Samaritan woman came to draw water, and Jesus asked her for a drink. He was alone at the time as his disciples had gone into the village to buy some food. The woman was surprised that a Jew would ask a "despised Samaritan" for anything—usually they wouldn't even speak to them!—and she remarked about this to Jesus.

*Jacob's well was on the property originally owned by Jacob (Genesis 33:18-19). It was not a spring-fed well, but a well into which water seeped from rain and dew, collecting at the bottom. Wells were almost always located outside the city along the main road. Twice each day, morning and evening, women came to draw water. This woman came at noon, however, probably to avoid meeting people who knew her reputation.*

He replied, "If you only knew what a wonderful gift God has for you, and who I am, you would ask me for some *living* water!"

"But you don't have a rope or a bucket," she said, "and this is a very deep well! Where would you get this living water? And besides, are you greater than our ancestor Jacob? How can you offer better water than this which he and his sons and cattle enjoyed?"

Jesus replied that people soon became thirsty again after drinking this water. "But the water I give them," he said, "becomes a perpetual spring within them, watering them forever with eternal life."

"Please, sir," the woman said, "give me some of that water! Then I'll never be thirsty again and won't have to make this long trip out here every day."

### THIRST QUENCHER

Many spiritual functions parallel physical functions. As our bodies hunger and thirst, so do our souls. But our souls need *spiritual* food and water. The woman confused the two kinds of water, perhaps because no one had ever talked with her about her spiritual hunger and thirst before. We would not think of depriving our bodies of food and water when they hunger or thirst. Why then should we deprive our souls? The living Word, Jesus Christ, and the written Word, the Bible, can satisfy our hungry and thirsty souls. The woman mistakenly believed that if she received the water Jesus offered, she would not have to return to the well each day. She was interested in Jesus' message because she thought it could make her life easier. But if that were always the case, people would accept Christ's message for the wrong reasons. Christ did not come to take away challenges, but to change us on the inside, helping us see our problems from God's perspective and empowering us to deal with them. Jesus wants to help you too. Let him change you from the inside out.

*February 20*

---

## Jesus talks to a woman at the well

**JOHN 4:16-26** *(Harmony 27b)*

Go and get your husband," Jesus told her.

"But I'm not married," the woman replied.

"All too true!" Jesus said. "For you have had five husbands, and you aren't even married to the man you're living with now."

"Sir," the woman said, "you must be a prophet. But say, tell me, why is it that you Jews insist that Jerusalem is the only place of worship, while we Samaritans claim it is here at Mount Gerizim, where our ancestors worshiped?"

Jesus replied, "The time is coming, ma'am, when we will no longer be concerned about whether to worship the Father here or in Jerusalem. For it's not *where* we worship that counts, but *how* we worship—is our worship spiritual and real? Do we have the Holy Spirit's help?

*The woman brought up a popular theological issue—the correct place to worship. But her question was a diversion to keep Jesus away from her deepest need. Jesus directed the conversation to a much more important point: The location of worship is not nearly as important as the attitude of the worshipers.*

For God is Spirit, and we must have his help to worship as we should. The Father wants this kind of worship from us. But you Samaritans know so little about him, worshiping blindly, while we Jews know all about him, for salvation comes to the world through the Jews."

The woman said, "Well, at least I know that the Messiah will come—the one they call Christ—and when he does, he will explain everything to us."

Then Jesus told her, "I am the Messiah!"

### THE HOLY SPIRIT'S HELP

"God is Spirit" means he is not a physical being limited to one place. He is present everywhere and he can be worshiped anywhere, at any time. It is not *where* we worship that counts, but *how* we worship. Is your worship genuine and true? Do you have the

Holy Spirit's help? How does the Holy Spirit help us worship? The Holy Spirit prays for us (Romans 8:26), teaches us the words of Christ (14:26), and tells us we are loved (Romans 5:5). Focus your worship on who God is and what he has done for you. Ask for the Holy Spirit's help.

## *February 21*

## Jesus tells about the spiritual harvest

*JOHN 4:27-38 (Harmony 28)*

Just then his disciples arrived. They were surprised to find him talking to a woman, but none of them asked him why, or what they had been discussing.

Then the woman left her waterpot beside the well and went back to the village and told everyone, "Come and meet a man who told me everything I ever did! Can this be the Messiah?" So the people came streaming from the village to see him.

Meanwhile, the disciples were urging Jesus to eat. "No," he said, "I have some food you don't know about."

"Who brought it to him?" the disciples asked each other.

Then Jesus explained: "My nourishment comes from doing the will of God who sent me, and from finishing his work. Do you think the work of harvesting will not begin until the summer ends four months from now? Look around you! Vast fields of human souls are ripening all around us, and are ready now for reaping. The reapers will be paid good wages and will be gathering eternal souls into the granaries of heaven! What joys await the sower and the reaper, both together! For it is true that one sows and someone else reaps. I sent you to reap where you didn't sow; others did the work, and you received the harvest."

*The "food" about which Jesus was speaking was his spiritual nourishment. It includes more than Bible study, prayer, and attending church. Spiritual nourishment also comes from doing God's will and helping to bring his work of salvation to completion. We are nourished not only by what we take in, but also by what we give out for God.*

### WAGES OF JOY

The wages Jesus offers are the joy of working for him and seeing the harvest of believers. These wages come to sower and reaper alike because both find joy in seeing new believers come into Christ's Kingdom. The phrase "others did the work" (4:38) may refer to the Old Testament prophets and to John the Baptist, who paved the way for the gospel. Sometimes Christians excuse themselves from witnessing by saying that their family or friends aren't ready to believe. Jesus makes it clear, however, that around us a continual harvest waits to be reaped. Don't let Jesus find you making excuses. Look around. You will find people ready to hear God's Word.

## February 22

---

# Many Samaritans believe in Jesus

### JOHN 4:39-42 *(Harmony 29)*

*M*any from the Samaritan village believed he was the Messiah because of the woman's report: "He told me everything I ever did!" When they came out to see him at the well, they begged him to stay at their village; and he did, for two days, long enough for many of them to believe in him after hearing him. Then they said to the woman, "Now we believe because we have heard him ourselves, not just because of what you told us. He is indeed the Savior of the world."

*The Samaritan woman immediately shared her experience with others. Despite her reputation, many took her invitation and came out to meet Jesus. Perhaps there are sins in our past of which we're ashamed. But Christ changes us. As people see these changes, they become curious. We share these opportunities to introduce people to Christ.*

#### BREAKING THE BARRIERS

After the Northern Kingdom, with its capital at Samaria, fell to the Assyrians, many Jews were deported to Assyria, and foreigners were brought in to settle the land and help keep the peace (2 Kings 17:24). The intermarriage between those foreigners and the remaining Jews resulted in a mixed race, impure in the opinion of Jews who lived in the Southern Kingdom. Thus the pure Jews hated this mixed race, called Samaritans, because they felt that their fellow Jews who had intermarried had betrayed their people and nation. The Samaritans had set up an alternate center for worship on Mount Gerizim (referred to in 4:20) to parallel the Temple at Jerusalem, but it had been destroyed 150 years earlier. The Jews did everything they could to avoid traveling through Samaria. But Jesus had no reason to live by such cultural restrictions. The route through Samaria was shorter, so that was the route he took. As a result, many Samaritans became believers. Never let cultural or social prejudices keep you from sharing the gospel.

## Jesus preaches in Galilee

### MATTHEW 4:12-17 (also in MARK 1:14-15; LUKE 4:14-15; JOHN 4:43-45) (Harmony 30)

*W*hen Jesus heard that John had been arrested, he left Judea and returned home to Nazareth in Galilee; but soon he moved to Capernaum, beside the Lake of Galilee, close to Zebulun and Naphtali. This fulfilled Isaiah's prophecy:

"The land of Zebulun and the land of Naphtali, beside the lake, and the country-side beyond the Jordan River, and Upper Galilee where so many foreigners live— there the people who sat in darkness have seen a great Light; they sat in the land of death, and the Light broke through upon them."

From then on, Jesus began to preach, "Turn from sin and turn to God, for the Kingdom of Heaven is near."

*Jesus moved from Nazareth, his hometown, to Capernaum, about twenty miles farther north. Capernaum became Jesus' home base during his ministry in Galilee. Capernaum was a thriving city with great wealth as well as great decadence. Because it was the headquarters for many Roman troops, word about Jesus could spread all over the Roman Empire. Jesus' move fulfilled the prophecy of Isaiah 9:1-2, which stated that the Messiah would be a light to the land of Zebulun and Naphtali, the region of Galilee where Capernaum was located. Zebulun and Naphtali were two of the original twelve tribes of Israel.*

#### THE KINGDOM

The "Kingdom of Heaven" has the same meaning as the "Kingdom of God" in Mark and Luke. Matthew used this phrase because the Jews, out of their intense reverence and respect, did not pronounce God's name. The Kingdom of Heaven began when God himself entered human history as a man. Today Jesus Christ reigns in the hearts of believers, but the Kingdom of Heaven will not be fully realized until all evil in the world is judged and removed. Christ came to earth first as a suffering servant; he will come again as King and Judge to rule victoriously over all the earth. The Kingdom of Heaven is still near because it has arrived in our hearts. When you feel overwhelmed by life and destroyed by circumstances, remember that this world isn't all there is. Jesus will return—the Kingdom of Heaven is near.

## Jesus heals a government official's son

*JOHN 4:46-54 (Harmony 31)*

n the course of his journey through Galilee he arrived at the town of Cana, where he had turned the water into wine. While he was there, a man in the city of Capernaum, a government official, whose son was very sick, heard that Jesus had come from Judea and was traveling in Galilee. This man went over to Cana, found Jesus, and begged him to come to Capernaum with him and heal his son, who was now at death's door.

Jesus asked, "Won't any of you believe in me unless I do more and more miracles?"

The official pled, "Sir, please come now before my child dies."

Then Jesus told him, "Go back home. Your son is healed!" And the man believed Jesus and started home. While he was on his way, some of his servants met him with the news that all was well—his son had recovered. He asked them when the lad had begun to feel better, and they replied, "Yesterday afternoon at about one o'clock his fever suddenly disappeared!" Then the father realized it was the same moment that Jesus had told him, "Your son is healed." And the officer and his entire household believed that Jesus was the Messiah.

This was Jesus' second miracle in Galilee after coming from Judea.

*Jesus' miracles were not mere illusions, the product of wishful thinking. Although the official's son was twenty miles away, he was healed when Jesus spoke the word. Distance was no problem because Christ has mastery over space. We can never put so much space between ourselves and Christ that he can no longer help us.*

### FAITH IN ACTION

This government official was probably in Herod's service. He had walked twenty miles to see Jesus and addressed him as "Sir," putting himself under Jesus even though he had legal authority over Jesus. This official not only believed Jesus could heal; he also obeyed Jesus by returning home, thus demonstrating his faith. It isn't enough for us to say we believe that Jesus can take care of our problems. We need to act as if he can. When you pray about a need or problem, live as though you believe Jesus can do what he says. Notice how the official's faith grew. First, he believed enough to ask Jesus to help his son. Second, he believed Jesus' assurance that his son would live, and he acted on it. Third, he and his whole house believed in Jesus. Faith is a gift that grows as we use it.

## Jesus is rejected at Nazareth

### *LUKE 4:16-30 (Harmony 32)*

When he came to the village of Nazareth, his boyhood home, he went as usual to the synagogue on Saturday, and stood up to read the Scriptures. The book of Isaiah the prophet was handed to him, and he opened it to the place where it says:

"The Spirit of the Lord is upon me; he has appointed me to preach Good News to the poor; he has sent me to heal the brokenhearted and to announce that captives shall be released and the blind shall see, that the downtrodden shall be freed from their oppressors, and that God is ready to give blessings to all who come to him."

*Jesus' remarks filled the people of Nazareth with rage because he was saying that God sometimes chooses to reach Gentiles rather than Jews. Jesus implied that his hearers were as unbelieving as the citizens of the Northern Kingdom of Israel in the days of Elijah and Elisha, a time notorious for its great wickedness.*

He closed the book and handed it back to the attendant and sat down, while everyone in the synagogue gazed at him intently. Then he added, "These Scriptures came true today!"

All who were there spoke well of him and were amazed by the beautiful words that fell from his lips. "How can this be?" they asked. "Isn't this Joseph's son?"

Then he said, "Probably you will quote me that proverb, 'Physician, heal yourself'—meaning, 'Why don't you do miracles here in your hometown like those you did in Capernaum?' But I solemnly declare to you that no prophet is accepted in his own hometown! For example, remember how Elijah the prophet used a miracle to help the widow of Zarephath—a foreigner from the land of Sidon. There were many Jewish widows needing help in those days of famine, for there had been no rain for three and a half years, and hunger stalked the land; yet Elijah was not sent to them. Or think of the prophet Elisha, who healed Naaman, a Syrian, rather than the many Jewish lepers needing help."

These remarks stung them to fury; and jumping up, they mobbed him and took him to the edge of the hill on which the city was built, to push him over the cliff. But he walked away through the crowd and left them.

Jesus was quoting from Isaiah 61:1-2. Isaiah pictured the deliverance of Israel from exile in Babylon as a Year of Jubilee when all debts are cancelled, all slaves are freed, and all property is returned to original owners (Leviticus 25). But the release from Babylonian exile had not brought the fulfillment the people had expected; they were still a conquered and oppressed people. So Isaiah must have been referring to a future messianic age. Jesus boldly announced, "These Scriptures came true today!" Jesus was proclaiming himself as the one who would bring this good news to pass, but in a way that the people would not yet be able to grasp. Even Jesus himself was not accepted as a prophet in his hometown. Many people have a similar attitude—an expert is anyone who carries a briefcase and comes from more than two hundred miles away. Don't be surprised when your Christian life and faith are not easily understood or accepted by those who know you well.

## February 26

# Four fishermen follow Jesus

### MARK 1:16-20 (also in MATTHEW 4:18-22) (Harmony 33)

One day as Jesus was walking along the shores of the Sea of Galilee, he saw Simon and his brother Andrew fishing with nets, for they were commercial fishermen.

Jesus called out to them, "Come, follow me! And I will make you fishermen for the souls of men!" At once they left their nets and went along with him.

A little farther up the beach, he saw Zebedee's sons, James and John, in a boat mending their nets. He called them too, and immediately they left their father Zebedee in the boat with the hired men and went with him.

*Fishing was a major industry around the Sea of Galilee. Fishing with nets was the most common method. Capernaum, the largest of the more than thirty fishing towns around the lake at that time, became Jesus' new home (Matthew 4:12-13).*

#### TRUE FOLLOWERS

We often assume that Jesus' disciples were great men of faith from the first time they met Jesus. But they had to grow in their faith just as all believers do (14:48-50, 66-72; John 14:1-9; 20:26-29). This is apparently not the only time Jesus called Peter (Simon), James, and John to follow him (see Luke 5:1-11 and John 1:35-42 for two other times). Although it took time for Jesus' call and his message to get through, the disciples still *followed.* In the same way, we may question and falter, but we must never stop following Jesus.

## Jesus teaches with great authority

*LUKE 4:31-37 (also in MARK 1:21-28) (Harmony 34)*

hen he returned to Capernaum, a city in Galilee, and preached there in the synagogue every Saturday. Here, too, the people were amazed at the things he said. For he spoke as one who knew the truth, instead of merely quoting the opinions of others as his authority.

Once as he was teaching in the synagogue, a man possessed by a demon began shouting at Jesus, "Go away! We want nothing to do with you, Jesus from Nazareth. You have come to destroy us. I know who you are—the Holy Son of God."

Jesus cut him short. "Be silent!" he told the demon. "Come out!" The demon threw the man to the floor as the crowd watched, and then left him without hurting him further.

*Why was Jesus allowed to teach in the synagogues? Jesus was taking advantage of the policy of allowing visitors to teach. Itinerant rabbis were always welcome to speak to those gathered each Sabbath in the synagogues. The apostle Paul also profited from this practice (see Acts 13:5; 14:1).*

Amazed, the people asked, "What is in this man's words that even demons obey him?" The story of what he had done spread like wildfire throughout the whole region.

### JESUS VS. SATAN

A man possessed by a demon was in the synagogue where Jesus was teaching. This man made his way into the place of worship and verbally abused Jesus. The people were amazed at Jesus' authority to drive out demons—evil (unclean) spirits ruled by Satan and sent to harass people and tempt them to sin. Demons are fallen angels who have joined Satan in rebellion against God. Demons can cause a person to become mute, deaf, blind, or insane. Jesus faced many demons during his time on earth, and he always exerted authority over them. Not only did the evil spirit leave this man; Luke records that the man was not even injured. Evil permeates our world, and it is no wonder that people are often fearful. But Jesus' power is far greater than Satan's. The first step toward conquering fear of evil is to recognize Jesus' authority and power. He has overcome all evil, including Satan himself.

# Jesus heals Peter's mother-in-law and many others

### LUKE 4:38-41 (also in MATTHEW 8:14-17; MARK 1:29-34) (Harmony 35)

*A*fter leaving the synagogue that day, he went to Simon's home where he found Simon's mother-in-law very sick with a high fever. "Please heal her," everyone begged. Standing at her bedside he spoke to the fever, rebuking it, and immediately her temperature returned to normal, and she got up and prepared a meal for them!

As the sun went down that evening, all the villagers who had any sick people in their homes, no matter what their diseases were, brought them to Jesus; and the touch of his hands healed every one! Some were possessed by demons; and the demons came out at his command, shouting, "You are the Son of God." But because they knew he was the Christ, he stopped them and told them to be silent.

*Why didn't Jesus want the demons to reveal who he was? (1) By commanding the demons to remain silent, Jesus proved his authority and power over them. (2) Jesus wanted the people to believe he was the Messiah because of what he said and did, not because of the demons' words. (3) Jesus wanted to reveal his identity as the Messiah according to his timetable, not according to Satan's timetable. Satan wanted the people to follow Jesus around for what they could get out of him, not because he was the Son of God who could truly set them free from sin's guilt and power.*

#### READY TO SERVE

Jesus healed Simon's (Peter's) mother-in-law so completely that not only did the fever leave, but her strength was restored, and immediately she got up and took care of others' needs. Peter's mother-in-law gives us a beautiful example to follow. Her response to Jesus' touch was to wait on Jesus and his disciples—immediately. Has God ever helped you through a dangerous or difficult situation? If so, you should ask, "How can I express my gratitude to him?" Because God has promised us all the rewards of his Kingdom, we should look for ways to serve him and his followers now. God gives us health so that we may serve others.

## Jesus preaches throughout Galilee

### *MARK 1:35-39 (also in MATTHEW 4:23-25; LUKE 4:42-44) (Harmony 36)*

he next morning he was up long before daybreak and went out alone into the wilderness to pray.

Later, Simon and the others went out to find him, and told him, "Everyone is asking for you."

But he replied, "We must go on to other towns as well, and give my message to them too, for that is why I came."

So he traveled throughout the province of Galilee, preaching in the synagogues and releasing many from the power of demons.

*The Romans divided the land of Israel into three separate regions: Galilee, Samaria, and Judea. Galilee was the northernmost region, an area about sixty miles long and thirty miles wide. Jesus did much of his ministry in this area, an ideal place for him to teach because there were more than 250 towns concentrated there, with many synagogues.*

**TIME TO PRAY**

Jesus took time to pray. Finding time to pray is not easy, but prayer is the vital link between us and God. Like Jesus, we must break away from others to talk with God, even if we have to get up very early in the morning to do it! If Jesus needed solitude for prayer and refreshment, how much more is this true for us? Don't become so busy that life turns into a flurry of activity, leaving no room for quiet fellowship alone with God. No matter how much you have to do, you should always have time for prayer.

## Jesus provides a miraculous catch of fish

### *LUKE 5:1-11 (Harmony 37)*

ne day as he was preaching on the shore of Lake Gennesaret, great crowds pressed in on him to listen to the Word of God. He noticed two empty boats standing at the water's edge while the fishermen washed their nets. Stepping into one of the boats, Jesus asked Simon, its owner, to push out a little into the water, so that he could sit in the boat and speak to the crowds from there.

When he had finished speaking, he said to Simon, "Now go out where it is deeper and let down your nets and you will catch a lot of fish!"

"Sir," Simon replied, "we worked hard all last night and didn't catch a thing. But if you say so, we'll try again."

And this time their nets were so full that they began to tear! A shout for help brought their partners in the other boat, and soon both boats were filled with fish and on the verge of sinking.

*Lake Gennesaret was also known as the Sea of Galilee or the Sea of Tiberias. Fishermen on the Sea of Galilee used nets, often bell-shaped, with lead weights around the edges. A net would be thrown flat onto the water, and the lead weights would cause it to sink around the fish. Then the fishermen would pull on a cord, drawing the net around the fish. Nets had to be kept in good condition, so they were washed to remove weeds and then mended.*

When Simon Peter realized what had happened, he fell to his knees before Jesus and said, "Oh, sir, please leave us—I'm too much of a sinner for you to have around." For he was awestruck by the size of their catch, as were the others with him, and his partners too—James and John, the sons of Zebedee. Jesus replied, "Don't be afraid! From now on you'll be fishing for the souls of men!"

And as soon as they landed, they left everything and went with him.

### DAY TO DAY WITH JESUS

This was the disciples' second call. After the first call (Matthew 4:18-22; Mark 1:16-20), Peter, Andrew, James, and John had gone back to fishing. They continued to watch Jesus, however, as he established his authority in the synagogue, healed the sick, and drove out demons. Here he also established his authority in their lives—he met them on their level and helped them in their work. Simon Peter was awestruck at this miracle, and his first response was to feel his own insignificance in comparison to this man's greatness. Peter knew that Jesus had healed the sick and driven out demons, but he was amazed that Jesus cared about his day-to-day routine and understood his needs. God is interested not only in saving us, but also in helping us in our daily activities. From this point on, they left their nets and remained with Jesus. For us, following Jesus means more than just acknowledging him as Savior. We must leave our past behind and commit our future to him.

## Jesus heals a man with leprosy

*MARK 1:40-45 (also in MATTHEW 8:1-4; LUKE 5:12-16)*
*(Harmony 38)*

nce a leper came and knelt in front of him and begged to be healed. "If you want to, you can make me well again," he pled. And Jesus, moved with pity, touched him and said, "I want to! Be healed!" Immediately the leprosy was gone—the man was healed!

Jesus then told him sternly, "Go and be examined immediately by the Jewish priest. Don't stop to speak to anyone along the way. Take along the offering prescribed by Moses for a leper who is healed, so that everyone will have proof that you are well again."

But as the man went on his way he began to shout the good news that he was healed; as a result, such throngs soon surrounded Jesus that he couldn't publicly enter a city anywhere, but had to stay out in the barren wastelands. And people from everywhere came to him there.

*Although leprosy was incurable, many different types of skin diseases were classified together as "leprosy." According to the Old Testament laws about leprosy (Leviticus 13–14), when a leper was cured, he or she had to go to a priest to be examined. Then the leper was to give an offering of thanks at the Temple. Jesus adhered to these laws by sending the man to the priest. This demonstrated Jesus' complete regard for God's Law. Sending a healed leper to a priest was also a way to verify Jesus' great miracle to the community.*

### THE HEALING TOUCH

Leprosy was a feared disease because it had no known cure, and some forms of it were highly contagious. Leprosy had an emotional impact and terror associated with it as AIDS does today. (Sometimes called Hansen's disease, leprosy still exists in a less contagious form that can be treated.) The priests monitored the disease, banishing lepers who were in a contagious stage to prevent the spread of infection and readmitting lepers whose disease was in remission. Because leprosy destroys the nerve endings, lepers often would unknowingly damage their fingers, toes, and noses. This man with leprosy had an advanced case, so he undoubtedly had lost much bodily tissue. Lepers were considered untouchable because people feared contracting their disease. Yet Jesus reached out and touched the leper to heal him.

The real value of a person is inside, not outside. Although a person's body may be diseased or deformed, the person inside is no less valuable to God. No person is too disgusting for God's touch. In a sense, we are all people with leprosy because we have all been deformed by the ugliness of sin. But by sending his Son Jesus, God has touched us, giving us the opportunity to be healed. When you feel repulsed by someone, remember how God feels about that person—and about you.

*March 4*

---

## Jesus heals a paralyzed man

*MARK 2:1-12 (also in MATTHEW 9:1-8; LUKE 5:17-26) (Harmony 39)*

Several days later he returned to Capernaum, and the news of his arrival spread quickly through the city. Soon the house where he was staying was so packed with visitors that there wasn't room for a single person more, not even outside the door. And he preached the Word to them. Four men arrived carrying a paralyzed man on a stretcher. They couldn't get to Jesus through the crowd, so they dug through the clay roof above his head and lowered the sick man on his stretcher, right down in front of Jesus.

*Houses in Bible times were built of stone. They had flat roofs made of mud mixed with straw. Outside stairways led to the roofs. These friends may have carried the paralyzed man up the outside stairs to the roof. They then could easily have taken apart the mud and straw mixture to make a hole through which to lower their friend to Jesus.*

When Jesus saw how strongly they believed that he would help, Jesus said to the sick man, "Son, your sins are forgiven!"

But some of the Jewish religious leaders said to themselves as they sat there, "What? This is blasphemy! Does he think he is God? For only God can forgive sins."

Jesus could read their minds and said to them at once, "Why does this bother you? I, the Messiah, have the authority on earth to forgive sins. But talk is cheap—anybody could say that. So I'll prove it to you by healing this man." Then, turning to the paralyzed man, he commanded, "Pick up your stretcher and go on home, for you are healed!"

The man jumped up, took the stretcher, and pushed his way through the stunned onlookers! Then how they praised God. "We've never seen anything like this before!" they all exclaimed.

### MOVED TO ACTION

It wasn't the paralyzed man's faith that impressed Jesus, but the faith of his friends. The paralyzed man's need moved his friends to action, and they brought him to Jesus. Jesus responded to their faith and healed the man. For better or worse, our faith affects others.

When you recognize someone's need, do you act? Many people have physical and spiritual needs you can meet, either by yourself or with others who are also concerned. Human need moved these four men; let it also move you to compassionate action. We cannot make another person a Christian, but we can do much through our words, actions, and love to give him or her a chance to respond. Look for opportunities to bring your friends to the living Christ.

*March 5*

---

## Jesus eats with sinners at Matthew's house

### MATTHEW 9:9-13 (also in MARK 2:13-17; LUKE 5:27-32) (Harmony 40)

As Jesus was going on down the road, he saw a tax collector, Matthew, sitting at a tax collection booth. "Come and be my disciple," Jesus said to him, and Matthew jumped up and went along with him.

Later, as Jesus and his disciples were eating dinner at Matthew's house, there were many notorious swindlers there as guests!

The Pharisees were indignant. "Why does your teacher associate with men like that?"

"Because people who are well don't need a doctor! It's the sick people who do!" was Jesus' reply. Then he added, "Now go away and learn the meaning of this verse of Scripture."

*The Pharisees constantly tried to trap Jesus, and they thought his association with these "lowlifes" was the perfect opportunity. They were more concerned with their own appearance of holiness than with helping people, with criticism than encouragement, with outward respectability than practical help.*

**LEAVE IT BEHIND!**
Matthew was a Jew who was appointed by the Romans to be the area's tax collector. He collected taxes from the citizens as well as from merchants passing through town. Tax collectors were expected to take a commission on the taxes they collected, but most of them overcharged and kept the profits. Thus, tax collectors were hated by the Jews because of their reputation for cheating and because of their support of Rome. When Jesus called Matthew to be one of his disciples, Matthew got up and followed, leaving a lucrative career. When God calls you to follow or obey him, do you do it with as much abandon as Matthew? Sometimes the decision to follow Christ requires difficult or painful choices. Like Matthew, we must decide to leave behind those things that would keep us from following Christ.

## Religious leaders ask Jesus about fasting

### *LUKE 5:33-39 (also in MATTHEW 9:14-17; MARK 2:18-22) (Harmony 41)*

Their next complaint was that Jesus' disciples were feasting instead of fasting. "John the Baptist's disciples are constantly going without food and praying," they declared, "and so do the disciples of the Pharisees. Why are yours wining and dining?"

Jesus asked, "Do happy men fast? Do wedding guests go hungry while celebrating with the groom? But the time will come when the bridegroom will be killed; then they won't want to eat."

Then Jesus used this illustration: "No one tears off a piece of a new garment to make a patch for an old one. Not only will the new garment be ruined, but the old garment will look worse with a new patch on it! And no one puts new wine into old wineskins, for the new wine bursts the old skins, ruining the skins and spilling the wine. New wine must be put into new wineskins. But no one after drinking the old wine seems to want the fresh and the new. 'The old ways are best,' they say."

*John's disciples fasted (went without food) as a sign of mourning for sin and to prepare for the Messiah's coming. Jesus' disciples did not need to fast because he is the Messiah and was with them! Jesus did not condemn fasting—he himself fasted (Luke 4:1-2). He emphasized that fasting must be done for the right reasons.*

#### SOFT HEARTS

"Wineskins" were goatskins sewed together at the edges to form watertight bags. Because new wine expands as it ages, it had to be put in new, pliable wineskins. A used skin, having become more rigid, would burst and spill the wine. Like old wineskins, the Pharisees were too rigid to accept Jesus, who could not be contained in their traditions or rules. Christianity required new approaches, new traditions, new structures. Our church programs and ministries should not be so structured that they have no room for a fresh touch of the Spirit, a new method, or a new idea. We, too, must be careful that our hearts do not become so hard that they prevent us from accepting the new way of thinking that Christ brings. We need to keep our hearts pliable so we can accept Jesus' life-changing message.

## Jesus heals a lame man by the pool

*JOHN 5:1-9 (Harmony 42a)*

*A*fterwards Jesus returned to Jerusalem for one of the Jewish religious holidays. Inside the city, near the Sheep Gate, was Bethesda Pool, with five covered platforms or porches surrounding it. Crowds of sick folks—lame, blind, or with paralyzed limbs—lay on the platforms (waiting for a certain movement of the water, for an angel of the Lord came from time to time and disturbed the water, and the first person to step down into it afterwards was healed).

*Some ancient authorities do not include the reference to an angel disturbing the waters. Whether or not this occurred, Jesus healed this man who had been waiting for years to be healed.*

One of the men lying there had been sick for thirty-eight years. When Jesus saw him and knew how long he had been ill, he asked him, "Would you like to get well?"

"I can't," the sick man said, "for I have no one to help me into the pool at the movement of the water. While I am trying to get there, someone else always gets in ahead of me."

Jesus told him, "Stand up, roll up your sleeping mat and go on home!"

Instantly, the man was healed! He rolled up the mat and began walking!

But it was on the Sabbath when this miracle was done.

### GOD MEETS NEEDS

Jesus appropriately asked, "Would you like to get well?" After thirty-eight years, this man's problem had become a way of life. No one had ever helped him. He had no hope of ever being healed and no desire to help himself. The man's situation looked hopeless. But no matter how trapped you feel in your infirmities, God can minister to your deepest needs. Don't let a problem or hardship cause you to lose hope. God may have special work for you to do in spite of your condition, or even because of it. Many have ministered effectively to hurting people because they have triumphed over their own hurts.

## Jesus heals a lame man by the pool

*JOHN 5:10-15 (Harmony 42b)*

o the Jewish leaders objected. They said to the man who was cured, "You can't work on the Sabbath! It's illegal to carry that sleeping mat!"

"The man who healed me told me to," was his reply.

"Who said such a thing as that?" they demanded.

The man didn't know, and Jesus had disappeared into the crowd. But afterwards Jesus found him in the Temple and told him, "Now you are well; don't sin as you did before, or something even worse may happen to you."

Then the man went to find the Jewish leaders and told them it was Jesus who had healed him.

*According to the Pharisees, carrying one's bed (a mat) on the Sabbath was work and was therefore unlawful. It did not break an Old Testament law, but merely the Pharisees' interpretation of God's command to "remember to observe the Sabbath as a holy day" (Exodus 20:8). This was just one of hundreds of rules they had added to the Old Testament Law.*

**THE GREATEST MIRACLE**

This man had been lame, or paralyzed, and suddenly he could walk. This was a great miracle. But he needed an even greater miracle—to have his sins forgiven. The man was delighted to be physically healed, but he had to turn from his sins and seek God's forgiveness to be spiritually healed. God's forgiveness is the greatest gift you will ever receive. Don't neglect his gracious offer.

## Jesus claims to be God's Son

*JOHN 5:16-23 (Harmony 43a)*

o they began harassing Jesus as a Sabbath breaker.

But Jesus replied, "My Father constantly does good, and I'm following his example."

Then the Jewish leaders were all the more eager to kill him because in addition to disobeying their Sabbath laws, he had spoken of God as his

Father, thereby making himself equal with God.

Jesus replied, "The Son can do nothing by himself. He does only what he sees the Father doing, and in the same way. For the Father loves the Son, and tells him everything he is doing; and the Son will do far more awesome miracles than this man's healing. He will even raise from the dead anyone he wants to, just as the Father does. And the Father leaves all judgment of sin to his Son, so that everyone will honor the Son,

*If God stopped every kind of work on the Sabbath, nature would fall into chaos, and sin would overrun the world. Genesis 2:2 says that God rested on the seventh day, but this doesn't mean that he stopped doing good. Jesus was teaching that when the opportunity to do good presents itself, we should act, even on the Sabbath.*

just as they honor the Father. But if you refuse to honor God's Son, whom he sent to you, then you are certainly not honoring the Father."

### LIVING FOR JESUS

Jesus was identifying himself with God, his Father. There could be no doubt as to his claim to be God. Jesus does not leave us the option to believe in God while ignoring God's Son. Because of his unity with God, Jesus lived as God wanted him to live. Because of our identification with Jesus, we must honor him and live as he wants us to live. The questions "What would Jesus do?" and "What would Jesus have me do?" may help you make the right choices.

*March 10*

## Jesus claims to be God's Son

*JOHN 5:24-30 (Harmony 43b)*

I say emphatically that anyone who listens to my message and believes in God who sent me has eternal life, and will never be damned for his sins, but has already passed out of death into life. And I solemnly declare that the time is coming, in fact, it is here, when the dead shall hear my voice—the voice of the Son of God—and those who listen shall live. The Father has life in himself, and has granted his Son to have life in himself, and to judge the sins of all mankind because he is the Son of Man. Don't be so surprised! Indeed the time is coming

*God is the source and Creator of life. Because Jesus is eternally existent with God, the Creator, he too is "the Life" (14:6) through whom we may live eternally (see 1 John 5:11).*

when all the dead in their graves shall hear the voice of God's Son, and shall rise again—those who have done good, to eternal life; and those who have continued in evil, to judgment.

"But I pass no judgment without consulting the Father. I judge as I am told. And my judgment is absolutely fair and just, for it is according to the will of God who sent me and is not merely my own."

### TO LIVE FOREVER

In saying that the dead will hear his voice, Jesus was talking about the spiritually dead who hear, understand, and accept him. Those who accept Jesus, the Word, will have eternal life. Jesus was also talking about the physically dead. He raised several dead people while he was on earth, and at his second coming, "the believers who are dead will be the first to rise to meet the Lord" (1 Thessalonians 4:16). "Eternal life"—living forever with God—begins when you accept Jesus Christ as Savior. At that moment, new life begins in you (2 Corinthians 5:17). It is a completed transaction. You still will face physical death, but when Christ returns, your body will be resurrected to live forever (1 Corinthians 15). Those who have rebelled against Christ will be resurrected too, but to hear God's judgment against them and to be sentenced to an eternity apart from him. There are those who wish to live well on earth, ignore God, and then see death as final rest. Jesus does not allow unbelieving people to see death as the end of it all. There is a judgment to face. You can help people face judgment and be saved from eternal death—tell them the Good News about Christ's eternal life.

## March 11

# Jesus supports his claim

### JOHN 5:31-40 (Harmony 44a)

When I make claims about myself they aren't believed, but someone else, yes, John the Baptist, is making these claims for me too. You have gone out to listen to his preaching, and I can assure you that all he says about me is true! But the truest witness I have is not from a man, though I have reminded you about John's witness so that you will believe in me and be saved. John shone brightly for a while, and you benefited and rejoiced, but I have a greater witness than John. I refer to the miracles I do; these have been assigned me by the Father, and they prove that the Father has sent me. And the Father himself has also testified about me, though not appearing to you personally, or speaking to you directly. But you are not listening to him, for you refuse to believe me—the one sent to you with God's message.

"You search the Scriptures, for you believe they give you eternal life. And the Scriptures point to me! Yet you won't come to me so that I can give you this life eternal!"

*Jesus claimed to be equal with God (John 5:18), to give everlasting life (5:24), to be the source of life (5:26), and to judge sin (5:27). These statements make it clear that Jesus was claiming to be divine—an almost unbelievable claim, but one that was supported by another witness, John the Baptist.*

**MISSING THE SAVIOR**

The religious leaders knew what the Bible said but failed to apply its words to their lives. They knew the teachings of the Scriptures but failed to see the Messiah to whom the Scriptures pointed. They knew the rules but missed the Savior. Entrenched in their own religious system, they refused to let the Son of God change their lives. Don't become so involved in "religion" that you miss Christ.

*March 12*

---

## Jesus supports his claim

*JOHN 5:41-47 (Harmony 44b)*

our approval or disapproval means nothing to me, for as I know so well, you don't have God's love within you. I know, because I have come to you representing my Father and you refuse to welcome me, though you readily enough receive those who aren't sent from him, but represent only themselves! No wonder you can't believe! For you gladly honor each other, but you don't care about the honor that comes from the only God!

"Yet it is not I who will accuse you of this to the Father—Moses will! Moses, on whose laws you set your hopes of heaven. For you have refused to believe Moses. He wrote about me, but you refuse to believe him, so you refuse to believe in me. And since you don't believe what he wrote, no wonder you don't believe me either."

*The Pharisees prided themselves on being the true followers of their ancestor Moses. They were trying to follow every one of his laws to the letter. Jesus' warning that Moses would accuse them stung them to fury. Moses wrote about Jesus (Genesis 3:15; Numbers 24:17; Deuteronomy 18:15), yet the religious leaders refused to believe Jesus when he came.*

Whose praise do you seek? The religious leaders enjoyed great prestige in Israel, but their stamp of approval meant nothing to Jesus. He was concerned about God's approval. This is a good principle for us. If even the highest officials in the world approve of our actions and God does not, we should be concerned. But if God approves, even though others don't, we should be content.

*March 13*

---

## The disciples pick wheat on the Sabbath

### MATTHEW 12:1-8 (also in MARK 2:23-28; LUKE 6:1-5) (Harmony 45)

*A*bout that time, Jesus was walking one day through some grainfields with his disciples. It was on the Sabbath, the Jewish day of worship, and his disciples were hungry; so they began breaking off heads of wheat and eating the grain.

But some Pharisees saw them do it and protested, "Your disciples are breaking the Law. They are harvesting on the Sabbath."

But Jesus said to them, "Haven't you ever read what King David did when he and his friends were hungry? He went into the Temple and they ate the special bread permitted to the priests alone. That was breaking the Law too. And haven't you ever read in the Law of Moses how the priests on duty in the Temple may work on the Sabbath? And truly, one is here who is greater than the Temple! But if you had known the meaning of this Scripture verse, 'I want you to be merciful more than I want your offerings,' you would not have condemned those who aren't guilty! For I, the Messiah, am master even of the Sabbath."

*This story of David and the consecrated bread is recorded in 1 Samuel 21:1-6. The special bread was replaced every week, and the old loaves were eaten by the priests. The loaves given to David were the old loaves that had just been replaced with fresh ones. Although the priests were the only ones allowed to eat this bread, God did not punish David because his need for food was more important than the priestly regulations. Jesus was saying, "If you condemn me, you must also condemn David."*

The Pharisees had established thirty-nine categories of actions forbidden on the Sabbath, based on interpretations of God's Law and on Jewish custom. Harvesting was one of those forbidden actions. By picking wheat and rubbing it in their hands, the disciples were technically harvesting, according to the religious leaders. Jesus and the disciples were picking grain because they were hungry, not because they wanted to harvest the grain for a profit. They were not working on the Sabbath. The Pharisees, however, could not (and did not want to) see beyond their law's technicalities.

Many of the Pharisees were so caught up in their man-made laws and traditions that they lost sight of what was good and right. The Ten Commandments prohibit work on the Sabbath (Exodus 20:8-11). That was the *letter* of the Law. But because the *purpose* of the Sabbath is to rest and to worship God, the priests were allowed to work by performing sacrifices and conducting worship services. This "work" was serving and worshiping God. Jesus always emphasized the intent of the Law, the meaning behind the letter. God is far more important than the created instruments of worship. If we become more concerned with the means of worship than with the One we worship, we will miss God even as we think we are worshiping him.

## *March 14*

### Jesus heals a man's hand on the Sabbath

**MARK 3:1-6 (also in MATTHEW 12:9-14; LUKE 6:6-11) (Harmony 46)**

While in Capernaum Jesus went over to the synagogue again, and noticed a man there with a deformed hand.

Since it was the Sabbath, Jesus' enemies watched him closely. Would he heal the man's hand? If he did, they planned to arrest him!

Jesus asked the man to come and stand in front of the congregation. Then turning to his enemies he asked, "Is it all right to do kind deeds on Sabbath days? Or is this a day for doing harm? Is it a day to save lives or to destroy them?" But they wouldn't answer him. Looking around at them angrily, for he was deeply disturbed by their indifference to human need, he said to the man, "Reach out your hand." He did, and instantly his hand was healed!

*The Pharisees plotted Jesus' death because they were outraged. Jesus had overruled their authority (Luke 6:11) and had exposed their evil attitudes in front of the entire crowd in the synagogue. Jesus had shown that the Pharisees were more loyal to their religious system than to God.*

At once the Pharisees went away and met with the Herodians to discuss plans for killing Jesus.

As the Pharisees watched the man with the deformed hand, they wondered if Jesus would heal him, thereby breaking the Sabbath. Their Sabbath rules said that people could be helped on the Sabbath only if their lives were in danger. Jesus healed on the Sabbath several times, and none of those healings was in response to an emergency. If Jesus had waited until another day, he would have been submitting to the Pharisees' authority, showing that their petty rules were equal to God's Law. If he healed the man on the Sabbath, the Pharisees could claim that because Jesus broke their rules, his power was not from God. But Jesus made it clear how ridiculous and petty their rules were. God is more concerned about people than rules. The best time to reach out to someone is when he or she needs help. The Pharisees placed their laws above human need. They were so concerned about Jesus' breaking one of their rules that they did not care about the man's deformed hand. What is your attitude toward others? If your convictions don't allow you to help certain people, those convictions may not be in tune with God's Word. Don't allow dogma to blind you to human need.

## March 15

## Large crowds follow Jesus

### MARK 3:7-12 (also in MATTHEW 12:15-21)
### (Harmony 47a)

eanwhile, Jesus and his disciples withdrew to the beach, followed by a huge crowd from all over Galilee, Judea, Jerusalem, Idumea, from beyond the Jordan River, and even from as far away as Tyre and Sidon. For the news about his miracles had spread far and wide and vast numbers came to see him for themselves.

He instructed his disciples to bring around a boat and to have it standing ready to rescue him in case he was crowded off the beach. For there had been many healings that day and as a result great numbers of sick people were crowding around him, trying to touch him.

And whenever those possessed by demons caught sight of him they would fall down before him shrieking, "You are the Son of God!" But he strictly warned them not to make him known.

*While Jesus was drawing fire from the religious leaders, he was gaining great popularity among the people. Some were curious, some sought healing, some wanted evidence to use against him, and others wanted to know if Jesus truly was the Messiah. Most of these leaders could only dimly guess at the real meaning of what was happening among them.*

**THE TRUE MESSIAH**

Jesus warned the demons not to reveal his identity because he did not want them to reinforce a popular misconception. The huge crowds were looking for a political and military leader who would free them from Rome's control, and they thought that the Messiah predicted by the Old Testament prophets would be this kind of man. Jesus wanted to teach the people about the kind of Messiah he was—one who was far different from their expectations. Christ's Kingdom is spiritual. It begins not with the overthrow of governments, but with the overthrow of sin in people's hearts. The demons knew that Jesus was the Son of God, but they refused to turn from their evil purposes. Knowing about Jesus, or even believing that he is God's Son, does not guarantee salvation. You must also want to follow and obey him (see also James 2:17). Have you allowed Christ to reign in your heart?

## *March 16*

## Large crowds follow Jesus

### *MATTHEW 12:15-21 (also in MARK 3:7-12)*
### *(Harmony 47b)*

*B*ut he knew what they were planning and left the synagogue, with many following him. He healed all the sick among them, but he cautioned them against spreading the news about his miracles. This fulfilled the prophecy of Isaiah concerning him:

"Look at my Servant.
See my Chosen One.
He is my Beloved, in whom my
    soul delights.
I will put my Spirit upon him,
And he will judge the nations.
He does not fight nor shout;
He does not raise his voice!
He does not crush the weak,
Or quench the smallest hope;
He will end all conflict with his
    final victory,
And his name shall be the hope
Of all the world."

*Jesus did not want those he healed to tell others about his miracles because he didn't want the people coming to him for the wrong reasons. That would hinder his teaching ministry and arouse false hopes about an earthly kingdom. But the news of Jesus' miracles spread, and many came to see for themselves.*

## THE SERVANT KING

The people expected the Messiah to be a king. This quotation from Isaiah's prophecy (Isaiah 42:1-4) showed that the Messiah was indeed a king, but it illustrated what *kind* of king—a quiet, gentle ruler who brings justice to the nations. His final victory puts the cross before a crown, brings justice without courtly pomp, and yields victory without an army. As a servant, he brings hope. He brings life by offering his own. Like the crowd in Jesus' day, we may want Christ to rule as a king and bring great and visible victories in our lives. But often Christ's work is quiet, and it happens according to *his* perfect timing, not ours. Take time to reflect on Christ's quiet work in your life. Thank him for what he has done and continue to stay close to him.

# March 17

## Jesus selects the twelve disciples

### MARK 3:13-19 (also in LUKE 6:12-16) (Harmony 48)

*A*fterwards he went up into the hills and summoned certain ones he chose, inviting them to come and join him there; and they did. Then he selected twelve of them to be his regular companions and to go out to preach and to cast out demons. These are the names of the twelve he chose: Simon (he renamed him "Peter"), James and John (the sons of Zebedee, but Jesus called them "Sons of Thunder"), Andrew, Philip, Bartholomew, Matthew, Thomas, James (the son of Alphaeus), Thaddaeus, Simon (a member of a political party advocating violent overthrow of the Roman government), Judas Iscariot (who later betrayed him).

*Why did Jesus choose twelve men? The number twelve corresponds to the twelve tribes of Israel (Matthew 19:28), showing the continuity between the old religious system and the new one based on Jesus' message. Many people followed Jesus, but these twelve received the most intense training. We see the impact of these men throughout the rest of the New Testament.*

### WILLING DISCIPLES

From the hundreds of people who followed him from place to place, Jesus chose twelve to "be his regular companions" and be sent out "to preach and to cast out demons." He did not choose these twelve to be his companions because of their faith; their faith often faltered. He didn't choose them because of their talent and ability; no one stood out with unusual ability. The disciples represented a wide range of backgrounds and life experiences, but apparently they had no more leadership potential than those who were not chosen. The one characteristic they all shared was their willingness to obey Jesus. After Jesus' ascension, they were filled with the Holy Spirit and empowered to carry out special roles in the growth of the early church. We should not disqualify ourselves from service to Christ because we do not have the expected credentials. Being a good disciple is simply a matter of following Jesus with a willing heart.

## *March 18*

## Jesus gives the Beatitudes

### *MATTHEW 5:1-2 (also in LUKE 6:17-19) (Harmony 49a)*

One day as the crowds were gathering, he went up the hillside with his disciples and sat down and taught them there.

*Matthew 5–7 is called the Sermon on the Mount because Jesus gave it on a hillside near Capernaum. This "sermon" probably covered several days of preaching. The Sermon on the Mount challenged the proud and legalistic religious leaders of the day. It called them back to the messages of the Old Testament prophets who, like Jesus, taught that heartfelt obedience is more important than legalistic observance.*

#### WHAT A DISCIPLE CAN EXPECT

Enormous crowds were following Jesus—he was the talk of the town, and everyone wanted to see him. The disciples, who were the closest associates of this popular man, were certainly tempted to feel important, proud, and possessive. Being with Jesus gave them not only prestige, but also opportunity for receiving money and power.

The crowds were gathering once again. But before speaking to them, Jesus pulled his disciples aside and warned them about the temptations they would face as his associates. Don't expect fame and fortune, Jesus was saying, but mourning, hunger, and persecution. Nevertheless, Jesus assured his disciples, they would be rewarded—but perhaps not in this life. There may be times when following Jesus will bring us great popularity. If we don't live by Jesus' words in this sermon, we will find ourselves using God's message only to promote our personal interests.

## Jesus gives the Beatitudes

### MATTHEW 5:3 (also in LUKE 6:20) (Harmony 49b)

umble men are very fortunate!" he told them, "for the Kingdom of Heaven is given to them."

*Each Beatitude tells how to be fortunate and happy. Other translations use the word "blessed." The Beatitudes don't promise laughter, pleasure, or earthly prosperity. To Jesus, "blessed" means the experience of hope and joy, independent of outward circumstances. To find hope and joy, the deepest form of happiness, follow Jesus no matter what the cost.*

#### REWARDS OF HUMILITY

With Jesus' announcement that the Kingdom was near (4:17), people were naturally asking, "How do I qualify to be in God's Kingdom?" Jesus said that God's Kingdom is organized differently from worldly kingdoms. In the Kingdom of Heaven, wealth and power and authority are unimportant. Kingdom people seek different blessings and benefits, and they have different attitudes. They desire humility rather than chasing after the things of the world that lead to pride. Are your attitudes a carbon copy of the world's selfishness, pride, and lust for power, or do they reflect the humility and self-sacrifice of Jesus, your King?

## Jesus gives the Beatitudes

### MATTHEW 5:4 (Harmony 49c)

hose who mourn are fortunate! for they shall be comforted."

*The Greek word for mourn is the strongest word in that language to designate it— thus it refers to mourning for the dead. People who mourn loved ones know there is no other hope but in the Savior. They experience the reality of the comfort brought by the certainty of eternal life.*

#### FORTUNATE MOURNERS

Jesus' words seem to contradict each other. How can people who mourn be fortunate? But God's way of living usually contradicts the world's. If you want to live for God you must be ready to say and do what seems strange to the world. You must be willing to give when others take, to love when others hate, to help when others abuse. By giving up your own rights in order to serve others, you will one day receive everything God has in store for you.

# March 21

## Jesus gives the Beatitudes

### MATTHEW 5:5 (Harmony 49d)

"The meek and lowly are fortunate! for the whole wide world belongs to them."

**MEEK, NOT WEAK**

Meek people are not wimps. Rather, they have gentle, disciplined spirits that allow them to truly enjoy life. Because they are humble, willing to learn, willing to forgive and be forgiven, willing to take life in stride, it is true that "the whole wide world belongs to them." Too often it seems that the movers, pushers, and shakers are the ones who own everything. But how much can they appreciate, really? Instead, it is the people who have learned balance in life and genuine humility who can enjoy all that God has given them. How much of "the whole wide world" have you accepted by God's grace? Can you set aside pride and desires in order to be one of God's meek and lowly ones?

*Being meek and lowly (humble) means having a true perspective on ourselves. It does not mean that we should put ourselves down. We see that we are sinners, saved only by God's grace; but we are saved and therefore have great worth in God's Kingdom. We should place ourselves in his hands to be used as he wants in order to spread his Word and share his love with others.*

# March 22

## Jesus gives the Beatitudes

### MATTHEW 5:6 (also in LUKE 6:21) (Harmony 49e)

"Happy are those who long to be just and good, for they shall be completely satisfied."

*Only God is truly just and good; We should long to be like him.*

## THE JUST AND GOOD

The reference in Luke reads, "What happiness there is for you who are now hungry, for you are going to be satisfied!" Some believe that the hunger about which Jesus was speaking is a hunger for righteousness, a desire to be "just and good," as here in Matthew's verse. Others say this is physical hunger. In any case, in a nation where riches were seen as a sign of God's favor, Jesus startled his hearers by pronouncing blessings on those who hunger. In doing so, however, he was in line with an ancient tradition. The Old Testament is filled with texts proclaiming God's concern for the poor and needy. See, for example, 1 Samuel 2:5; Psalm 146:7; Isaiah 58:6-7; and Jesus' own mother's prayer in Luke 1:53. This promise gives hope to all who are hungry and poor. When you experience loss and are struggling financially, remember God's covenant and look for God's blessings in the midst of poverty.

*March 23*

---

# Jesus gives the Beatitudes

### MATTHEW 5:7 (Harmony 49f)

*H*appy are the kind and merciful, for they shall be shown mercy."

*James wrote that, "If you have been merciful, then God's mercy toward you will win out over his judgment against you" (James 2:13). In other words, not showing mercy places us only under God's judgment, but showing mercy places us under God's mercy as well. Merciful actions are evidence of a vital relationship with Christ.*

## THE KIND AND MERCIFUL

Kindness and mercy go hand in hand. Mercy is often used to describe God—the mercy we receive from him allows us to be saved. It is God's mercy alone that brought Jesus to the cross for undeserving sinners. Precisely because of this incredible mercy, believers ought to demonstrate that quality toward others. If we withhold mercy from others after having received it from God, we show that we don't understand or appreciate God's mercy toward us. Showing mercy means we don't make hasty criticisms, we don't set down demands and expectations of others, we show great patience, and we treat others with the same kindness, generosity, compassion, and understanding that God shows to us every day.

## Jesus gives the Beatitudes

### MATTHEW 5:8 *(Harmony 49g)*

 appy are those whose hearts are pure, for they shall see God."

*The word for pure means unmixed, without alloy, as with a pure metal. Pure people are transparent with unmixed motives. Their integrity shines through without question. Their only goal is to do God's will.*

**PURE HAPPINESS**

A follower of Christ becomes pure and holy through believing and obeying the Word of God (Hebrews 4:12). He or she has already accepted forgiveness through Christ's sacrificial death (Hebrews 7:26-27). But daily application of God's Word purifies our minds and hearts. Scripture points out sin, motivates us to confess, renews our relationship with Christ, and guides us back to the right path. Continue to read, study and apply God's Word, allowing it to purify your life.

## Jesus gives the Beatitudes

### MATTHEW 5:9 *(Harmony 49h)*

appy are those who strive for peace—they shall be called the sons of God."

*Because of Christ's death, we have peace with God and peace with one another. We are no longer foreigners or aliens to God; and we are all being built into a holy temple with Christ as our chief cornerstone.*

**WORKING FOR PEACE**

Many barriers can divide us from other Christians: age, appearance, intelligence, political persuasion, economic status, race, theological perspective. One of the best ways to stifle Christ's love is to be friendly with only those people that we like. Fortunately, Christ has knocked down the barriers and has unified all believers in one family. His cross should be the focus of our unity. The Holy Spirit helps us look beyond the barriers to the unity we are called to enjoy. People who want peace allow the Holy Spirit to work in their lives and strive for peace with others. While we should try to live at peace with everyone

(Romans 12:18), conflict with the world and its authorities is sometimes inevitable for a Christian (John 15:18; Acts 5:29). There will be situations where you cannot obey both God and man. Then you must obey God.

*March 26*

---

## Jesus gives the Beatitudes

### MATTHEW 5:10 *(Harmony 49i)*

"Happy are those who are persecuted because they are good, for the Kingdom of Heaven is theirs."

**TOUGH HAPPINESS**

Jesus said that persecuted people can be happy! Persecution can be good because (1) it takes our eyes off earthly rewards, (2) it strips away superficial belief, (3) it strengthens the faith of those who endure, and (4) it serves as an example to others who follow. The fact that we are being persecuted proves that we have been faithful; faithless people would be unnoticed. Later, two of the disciples, Peter and John, would be physically abused for their faith (see Acts 5:17-41). Yet because they knew how Jesus had suffered, they praised God that he had allowed them to be persecuted like their Lord. If you are mocked or persecuted for your faith, it isn't because you're doing something wrong, but because God has counted you "worthy to suffer dishonor for his name" (Acts 5:41). You can then be happy in the middle of persecution, for you have understood what it means to have the Kingdom of Heaven within you.

*Notice the progression in the Beatitudes. People who live differently from society, exposing its evil values by their humility, kindness, gentleness, and peacemaking, will find themselves at odds and persecuted for their beliefs and lifestyle. Jesus would later warn his disciples, "The people of the world will persecute you because you belong to me, for they don't know God who sent me" (John 15:21).*

## Jesus gives the Beatitudes

### MATTHEW 5:11 (also in LUKE 6:22) (Harmony 49j)

*W*hen you are reviled and persecuted and lied about because you are my followers—wonderful!"

**REJOICING IN PERSECUTION**

All believers face trials when they live for Christ in a hostile world. We must accept trials as part of the refining process that burns away impurities and prepares us to meet Christ. Trials teach us patience and help us grow to be the kind of people God wants. Those who stand for Christ will be persecuted because the world is ruled by Christ's greatest enemy. But just as the small group of early believers stood against persecution, so we must be willing to stand for our faith with patience, endurance, and courage.

*Why would Christians even face persecution? The early Christians were misunderstood, harassed, and many were tortured and even put to death. Persecution from Rome came for several reasons: (1) Christians refused to worship the emperor as a god and thus were viewed as atheists and traitors. (2) Christians refused to worship at heathen temples, so business for these money-making enterprises dropped wherever Christianity took hold. (3) Christians didn't support the Roman ideals of self, power, and conquest; and the Romans scorned the Christian ideal of self-sacrificing service. (4) Christians exposed and rejected the horrible immorality of heathen culture.*

## Jesus gives the Beatitudes

### MATTHEW 5:12 (also in LUKE 6:23) (Harmony 49k)

*B*e *happy* about it! Be *very glad!* for a *tremendous reward* awaits you up in heaven. And remember, the ancient prophets were persecuted too."

**FUTURE REWARDS**

Persecution would become a harsh reality for many early Christians. At the time the apostle John wrote Revelation, the Roman government had stepped up its persecution of

Christians, causing John to wonder if the church could survive and stand against the opposition. But Jesus appeared in glory and splendor, reassuring John that he and his fellow believers had access to God's strength to face these trials (see Revelation 1:17-18) and that tremendous rewards awaited them. If you are facing difficult problems, remember that the power available to John and the early church is also available to you. In the end, all believers will finally be with God in heaven. All who have been faithful through the ages will sing before

*We can be comforted to know that God's greatest prophets were persecuted. Read about Jeremiah (Jeremiah 38:1-6); Isaiah (tradition says he was killed by King Manasseh; see 2 Kings 21:16); Amos (Amos 7:10-13); Zechariah (2 Chronicles 24:20-22); and Elijah (1 Kings 19:2).*

God's throne (Revelation 7:14-17). Their tribulations and sorrows will be over: There will be no more tears for sin, for all sins will have been forgiven; no more tears for suffering, for all suffering will be over; no more tears for death, for all believers will have been resurrected to die no more.

## March 29

---

## Jesus gives the Beatitudes

### LUKE 6:24-26 *(Harmony 49l)*

*B*ut, oh, the sorrows that await the rich. For they have their only happiness down here. They are fat and prosperous now, but a time of awful hunger is before them. Their careless laughter now means sorrow then. And what sadness is ahead for those praised by the crowds—for *false* prophets have *always* been praised."

**THE POOR RICH**

Despite overwhelming evidence to the contrary, most people still believe that money brings happiness. Rich people craving greater riches can be caught in an endless cycle that only ends in ruin and destruction. How can you keep away from the love of money? (1) Realize that one day riches will all be gone. (2) Be content with what you have. (3) Monitor what you are willing to do to get more money. (4) Love people more than money. (5) Love God's work more than money. (6) Freely share what you have with others.

*There were many false prophets in Old Testament times. They were praised by kings and crowds because their predictions—prosperity and victory in war—were exactly what the people wanted to hear. But popularity is no guarantee of truth, and human flattery does not bring God's approval. Sadness lies ahead for those who chase after the crowd's praise rather than God's truth.*

## Jesus teaches about salt and light

**MATTHEW 5:13** *(Harmony 50a)*

ou are the world's seasoning, to make it tolerable. If you lose your flavor, what will happen to the world? And you yourselves will be thrown out and trampled underfoot as worthless."

### GOOD TASTE

If a seasoning has no flavor, it has no value. If Christians make no effort to affect the world around them, they are of little value to God. If we are too much like the world, we are worthless. Christians should not blend in with everyone else. Instead, we should affect others positively, just as seasoning brings out the best flavor in food. God wants to be active in your life, bringing out the best in you as

*In Leviticus 2:13 we read that the offerings were seasoned with salt as a reminder of the people's covenant (contract) with God. Salt is a good symbol of God's activity in a person's life because it penetrates, preserves, and aids in healing.*

well. Let him become part of you, penetrating every aspect of your life, preserving you from the evil all around, and healing you of your sins and shortcomings.

---

## Jesus teaches about salt and light

**MATTHEW 5:14-16** *(Harmony 50b)*

ou are the world's light—a city on a hill, glowing in the night for all to see. Don't hide your light! Let it shine for all; let your good deeds glow for all to see, so that they will praise your heavenly Father."

### GOOD LIGHT

Can you hide a city that is sitting on top of a hill? Its light at night can be seen for miles. If we live for Christ, we will glow like lights, showing others what Christ is like. We hide our light by (1) being quiet when we

*Light represents what is good, pure, true, holy, and reliable. Darkness represents what is sinful and evil. Light is also related to truth in that light exposes whatever exists, whether it is good or bad. In the dark, good and evil look alike; in the light, they can be clearly distinguished. Just as darkness cannot exist in the presence of light, sin cannot exist in the presence of a holy God.*

should speak, (2) going along with the crowd, (3) denying the light, (4) letting sin dim our light, (5) not explaining our light to others, or (6) ignoring the needs of others. If we want to have a relationship with God, we must put aside our sinful ways of living. To claim that we belong to him but then to go out and live for ourselves is hypocrisy. Be a beacon of truth—don't shut your light off from the rest of the world.

## Jesus teaches about the Law

### *MATTHEW 5:17-20 (Harmony 51)*

*D*on't misunderstand why I have come—it isn't to cancel the laws of Moses and the warnings of the prophets. No, I came to fulfill them and to make them all come true. With all the earnestness I have I say: Every law in the Book will continue until its purpose is achieved. And so if anyone breaks the least commandment and teaches others to, he shall be the least in the Kingdom of Heaven. But those who teach God's laws *and obey them* shall be great in the Kingdom of Heaven.

"But I warn you—unless your goodness is greater than that of the Pharisees and other Jewish leaders, you can't get into the Kingdom of Heaven at all!"

*If Jesus did not come to destroy the Law, does that mean all the Old Testament laws still apply to us today? In the Old Testament, there were three categories of law: ceremonial, civil, and moral. The ceremonial law related specifically to Israel's worship. Its primary purpose was to point forward to Jesus Christ. The civil law applied to daily living in Israel. The moral law (such as the Ten Commandments) is the direct command of God, and it still requires strict obedience from God's people.*

#### GREATER RIGHTEOUSNESS

The Pharisees were exacting and scrupulous in their attempts to follow their laws. So how can Jesus reasonably call us to a greater righteousness than theirs? The Pharisees' weakness was that they were content to obey the laws outwardly without allowing God to change their hearts (or attitudes). Jesus was saying, therefore, that the *quality* of our goodness should be greater than that of the Pharisees. They looked pious, but they were far from the Kingdom of God. God judges our hearts as well as our works, for it is in the heart that our real allegiance lies. Jesus was saying that his listeners needed a different kind of righteousness altogether (love and obedience), not just a more intense version of the Pharisees' righteousness (legal compliance). Our righteousness must (1) come from what God does in us, not what we can do by ourselves; (2) be God-centered, not self-centered; (3) be based on reverence for God, not approval from people; and (4) go beyond keeping the Law to living by the principles behind the Law.

## Jesus teaches about anger

### MATTHEW 5:21-22 *(Harmony 52a)*

*U*nder the laws of Moses the rule was, 'If you murder, you must die.' But I have added to that rule and tell you that if you are only *angry,* even in your own home, you are in danger of judgment! If you call your friend an idiot, you are in danger of being brought before the court. And if you curse him, you are in danger of the fires of hell."

*When Jesus said, "But I have added to that rule," he was not doing away with the Law or adding his own beliefs. Rather, he was giving a fuller understanding of why God made the specific law in the first place.*

**THOUGHT CONTROL**

Killing is a terrible sin, but *anger* is a great sin too because it also violates God's command to love. Anger in this case refers to a seething, brooding bitterness against someone. It is a dangerous emotion that always threatens to leap out of control, leading to violence, emotional hurt, increased mental stress, and spiritual damage. Anger keeps us from developing a spirit pleasing to God. Have you ever been proud that you didn't strike out and say what was really on your mind? Self-control is good, but Christ wants us to practice thought control as well. Jesus said that we will be held accountable even for our attitudes.

## Jesus teaches about anger

### MATTHEW 5:23-26 *(Harmony 52b)*

*S*o if you are standing before the altar in the Temple, offering a sacrifice to God, and suddenly remember that a friend has something against you, leave your sacrifice there beside the altar and go and apologize and be reconciled to him, and then come and offer your sacrifice to God. Come to terms quickly with your enemy before it is too late and he drags you into

*In Jesus' day, someone who couldn't pay a debt was thrown into prison until someone paid his debt. It is practical advice to resolve our differences with our enemies before their anger causes more trouble (Proverbs 25:8-10).*

court and you are thrown into a debtor's cell, for you will stay there until you have paid the last penny."

## GET THINGS RIGHT

Broken relationships can hinder our relationship with God. If we have a problem or grievance with a friend, we should resolve the problem as soon as possible. We are hypocrites if we claim to love God while we hate others. A person's attitude toward others reflects his or her relationship with God. You may not get into a disagreement that takes you to court, but even small conflicts mend more easily if you try to make peace right away. In a broader sense, these verses advise us to get things right with our brothers and sisters before we have to stand before God.

*April 4*

# Jesus teaches about lust

### MATTHEW 5:27-30 *(Harmony 53)*

The laws of Moses said, 'You shall not commit adultery.' But I say: Anyone who even looks at a woman with lust in his eye has already committed adultery with her in his heart. So if your eye—even if it is your best eye!—causes you to lust, gouge it out and throw it away. Better for part of you to be destroyed than for all of you to be cast into hell. And if your hand—even your right hand—causes you to sin, cut it off and throw it away. Better that than find yourself in hell."

*When Jesus said to get rid of your hand or your eye, he was speaking figuratively. He didn't mean literally to gouge out your eye, because even a blind person can lust. We sometimes tolerate sins in our lives that, left unchecked, could eventually destroy us. It is better to experience the pain of removal (getting rid of a bad habit or something we treasure, for instance) than to allow the sin to bring judgment and condemnation.*

## DESIRES

The Old Testament law said that it was wrong for a person to have sex with someone other than his or her spouse (Exodus 20:14). But Jesus said that the *desire* to have sex with someone other than your spouse is mental adultery and thus sin. Jesus emphasized that if the *act* is wrong, then so is the *intention*. To be faithful to your spouse with your body but not your mind is to break the trust so vital to a strong marriage. Jesus is not condemning natural interest in the opposite sex or even healthy sexual desire, but rather the deliberate and repeated filling of one's mind with fantasies that would be evil if acted out. Sinful desires can be just as damaging as sinful actions. Left unchecked, wrong desires will result in wrong actions and turn people away from God. Guard your thoughts—don't give sin a foothold through lust.

*April 5*

---

## Jesus teaches about divorce

**MATTHEW 5:31-32** *(Harmony 54)*

he law of Moses says, 'If anyone wants to be rid of his wife, he can divorce her merely by giving her a letter of dismissal.' But I say that a man who divorces his wife, except for fornication, causes her to commit adultery if she marries again. And he who marries her commits adultery."

#### A LIFETIME COMMITMENT

Divorce is as hurtful and destructive today as it was in Jesus' day. God intends marriage to be a lifetime commitment (Genesis 2:24). When entering into marriage, people should never consider divorce an option for solving problems or a way out of a relationship that seems dead. In these verses, Jesus is also attacking those who purposefully abuse the marriage contract, using divorce to satisfy their lustful desire to marry someone else. Are your actions today helping your marriage grow stronger, or are you tearing it apart?

*Jesus said that divorce is not permissible except for unfaithfulness. This does not mean that divorce should automatically occur when a spouse commits adultery. "Fornication" implies a sexually immoral lifestyle, not a confessed and repented act of adultery. Those who discover that their partner has been unfaithful should first make every effort to forgive, reconcile, and restore their relationship.*

## Jesus teaches about vows

### *MATTHEW 5:33-37 (Harmony 55)*

*A*gain, the law of Moses says, 'You shall not break your vows to God but must fulfill them all.' But I say: Don't make any vows! And even to say 'By heavens!' is a sacred vow to God, for the heavens are God's throne. And if you say 'By the earth!' it is a sacred vow, for the earth is his footstool. And don't swear 'By Jerusalem!' for Jerusalem is the capital of the great King. Don't even swear 'By my head!' for you can't turn one hair white or black. Say just a simple 'Yes, I will' or 'No, I won't.' Your word is enough. To strengthen your promise with a vow shows that something is wrong."

*The Bible condemns making vows or taking oaths casually, giving your word while knowing that you won't keep it, or swearing falsely in God's name (Exodus 20:7; Leviticus 19:12; Numbers 30:1-2; Deuteronomy 19:16-20). Oaths are needed in certain situations only because we live in a sinful society that breeds distrust.*

#### PROMISES, PROMISES

Jesus was emphasizing the importance of telling the truth. People were breaking promises and using sacred language casually and carelessly. Keeping oaths and promises is important; it builds trust and makes committed human relationships possible. Are you known as a person of your word? Truthfulness seems so rare that we feel we must end our statements with "I promise." If we tell the truth all the time, we will have less pressure to back up our words with an oath or promise.

## Jesus teaches about retaliation

### *MATTHEW 5:38-42 (Harmony 56)*

*T*he law of Moses says, 'If a man gouges out another's eye, he must pay with his own eye. If a tooth gets knocked out, knock out the tooth of the one who did it.' But I say: Don't resist violence! If you are slapped on one

*God's purpose behind this law was to limit vengeance and help the court administer punishment that was neither too strict nor too lenient.*

cheek, turn the other too. If you are ordered to court, and your shirt is taken from you, give your coat too. If the military demand that you carry their gear for a mile, carry it two. Give to those who ask, and don't turn away from those who want to borrow."

### GETTING EVEN

When we are wronged, often our first reaction is to get even. Jesus said, however, that we should do *good* to those who wrong us! Our desire should not be to keep score, but to love and forgive. This is not natural—it is supernatural. Only God can give us the strength to love as he does. Instead of planning vengeance, pray for those who hurt you.

## *April 8*

# Jesus teaches about loving enemies

*LUKE 6:27-36 (also in MATTHEW 5:43-48)*
*(Harmony 57)*

*L*isten, all of you. Love your *enemies*. Do *good* to those who *hate* you. Pray for the happiness of those who *curse* you; implore God's blessing on those who *hurt* you.

"If someone slaps you on one cheek, let him slap the other too! If someone demands your coat, give him your shirt besides. Give what you have to anyone who asks you for it; and when things are taken away from you, don't worry about getting them back. Treat others as you want them to treat you.

*Jesus wasn't talking about having affection for enemies; he was talking about an act of the will. You can't "fall into" this kind of love—it takes conscious effort. We must trust the Holy Spirit to help us show love to those for whom we may not feel love.*

"Do you think you deserve credit for merely loving those who love you? Even the godless do that! And if you do good only to those who do you good—is that so wonderful? Even sinners do that much! And if you lend money only to those who can repay you, what good is that? Even the most wicked will lend to their own kind for full return!

"Love your *enemies!* Do good to *them!* Lend to *them!* And don't be concerned about the fact that they won't repay. Then your reward from heaven will be very great, and you will truly be acting as sons of God: for he is kind to the *unthankful* and to those who are *very wicked*.

"Try to show as much compassion as your Father does."

**LOVING YOUR ENEMIES**

By telling us not to retaliate, Jesus keeps us from taking the law into our own hands. By loving and praying for our enemies, we can overcome evil with good. If you love your enemies and treat them well, you will truly show that Jesus is Lord of your life. This is possible only for those who give themselves fully to God, because only he can deliver people from natural selfishness. Loving our enemies means acting in their best interests. We can pray for them and think of ways to help them. Jesus loved the whole world, even though the world was in rebellion against God. Jesus asks us to follow his example by loving our enemies. Grant your enemies the same respect and rights as you desire for yourself.

*April 9*

## Jesus teaches about giving to the needy

### MATTHEW 6:1-4 *(Harmony 58)*

Take care! Don't do your good deeds publicly, to be admired, for then you will lose the reward from your Father in heaven. When you give a gift to a beggar, don't shout about it as the hypocrites do—blowing trumpets in the synagogues and streets to call attention to their acts of charity! I tell you in all earnestness, they have received all the reward they will ever get. But when you do a kindness to someone, do it secretly—don't tell your left hand what your right hand is doing. And your Father, who knows all secrets, will reward you."

*The term hypocrites, as used here, describes people who do good acts for appearances only—not out of compassion or other good motives. Their actions may be good, but their motives are hollow.*

**GOOD SECRETS**

When Jesus says not to tell the left hand what the right hand is doing, he is teaching that our motives for giving to God and to others must be pure. It's easier to do what is right when we gain recognition and praise. To be sure that our motives are not selfish, we should do our good works quietly or in secret, with no thought of reward. Our actions should not be self-centered, but God-centered; done not to make us look good, but to make God look good. The reward God promises is not material, and it is never given to those who seek it. Doing something only for ourselves is not a loving sacrifice. With your next good deed, ask, "Would I still do this if no one would ever know I did it?"

## Jesus teaches about prayer

### *MATTHEW 6:5-8 (Harmony 59a)*

*A*nd now about prayer. When you pray, don't be like the hypocrites who pretend piety by praying publicly on street corners and in the synagogues where everyone can see them. Truly, that is all the reward they will ever get. But when you pray, go away by yourself, all alone, and shut the door behind you and pray to your Father secretly, and your Father, who knows your secrets, will reward you.

*Some people, especially the religious leaders, wanted to be seen as "holy," and public prayer was one way to get attention. Jesus saw through their self-righteous acts, however, and taught that the essence of prayer is not public style but private communication with God.*

"Don't recite the same prayer over and over as the heathen do, who think prayers are answered only by repeating them again and again. Remember, your Father knows exactly what you need even before you ask him!"

#### OVER AND OVER

Repeating the same words over and over like a magic incantation is no way to ensure that God will hear your prayer. It's not wrong to come to God many times with the same requests—Jesus encourages *persistent* prayer. But he condemns the shallow repetition of words that are not offered with a sincere heart. We can never pray too much if our prayers are honest and sincere. Before you start to pray, make sure you mean what you say.

## Jesus teaches about prayer

### *MATTHEW 6:9-15 (Harmony 59b)*

*P*ray along these lines: 'Our Father in heaven, we honor your holy name. We ask that your Kingdom will come now. May your will be done here on earth, just as it is in heaven.

*This is often called the Lord's Prayer because Jesus gave it to the disciples. It can be a pattern for our prayers.*

Give us our food again today, as usual, and forgive us our sins, just as we have forgiven those who have sinned against us. Don't bring us into temptation, but deliver us from the Evil One. Amen.' Your heavenly Father will forgive you if you forgive those who sin against you; but if *you* refuse to forgive *them, he* will not forgive *you.*"

### FORGIVENESS

Jesus gives a startling warning about forgiveness: If we refuse to forgive others, God will also refuse to forgive us. Why? Because when we don't forgive others, we are denying our common ground as sinners in need of God's forgiveness. God's forgiveness of sin is not the direct result of our forgiving others, but it is based on our realizing what forgiveness means (see Ephesians 4:32). It is easy to ask God for forgiveness but difficult to grant it to others. Whenever we ask God to forgive us for sin, we should ask ourselves, "Have I forgiven the people who have wronged me?"

*April 12*

## Jesus teaches about fasting

### *MATTHEW 6:16-18 (Harmony 60)*

*A*nd now about fasting. When you fast, declining your food for a spiritual purpose, don't do it publicly, as the hypocrites do, who try to look wan and disheveled so people will feel sorry for them. Truly, that is the only reward they will ever get. But when you fast, put on festive clothing, so that no one will suspect you are hungry, except your Father who knows every secret. And he will reward you."

*By separating yourself from the daily routine of food preparation and eating, you can devote extra time to prayer. Hunger pangs remind you of your weakness and your dependence upon God. Fasting still can be helpful today as you seek God's will in special situations.*

### SPIRITUAL DISCIPLINE

Fasting—going without food in order to spend time in prayer—is noble *and* difficult. It gives us time to pray, teaches self-discipline, reminds us that we can live with a lot less, and helps us appreciate God's gifts. Jesus was not condemning fasting, but hypocrisy—fasting in order to gain public approval. Fasting was mandatory for the Jewish people once a year, on the Day of Atonement (Leviticus 23:32). The Pharisees voluntarily fasted twice a week to impress the people with their "holiness." Jesus commended acts of self-sacrifice done quietly and sincerely. He wanted people to adopt spiritual disciplines for the right reasons, not from a selfish desire for praise.

## Jesus teaches about money

### MATTHEW 6:19-24 *(Harmony 61)*

*D*on't store up treasures here on earth where they can erode away or may be stolen. Store them in heaven where they will never lose their value and are safe from thieves. If your profits are in heaven, your heart will be there too.

"If your eye is pure, there will be sunshine in your soul. But if your eye is clouded with evil thoughts and desires, you are in deep spiritual darkness. And oh, how deep that darkness can be!

"You cannot serve two masters: God and money. For you will hate one and love the other, or else the other way around."

*Spiritual vision is the capacity to see clearly what God wants us to do and to see the world from his point of view. But this spiritual insight can be easily clouded. Self-serving desires, interests, and goals block that vision. Serving God is the best way to restore it. A "pure" eye is one that is fixed on God.*

**ONE MASTER**

Jesus says we can have only one master. We live in a materialistic society where many people serve money. They spend all their lives collecting and storing it, only to die and leave it behind. Their desire for money and what it can buy far outweighs their commitment to God and spiritual matters. You will spend much of your time and energy thinking about whatever you have stored up. Don't fall into the materialism trap, because "the love of money is the first step toward all kinds of sin" (1 Timothy 6:10). Can you honestly say that God, and not money, is your master? One test is to ask which one occupies more of your thoughts, time, and efforts.

## Jesus teaches about worry

### MATTHEW 6:25-30 *(Harmony 62a)*

*S*o my counsel is: Don't worry about *things*—food, drink, and clothes. For you already have life and a body—and they are far more important than what to eat and wear. Look at the birds! They don't worry about what to eat—they don't need to sow or reap or store up food—for your heavenly Father feeds them. And you are far more valuable to him than they are. Will all your worries add a single moment to your life?

"And why worry about your clothes? Look at the field lilies! They don't worry about theirs. Yet King Solomon in all his glory was not clothed as beautifully as they. And if God cares so wonderfully for flowers that are here today and gone tomorrow, won't he more surely care for you, O men of little faith?"

*Jesus refers to King Solomon "in all his glory." When Solomon asked for wisdom, God promised him riches and honor as well (1 Kings 3:13). Solomon's riches became legendary. Yet the great glory of his expensive robes and jewels cannot compare with the beauty of God's creation in the form of the tiniest flowers.*

### WHY WORRY?

Because of the ill effects of worry, Jesus tells us not to worry about those needs that God promises to supply. Worry may (1) damage your health, (2) cause the object of your worry to consume your thoughts, (3) disrupt your productivity, (4) negatively affect the way you treat others, and (5) reduce your ability to trust in God. How many ill effects of worry are you experiencing? Here is the difference between worry and genuine concern—worry immobilizes, but concern moves you to action. Take your worry and turn it into prayer. Do you want to worry less? Then pray more! Whenever you start to worry, stop and pray.

*April 15*

---

## Jesus teaches about worry

### MATTHEW 6:31-34 (Harmony 62b)

*S*o don't worry at all about having enough food and clothing. Why be like the heathen? For they take pride in all these things and are deeply concerned about them. But your heavenly Father already knows perfectly well that you need them, and he will give them to you if you give him first place in your life and live as he wants you to.

"So don't be anxious about tomorrow. God will take care of your tomorrow too. Live one day at a time."

*Planning for tomorrow is time well spent; worrying about tomorrow is time wasted. Sometimes it's difficult to tell the difference. Careful planning is thinking ahead about goals, steps, and schedules, and trusting in God's guidance.*

### WHO'S ON FIRST?

To "give him first place in your life" means to turn to God *first* for help, to fill your thoughts with his desires, to take his character for your pattern, and to serve and obey him in everything. What is really important to you? People, objects, goals, and other desires all compete for priority. Any of these can quickly bump God out of first place if you don't actively choose to give him first place in *every* area of your life.

*April 16*

## Jesus teaches about criticizing others

### *LUKE 6:37-42 (also in MATTHEW 7:1-6)*
### *(Harmony 63)*

*N*ever criticize or condemn—or it will all come back on you. Go easy on others; then they will do the same for you. For if you give, you will get! Your gift will return to you in full and overflowing measure, pressed down, shaken together to make room for more, and running over. Whatever measure you use to give—large or small—will be used to measure what is given back to you."

*An object in the eye quickly blurs a person's vision, causing him or her to see things imagined, blurred, or double. When one's vision is clear, that person will be better able to help someone else remove a speck in his or her eye (if one actually exists).*

Here are some of the story-illustrations Jesus used in his sermons: "What good is it for one blind man to lead another? He will fall into a ditch and pull the other down with him. How can a student know more than his teacher? But if he works hard, he may learn as much.

"And why quibble about the speck in someone else's eye—his little fault—when a board is in your own? How can you think of saying to him, 'Brother, let me help you get rid of that speck in your eye,' when you can't see past the board in yours? Hypocrite! First get rid of the board, and then perhaps you can see well enough to deal with his speck!"

#### VISION TEST

Jesus doesn't mean we should ignore wrongdoing, but we should not be so worried about others' sins that we overlook our own. Jesus tells us to examine our own motives and conduct instead of judging others. The traits that bother us in others are often the habits we dislike in ourselves. Our untamed bad habits and behavior patterns are the very ones that we most want to change in others. Do you find it easy to magnify others' faults while excusing your own? If you are ready to criticize someone, check to see if you deserve the same criticism. Judge yourself first, and then lovingly forgive and help your neighbor. Remember your own "boards" when you feel like criticizing, and you may find that you have less to say.

## April 17

## Jesus teaches about asking, seeking, knocking

### MATTHEW 7:7-11 (Harmony 64a)

Ask, and you will be given what you ask for. Seek, and you will find. Knock, and the door will be opened. For everyone who asks, receives. Anyone who seeks, finds. If only you will knock, the door will open. If a child asks his father for a loaf of bread, will he be given a stone instead? If he asks for fish, will he be given a poisonous snake? Of course not! And if you hard-hearted, sinful men know how to give good gifts to your children, won't your Father in heaven even more certainly give good gifts to those who ask him for them?"

*Jesus tells us to persist in pursuing God. People often give up after a few half-hearted efforts and conclude that God cannot be found. But knowing God takes faith, focus, and follow-through, and Jesus assures us that we will be rewarded.*

**ASKING FOR SNAKES**

The child in Jesus' example asked his father for bread and fish—good and necessary items. If the child had asked for a poisonous snake, would the wise father have granted his request? Sometimes God knows we are praying for "snakes" and does not give us what we ask for, even though we persist in our prayers. As we learn to know God better as a loving Father, we learn to ask for what is good for us, and then he grants it.

## Jesus teaches about asking, seeking, knocking

### MATTHEW 7:12 *(Harmony 64b)*

o for others what you want them to do for you. This is the teaching of the laws of Moses in a nutshell."

*Jesus called this "the laws of Moses in a nutshell." If we do to others what we want done to us, we will naturally keep all the laws. This looks at God's Law positively. Rather than worrying about all we should not do, we should concentrate on all we can do to show our love for God and others.*

**GOLDEN ACTIONS**

This is commonly known as the Golden Rule. In many religions it is stated negatively: "Don't do to others what you don't want done to you." By stating it positively, Jesus made it more significant. It is not very difficult to refrain from harming others; it is much more difficult to take the initiative in doing something good for them. The Golden Rule as Jesus formulated it is the foundation of active goodness and mercy—the kind of love God shows to us every day. Think of a good and merciful action you can do today.

## Jesus teaches about the way to heaven

### MATTHEW 7:13-14 *(Harmony 65)*

eaven can be entered only through the narrow gate! The highway to hell is broad, and its gate is wide enough for all the multitudes who choose its easy way. But the Gateway to Life is small, and the road is narrow, and only a few ever find it.

**ONE WAY**

The gate that leads to eternal life is called "narrow." This does not mean that it is difficult to become a Christian, but that there is only *one* way to live eternally with God, and only a few decide to take that way. Believing in Jesus is the only way to heaven because he alone died for our

*In John 10:7, Jesus calls himself "the Gate for the sheep." Jesus is the only way into God's Kingdom. Only by accepting his sacrifice on your behalf can you find eternal life.*

sins and opened the way. Going Jesus' way may not be popular, but it is true and right. Thank God there *is* one way!

## Jesus teaches about fruit in people's lives

*MATTHEW 7:15-20 (also in LUKE 6:43-45) (Harmony 66)*

*B*eware of false teachers who come disguised as harmless sheep, but are wolves and will tear you apart. You can detect them by the way they act, just as you can identify a tree by its fruit. You need never confuse grapevines with thorn bushes or figs with thistles. Different kinds of fruit trees can quickly be identified by examining their fruit. A variety that produces delicious fruit never produces an inedible kind. And a tree producing an inedible kind can't produce what is good. So the trees having the inedible fruit are chopped down and thrown on the fire. Yes, the way to identify a tree or a person is by the kind of fruit produced."

*False prophets were common in Old Testament times. They prophesied only what the king and the people wanted to hear, claiming it was God's message. False teachers are just as common today. Jesus says to beware of those whose words sound religious but who are motivated by money, fame, or power.*

**FRUIT CHECK**

We should evaluate teachers' words by examining their lives. Just as trees are consistent in the kind of fruit they produce, good teachers consistently exhibit good behavior and high moral character as they attempt to live out the truths of Scripture. This does not mean we should throw out church teachers, pastors, and others who are less than perfect. Every one of us is subject to sin, and we must show the same mercy to others that we need for ourselves. When Jesus talks about bad trees, he means teachers who deliberately teach false doctrine. We must examine the teachers' motives, the direction they are taking, and the results they are seeking.

## Jesus teaches about those who build houses on rock and sand

*MATTHEW 7:21-29 (also in LUKE 6:46-49) (Harmony 67)*

*N*ot all who sound religious are really godly people. They may refer to me as 'Lord,' but still won't get to heaven. For the decisive question is whether they obey my Father in heaven. At the Judgment many will tell me, 'Lord, Lord, we told others about you and used your name to cast out demons and to do many other great miracles.' But I will reply, 'You have never been mine. Go away, for your deeds are evil.'

"All who listen to my instructions and follow them are wise, like a man who builds his house on solid rock. Though the rain comes in torrents, and the floods rise

*Living on the edge of a desert, Jesus' listeners were well aware of sand—its shifts and sudden movements in the wind. Tents were used on sand, not houses. The people were also very aware of the deceptive nature of water, having experienced violent storms on the Sea of Galilee.*

and the storm winds beat against his house, it won't collapse, for it is built on rock.

"But those who hear my instructions and ignore them are foolish, like a man who builds his house on sand. For when the rains and floods come, and storm winds beat against his house, it will fall with a mighty crash." The crowds were amazed at Jesus' sermons, for he taught as one who had great authority, and not as their Jewish leaders.

#### A SOLID FOUNDATION

Like a house of cards, the fool's life crumbles under pressure. Most people do not deliberately seek to build on a false or inferior foundation; instead, they just don't think about their life's purpose. Many people are headed for destruction, not out of stubbornness but out of thoughtlessness. Part of our responsibility as believers is to help others stop and think about where their lives are headed and to point out the consequences of ignoring Christ's message. Obeying God is like building a house on a strong, solid foundation that stands firm when storms come. When life is calm, our foundations don't seem to matter. But when crises come, our foundations are tested. Be sure your life is built on the solid foundation of knowing and trusting Jesus Christ.

*April 22*

## A Roman soldier demonstrates faith

*LUKE 7:1-10 (also in MATTHEW 8:5-13) (Harmony 68)*

hen Jesus had finished his sermon he went back into the city of Capernaum.

Just at that time the highly prized slave of a Roman army captain was sick and near death. When the captain heard about

Jesus, he sent some respected Jewish elders to ask him to come and heal his slave. So they began pleading earnestly with Jesus to come with them and help the man. They told him what a wonderful person the captain was.

"If anyone deserves your help, it is he," they said, "for he loves the Jews and even paid personally to build us a synagogue!"

*Since he was well aware of the Jewish hatred for Roman soldiers, the Roman army captain may not have wanted to interrupt a Jewish gathering. As a centurion, he daily delegated work and sent groups on missions, so this was how he chose to get his message to Jesus.*

Jesus went with them; but just before arriving at the house, the captain sent some friends to say, "Sir, don't inconvenience yourself by coming to my home, for I am not worthy of any such honor or even to come and meet you. Just speak a word from where you are, and my servant boy will be healed! I know, because I am under the authority of my superior officers, and I have authority over my men. I only need to say 'Go!' and they go; or 'Come!' and they come; and to my slave, 'Do this or that,' and he does it. So just say, 'Be healed!' and my servant will be well again!"

Jesus was amazed. Turning to the crowd he said, "Never among all the Jews in Israel have I met a man with faith like this."

And when the captain's friends returned to his house, they found the slave completely healed.

### BETWEEN YOU AND JESUS

This army captain was a *centurion,* in charge of one hundred men in the Roman army. This man turned to Jesus not as a last resort or magic charm, but because he believed Jesus was sent from God. Yet he didn't come himself to Jesus, and he didn't expect Jesus to come to him. Just as this captain did not need to be present to have his orders carried out, so Jesus didn't need to be present to heal. The captain's faith was especially amazing because he was a Gentile who had not been brought up to know a loving God. The Roman army captain could have let many obstacles stand between him and Jesus—pride, doubt, money, language, distance, time, self-sufficiency, power, race. But he didn't. Neither should we.

## Jesus raises a widow's son from the dead

### *LUKE 7:11-17 (Harmony 69)*

*N*ot long afterwards Jesus went with his disciples to the village of Nain, with the usual great crowd at his heels. A funeral procession was coming out as he approached the village gate. The boy who had died was the only son of his widowed mother, and many mourners from the village were with her.

When the Lord saw her, his heart overflowed with sympathy. "Don't cry!" he said. Then he walked over to the coffin and touched it, and the bearers stopped. "Laddie," he said, "come back to life again."

Then the boy sat up and began to talk to those around him! And Jesus gave him back to his mother.

A great fear swept the crowd, and they exclaimed with praises to God, "A mighty prophet has risen among us," and, "We have seen the hand of God at work today."

*Honoring the dead was important in Jewish tradition. A funeral procession—the relatives of the dead person following the body, which was wrapped and carried on a kind of stretcher—would make its way through town, and bystanders would be expected to join the procession. In addition, hired mourners would cry aloud and draw attention to the procession.*

The report of what he did that day raced from end to end of Judea and even out across the borders.

#### ACCEPT THE GIFT

This story illustrates salvation. The whole world was dead in sin (Ephesians 2:1), just as the widow's son was dead. Being dead, we could do nothing to help ourselves—we couldn't even ask for help. But God had compassion on us, and he sent Jesus to raise us to life with him (Ephesians 2:4-7). The dead boy did not earn his second chance at life, and we cannot earn our new life in Christ. But we can accept God's gift of life, praise God for it, and use our lives to do his will.

## Jesus eases John's doubt

*LUKE 7:18-28 (also in MATTHEW 11:1-15)*
*(Harmony 70a)*

The disciples of John the Baptist soon heard of all that Jesus was doing. When they told John about it, he sent two of his disciples to Jesus to ask him, "Are you really the Messiah? Or shall we keep on looking for him?"

The two disciples found Jesus while he was curing many sick people of their various diseases—healing the lame and the blind and casting out evil spirits. When they asked him John's question, this was his reply: "Go back to John and tell him all you have seen and heard here today: how those who were blind can see. The lame are walking without a limp.

*Of all people, no one fulfilled his God-given purpose better than John. Yet in God's Kingdom, all who come after John have a greater spiritual heritage because they have clearer knowledge of the purpose of Jesus' death and resurrection.*

The lepers are completely healed. The deaf can hear again. The dead come back to life. And the poor are hearing the Good News. And tell him, 'Blessed is the one who does not lose his faith in me.'"

After they left, Jesus talked to the crowd about John. "Who is this man you went out into the Judean wilderness to see?" he asked. "Did you find him weak as grass, moved by every breath of wind? Did you find him dressed in expensive clothes? No! Men who live in luxury are found in palaces, not out in the wilderness. But did you find a prophet? Yes! And more than a prophet. He is the one to whom the Scriptures refer when they say, 'Look! I am sending my messenger ahead of you, to prepare the way before you.' In all humanity there is no one greater than John. And yet the least citizen of the Kingdom of God is greater than he."

### DEALING WITH DOUBTS

John was confused because the reports he received about Jesus were unexpected and incomplete. John's doubts were natural, and Jesus didn't rebuke him for them. Instead, Jesus responded in a way that John would understand: Jesus explained that he had accomplished what the Messiah was supposed to accomplish. God can handle our doubts, and he welcomes our questions. Do you have questions about Jesus—about who he is or what he expects of you? Admit them to yourself and to God, and begin looking for answers. Only as you face your doubts honestly can you begin to resolve them.

## Jesus eases John's doubt

*LUKE 7:29-35 (also in MATTHEW 11:16-19)*
*(Harmony 70b)*

**A**nd all who heard John preach—even the most wicked of them—agreed that God's requirements were right, and they were baptized by him. All, that is, except the Pharisees and teachers of Moses' law. They rejected God's plan for them and refused John's baptism.

"What can I say about such men?" Jesus asked. "With what shall I compare them? They are like a group of children who complain to their friends, 'You don't like it if we play "wedding" and you don't like it if we play "funeral"!' For John the Baptist used to go without food and never took a drop of liquor all his life, and you said, 'He must be crazy!' But I eat my food and drink my wine, and you say, 'What a glutton Jesus is! And he drinks! And has the lowest sort of friends!' But I am sure you can always justify your inconsistencies."

*The tax collectors (who embodied evil in most people's minds) and common people heard John's message and repented. In contrast, the Pharisees and experts in the Law—religious leaders—rejected his words. Wanting to live their own way, they justified their own point of view and refused to listen to other ideas.*

**HYPOCRISY**

The religious leaders hated anyone who spoke the truth and exposed their own hypocrisy, and they did not bother to be consistent in their faultfinding. They criticized John the Baptist because he fasted and drank no wine; they criticized Jesus because he ate heartily and drank wine with tax collectors and "lowlifes." Their real objection to both men, of course, had nothing to do with dietary habits. What the Pharisees and experts in the Law couldn't stand was being exposed for their hypocrisy. Most of us can find compelling reasons to do or believe whatever suits our purposes. If we do not examine our ideas in the light of God's truth, however, we may be just as obviously self-serving as the Pharisees.

## Jesus promises rest for the soul

*MATTHEW 11:20-24 (Harmony 71a)*

hen he began to pour out his denunciations against the cities where he had done most of his miracles, because they hadn't turned to God.

"Woe to you, Chorazin, and woe to you, Bethsaida! For if the miracles I did in your streets had been done in wicked Tyre and Sidon, their people would have repented long ago in shame and humility. Truly, Tyre and Sidon will be better off on the Judgment Day than you! And Capernaum, though highly honored, shall go down to hell! For if the marvelous miracles I did in you had been done in Sodom, it would still be here today. Truly, Sodom will be better off at the Judgment Day than you."

*God had promised to spare Sodom if only ten godly people could be found in the city (Genesis 18:32), and not even ten could be found. The cities of Tyre and Sidon on the sea were beautiful, but the beauty was a source of pride, guaranteeing their judgment.*

### NO EXCUSES

Tyre, Sidon, and Sodom were ancient cities with a long-standing reputation for wickedness (Genesis 18–19; Ezekiel 27–28). Each was destroyed by God for its evil. The people of Bethsaida, Chorazin, and Capernaum saw Jesus firsthand, and yet they stubbornly refused to repent of their sins and believe in him. Jesus said that if some of the wickedest cities in the world had seen him, they would have repented. Because Bethsaida, Chorazin, and Capernaum saw Jesus and didn't believe, they would suffer even greater punishment than that of the wicked cities who didn't see Jesus. Similarly, nations and cities with churches on every corner and Bibles in every home will have no excuse on Judgment Day if they do not repent and believe. What evidence do you have for the truth of the gospel? How have you responded to the truth?

## Jesus promises rest for the soul

### MATTHEW 11:25-30 *(Harmony 71b)*

*A*nd Jesus prayed this prayer: "O Father, Lord of heaven and earth, thank you for hiding the truth from those who think themselves so wise, and for revealing it to little children. Yes, Father, for it pleased you to do it this way! . . .

"Everything has been entrusted to me by my Father. Only the Father knows the Son, and the Father is known only by the Son and by those to whom the Son reveals him. Come to me and I will give you rest—all of you who work so hard beneath a heavy yoke. Wear my yoke—for it fits perfectly—and let me teach you; for I am gentle and humble, and you shall find rest for your souls; for I give you only light burdens."

*Jesus mentions two kinds of people in his prayer: The "wise"—arrogant in their own knowledge—and the "little children"—humbly open to receive the truth of God's Word. Are you wise in your own eyes, or do you seek the truth in childlike faith, realizing that only God holds all the answers?*

**THE YOKE**

A yoke is a heavy wooden harness that fits over the shoulders of oxen. It is attached to a piece of equipment the oxen are to pull. A person may be carrying heavy burdens of (1) sin, (2) excessive demands of religious leaders (23:4; Acts 15:10), (3) oppression and persecution, or (4) weariness in the search for God. Jesus frees people from all these burdens. The rest that Jesus promises is love, healing, and peace with God, not the end of all labor. A relationship with God changes meaningless, wearisome toil into spiritual productivity and purpose. Come to Jesus with your burdens. Turn them over to him—he will give you rest.

## A sinful woman anoints Jesus' feet

### LUKE 7:36-50 *(Harmony 72)*

*O*ne of the Pharisees asked Jesus to come to his home for lunch and Jesus accepted the invitation. As they sat down to eat, a woman of the streets—a prostitute—heard he was there and brought an exquisite flask filled with expensive perfume. Going in, she knelt behind him at his feet, weeping, with her tears falling down upon his feet; and she wiped them off with her hair and kissed them and poured the perfume on them.

*In Jesus' day, it was customary to recline while eating. Dinner guests would lie on couches with their heads near the table, propping themselves up on one elbow and stretching their feet out behind them. The woman could easily anoint Jesus' feet without approaching the table.*

When Jesus' host, a Pharisee, saw what was happening and who the woman was, he said to himself, "This proves that Jesus is no prophet, for if God had really sent him, he would know what kind of woman this one is!"

Then Jesus spoke up and answered his thoughts. "Simon," he said to the Pharisee, "I have something to say to you."

"All right, Teacher," Simon replied, "go ahead."

Then Jesus told him this story: "A man loaned money to two people—$5,000 to one and $500 to the other. But neither of them could pay him back, so he kindly forgave them both, letting them keep the money! Which do you suppose loved him most after that?"

"I suppose the one who had owed him the most," Simon answered.

"Correct," Jesus agreed.

Then he turned to the woman and said to Simon, "Look! See this woman kneeling here! When I entered your home, you didn't bother to offer me water to wash the dust from my feet, but she has washed them with her tears and wiped them with her hair. You refused me the customary kiss of greeting, but she has kissed my feet again and again from the time I first came in. You neglected the usual courtesy of olive oil to anoint my head, but she has covered my feet with rare perfume. Therefore her sins—and they are many—are forgiven, for she loved me much; but one who is forgiven little, shows little love."

And he said to her, "Your sins are forgiven."

Then the men at the table said to themselves, "Who does this man think he is, going around forgiving sins?"

And Jesus said to the woman, "Your faith has saved you; go in peace."

### COMPLETE FORGIVENESS

Simon had committed several social errors in neglecting to wash Jesus' feet (a courtesy extended to guests because sandaled feet got very dirty), anoint his head with oil, and offer him the kiss of greeting. Did Simon perhaps feel that he was too good to treat Jesus as an equal? The sinful woman, by contrast, lavished tears, expensive perfume, and kisses on her Savior. In this story it is the grateful prostitute, and not the stingy religious leader, whose sins were forgiven. Although it is God's grace through faith that saves us, and not acts of love or generosity, this woman's act demonstrated her true faith, and Jesus honored her faith. Overflowing love is the natural response to forgiveness and the appropriate consequence of faith. But only those who realize the depth of their sin can appreciate the complete forgiveness God offers them. Do you appreciate the wideness of God's mercy? Are you grateful for his forgiveness?

*April 29*

---

## Women accompany Jesus and his disciples

*LUKE 8:1-3 (Harmony 73)*

Not long afterwards he began a tour of the cities and villages of Galilee to announce the coming of the Kingdom of God, and took his twelve disciples with him. Some women went along, from whom he had cast out demons or whom he had healed; among them were Mary Magdalene (Jesus had cast out seven demons from her), Joanna, Chuza's wife (Chuza was King Herod's business manager and was in charge of his palace and domestic affairs), Susanna, and many others who were contributing from their private means to the support of Jesus and his disciples.

*God styles and equips men and women for various tasks, but all lead to the same goal—honoring God. Man gives life to woman; woman gives life to the world. Each role carries exclusive privileges that should eliminate any attitudes about an inferior or superior sex.*

**EQUALITY**

Jesus lifted women up from the agony of degradation and servitude to the joy of fellowship and service. In Jewish culture, women were not supposed to learn from rabbis. By allowing these women to travel with him, Jesus was showing that all people are equal under God. These women supported Jesus' ministry with their own money. They owed a great debt to him because he had driven demons out of some and had healed others. Here we catch a glimpse of a few of the people behind the scenes in Jesus' ministry. The ministry of those in the foreground is often supported by those whose work is less visible but just as essential. Offer your resources to God, whether or not you will be on center stage.

## Religious leaders accuse Jesus of being Satan

*MATTHEW 12:22-32 (also in MARK 3:20-30)*
*(Harmony 74a)*

hen a demon-possessed man—he was both blind and unable to talk—was brought to Jesus, and Jesus healed him so that he could both speak and see. The crowd was amazed. "Maybe Jesus is the Messiah!" they exclaimed.

But when the Pharisees heard about the miracle, they said, "He can cast out demons because he is Satan, king of devils."

*The Pharisees had already accused Jesus of being in league with Satan (9:34).*

Jesus knew their thoughts and replied, "A divided kingdom ends in ruin. A city or home divided against itself cannot stand. And if Satan is casting out Satan, he is fighting himself and destroying his own kingdom. And if, as you claim, I am casting out demons by invoking the powers of Satan, then what power do your own

*They were trying to discredit him by using an emotional argument. Refusing to believe that Jesus came from God, they said he was from Satan. Jesus easily exposed the foolishness of their argument.*

people use when they cast them out? Let them answer your accusation! But if I am casting out demons by the Spirit of God, then the Kingdom of God has arrived among you. One cannot rob Satan's kingdom without first binding Satan. Only then can his demons be cast out! Anyone who isn't helping me is harming me.

"Even blasphemy against me or any other sin can be forgiven—all except one: speaking against the Holy Spirit shall never be forgiven, either in this world or in the world to come."

#### THE UNFORGIVABLE SIN

The Pharisees had blasphemed against the Spirit by attributing the power by which Christ did miracles to Satan (12:24) instead of the Holy Spirit. The unforgivable sin is the deliberate refusal to acknowledge God's power in Christ. It indicates a deliberate and irreversible hardness of heart. Sometimes believers worry that they have accidently committed this unforgivable sin. But only those who have turned their backs on God and rejected all faith have any need to worry. Jesus said they can't be forgiven—not because their sin is worse than any other, but because they will never ask for forgiveness. Whoever rejects the prompting of the Holy Spirit removes himself or herself from the only force that can lead him or her to repentance and restoration to God.

## Religious leaders accuse Jesus of being Satan

### MATTHEW 12:33-37 *(Harmony 74b)*

*A* tree is identified by its fruit. A tree from a select variety produces good fruit; poor varieties don't. You brood of snakes! How could evil men like you speak what is good and right? For a man's heart determines his speech. A good man's speech reveals the rich treasures within him. An evil-hearted man is filled with venom, and his speech reveals it. And I tell you this, that you must give account on Judgment Day for every idle word you speak. Your words now reflect your fate then: either you will be justified by them or you will be condemned."

*Jesus Christ has been given the authority to judge all the earth (Romans 14:9-11; Philippians 2:9-11). Although his judgment is already at work in our lives, there will be a future, final judgment when Christ returns (Matthew 25:31-46) and everyone's life is reviewed and evaluated.*

**MOUTH WASH**

Jesus reminds us that what we say reveals what is in our hearts. What kinds of words come from your mouth? That is an indication of what your heart is really like. You can't solve your heart problem, however, just by cleaning up your speech. You must allow the Holy Spirit to fill you with new attitudes and motives; then your speech will be cleansed at its source.

## Religious leaders ask Jesus for a miracle

### MATTHEW 12:38-42 *(Harmony 75a)*

*O* ne day some of the Jewish leaders, including some Pharisees, came to Jesus asking him to show them a miracle.

But Jesus replied, "Only an evil, faithless nation would ask for further proof; and none will be given except what happened to Jonah the prophet! For as Jonah was in the great fish for three days and three nights, so I, the Messiah, shall be in the heart of the earth three days and three nights. The men of Nineveh shall arise against this nation at the judgment and condemn you. For when Jonah preached to them, they repented and turned to God from all their evil ways. And now one greater than Jonah is here—and you refuse to believe him. The queen of Sheba shall rise against this nation in the judgment and condemn it; for she came from a distant land to hear the wisdom of Solomon; and now one greater than Solomon is here—and you refuse to believe him."

*Jonah was a prophet sent to the Assyrian city of Nineveh (see the book of Jonah). Because Assyria was such a cruel and warlike nation, Jonah tried to run from his assignment and ended up spending three days in the stomach of a huge fish. When Jonah got out, he grudgingly went to Nineveh, preached God's message, and saw the city repent. By contrast, when Jesus came to his people, they refused to repent.*

**MORE EVIDENCE?**

The Pharisees were asking for another miraculous sign, but they were not sincerely seeking to know Jesus. Jesus knew they had already seen enough miraculous proof to convince them that he was the Messiah if they would just open their hearts. But they had already decided not to believe in him, and more miracles would not change that.

Many people have said, "If I could just see a real miracle, then I could really believe in God." But Jesus' response to the Pharisees applies to us. We have plenty of evidence—Jesus' birth, death, resurrection, and ascension, and centuries of his work in believers around the world. Instead of looking for additional evidence or miracles, accept what God has already given and move forward. He may use your life as evidence to reach another person.

*May 3*

## Religious leaders ask Jesus for a miracle

### MATTHEW 12:43-45 (Harmony 75b)

This evil nation is like a man possessed by a demon. For if the demon leaves, it goes into the deserts for a while, seeking rest but finding none. Then it says, 'I will return to the man I came from.' So it returns and finds the man's heart clean but empty! Then the demon finds seven other spirits more evil than itself, and all enter the man and live in him. And so he is worse off than before."

*Jesus told this parable to warn the Jewish religious leaders who were opposing him. The nation had benefited from the exorcisms and miracles of Jesus. But because they rejected the Savior, the nation would now be defenseless against evil and worse off than before—just like the man in the parable..*

Jesus was describing the attitude of the nation of Israel, and the religious leaders in particular. Just cleaning up one's life without filling it with God leaves plenty of room for Satan to enter. The book of Ezra records how the people rid themselves of idolatry but failed to replace it with love for God and obedience to him. Ridding our lives of sin is only the first step. We must also take the second step: filling our lives with God's Word and the Holy Spirit. Unfilled and complacent people are easy targets for Satan.

*May 4*

---

## Jesus describes his true family

### *MARK 3:31-35 (also in MATTHEW 12:46-50; LUKE 8:19-21) (Harmony 76)*

Now his mother and brothers arrived at the crowded house where he was teaching, and they sent word for him to come out and talk with them. "Your mother and brothers are outside and want to see you," he was told.

He replied, "Who is my mother? Who are my brothers?" Looking at those around him he said, "These are my mother and brothers! Anyone who does God's will is my brother, and my sister, and my mother."

*Jesus' family did not yet fully understand his ministry. Jesus explained that in our spiritual family, the relationships are ultimately more important and longer lasting than those formed in our physical families.*

### GOD'S FAMILY

God's family is accepting and doesn't exclude anyone. Although Jesus cared for his mother and brothers, he also cared for all those who loved him. Jesus did not show partiality; he allowed everyone the privilege of obeying God and becoming part of his family. In our increasingly computerized, impersonal world, warm relationships among members of God's family take on major importance. The church can give the loving, personalized care found nowhere else.

## Jesus tells the parable of the four soils

*MARK 4:1-9 (also in MATTHEW 13:1-9; LUKE 8:4-8)*
*(Harmony 77)*

Once again an immense crowd gathered around him on the beach as he was teaching, so he got into a boat and sat down and talked from there. His usual method of teaching was to tell the people stories. One of them went like this:

"Listen! A farmer decided to sow some grain. As he scattered it across his field, some of it fell on a path, and the birds came and picked it off the hard ground and ate it. Some fell on thin soil with underlying rock. It grew up quickly enough, but soon wilted beneath the hot sun and died because the roots had no nourishment in the shallow soil. Other seeds fell among thorns that shot up and crowded the young plants so that they produced no grain. But some of the seeds fell into good soil and yielded thirty times as much as he had planted—some of it even sixty or a hundred times as much! If you have ears, listen!"

*Jesus taught the people by telling parables, short stories using familiar scenes to explain spiritual truth. This method of teaching compels the listener to think. It conceals the truth from those who are too stubborn or prejudiced to hear what is being taught. Most parables have one main point, so we must be careful not to go beyond what Jesus intended to teach.*

**KEEP ON SOWING**

This parable should encourage spiritual "sowers"—those who teach, preach, and lead others. The farmer sowed good seed, but not all the seed sprouted, and even the plants that grew had varying yields. Don't be discouraged if you do not always see results as you faithfully teach the Word. Belief does not follow a formula (for example, a 4:1 ratio of seeds planted to seeds sprouted). Rather, it is a miracle of God's Holy Spirit as he uses your words to lead others to him.

## Jesus explains the parable of the four soils

### *MARK 4:10-25 (also in MATTHEW 13:10-23; LUKE 8:9-18) (Harmony 78)*

*A*fterwards, when he was alone with the Twelve and with his other disciples, they asked him, "What does your story mean?"

He replied, "You are permitted to know some truths about the Kingdom of God that are hidden to those outside the Kingdom:

"'Though they see and hear, they will not understand or turn to God, or be forgiven for their sins.'

"But if you can't understand *this* simple illustration, what will you do about all the others I am going to tell?

"The farmer I talked about is anyone who brings God's message to others, trying to plant good seed within their lives. The hard pathway, where some of the seed fell, represents the hard hearts of some of those who hear God's message; Satan comes at once to try to make them forget it. The rocky soil represents the hearts of those who hear the message with joy, but, like young plants in such soil, their roots don't go very deep, and though at first they get along fine, as soon as persecution begins, they wilt.

*We hear with our ears, but there is a deeper kind of listening with the mind and heart that is necessary in order to gain spiritual understanding from Jesus' words. Some people in the crowd were looking for evidence to use against Jesus; others truly wanted to learn and grow. Jesus' words were for the honest seekers.*

"The thorny ground represents the hearts of people who listen to the Good News and receive it, but all too quickly the attractions of this world and the delights of wealth, and the search for success and lure of nice things come in and crowd out God's message from their hearts, so that no crop is produced.

"But the good soil represents the hearts of those who truly accept God's message and produce a plentiful harvest for God—thirty, sixty, or even a hundred times as much as was planted in their hearts." Then he asked them, "When someone lights a lamp, does he put a box over it to shut out the light? Of course not! The light couldn't be seen or used. A lamp is placed on a stand to shine and be useful.

"All that is now hidden will someday come to light. If you have ears, listen! And be sure to put into practice what you hear. The more you do this, the more you will understand what I tell you. To him who has shall be given; from him who has not shall be taken away even what he has."

### SOILED AGAIN

The four soils represent four different ways people respond to God's message. Usually we think that Jesus was talking about four different kinds of people. But he may also have been talking about (1) different times or phases in a person's life, or (2) how we willingly receive God's message in some areas of our lives and resist it in others. For example, you may be open to God about your future, but closed concerning how you spend your money. You may respond like good soil to God's demand for worship, but like rocky soil to his demand to give to people in need. We must strive to be like good soil in every area of our lives at all times.

*May 7*

## Jesus tells the parable of the growing seed

*MARK 4:26-29 (Harmony 79)*

ere is another story illustrating what the Kingdom of God is like:

"A farmer sowed his field and went away, and as the days went by, the seeds grew and grew without his help. For the soil made the seeds grow. First the stalks pushed through, and later the heads of wheat formed, and finally the grain ripened, and then the farmer came at once with his sickle and harvested it."

### KINGDOM GROWTH

This parable about the Kingdom of God, recorded only by Mark, reveals that spiritual growth is a continual, gradual process that is finally consummated in a harvest of spiritual maturity. We can understand the process of spiritual growth by comparing it to the slow but certain growth of a plant. God's Kingdom grows. We don't know how. We do our part, and God does his, so that in due time a harvest is ready. Are you doing your part in helping the Kingdom of God grow to maturity?"

*Seed was sown by hand. As the farmer walked across the field he threw handfuls of seed onto the ground from a large bag slung across his shoulders.*

## Jesus tells the parable of the weeds

### *MATTHEW 13:24-30 (Harmony 80)*

ere is another illustration Jesus used: "The Kingdom of Heaven is like a farmer sowing good seed in his field; but one night as he slept, his enemy came and sowed thistles among the wheat. When the crop began to grow, the thistles grew too.

"The farmer's men came and told him, 'Sir, the field where you planted that choice seed is full of thistles!'

"'An enemy has done it,' he exclaimed.

"'Shall we pull out the thistles?' they asked.

"'No,' he replied. 'You'll hurt the wheat if you do. Let both grow together until the

*The Kingdom of Heaven is not a geographic location, but a spiritual realm where God rules and where we share in his eternal life. We join that Kingdom when we trust in Christ as Savior.*

harvest, and I will tell the reapers to sort out the thistles and burn them, and put the wheat in the barn.'"

#### THE COMING HARVEST

The young thistles (weeds) and the young blades of wheat look the same and can't be distinguished until they are grown and ready for harvest. Thistles (unbelievers) and wheat (believers) must live side by side in this world. God allows unbelievers to remain for a while, just as a farmer allows weeds to remain in his field so the surrounding wheat isn't uprooted with them. At the harvest, however, the weeds will be uprooted and thrown away. God's harvest (judgment) of all people is coming. We are to make ourselves ready by making sure that our faith is sincere.

## Jesus tells the parable of the mustard seed

### *MARK 4:30-34 (also in MATTHEW 13:31-32)* *(Harmony 81)*

esus asked, "How can I describe the Kingdom of God? What story shall I use to illustrate it? It is like a tiny mustard seed! Though this is one of the smallest of seeds, yet it grows to become one of the largest of plants, with long branches where birds can build their nests and be sheltered."

He used many such illustrations to teach the people as much as they were ready to understand. In fact, he taught only by illustrations in his public teaching, but afterwards, when he was alone with his disciples, he would explain his meaning to them.

*The mustard seed was the smallest seed a farmer used. Jesus used this parable to show that the Kingdom has small beginnings but will grow and produce great results.*

### WORLDWIDE FELLOWSHIP

Jesus adapted his methods to his audience's ability and desire to understand. He didn't speak in parables to confuse people, but to challenge sincere seekers to discover the meaning of his words. Jesus used this parable to explain that although Christianity had very small beginnings, it would grow into a worldwide community of believers. When you feel alone in your stand for Christ, realize that God is building a worldwide Kingdom. He has faithful followers in every part of the world, and your faith, no matter how small, can join with that of others to accomplish great things.

*May 10*

## Jesus tells the parable of the yeast

### MATTHEW 13:33-35 *(Harmony 82)*

He also used this example:

"The Kingdom of Heaven can be compared to a woman making bread. She takes a measure of flour and mixes in the yeast until it permeates every part of the dough."

Jesus constantly used these illustrations when speaking to the crowds. In fact, because the prophets said that he would use so many, he never spoke to them without at least one illustration. For it had been prophesied, "I will talk in parables; I will explain mysteries hidden since the beginning of time."

*All the parables in Matthew 13 teach us about God and his Kingdom. They explain what the Kingdom is really like as opposed to our expectations of it.*

### JUST ONE SEED

In other Bible passages, yeast is used as a symbol of evil or uncleanness. Here it is a positive symbol of growth. Although yeast looks like a minor ingredient, it permeates the whole loaf. Although the Kingdom began small and was nearly invisible, it would soon grow and have a great impact on the world. You may wonder what kind of impact you as just one person can make on your world. But as the Kingdom grows from one small seed, so it grows from individual believers who serve God. Ask God what you can do to help his Kingdom grow.

*May 11*

## Jesus explains the parable of the weeds

### MATTHEW 13:36-43 *(Harmony 83)*

hen, leaving the crowds outside, he went into the house. His disciples asked him to explain to them the illustration of the thistles and the wheat.

"All right," he said. "I am the farmer who sows the choice seed. The field is the world, and the seed represents the people of the Kingdom; the thistles are the people belonging to Satan. The enemy who sowed the thistles among the wheat is the devil; the harvest is the end of the world, and the reapers are the angels.

*Those who receive God's favor stand in bright contrast to those who receive his judgment. The wailing indicates sorrow or remorse, and gnashing of teeth shows extreme anxiety or pain.*

"Just as in this story the thistles are separated and burned, so shall it be at the end of the world: I will send my angels, and they will separate out of the Kingdom every temptation and all who are evil, and throw them into the furnace and burn them. There shall be weeping and gnashing of teeth. Then the godly shall shine as the sun in their Father's Kingdom. Let those with ears listen!"

#### FINAL JUDGMENT
At the end of the world, angels will separate the evil from the good. There are true and false believers in churches today, but we should be cautious in our judgments because only Christ is qualified to make the final separation. If you start judging, you may damage some of the good "plants." It's more important to judge our own response to God than to analyze others' responses.

## Jesus tells the parable of hidden treasure

### MATTHEW 13:44 *(Harmony 84)*

he Kingdom of Heaven is like a treasure a man discovered in a field. In his excitement, he sold everything he owned to get enough money to buy the field—and get the treasure, too!"

*Believers live in this world, but they're not "of" it; their home is really in heaven. We often feel like strangers in a world that would prefer to ignore God. But we have citizenship in the Kingdom of Heaven.*

**TOTAL RULE**

The Kingdom of Heaven is more valuable than anything else we can have, and a person must be willing to give up everything to obtain it. The man who discovered the treasure in the field stumbled upon it by accident but knew its value when he found it. When we decide to become part of God's Kingdom, we are accepted by God. Yet to truly experience citizenship in that Kingdom, we may need to give up some actions or attitudes. Have you set aside "the world" in order to have God's Kingdom? Do you live so that people know your true citizenship?"

## Jesus tells the parable of the pearl merchant

### MATTHEW 13:45-46 *(Harmony 85)*

gain, the Kingdom of Heaven is like a pearl merchant on the lookout for choice pearls. He discovered a real bargain—a pearl of great value—and sold everything he owned to purchase it!"

*Heaven is where God dwells, and it operates according to God's principles and values. It is eternal and unshakable. Our hope is in the certainty of heaven.*

**THE KINGDOM'S VALUE**

The merchant was earnestly searching for the pearl of great value, and when he found it he sold everything he had to purchase it. Why is the Kingdom so valuable? Someday, after God judges and destroys all sin, the Kingdom of Heaven will rule every corner of this earth. We will be with Christ in a way not possible in this life. John saw this day in a vision, and he cried out, "Look, the home of God is now among men, and he will live with them and they will be his people; yes, God himself will be among them" (Revelation 21:3). Our true loyalty is not to the things of this earth which will be destroyed. It is to God's truth, his way of life, his perfect creation. Can you willingly put aside everything else in order to have God and his Kingdom?

*May 14*

## Jesus tells the parable of the fishing net

### *MATTHEW 13:47-52 (Harmony 86)*

Again, the Kingdom of Heaven can be illustrated by a fisherman—he casts a net into the water and gathers in fish of every kind, valuable and worthless. When the net is full, he drags it up onto the beach and sits down and sorts out the edible ones into crates and throws the others away. That is the way it will be at the end of the world—the angels will come and separate the wicked people from the godly, casting the wicked into the fire; there shall be weeping and gnashing of teeth. Do you understand?"

*Revelation 14:14-17 describes Christ separating the faithful from the unfaithful like a farmer harvesting his crops. This will be a time of joy for Christians.*

"Yes," they said, "we do."

Then he added, "Those experts in Jewish law who are now my disciples have double treasures—from the Old Testament as well as from the New!"

#### FINAL SORTING

The parable of the fishing net has the same meaning as the parable of the wheat and thistles. We are to obey God and tell others about his grace and goodness, but we cannot dictate who is part of the Kingdom of Heaven and who is not. This sorting will be done at the Last Judgment by those infinitely more qualified than we. The Day of Judgment is that final day when we will appear before Christ and be held accountable for our lives. With God living in us through Christ, we have no reason to fear this day, because we have been saved from punishment. Instead, we can look forward to the Judgment because it will mean the end of sin and the beginning of a face-to-face relationship with Jesus Christ. Be careful of judging others' relationship with God. Only God is the true and reliable Judge.

## Jesus calms the storm

*MARK 4:35-41 (also in MATTHEW 8:23-27;*
*LUKE 8:22-25) (Harmony 87)*

As evening fell, Jesus said to his disciples, "Let's cross to the other side of the lake." So they took him just as he was and started out, leaving the crowds behind (though other boats followed). But soon a terrible storm arose. High waves began to break into the boat until it was nearly full of water and about to sink. Jesus was asleep at the back of the boat with his head on a cushion. Frantically they wakened him, shouting, "Teacher, don't you even care that we are all about to drown?"

Then he rebuked the wind and said to the sea, "Quiet down!" And the wind fell, and there was a great calm!

And he asked them, "Why were you so fearful? Don't you even yet have confidence in me?"

*The Sea of Galilee is an unusual body of water. It is relatively small (thirteen miles long, seven miles wide), but it is 150 feet deep, and the shoreline is 680 feet below sea level. Sudden storms can appear over the surrounding mountains with little warning, stirring the water into violent twenty-foot waves.*

And they were filled with awe and said among themselves, "Who is this man, that even the winds and seas obey him?"

#### CALMING THE STORMS

Although the disciples had witnessed many miracles, they panicked in this storm. As experienced sailors, they knew its danger; what they did not know was that Christ could control the forces of nature. There is often a stormy area of our human nature where we feel God can't or won't work. When we truly understand who God is, however, we will realize that he controls both the storms of nature and the storms of the troubled heart. Jesus' power that calmed this storm can also help us deal with the problems we face. Jesus is willing to help if we only ask him. We should never discount his power, even in terrible trials.

## Jesus sends the demons into a herd of pigs

### MARK 5:1-10 (also in MATTHEW 8:28-29; LUKE 8:26-31) (Harmony 88a)

*W*hen they arrived at the other side of the lake, a demon-possessed man ran out from a graveyard, just as Jesus was climbing from the boat.

This man lived among the gravestones and had such strength that whenever he was put into handcuffs and shackles—as he often was—he snapped the handcuffs from his wrists and smashed the shackles and walked away. No one was strong enough to control him. All day long and through the night he would wander among the tombs and in the wild hills, screaming and cutting himself with sharp pieces of stone.

*The demons begged Jesus not to send them to "some distant land" (to spare them from the abyss, which is also mentioned in Revelation 9:1 and 20:1-3 as the place of confinement for Satan and his messengers). The demons, of course, knew all about this place of confinement, and they didn't want to go there.*

When Jesus was still far out on the water, the man had seen him and had run to meet him, and fell down before him.

Then Jesus spoke to the demon within the man and said, "Come out, you evil spirit." It gave a terrible scream, shrieking, "What are you going to do to me, Jesus, Son of the Most High God? For God's sake, don't torture me!"

"What is your name?" Jesus asked, and the demon replied, "Legion, for there are many of us here within this man."

Then the demons begged him again and again not to send them to some distant land.

#### CHRIST'S AUTHORITY

These demons recognized Jesus and his authority immediately. They knew who Jesus was and what his great power could do to them. Demons, Satan's messengers, are powerful and destructive. Still active today, they attempt to distort and destroy people's relationship with God. Demons and demon-possession are real. It is vital that believers recognize the power of Satan and his demons, but we shouldn't let curiosity lead us to get involved with demonic forces (Deuteronomy 18:10-12). Demons have no authority over those who trust in Jesus. If we resist the devil, he will leave us alone (James 4:7).

## Jesus sends the demons into a herd of pigs

*MARK 5:11-20 (also in MATTHEW 8:30-34;*
*LUKE 8:32-39) (Harmony 88b)*

ow as it happened there was a huge herd of hogs rooting around on the hill above the lake. "Send us into those hogs," the demons begged.

And Jesus gave them permission. Then the evil spirits came out of the man and entered the hogs, and the entire herd plunged down the steep hillside into the lake and drowned.

The herdsmen fled to the nearby towns and countryside, spreading the news as they ran. Everyone rushed out to see for themselves. And a large crowd soon gathered where Jesus was; but as they saw the man sitting there, fully clothed and perfectly sane, they were frightened. Those who saw what happened were telling everyone about it, and the crowd began pleading with Jesus to go away and leave them alone! So he got back into the boat. The man who had been possessed by the demons begged Jesus to let him go along. But Jesus said no.

*Why didn't Jesus send these demons to the abyss? His time for that has not yet come. But it will come. The book of Revelation portrays the future victory of Jesus over Satan, his demons, and all evil.*

"Go home to your friends," he told him, "and tell them what wonderful things God has done for you; and how merciful he has been."

So the man started off to visit the Ten Towns of that region and began to tell everyone about the great things Jesus had done for him; and they were awestruck by his story.

### WHAT'S MORE IMPORTANT?

The demons destroyed the hogs, which hurt the finances of those tending the hogs, but can hogs and money compare with a human life? A man had been freed from the devil's power, but the people thought only about their livestock. People have always tended to value financial gain above needy people. Throughout history, most wars have been fought to protect economic interests. Much injustice and oppression, both at home and abroad, is the direct result of some individual's or company's urge to get rich. People are continually being sacrificed to the god of money. Don't think more highly of "swine" than of people. Think carefully about how your decisions will affect other human beings, and be willing to choose a simpler lifestyle if it will keep other people from being harmed.

## Jesus heals a bleeding woman and restores a girl to life

*MARK 5:21-34 (also in MATTHEW 9:18-22;*
*LUKE 8:40-48) (Harmony 89a)*

*W*hen Jesus had gone across by boat to the other side of the lake, a vast crowd gathered around him on the shore.

The leader of the local synagogue, whose name was Jairus, came and fell down before him, pleading with him to heal his little daughter.

"She is at the point of death," he said in desperation. "Please come and place your hands on her and make her live."

Jesus went with him, and the crowd thronged behind. In the crowd was a woman who had been sick for twelve years with a hemorrhage. She had suffered much from many doctors through the years and had become poor from paying

*It isn't that Jesus didn't know who had touched him; it's that he wanted the woman to step forward and identify herself. Jesus wanted to teach her that his cloak did not contain magical properties, but that her faith in him had healed her.*

them, and was no better but, in fact, was worse. She had heard all about the wonderful miracles Jesus did, and that is why she came up behind him through the crowd and touched his clothes.

For she thought to herself, "If I can just touch his clothing, I will be healed." And sure enough, as soon as she had touched him, the bleeding stopped and she knew she was well!

Jesus realized at once that healing power had gone out from him, so he turned around in the crowd and asked, "Who touched my clothes?"

His disciples said to him, "All this crowd pressing around you, and you ask who touched you?"

But he kept on looking around to see who it was who had done it. Then the frightened woman, trembling at the realization of what had happened to her, came and fell at his feet and told him what she had done. And he said to her, "Daughter, your faith has made you well; go in peace, healed of your disease."

#### AVAILABLE POWER

Many people surrounded Jesus as he made his way toward Jairus's house. It was virtually impossible to get through the multitude, but one woman fought her way desperately through the crowd in order to touch Jesus. As soon as she did so, she was healed. What a difference there is between the crowds that are curious about Jesus and the few who reach out and touch him! Today, many people are vaguely familiar with Jesus, but nothing in their lives is changed or bettered by this passing acquaintance. It is only faith that releases God's healing power. Are you just curious about God, or do you reach out to him in faith, knowing that his mercy will bring healing to your body, soul, and spirit?

## *May 19*

## Jesus heals a bleeding woman and restores a girl to life

*MARK 5:35-43 (also in MATTHEW 9:23-26; LUKE 8:49-56) (Harmony 89b)*

While he was still talking to her, messengers arrived from Jairus's home with the news that it was too late—his daughter was dead and there was no point in Jesus' coming now. But Jesus ignored their comments and said to Jairus, "Don't be afraid. Just trust me."

Then Jesus halted the crowd and wouldn't let anyone go on with him to Jairus's home except Peter and James and John. When they arrived, Jesus saw that all was in great confusion, with unrestrained weeping and wailing. He went inside and spoke to the people. "Why all this weeping and commotion?" he asked. "The child isn't dead; she is only asleep!"

They laughed at him in bitter derision, but he told them all to leave, and taking the little girl's father and mother and his three disciples, he went into the room where she was lying.

*Jesus told the girl's parents not to spread the news of the miracle. He wanted the facts to speak for themselves, and the time was not yet right for a major confrontation with the religious leaders. Jesus still had much to accomplish, and he didn't want people following him just to see his miracles.*

Taking her by the hand he said to her, "Get up, little girl!" (She was twelve years old.) And she jumped up and walked around! Her parents just couldn't get over it. Jesus instructed them very earnestly not to tell what had happened and told them to give her something to eat.

### POWER OVER DEATH

The leader of the synagogue didn't come to Jesus until his daughter was near death—it was too late for anyone else to help. But Jesus simply went to the girl and raised her! In our lives Christ can make a difference when it is too late for anyone else to help. He can bring healing to broken relationships, release from addicting habits, and forgiveness and healing to emotional scars. If your situation looks hopeless, remember that Christ can do the impossible.

*May 20*

## Jesus heals the blind and mute

*MATTHEW 9:27-34 (Harmony 90)*

As Jesus was leaving her home, two blind men followed along behind, shouting, "O Son of King David, have mercy on us."

They went right into the house where he was staying, and Jesus asked them, "Do you believe I can make you see?"

"Yes, Lord," they told him, "we do."

Then he touched their eyes and said, "Because of your faith it will happen."

And suddenly they could see! Jesus sternly warned them not to tell anyone about it, but instead they spread his fame all over the town.

*While the Pharisees questioned, debated, and dissected Jesus, people were being healed and lives changed right in front of them. Their skepticism was based not on insufficient evidence but on jealousy of Jesus' popularity.*

Leaving that place, Jesus met a man who couldn't speak because a demon was inside him. So Jesus cast out the demon, and instantly the man could talk. How the crowds marveled! "Never in all our lives have we seen anything like this," they exclaimed.

But the Pharisees said, "The reason he can cast out demons is that he is demon-possessed himself—possessed by Satan, the demon king!"

### HEALING POWER

These blind men were persistent. They went right into the house where Jesus was staying. They knew Jesus could heal them. "Son of King David" was a popular way of addressing Jesus as the Messiah because it was known that the Messiah would be a descendant of David (Isaiah 9:7). This is the first time the title is used in Matthew. Jesus' ability to give sight to the blind was prophesied in Isaiah 29:18; 35:5; 42:7. These men let nothing stop them from finding the Messiah. That's real faith in action. If you believe Jesus is the answer to your every need, don't let anything or anyone stop you from reaching him.

## The people of Nazareth refuse to believe

### MARK 6:1-6 (also in MATTHEW 13:53-58) (Harmony 91)

*S*oon afterwards he left that section of the country and returned with his disciples to Nazareth, his hometown. The next Sabbath he went to the synagogue to teach, and the people were astonished at his wisdom and his miracles because he was just a local man like themselves.

"He's no better than we are," they said. "He's just a carpenter, Mary's boy, and a brother of James and Joseph, Judas and Simon. And his sisters live right here among us." And they were offended!

Then Jesus told them, "A prophet is honored everywhere except in his hometown and among his relatives and by his own family." And because of their unbelief he couldn't do any mighty miracles among them except to place his hands on a few sick people and heal them. And he could hardly accept the fact that they wouldn't believe in him.

*Jesus could have done greater miracles in Nazareth, but he chose not to because of the people's pride and unbelief. The miracles he did had little effect on the people because they did not accept his message or believe that he was from God.*

Then he went out among the villages, teaching.

#### SEEING THE REAL JESUS

Jesus was teaching effectively and wisely, but the people of his hometown saw him as only a carpenter. "He's no better than we are—he's just a common laborer," they said. They were offended that others could be impressed by Jesus and follow him. They rejected his authority because he was one of their peers. They thought they knew him, but their preconceived notions about who he was made it impossible for them to accept his message. Don't let prejudice blind you to truth. As you learn more about Jesus, try to see him for who he really is.

## Jesus urges the disciples to pray for workers

### MATTHEW 9:35-38 *(Harmony 92)*

*J*esus traveled around through all the cities and villages of that area, teaching in the Jewish synagogues and announcing the Good News about the Kingdom. And wherever he went he healed people of every sort of illness. And what pity he felt for the crowds that came, because their problems were so great and they didn't know what to do or where to go for help. They were like sheep without a shepherd.

"The harvest is so great, and the workers are so few," he told his disciples. "So pray to the one in charge of the harvesting, and ask him to recruit more workers for his harvest fields."

*The gospel of the Kingdom was that the promised and long-awaited Messiah had finally come. His healing miracles were a sign that his teaching was true.*

### HELP WANTED

Jesus looked at the crowds following him and referred to them as a field ripe for harvest. Many people are ready to give their lives to Christ if someone would show them how. Jesus commands us to pray that people will respond to this need for workers. Often when we pray for something, God answers our prayers by using *us.* Be prepared for God to use you to show another person the way to him. Jesus needs workers who know how to deal with people's problems. We can comfort others and show them the way to live because we have been helped with our problems by God and his laborers.

## Jesus sends out the twelve disciples

### MATTHEW 10:1-15 *(also in MARK 6:7-13; LUKE 9:1-6) (Harmony 93)*

*J*esus called his twelve disciples to him and gave them authority to cast out evil spirits and to heal every kind of sickness and disease.

Here are the names of his twelve disciples: Simon (also called

Peter), Andrew (Peter's brother), James (Zebedee's son), John (James's brother), Philip, Bartholomew, Thomas, Matthew (the tax collector), James (Alphaeus's son), Thaddaeus, Simon (a member of "The Zealots," a subversive political party), Judas Iscariot (the one who betrayed him).

*Jesus asked his disciples to go only to the Jews because he came first to the Jews (Romans 1:16). God chose them to tell the rest of the world about him. Jewish disciples and apostles preached the gospel of the risen Christ all around the Roman Empire, and soon Gentiles were pouring into the church. The Bible clearly teaches that God's message of salvation is for all people.*

Jesus sent them out with these instructions: "Don't go to the Gentiles or the Samaritans, but only to the people of Israel—God's lost sheep. Go and announce to them that the Kingdom of Heaven is near. Heal the sick, raise the dead, cure the lepers, and cast out demons. Give as freely as you have received!

"Don't take any money with you; don't even carry a duffle bag with extra clothes and shoes, or even a walking stick; for those you help should feed and care for you. Whenever you enter a city or village, search for a godly man and stay in his home until you leave for the next town. When you ask permission to stay, be friendly, and if it turns out to be a godly home, give it your blessing; if not, keep the blessing. Any city or home that doesn't welcome you—shake off the dust of that place from your feet as you leave. Truly, the wicked cities of Sodom and Gomorrah will be better off at Judgment Day than they."

### USED BY GOD

The list of Jesus' twelve disciples doesn't give us many details—probably because there weren't many impressive details to tell. Jesus called people from all walks of life—fishermen, political activists, tax collectors. He called common people and uncommon leaders, rich and poor, educated and uneducated. Today many people think only certain people are fit to follow Christ, but this was not the attitude of the Master himself. Jesus *called* his twelve disciples. He didn't draft them, force them, or ask them to volunteer; he chose them to serve him in a special way. Christ calls us today. He doesn't twist our arms and make us do something we don't want to do. We can choose to join him or remain behind. God can use anyone, no matter how insignificant he or she appears. God uses ordinary people to do his extraordinary work. Be one who is used by God.

## Jesus prepares the disciples for persecution

*MATTHEW 10:16-23 (Harmony 94a)*

am sending you out as sheep among wolves. Be as wary as serpents and harmless as doves. But beware! For you will be arrested and tried, and whipped in the synagogues. Yes, and you must stand trial before governors and kings for my sake. This will give you the opportunity to tell them about me, yes, to witness to the world.

"When you are arrested, don't worry about what to say at your trial, for you will be given the right words at the right time. For it won't be you doing the talking—it will be the Spirit of your heavenly Father speaking through you!

*Enduring to the end is not a way to be saved but rather the evidence that a person is really committed to Jesus. Persistence is not a means to earn salvation; it is the by-product of a truly devoted life.*

"Brother shall betray brother to death, and fathers shall betray their own children. And children shall rise against their parents and cause their deaths. Everyone shall hate you because you belong to me. But all of you who endure to the end shall be saved.

"When you are persecuted in one city, flee to the next! I will return before you have reached them all!"

#### BE PREPARED

Jesus told the disciples that when arrested for preaching the gospel, they should not worry about what to say in their defense—God's Spirit would speak through them. This promise was fulfilled in Acts 4:8-14 and elsewhere. Some mistakenly think this means that we don't have to prepare to present the gospel because God will take care of everything. Scripture teaches, however, that we are to make carefully prepared, thoughtful statements (Colossians 4:6). Jesus is not telling us to stop preparing but to stop worrying.

## Jesus prepares the disciples for persecution

*MATTHEW 10:24-33 (Harmony 94b)*

*A* student is not greater than his teacher. A servant is not above his master. The student shares his teacher's fate. The servant shares his master's! And since I, the master of the household, have been called 'Satan,' how much more will you! But don't be afraid of those who threaten you. For the time is coming when the truth will be revealed: their secret plots will become public information.

*The Pharisees did, in fact, call Jesus "Satan" (see Matthew 9:34). Good is sometimes labeled evil. If Jesus, who is perfect, was called evil, his followers should expect that similar accusations will be directed at them. But those who endure will be vindicated (10:22).*

"What I tell you now in the gloom, shout abroad when daybreak comes. What I whisper in your ears, proclaim from the housetops!

"Don't be afraid of those who can kill only your bodies—but can't touch your souls! Fear only God who can destroy both soul and body in hell. Not one sparrow (What do they cost? Two for a penny?) can fall to the ground without your Father knowing it. And the very hairs of your head are all numbered. So don't worry! You are more valuable to him than many sparrows.

"If anyone publicly acknowledges me as his friend, I will openly acknowledge him as my friend before my Father in heaven. But if anyone publicly denies me, I will openly deny him before my Father in heaven."

### COVERED BY GOD

Jesus said that God is aware of everything that happens, even to sparrows, and you are far more valuable to him than they are. You are so valuable that God sent his only Son to die for you (John 3:16). Because God places such value on you, you need never fear personal threats or difficult trials. These can't shake God's love or dislodge his Spirit from within you.

But this doesn't mean that God will take away all your troubles (see 10:16). The real test of value is how well something holds up under the wear, tear, and abuse of everyday life. Those who stand up for Christ in spite of their troubles truly have lasting value and will receive great rewards (see 5:11-12). Despite your struggles and trials, remember that you are valuable to God and that he is making you more like Christ (Romans 8:29).

## Jesus prepares the disciples for persecution

### MATTHEW 10:34-39 *(Harmony 94c)*

*D*on't imagine that I came to bring peace to the earth! No, rather, a sword. I have come to set a man against his father, and a daughter against her mother, and a daughter-in-law against her mother-in-law—a man's worst enemies will be right in his own home! If you love your father and mother more than you love me, you are not worthy of being mine; or if you love your son or daughter more than me, you are not worthy of being mine. If you refuse to take up your cross and follow me, you are not worthy of being mine.

"If you cling to your life, you will lose it; but if you give it up for me, you will save it."

*To take our cross and follow Jesus means to be willing to publicly identify with him, to experience almost certain opposition, and to be committed to face even suffering and death for his sake.*

**FREE TO FOLLOW**

Matthew 10:39 is a positive and negative statement of the same truth: Clinging to this life may cause us to forfeit the best from Christ in this world *and* in the next. The more we love this life's rewards (leisure, power, popularity, financial security), the more we will discover how empty they really are. The best way to enjoy life, therefore, is to loosen our greedy grasp on earthly rewards so that we can be free to follow Christ. In doing so, we will inherit eternal life and begin at once to experience the benefits of following Christ. To what are you holding tightly for security and meaning in life? Let go!

*May 27*

## Jesus prepares the disciples for persecution

### MATTHEW 10:40-42 *(Harmony 94d)*

*T*hose who welcome you are welcoming me. And when they welcome me they are welcoming God who sent me. If you welcome a prophet because he is a man of God, you will be given the same reward a prophet gets. And if you welcome good and godly men because of their godliness, you will be given a reward like theirs.

"And if, as my representatives, you give even a cup of cold water to a little child, you will surely be rewarded."

*Jesus gave the disciples a principle to guide their actions as they ministered to others: "Give as freely as you have received" (10:8). Because God has showered us with his blessings, we should give generously to others of our time, love, and possessions.*

### LOVE'S MEASUREMENT

How much we love God can be measured by how well we treat others. Jesus' example of giving a cup of cold water to a thirsty child is a good model of unselfish service. A child usually can't or won't return a favor. God notices every good deed we do or don't do as if he were the one receiving it. Is there something unselfish you can do for someone else today? Although no one else may see you, God will notice.

## May 28

## Herod kills John the Baptist

***MARK 6:14-16 (also in MATTHEW 14:1-2; LUKE 9:7-9) (Harmony 95a)***

King Herod soon heard about Jesus, for his miracles were talked about everywhere. The king thought Jesus was John the Baptist come back to life again. So the people were saying, "No wonder he can do such miracles." Others thought Jesus was Elijah the ancient prophet, now returned to life again; still others claimed he was a new prophet like the great ones of the past.

"No," Herod said, "it is John, the man I beheaded. He has come back from the dead."

*Herod was a tetrarch— one of four rulers over the four districts of Palestine. His territory included the regions of Galilee and Perea. He was the son of Herod the Great, who ordered the killing of the babies in Bethlehem (Matthew 2:16). Also known as Herod Antipas, he heard Jesus' case before Jesus' crucifixion (Luke 23:6-12).*

### CHRIST'S TRUE IDENTITY

It was so difficult for the people to accept Jesus as the Son of God that they tried to come up with other solutions—most of which sound quite unbelievable to us. Many thought that he must be someone who had come back to life, perhaps John the Baptist or another prophet. Some suggested that he was Elijah, the great prophet who did not die but was taken to heaven in a chariot of fire (2 Kings 2:1-11). Very few found the correct answer, as Peter did (Luke 9:20).

Many people still find it difficult to accept Jesus as the fully human yet fully divine Son of God. People are still trying to find alternate explanations—a great prophet, a radical political leader, a self-deceived rabble-rouser. None of these explanations can account for Jesus' miracles or, especially, his glorious resurrection—so these realities too have to be explained away. In the end, the attempts to explain away Jesus are far more difficult to believe than the truth. People still have to make up their minds about Jesus. Some think that if they can name what he is—prophet, teacher, good man—they can weaken the power of his claim on their lives. But what they *think* does not change who Jesus *is*. Jesus is the God-man; he is God. Does he rule in your life?

*May 29*

---

## Herod kills John the Baptist

***MARK 6:17-29 (also in MATTHEW 14:3-12)*** *(Harmony 95b)*

For Herod had sent soldiers to arrest and imprison John because he kept saying it was wrong for the king to marry Herodias, his brother Philip's wife. Herodias wanted John killed in revenge, but without Herod's approval she was powerless. And Herod respected John, knowing that he was a good and holy man, and so he kept him under his protection. Herod was disturbed whenever he talked with John, but even so he liked to listen to him.

*Philip, Herod's half brother, was another of Palestine's four rulers. His territories were Iturea and Trachonitis, northeast of the Sea of Galilee (Luke 3:1). Philip's wife, Herodias, left Philip to live with Herod Antipas. John the Baptist condemned Herod and Herodias for living immorally.*

Herodias's chance finally came. It was Herod's birthday and he gave a stag party for his palace aides, army officers, and the leading citizens of Galilee. Then Herodias's daughter came in and danced before them and greatly pleased them all.

"Ask me for anything you like," the king vowed, "even half of my kingdom, and I will give it to you!"

She went out and consulted her mother, who told her, "Ask for John the Baptist's head!"

So she hurried back to the king and told him, "I want the head of John the Baptist—right now—on a tray!"

Then the king was sorry, but he was embarrassed to break his oath in front of his guests. So he sent one of his bodyguards to the prison to cut off John's head and bring it to him. The soldier killed John in the prison, and brought back his head on a tray, and gave it to the girl and she took it to her mother.

When John's disciples heard what had happened, they came for his body and buried it in a tomb.

### DETERMINE TO DO RIGHT

As a ruler under Roman authority, Herod had no kingdom to give. The offer of half his kingdom was Herod's way to say that he would give Herodias's daughter almost anything she wanted. When Herodias asked for John's head, Herod would have been greatly embarrassed in front of his guests if he had denied her request. Words are powerful. Because they can lead to great sin, we should use them with great care. How easy it is to give in to the crowd and to let ourselves be pressured into doing wrong. Don't get in a situation where it will be too embarrassing to do what is right. Determine to do what is right, no matter how embarrassing or painful it may be.

*May 30*

---

## Jesus feeds five thousand

### MARK 6:30-34 (also in MATTHEW 14:13-14; LUKE 9:10-11; JOHN 6:1-4) (Harmony 96a)

 he apostles now returned to Jesus from their tour and told him all they had done and what they had said to the people they visited.

Then Jesus suggested, "Let's get away from the crowds for a while and rest." For so many people were coming and going that they scarcely had time to eat. So they left by boat for a quieter spot. But many people saw them leaving and ran on ahead along the shore and met them as they landed. So the usual vast crowd was there as he stepped from the boat; and he had pity on them

*When the disciples had returned from their mission, Jesus took them away to rest. Doing God's work is very important, but Jesus recognized that to do it effectively we need periodic rest and renewal.*

because they were like sheep without a shepherd, and he taught them many things they needed to know.

### JESUS LOVED PEOPLE

Jesus had tried to slip quietly away from the crowds, but they found out where he was going and followed him. Instead of showing impatience at this interruption, Jesus welcomed the people and ministered to their needs. This crowd was as pitiful as a flock of sheep without a shepherd. Sheep are easily scattered; without a shepherd they are in grave danger. Jesus was the Shepherd who could teach them what they needed to know and keep them from straying from God. How do you see people who interrupt your schedule—as nuisances, or as the reason for your life and ministry?

*May 31*

## Jesus feeds five thousand

*MARK 6:35-44 (also in MATTHEW 14:15-21; LUKE 9:12-17; JOHN 6:5-13) (Harmony 96b)*

*L*ate in the afternoon his disciples came to him and said, "Tell the people to go away to the nearby villages and farms and buy themselves some food, for there is nothing to eat here in this desolate spot, and it is getting late."

But Jesus said, *"You* feed them."

"With what?" they asked. "It would take a fortune to buy food for all this crowd!"

"How much food do we have?" he asked. "Go and find out."

They came back to report that there were five loaves of bread and two fish. Then Jesus told the crowd to sit down, and soon colorful groups of fifty or a hundred each were sitting on the green grass.

*The text states that there were five thousand men present, besides women and children. Therefore the total number of people Jesus fed could have been ten to fifteen thousand. The number of men is listed separately because in the Jewish culture of the day, men and women usually ate separately when in public. The children ate with the women.*

He took the five loaves and two fish and looking up to heaven, gave thanks for the food. Breaking the loaves into pieces, he gave some of the bread and fish to each disciple to place before the people. And the crowd ate until they could hold no more!

There were about 5,000 men there for that meal, and afterwards twelve basketfuls of scraps were picked up off the grass!

## GIVE WHAT YOU HAVE

Jesus multiplied five loaves and two fish to feed more than five thousand people. What he was originally given seemed insufficient, but in his hands it became more than enough. We often feel that our contribution to Jesus is meager, but he can use and multiply whatever we give him, whether it is talent, time, or treasure. It is when we give them to Jesus that our resources are multiplied. God gives in abundance. He takes whatever we can offer him in time, ability, or resources and multiplies its effectiveness beyond our wildest expectations. If you take the first step in making yourself available to God, he will show you how greatly you can be used to advance the work of his Kingdom.

## Jesus walks on water

### MATTHEW 14:22-24 (also in MARK 6:45-46; JOHN 6:16-18) (Harmony 97a)

mmediately after this, Jesus told his disciples to get into their boat and cross to the other side of the lake while he stayed to get the people started home.

Then afterwards he went up into the hills to pray. Night fell, and out on the lake the disciples were in trouble. For the wind had risen and they were fighting heavy seas.

*The miraculous feeding of the five thousand occurred on the shores of the Sea of Galilee. Jesus sent his disciples across the lake while he went up into the rolling hills to spend time in prayer.*

**TIME ALONE**

Seeking solitude was an important priority for Jesus (see also 14:13). He made room in his busy schedule to be alone with the Father. Spending time with God in prayer nurtures a vital relationship and equips us to meet life's challenges and struggles. Finding time to pray is not easy, but prayer is the vital link between us and God. Like Jesus, we must break away from others to talk with God, even if we have to get up very early in the morning to do it! Develop the discipline of spending time alone with God—it will help you grow spiritually and become more and more like Christ.

## Jesus walks on water

### MATTHEW 14:25-33 (also in MARK 6:47-52; JOHN 6:19-21) (Harmony 97b)

bout four o'clock in the morning Jesus came to them, walking on the water! They screamed in terror, for they thought he was a ghost.

But Jesus immediately spoke to them, reassuring them. "Don't be afraid!" he said.

Then Peter called to him: "Sir, if it is really you, tell me to come over to you, walking on the water."

"All right," the Lord said, "come along!"

So Peter went over the side of the boat and walked on the water toward Jesus. But when he looked around at the high waves, he was terrified and began to sink. "Save me, Lord!" he shouted.

*The disciples were afraid, but Jesus' presence calmed their fears. We all experience fear. Do we try to deal with it ourselves, or do we let Jesus deal with it? In times of fear and uncertainty, it is calming to know that Christ is always with us.*

Instantly Jesus reached out his hand and rescued him. "O man of little faith," Jesus said. "Why did you doubt me?" And when they had climbed back into the boat, the wind stopped.

The others sat there, awestruck. "You really are the Son of God!" they exclaimed.

#### TRANSFER THE TRUTH

The disciples didn't want to believe, perhaps because (1) they couldn't accept the fact that this human named Jesus was really the Son of God; (2) they dared not believe that the Messiah would choose them as his followers—it was too good to be true; (3) they still did not understand the real purpose for Jesus' coming to earth. Their disbelief took the form of misunderstanding.

Even after watching Jesus miraculously feed five thousand people, they still could not take the final step of faith and believe that he was God's Son. If they had, they would not have been amazed that Jesus could walk on water. The disciples did not transfer the truth they already knew about Jesus to their own lives. We read that Jesus walked on the water, and yet we often marvel that he is able to work in our lives. We must not only believe that these miracles really occurred; we must also transfer the truth to our own life situations.

*June 3*

## Jesus heals all who touch him

### MARK 6:53-56 (also in MATTHEW 14:34-36)
(Harmony 98)

 hen they arrived at Gennesaret on the other side of the lake, they moored the boat and climbed out. The people standing around there recognized him at once, and ran throughout the whole area to spread the news of his arrival, and began carrying sick folks to him on mats and stretchers. Wherever he went—in villages and cities, and out on the farms—they laid the sick in the market plazas and streets, and begged him to let them at least touch the fringes of his clothes; and as many as touched him were healed.

*Gennesaret was a small fertile plain located on the west side of the Sea of Galilee. Capernaum, Jesus' home, sat at the northern edge of this plain.*

### THE GREAT HEALER

The people recognized Jesus as a great healer, but how many understood who he truly was? They came to Jesus for physical healing, but did they come for spiritual healing? They came to prolong their lives on earth, but did they come to secure their eternal lives? People may seek Jesus to learn valuable lessons from his life or in hopes of finding relief from pain. But we miss Jesus' whole message if we seek him only to heal our bodies but not our souls; if we look to him for help only in this life, rather than for his eternal plan for us. Only when we understand the real Jesus Christ can we appreciate how he can truly change our lives.

*June 4*

## Jesus is the true Bread from heaven

### JOHN 6:22-29 (Harmony 99a)

The next morning, back across the lake, crowds began gathering on the shore waiting to see Jesus. For they knew that he and his disciples had come over together and that the disciples had gone off in their boat, leaving him behind. Several small boats from Tiberias were nearby, so when the people saw that Jesus wasn't there, nor his disciples, they got into the boats and went across to Capernaum to look for him.

When they arrived and found him, they said, "Sir, how did you get here?" Jesus replied, "The truth of the matter is that you want to be with me because I fed you, not because you believe in me. But you shouldn't be so concerned about perishable things like food. No, spend your

*Jesus criticized the people who only followed him for the physical and temporal benefits and not for the satisfying of their spiritual hunger. Many people use religion to gain prestige, comfort, or even political votes. But those are self-centered motives.*

energy seeking the eternal life that I, the Messiah, can give you. For God the Father has sent me for this very purpose."

They replied, "What should we do to satisfy God?"

Jesus told them, "This is the will of God, that you believe in the one he has sent."

### WE MUST BELIEVE

Many sincere seekers for God are puzzled about what he wants them to do. The world's religions are humankind's attempts to answer this question. But Jesus' reply is brief and simple: We must believe on him whom God has sent. Satisfying God does not come from the work we *do,* but from whom we *believe.* The first step is accepting that Jesus is who he claims to be. All spiritual development is built on this affirmation. Declare to Jesus that he is "the Christ, the Messiah, Son of the living God" (Matthew 16:16), and embark on a life of belief that is satisfying to your Creator.

*June 5*

## Jesus is the true Bread from heaven

**JOHN 6:30-40** *(Harmony 99b)*

They replied, "You must show us more miracles if you want us to believe you are the Messiah. Give us free bread every day, like our fathers had while they journeyed through the wilderness! As the Scriptures say, 'Moses gave them bread from heaven.'"

Jesus said, "Moses didn't give it to them. My Father did. And now he offers you true Bread from heaven. The true Bread is a Person—the one sent by God from heaven, and he gives life to the world."

*Jesus did not work independently of God the Father, but in union with him. His purpose was to do the will of God, not to satisfy human desires.*

"Sir," they said, "give us that bread every day of our lives!"

Jesus replied, "I am the Bread of Life. No one coming to me will ever be hungry again. Those believing in me will never thirst. But the trouble is, as I have told you before, you haven't believed even though you have seen me. But some will come to me—those the Father has given me—and I will never, never reject them. For I have come here from heaven to do the will of God who sent me, not to have my own way. And this is the will of God, that I should not lose even one of all those he has given me, but that I should raise them to eternal life at the Last Day.

For it is my Father's will that everyone who sees his Son and believes on him should have eternal life—that I should raise him at the Last Day."

### SPIRITUAL HUNGER

People eat bread to satisfy physical hunger and to sustain physical life. We can satisfy spiritual hunger and sustain spiritual life only by a right relationship with Jesus Christ. No wonder he called himself the Bread of Life. But bread must be eaten to sustain life, and Christ must be invited into our daily walk to sustain spiritual life.

*June 6*

## The Jews disagree that Jesus is from heaven

*JOHN 6:41-51 (Harmony 100a)*

Then the Jews began to murmur against him because he claimed to be the Bread from heaven.

"What?" they exclaimed. "Why, he is merely Jesus the son of Joseph, whose father and mother we know. What is this he is saying, that he came down from heaven?"

But Jesus replied, "Don't murmur among yourselves about my saying that. For no one can come to me unless the Father who sent me draws him to me, and at the Last Day I will cause all such to rise again from the dead. As it is written in the Scriptures, 'They shall all be taught of God.' Those the Father speaks to, who learn the truth from him, will be attracted to me. (Not that anyone actually sees the Father, for only I have seen him.)

*The religious leaders grumbled because they could not accept Jesus' claim of divinity. They saw him only as a carpenter from Nazareth. They refused to believe that Jesus was God's divine Son, and they could not tolerate his message.*

"How earnestly I tell you this—anyone who believes in me already has eternal life! Yes, I am the Bread of Life! When your fathers in the wilderness ate bread from the skies, they all died. But the Bread from heaven gives eternal life to everyone who eats it. I am that Living Bread that came down out of heaven. Anyone eating this Bread shall live forever; this Bread is my flesh given to redeem humanity.

### SATISFACTION

The religious leaders frequently asked Jesus to prove to them why he was better than the prophets they already had. Jesus was referring to the manna that Moses had given their ancestors in the wilderness (see Exodus 16). That bread was physical and temporal. The people had eaten it, and it had sustained them for a day. But they had to get more bread every day, and this bread could not keep them from dying. Jesus, who is much greater than Moses, offers himself as the spiritual Bread from heaven that satisfies completely and leads to eternal life. God, not man, plays the most active role in salvation. When someone chooses to believe in Jesus Christ as Savior, he or she does so only in response to the urging of God's Holy Spirit. God does the urging and gives the faith; then we decide whether or not to believe. Thus no one can believe in Jesus without God's help. If you know Christ as Savior, thank him for his powerful work in your life.

## June 7

---

## The Jews disagree that Jesus is from heaven

*JOHN 6:52-59 (Harmony 100b)*

Then the Jews began arguing with each other about what he meant. "How can this man give us his flesh to eat?" they asked.

So Jesus said it again, "With all the earnestness I possess I tell you this: Unless you eat the flesh of the Messiah and drink his blood, you cannot have eternal life within you. But anyone who does eat my flesh and drink my blood has eternal life, and I will raise him at the Last Day. For my flesh is the true food, and my blood is the true drink. Everyone who eats my flesh and drinks my blood is in me, and I in him. I live by the power of the living Father who sent me, and in the same way those who partake of me shall live because of me! I am the true Bread from heaven; and anyone who eats this Bread shall live forever, and not die as your fathers did—though they ate bread from heaven." (He preached this sermon in the synagogue in Capernaum.)

*Those who put their faith in Christ will be resurrected from physical death to everlasting life with God when Christ comes again (see 1 Corinthians 15:52; 1 Thessalonians 4:16).*

### THE LIVING BREAD

How can Jesus give us his flesh as bread to eat? This was a shocking message—to eat flesh and drink blood sounded cannibalistic. The idea of drinking any blood, let alone human blood, was repugnant to the religious leaders because the Law forbade it (Leviticus 17:10-11). Jesus was not talking about literal blood, of course; he was saying that his life had to become their own. But they could not accept this concept. The apostle Paul later used the body and blood imagery in talking about communion (see 1 Corinthians 11:23-26). To eat Living Bread means to accept Christ into our lives and become united with him. We are united with Christ in two ways: (1) by believing in his death (the sacrifice of his flesh) and resurrection and (2) by devoting ourselves to living as he requires, depending on his teaching for guidance and trusting in the Holy Spirit for power. If you are united with Christ, he is living through you by his Holy Spirit. In what ways do you reflect Christ to your family and friends?

## June 8

## Many disciples desert Jesus

**JOHN 6:60-65** *(Harmony 101a)*

Even his disciples said, "This is very hard to understand. Who can tell what he means?"

Jesus knew within himself that his disciples were complaining and said to them, "Does *this* offend you? Then what will you think if you see me, the Messiah, return to heaven again? Only the Holy Spirit gives eternal life. Those born only once, with physical birth, will never receive this gift. But now I have told you how to get this true spiritual life. But some of you don't believe me." (For Jesus knew from the beginning who didn't believe and knew the one who would betray him.)

And he remarked, "That is what I meant when I said that no one can come to me unless the Father attracts him to me."

*The Holy Spirit gives spiritual life; without the work of the Holy Spirit we cannot even see our need for new life (14:17). All spiritual renewal begins and ends with God. He reveals truth to us, lives within us, and then enables us to respond to that truth.*

### WHY TURN AWAY?

Why were Jesus' words so difficult for many of his followers to understand? (1) They may have realized that he wasn't going to be the conquering Messiah-King they expected. (2) He refused to give in to their self-centered requests. (3) He emphasized faith, not works. (4) His teachings were difficult to understand, and some of his words were offensive. As we grow in our faith, we may be tempted to turn away because Jesus' lessons are difficult. Will your response be to give up, ignore certain teachings, or reject Christ? Instead, ask God to show you what the teachings mean and how they apply to your life. Then have the courage to act on God's truth.

## Many disciples desert Jesus

*JOHN 6:66-71 (Harmony 101b)*

At this point many of his disciples turned away and deserted him.

Then Jesus turned to the Twelve and asked, "Are you going too?"

Simon Peter replied, "Master, to whom shall we go? You alone have the words that give eternal life, and we believe them and know you are the holy Son of God."

Then Jesus said, "I chose the twelve of you, and one is a devil." He was speaking of Judas, son of Simon Iscariot, one of the Twelve, who would betray him.

*The more the people heard Jesus' real message, the more they divided into two camps— the honest seekers who wanted to understand more, and those who rejected Jesus because they didn't like what they had heard.*

### NO OTHER WAY

After many of Jesus' followers had deserted him, he asked the twelve disciples if they were also going to leave. Peter replied, "To whom shall we go?" In his straightforward way, Peter answered for all of us—there is no other way. Though there are many philosophies and self-styled authorities, Jesus alone has the words of eternal life. People look everywhere for eternal life and miss Christ, the only source. Many people today turn away; others pretend to follow, going to church for status, approval of family and friends, or business contacts. But there are only two real responses to Jesus—you either accept him or reject him. How have you responded to Christ?

## Jesus teaches about inner purity

*MARK 7:1-13 (also in MATTHEW 15:1-9) (Harmony 102a)*

One day some Jewish religious leaders arrived from Jerusalem to investigate him, and noticed that some of his disciples failed to follow the usual Jewish rituals before eating. (For the Jews, especially the Pharisees, will never eat until they have sprinkled their arms to the elbows, as required by their ancient traditions. So when they come home from the market, they must always sprinkle themselves in this way before touching any food. This is but one of many examples of laws and regulations they have clung to for centuries, and still follow, such as their ceremony of cleansing for pots, pans, and dishes.)

*The Pharisees added hundreds of their own petty rules and regulations to God's holy laws, and then they tried to force people to follow these rules. These men claimed to know God's will in every detail of life.*

So the religious leaders asked him, "Why don't your disciples follow our age-old customs? For they eat without first performing the washing ceremony."

Jesus replied, "You bunch of hypocrites! Isaiah the prophet described you very well when he said, 'These people speak very prettily about the Lord but they have no love for him at all. Their worship is a farce, for they claim that God commands the people to obey their petty rules.' How right Isaiah was! For you ignore God's specific orders and substitute your own traditions. You are simply rejecting God's Laws and trampling them under your feet for the sake of tradition.

"For instance, Moses gave you this law from God: 'Honor your father and mother.' And he said that anyone who speaks against his father or mother must die. But you say it is perfectly all right for a man to disregard his needy parents, telling them, 'Sorry, I can't help you! For I have given to God what I could have given to you.' And so you break the Law of God in order to protect your man-made tradition. And this is only one example. There are many, many others."

### HYPOCRISY
Hypocrisy is pretending to be something you are not and have no intention of being. Jesus called the Pharisees hypocrites because they worshiped God for the wrong reasons. Their worship was not motivated by love, but by a desire to attain profit, to appear holy, and to increase their status. We become hypocrites when we (1) pay more attention to reputation than to character, (2) carefully follow certain religious practices while allowing our hearts to remain distant from God, and (3) emphasize our virtues but others' sins. Why do you go to church?

## Jesus teaches about inner purity

### MARK 7:14-19 (also in MATTHEW 15:10-17)
### (Harmony 102b)

hen Jesus called to the crowd to come and hear. "All of you listen," he said, "and try to understand. Your souls aren't harmed by what you eat, but by what you think and say!"

Then he went into a house to get away from the crowds, and his disciples asked him what he meant by the statement he had just made.

"Don't you understand either?" he asked. "Can't you see that what you eat won't harm your soul? For food doesn't come in contact with your heart, but only passes through the digestive system." (By saying this he showed that every kind of food is kosher.)

*It is idolatry to claim that your interpretation of God's Word is as important as God's Word itself. It is especially dangerous to set up unbiblical standards for others to follow. Instead, look to Christ for guidance about your own behavior, and let him lead others in the details of their lives.*

**INSIDE OUT**

Do we worry more about what is in our diets than what is in our hearts and minds? As they interpreted the dietary laws (Leviticus 11), the Jews believed they could be clean before God because of what they refused to eat. But Jesus pointed out that sin actually begins in the attitudes and intentions of the inner person. Jesus did not degrade the law, but he paved the way for the change made clear in Acts 10:9-29 when God removed the cultural restrictions regarding food. We are not pure because of outward acts—we become pure on the inside as Christ renews our minds and transforms us into his image.

## Jesus teaches about inner purity

### MARK 7:20-23 (also in MATTHEW 15:18-20)
### (Harmony 102c)

nd then he added, "It is the thought-life that pollutes. For from within, out of men's hearts, come evil thoughts of lust, theft, murder, adultery, wanting what belongs to others, wickedness, deceit, lewdness, envy, slander, pride, and all other folly. All these vile things come from within; they are what pollute you and make you unfit for God."

### A SINGLE THOUGHT

An evil action begins with a single thought. Allowing our minds to dwell on lust, envy, hatred, or revenge will lead to sin. Don't defile yourself by focusing on evil. What we put into our minds determines what comes out in our words and

*There is a downward spiral. First, people reject a command of God; next, they make up their own ideas about God. Then they allow evil thoughts to lead them into evil actions. Finally, they grow to hate God. Only Christ can break the progression and help people escape the downward spiral.*

actions. The apostle Paul tells us to program our minds with thoughts that are true, noble, right, just, pure, lovely, of good report, virtuous, and praiseworthy (Philippians 4:8). Do you have problems with impure thoughts and daydreams? Examine what you are putting into your mind through television, books, conversations, movies, and magazines. Replace harmful input with wholesome material. Above all, read God's Word and pray. Ask God to help you focus your mind on what is good and pure. It takes practice, but it can be done.

## June 13

## Jesus sends a demon out of a girl

### MARK 7:24-30 (also in MATTHEW 15:21-28)
*(Harmony 103)*

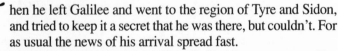hen he left Galilee and went to the region of Tyre and Sidon, and tried to keep it a secret that he was there, but couldn't. For as usual the news of his arrival spread fast.

Right away a woman came to him whose little girl was possessed by a demon. She had heard about Jesus and now she came and fell at his feet, and pled with him to release her child from the demon's control. (But she was Syrophoenician—a "despised Gentile"!)

Jesus told her, "First I should help my own family—the Jews. It isn't right to take the children's food and throw it to the dogs."

She replied, "That's true, sir, but even the puppies under the table are given some scraps from the children's plates."

"Good!" he said. "You have answered well—so well that I have

*Dog was a term the Jews commonly applied to Gentiles because the Jews considered these heathen people no more likely than dogs to receive God's blessing. Jesus was not degrading the woman by using this term; he was reflecting the Jews' attitude so as to contrast it with his own.*

healed your little girl. Go on home, for the demon has left her!"

And when she arrived home, her little girl was lying quietly in bed, and the demon was gone.

### AVAILABLE TO ALL

Jesus' words do not contradict the truth that God's message is for all people (Psalm 22:27; Isaiah 56:7; Matthew 28:19; Romans 15:9-12). Remember, when Jesus said these words, he was in Gentile territory on a mission to Gentile people. He ministered to Gentiles on many other occasions also. Jesus was simply telling the woman that Jews were to have the first opportunity to accept him as the Messiah because God wanted them to present the message of salvation to the rest of the world (see Genesis 12:3). Jesus was not rejecting the Syrophoenician woman. He may have wanted to test her faith, or he may have wanted to use the situation as another opportunity to teach that faith is available to all kinds of people. Ironically, many Jews would lose God's spiritual healing because of their rejection of Jesus, while many Gentiles, whom the Jews rejected, would find salvation because of their recognition of Jesus. Who do you know who seems to be beyond the gospel? Don't count them out. Continue to pray that God will bring others to faith, and look for ways to tell others about God's love.

*June 14*

---

## The crowd marvels at Jesus' healings

### MARK 7:31-37 (also in MATTHEW 15:29-31)
### (Harmony 104)

From Tyre he went to Sidon, then back to the Sea of Galilee by way of the Ten Towns. A deaf man with a speech impediment was brought to him, and everyone begged Jesus to lay his hands on the man and heal him.

Jesus led him away from the crowd and put his fingers into the man's ears, then spat and touched the man's tongue with the spittle. Then, looking up to heaven, he sighed and commanded, "Open!" Instantly the man could hear perfectly and speak plainly!

Jesus told the crowd not to spread the news, but the more he forbade them, the more they made it known, for they were

*Jesus asked the people not to talk about this healing because he didn't want to be seen simply as a miracle worker. He didn't want the people to miss his real message. We must not be so concerned about what Jesus can do for us that we forget to listen to his message.*

overcome with utter amazement. Again and again they said, "Everything he does is wonderful; he even corrects deafness and stammering!"

### HEALING POWER
A great crowd was brought to Jesus to be healed, and he healed them all. Jesus is still able to heal broken lives, and we can be the ones who bring suffering people to him. Who do you know who needs Christ's healing touch? You can bring them to Jesus by prayer or through explaining to them the reason for the hope that you have (1 Peter 3:15). Then let Christ do the healing.

*June 15*

## Jesus feeds four thousand

### MARK 8:1-9 *(also in MATTHEW 15:32-39) (Harmony 105)*

One day about this time as another great crowd gathered, the people ran out of food again. Jesus called his disciples to discuss the situation.

"I pity these people," he said, "for they have been here three days and have nothing left to eat. And if I send them home without feeding them, they will faint along the road! For some of them have come a long distance."

*Magadan was located on the west shore of the Sea of Galilee. Also known as Magdala or Dalmanutha (8:10), this was Mary Magdalene's hometown.*

"Are we supposed to find food for them here in the desert?" his disciples scoffed.

"How many loaves of bread do you have?" he asked.

"Seven," they replied. So he told the crowd to sit down on the ground. Then he took the seven loaves, thanked God for them, broke them into pieces and passed them to his disciples; and the disciples placed them before the people. A few small fish were found, too, so Jesus also blessed these and told the disciples to serve them.

And the whole crowd ate until they were full, and afterwards he sent them home. There were about 4,000 people in the crowd that day and when the scraps were picked up after the meal, there were seven very large basketfuls left over!

### FOOD FOR THOUGHT
This is a different miracle from the feeding of the five thousand described earlier. At that time, those fed were mostly Jews. This time Jesus was ministering to a

non-Jewish crowd in the Gentile region of the Decapolis. Jesus had already fed more than five thousand people with five loaves and two fish. Here, in a similar situation, the disciples were again perplexed. How easily we despair when faced with difficult situations. Like the disciples, we often forget that if God has cared for us in the past, he will do the same now. When facing a perplexing problem or a tough task, remember how God cared for you and trust him to work faithfully again.

## *June 16*

## Religious leaders ask for a sign in the sky

### *MATTHEW 16:1-4 (also in MARK 8:10-12) (Harmony 106)*

One day the Pharisees and Sadducees came to test Jesus' claim of being the Messiah by asking him to show them some great demonstrations in the skies.

He replied, "You are good at reading the weather signs of the skies—red sky tonight means fair weather tomorrow; red sky in the morning means foul weather all day—but you can't read the obvious signs of the times! This evil, unbelieving nation is asking for some strange sign in the heavens, but no further proof will be given except the miracle that happened to Jonah." Then Jesus walked out on them.

*The Pharisees had tried to explain away Jesus' previous miracles by claiming they were done by luck, coincidence, or evil power. Here they demanded a sign from heaven—something only God could do. Jesus refused their demand because he knew that even this kind of miracle would not convince them. They had already decided not to believe.*

#### MIRACLES

These Jewish leaders said they wanted to see a miracle so that they could believe. But Jesus knew that miracles never convince the skeptical. Jesus had been healing, raising people from the dead, and feeding thousands, and still people wanted him to prove himself. Do you doubt Christ because you haven't *seen* a miracle? Do you expect God to prove himself to you personally before you believe? Jesus says, "Blessed are those who haven't seen me and believe anyway" (John 20:29). We have all the miracles recorded in the Old and New Testaments, two thousand years of church history, and the witness of thousands of believers. With all this evidence, those who won't believe are either too proud or too stubborn. If you simply step forward in faith and believe, then you will begin to see the miracles that God can do with your life!

## Jesus warns against wrong teaching

### MARK 8:13-21 (also in MATTHEW 16:5-12)
*(Harmony 107)*

So he got back into the boat and left them, and crossed to the other side of the lake. But the disciples had forgotten to stock up on food before they left and had only one loaf of bread in the boat.

As they were crossing, Jesus said to them very solemnly, "Beware of the yeast of King Herod and of the Pharisees."

"What does he mean?" the disciples asked each other. They finally decided that he must be talking about their forgetting to bring bread.

*Yeast in this passage symbolizes evil. Just as only a small amount of yeast is needed to make a batch of bread rise, so the hard-heartedness of the religious and political leaders could permeate and contaminate the entire society and make it rise up against Jesus.*

Jesus realized what they were discussing and said, "No, that isn't it at all! Can't you understand? Are your hearts too hard to take it in? 'Your eyes are to see with—why don't you look? Why don't you open your ears and listen?' Don't you remember anything at all?

"What about the 5,000 men I fed with five loaves of bread? How many basketfuls of scraps did you pick up afterwards?"

"Twelve," they said.

"And when I fed the 4,000 with seven loaves, how much was left?"

"Seven basketfuls," they said.

"And yet you think I'm worried that we have no bread?"

#### OPEN HEARTS AND MINDS

How could the disciples experience so many of Jesus' miracles and yet be so slow to comprehend who he was? They had already seen Jesus feed over five thousand people with five loaves and two fish (6:35-44), yet here they doubted whether he could feed another large group.

Sometimes we are also slow to catch on. Although Christ has brought us through trials and temptations in the past, we don't believe that he will do it in the future. Is your heart too closed to take in all that God can do for you? Don't be like the disciples. Remember what Christ has done, and have faith that he will do it again.

## Jesus restores sight to a blind man

### *MARK 8:22-26* (Harmony 108)

*W*hen they arrived at Bethsaida, some people brought a blind man to him and begged him to touch and heal him. Jesus took the blind man by the hand and led him out of the village, and spat upon his eyes, and laid his hands over them.

"Can you see anything now?" Jesus asked him.

The man looked around. "Yes!" he said, "I see men! But I can't see them very clearly; they look like tree trunks walking around!"

*Jesus took the man out of the village to heal him and then told him not to go back into the village. Jesus had compassion to heal, but he did not want to be seen as merely a miracle worker.*

Then Jesus placed his hands over the man's eyes again and as the man stared intently, his sight was completely restored, and he saw everything clearly, drinking in the sights around him.

Jesus sent him home to his family. "Don't even go back to the village first," he said.

#### OPEN EYES

Why did Jesus touch the man a second time before he could see? This miracle was not too difficult for Jesus, but he chose to do it in stages, possibly to show the disciples that some healing would be gradual rather than instantaneous or to demonstrate that spiritual truth is not always perceived clearly at first. Before Jesus left, however, the man was healed completely. Sometimes it takes time for us to understand. Christ stays with us, helping us to finally "see" clearly. Trust him to help you when you don't understand.

## Peter says Jesus is the Messiah

*MATTHEW 16:13-20 (also in MARK 8:27-30;*
*LUKE 9:18-20) (Harmony 109)*

*W*hen Jesus came to Caesarea Philippi, he asked his disciples, "Who are the people saying I am?"

"Well," they replied, "some say John the Baptist; some, Elijah; some, Jeremiah or one of the other prophets."

Then he asked them, "Who do *you* think I am?"

Simon Peter answered, "The Christ, the Messiah, the Son of the living God."

"God has blessed you, Simon, son of Jonah," Jesus said, "for my Father in heaven has personally revealed this to you—this is not from any human source. You are Peter, a stone; and upon this rock I will build my church; and all the powers of hell shall not prevail against it. And I will give you the keys of the Kingdom of Heaven; whatever doors you lock on earth shall be locked in heaven; and whatever doors you open on earth shall be open in heaven!"

*The rock on which Jesus would build his church has been identified as: (1) Jesus himself (his work of salvation by dying for us on the cross); (2) Peter (the first great leader of the church at Jerusalem); (3) the confession of faith that Peter gave and that all subsequent true believers would give.*

Then he warned the disciples against telling others that he was the Messiah.

### WHO DO YOU SAY HE IS?

The disciples answered Jesus' question with the common view—that Jesus was one of the great prophets come back to life. This belief may have stemmed from Deuteronomy 18:18, where God said he would raise up a prophet from among the people. Peter, however, confessed Jesus as divine and as the promised and long-awaited Messiah. It is not enough to know what others say about Jesus: You must know, understand, and accept for yourself that he is the Messiah. You must move from curiosity to commitment, from admiration to adoration. If Jesus were to ask you this question, how would you answer? Is he your Lord and Messiah?

## Jesus predicts his death the first time

### MARK 8:31–9:1 (also in MATTHEW 16:21-28; LUKE 9:21-27) (Harmony 110)

*T*hen he began to tell them about the terrible things he would suffer, and that he would be rejected by the elders and the chief priests and the other Jewish leaders—and be killed, and that he would rise again three days afterwards. He talked about it quite frankly with them, so Peter took him aside and chided him. "You shouldn't say things like that," he told Jesus.

Jesus turned and looked at his disciples and then said to Peter very sternly, "Satan, get behind me! You are looking at this only from a human point of view and not from God's."

Then he called his disciples and the crowds to come over and listen. "If any of you wants to be my follower," he told them, "you must put aside your own pleasures and shoulder your cross, and follow me closely. If you insist on saving your life, you will lose it. Only those who throw away their lives for my sake and for the sake of the Good News will ever know what it means to really live.

"And how does a man benefit if he gains the whole world and loses his soul in the process? For is anything worth more than his soul? And anyone who is ashamed of me and my message in these days of unbelief and sin, I, the Messiah, will be ashamed of him when I return in the glory of my Father, with the holy angels."

Jesus went on to say to his disciples, "Some of you who are standing here right now will live to see the Kingdom of God arrive in great power!"

*In this moment Peter was not considering God's purposes, but only his own natural human desires and feelings. Peter wanted Christ to be king, but not the suffering servant prophesied in Isaiah 53. He was ready to receive the glory of following the Messiah, but not the persecution.*

#### LOST AND FOUND

Many people spend all their energy seeking pleasure. Jesus said, however, that a world of pleasure centered on possessions, position, or power is ultimately worthless. Whatever you have on earth is only temporary; it cannot be exchanged for your soul. If you work hard at getting what you want, you might eventually have a "pleasurable" life, but in the end you will find it hollow and empty. We should be willing to lose our lives for the sake of the gospel, not because our lives are useless, but because nothing—not even life itself—can compare to what we gain with Christ. Jesus wants us to *choose* to follow him rather than to lead a life of sin and self-satisfaction. He wants us to stop trying to control our own destiny and to let him direct us. This makes good sense because, as the Creator, Christ knows better than we do what real life is about. He asks for submission, not self-hatred; he asks us only to lose our self-centered determination to be in charge.

## *June 21*

## Jesus is transfigured on the mountain

### *LUKE 9:28-31 (also in MATTHEW 17:1-3; MARK 9:2-4)*
*(Harmony 111a)*

ight days later he took Peter, James, and John with him into the hills to pray. And as he was praying, his face began to shine, and his clothes became dazzling white and blazed with light. Then two men appeared and began talking with him—Moses and Elijah! They were splendid in appearance, glorious to see; and they were speaking of his death at Jerusalem, to be carried out in accordance with God's plan.

### THE INNER CIRCLE

When Jesus said that some of his disciples would see the Kingdom of God arrive (9:27), he may have been referring to the three disciples who would see the Transfiguration. We don't know why Jesus singled out Peter, James, and John for this special revelation of his glory and purity. Perhaps they were the ones most ready to understand and accept this great truth. These three disciples were the inner circle of the group of twelve. They were among the first to hear Jesus' call (Mark 1:16-19). They headed the Gospel lists of disciples (Mark 3:16-17). And they were present at certain healings where others were excluded (Luke 8:51). God calls different people to certain areas of service for him. Some are more visible than others, but all are needed to accomplish his work in the world. Are you doing what God called you to do?

*Moses and Elijah were the two greatest prophets in the Old Testament. Moses represents the Law, or the old covenant. He wrote the Pentateuch, and he predicted the coming of a great prophet (Deuteronomy 18:15-19). Elijah represents the prophets who foretold the coming of the Messiah (Malachi 4:5-6). Moses' and Elijah's presence with Jesus confirmed Jesus' messianic mission—to fulfill God's Law and the words of God's prophets.*

## Jesus is transfigured on the mountain

### *LUKE 9:32-36 (also in MATTHEW 17:4-13; MARK 9:5-13) (Harmony 111b)*

eter and the others had been very drowsy and had fallen asleep. Now they woke up and saw Jesus covered with brightness and glory, and the two men standing with him. As Moses and Elijah were starting to leave, Peter, all confused and not even knowing what he was saying, blurted out, "Master, this is wonderful! We'll put up three shelters—one for you and one for Moses and one for Elijah!"

But even as he was saying this, a bright cloud formed above them; and terror gripped them as it covered them. And a voice from the cloud said, *"This* is my Son, my Chosen One; listen to *him."*

Then, as the voice died away, Jesus was there alone with his disciples. They didn't tell anyone what they had seen until long afterwards.

#### GOD'S SON

The Transfiguration revealed Christ's divine nature. God's voice exalted Jesus above Moses and Elijah as the long-awaited Messiah with full divine authority. Moses represented the Law, and Elijah, the prophets. Their appearance showed Jesus as the fulfillment of both the Old Testament Law and the prophetic promises.

Jesus was not a reincarnation of Elijah or Moses. He was not merely one of the prophets. As God's only Son, he far surpasses them in authority and power. Many voices try to tell us how to live and how to know God personally. Some of these are helpful; many are not. We must first listen to the Bible, and then evaluate all other authorities in light of God's revelation.

*Jesus told Peter, James, and John not to speak about what they had seen because they would not fully understand it until Jesus had risen from the dead. Then they would realize that only through dying could Jesus show his power over death and his authority to be King of all. The disciples could not be powerful witnesses for God until they had grasped this truth.*

## Jesus heals a demon-possessed boy

### MARK 9:14-29 (also in MATTHEW 17:14-21; LUKE 9:37-43) (Harmony 112)

At the bottom of the mountain they found a great crowd surrounding the other nine disciples, as some Jewish leaders argued with them. The crowd watched Jesus in awe as he came toward them, and then ran to greet him. "What's all the argument about?" he asked.

One of the men in the crowd spoke up and said, "Teacher, I brought my son for you to heal—he can't talk because he is possessed by a demon. And whenever the demon is in control of him it dashes him to the ground and makes him foam at the mouth and grind his teeth and become rigid. So I begged your disciples to cast out the demon, but they couldn't do it."

*Why couldn't the disciples drive out the evil spirit that had caused the boy to be mute? They had special authority to do so, but perhaps their faith was faltering. Mark tells this story to show that the battle with Satan is a difficult, ongoing struggle.*

Jesus said to his disciples, "Oh, what tiny faith you have; how much longer must I be with you until you believe? How much longer must I be patient with you? Bring the boy to me."

So they brought the boy, but when he saw Jesus, the demon convulsed the child horribly, and he fell to the ground writhing and foaming at the mouth.

"How long has he been this way?" Jesus asked the father.

And he replied, "Since he was very small, and the demon often makes him fall into the fire or into water to kill him. Oh, have mercy on us and do something if you can."

"If I can?" Jesus asked. *"Anything* is possible if you have faith."

The father instantly replied, "I *do* have faith; oh, help me to have *more!"*

When Jesus saw the crowd was growing, he rebuked the demon.

"O demon of deafness and dumbness," he said, "I command you to come out of this child and enter him no more!"

Then the demon screamed terribly and convulsed the boy again and left him; and the boy lay there limp and motionless, to all appearance dead. A murmur ran through the crowd—"He is dead." But Jesus took him by the hand and helped him to his feet and he stood up and was all right! Afterwards, when Jesus was alone in the house with his disciples, they asked him, "Why couldn't we cast that demon out?"

Jesus replied, "Cases like this require prayer."

### ANYTHING WITH FAITH

Jesus' words do not mean that we can automatically obtain anything we want if we just think positively. Jesus meant that anything is *possible* if we believe, because nothing is too difficult for God. We cannot have everything we pray for as if by magic; but with faith, we can have everything we need to serve him. The attitude of trust and confidence that the Bible calls *belief* or *faith* (Hebrews 11:1, 6) is not something we can obtain without help. Faith is a gift from God (Ephesians 2:8-9). No matter how much faith we have, we never reach the point of being self-sufficient. Faith is not stored away like money in the bank. Growing in faith is a constant process of daily renewing our trust in Jesus.

*June 24*

## Jesus predicts his death the second time

*MARK 9:30-32 (also in MATTHEW 17:22-23; LUKE 9:44-45) (Harmony 113)*

*L*eaving that region they traveled through Galilee where he tried to avoid all publicity in order to spend more time with his disciples, teaching them. He would say to them, "I, the Messiah, am going to be betrayed and killed and three days later I will return to life again."

But they didn't understand and were afraid to ask him what he meant.

### CALLED TO BELIEVE

Once again Jesus predicted his death (see also Matthew 16:21); but more important, he told of his resurrection. Unfortunately, the disciples heard only the first part of Jesus' words and became discouraged. They couldn't understand why Jesus wanted to go back to Jerusalem where he would walk right into trouble.

*At times, Jesus limited his public ministry in order to train his disciples in depth. He knew the importance of equipping them to carry on when he returned to heaven. Leaving Caesarea Philippi, Jesus began his last tour through the region of Galilee.*

The disciples didn't fully comprehend the purpose of Jesus' death and resurrection until Pentecost (Acts 2). The disciples didn't understand why Jesus kept talking about his death because they expected him to set up a political kingdom. His death, they thought, would dash their hopes. They didn't know that Jesus' death and resurrection would make his Kingdom possible. We shouldn't get upset at ourselves for being slow to understand everything about Jesus. After all, the disciples were with him, saw his miracles, heard his words, and still had difficulty understanding. Despite their questions and doubts, however, they believed. We should do no less.

## June 25

### Peter finds the coin in the fish's mouth

*MATTHEW 17:24-27 (Harmony 114)*

On their arrival in Capernaum, the Temple tax collectors came to Peter and asked him, "Doesn't your master pay taxes?"

"Of course he does," Peter replied.

Then he went into the house to talk to Jesus about it, but before he had a chance to speak, Jesus asked him, "What do you think, Peter? Do kings levy assessments against their own people or against conquered foreigners?"

"Against the foreigners," Peter replied.

"Well, then," Jesus said, "the citizens are free! However, we don't want to offend them, so go down to the shore and throw in a line, and open the mouth of the first fish you catch. You will find a coin to cover the taxes for both of us; take it and pay them."

*All Jewish males had to pay a Temple tax to support Temple upkeep (Exodus 30:11-16). Tax collectors set up booths to collect these taxes. Only Matthew records this incident, perhaps because he had been a tax collector himself.*

#### GOOD AMBASSADORS

As usual, Peter answered a question without really knowing the answer, putting Jesus and the disciples in an awkward position. Jesus used this situation, however, to emphasize his kingly role. Just as kings pay no taxes and collect none from their family, Jesus, the King, owed no taxes. But he supplied the tax payment for both himself and Peter rather than offend those who didn't understand his kingship. As God's people, we are foreigners on earth because our loyalty is always to our real King—Jesus. Still we have to cooperate with the authorities and be responsible citizens. An ambassador to another country keeps the local laws in order to represent well the one who sent him. We are Christ's ambassadors (2 Corinthians 5:20). Are you being a good foreign ambassador for him to this world?

# The disciples argue about who would be the greatest

*MARK 9:33-37 (also in MATTHEW 18:1-6;*
*LUKE 9:46-48) (Harmony 115)*

And so they arrived at Capernaum. When they were settled in the house where they were to stay, he asked them, "What were you discussing out on the road?"

But they were ashamed to answer, for they had been arguing about which of them was the greatest!

He sat down and called them around him and said, "Anyone wanting to be the greatest must be the least—the servant of all!"

Then he placed a little child among them; and taking the child in his arms he said to them, "Anyone who welcomes a little child like this in my name is welcoming me, and anyone who welcomes me is welcoming my Father who sent me!"

*Children are trusting by nature. They trust adults, and through that trust their capacity to trust God grows. God holds parents and other adults who influence young children accountable for how they affect these little ones' ability to trust.*

### THE GREATEST

The disciples, caught up in their constant struggle for personal success, were embarrassed to answer Jesus' question. It is always painful to compare our motives with Christ's. It is not wrong for believers to be industrious or ambitious. But when ambition pushes obedience and service to one side, it becomes sin. Pride or insecurity can cause us to overvalue position and prestige. In God's Kingdom, such motives are destructive. The only safe ambition is directed toward Christ's Kingdom, not our own advancement. It is possible for thoughtless, selfish people to gain a measure of greatness in the world's eyes, but enduring greatness is measured only by God's standards. What do you use as your measure of greatness—personal achievement or unselfish service?

## The disciples forbid another to use Jesus' name

### *MARK 9:38-42 (also in LUKE 9:49-50) (Harmony 116)*

One of his disciples, John, told him one day, "Teacher, we saw a man using your name to cast out demons; but we told him not to, for he isn't one of our group."

"Don't forbid him!" Jesus said. "For no one doing miracles in my name will quickly turn against me. Anyone who isn't against us is for us. If anyone so much as gives you a cup of water because you are Christ's—I say this solemnly—he won't lose his reward. But if someone causes one of these little ones who believe in me to lose faith—it would be better for that man if a huge millstone were tied around his neck and he were thrown into the sea."

*In 9:40, Jesus was not saying that being indifferent or neutral toward him is as good as being committed. The statement is spoken in a different way in Matthew 12:30: "Anyone who isn't helping me is harming me." In both cases Jesus was pointing out that neutrality toward him is not possible.*

### COMMON FAITH, COMMON GOAL

The disciples were jealous of a man who healed in Jesus' name because they were more concerned about their own group's position than about helping to free those troubled by demons. We do the same when we refuse to participate in worthy causes because (1) other people or groups are not affiliated with our denomination, (2) these projects do not involve the kind of people with whom we feel most comfortable, (3) others don't do things the way we are used to doing things, (4) our efforts won't receive enough recognition. Correct theology is important but should never be an excuse to avoid helping people in need. People who are on Jesus' side have the same goal of building up the Kingdom of God, and they should not let their differences interfere with this goal. Those who share a common faith in Christ should cooperate. People don't have to be just like us to be following Jesus with us.

## Jesus warns against temptation

*MARK 9:43-50 (also in MATTHEW 18:7-9) (Harmony 117)*

f your hand does wrong, cut it off. Better live forever with one hand than be thrown into the unquenchable fires of hell with two! If your foot carries you toward evil, cut it off! Better be lame and live forever than have two feet that carry you to hell.

"And if your eye is sinful, gouge it out. Better enter the Kingdom of God half blind than have two eyes and see the fires of hell, where the worm never dies, and the fire never goes out—where all are salted with fire.

"Good salt is worthless if it loses its saltiness; it can't season anything. So don't lose your flavor! Live in peace with each other."

*Jesus used startling language to stress the importance of cutting sin out of our lives. Painful discipline is required of his true followers. Giving up a relationship, job, or habit that is against God's will may seem just as painful as cutting off a hand. Nothing should stand in the way of faith.*

### SALTY ENOUGH?

Jesus used salt to illustrate three qualities that should be found in his people: (1) *We should remember God's faithfulness,* just as salt when used with a sacrifice recalled God's covenant with his people (Leviticus 2:13). (2) *We should make a difference in the "flavor" of the world we live in,* just as salt changes meat's flavor (see Matthew 5:13). (3) *We should counteract the moral decay in society,* just as salt preserves food from decay. When we lose this desire to "salt" the earth with the love and message of God, we become useless to him. Think of how you can be salty this week.

## Jesus warns against looking down on others

*MATTHEW 18:10-14 (Harmony 118)*

eware that you don't look down upon a single one of these little children. For I tell you that in heaven their angels have constant access to my Father. And I, the Messiah, came to save the lost.

"If a man has a hundred sheep, and one wanders away and is lost, what will he do? Won't he leave the ninety-nine others and go out into the hills to search for the lost one? And if he finds it, he will rejoice over it more than over the ninety-nine others safe at home! Just so, it is not my Father's will that even one of these little ones should perish."

*Certain angels are assigned to watch over children, and they have direct access to God. If their angels have constant access to God, the least we can do is to allow children to approach us easily in spite of our far-too-busy schedules.*

### GUIDANCE

Just as a shepherd is concerned enough about one lost sheep to go search the hills for it, so God is concerned about every human being he has created (he is "not willing that any should perish" [2 Peter 3:9]). You come in contact with children who need Christ at home, at school, in church, and in the neighborhood. Steer them toward Christ by your example, your words, and your acts of kindness.

*June 30*

## Jesus teaches how to treat a believer who sins

*MATTHEW 18:15-18 (Harmony 119a)*

f a brother sins against you, go to him privately and confront him with his fault. If he listens and confesses it, you have won back a brother. But if not, then take one or two others with you and go back to him again, proving everything you say by these witnesses. If he still refuses to listen, then take your case to the church, and if the church's verdict favors you, but he won't accept it, then the church should excommunicate him. And I tell you this—whatever you bind on earth is bound in heaven, and whatever you free on earth will be freed in heaven."

*This binding and loosing refers to the decisions of the church in conflicts. Among believers, there is no court of appeals beyond the church. Ideally, the church's decisions should be God-guided and based on discernment of his Word. Believers have the responsibility to bring their problems to the church, and the church has the responsibility to use God's guidance in seeking to resolve them.*

### SINNED AGAINST

These are Jesus' guidelines for dealing with those who sin against us. They were meant for (1) Christians, not unbelievers, (2) sins committed against *you* and not others, and (3) conflict resolution in the context of the church, not the community at large. Jesus' words are not a license for a frontal attack on every person who hurts or slights us. They are not a license to start a destructive gossip campaign or to call for a church trial. They are designed to reconcile those who disagree so that all Christians can live in harmony.

When someone wrongs us, we often do the opposite of what Jesus recommends. We turn away in hatred or resentment, seek revenge, or engage in gossip. By contrast, we should go to that person *first,* as difficult as that may be. Then we should forgive that person as often as he or she needs it (18:21-22). This will create a much better chance of restoring the relationship.

*July 1*

## Jesus teaches how to treat a believer who sins

*MATTHEW 18:19-20 (Harmony 119b)*

also tell you this—if two of you agree down here on earth concerning anything you ask for, my Father in heaven will do it for you. For where two or three gather together because they are mine, I will be right there among them."

**PRAYER POWER**

Jesus looked ahead to a new day when he would be present with his followers, not physically, but through his Holy Spirit. In the body of believers (the church), the sincere agreement of two people is more powerful than the superficial agreement of thousands because Christ's Holy Spirit is with them too. Two or more believers, filled with the Holy Spirit, will pray according to God's will, not their own; thus their requests will be granted. Although God is all-powerful and all-knowing, he has chosen to let us help him change the world through our prayers. How this works is a mystery to us because of our limited understanding, but it is a reality. Our earnest prayers will have powerful results (James 5:16). Make prayer a regular part of your life, alone and with other believers.

*God is three persons in one—Father, Son, and Holy Spirit. God became a man in Jesus so that Jesus could die for our sins. When Jesus ascended into heaven, his physical presence left the earth, but he promised to send the Holy Spirit so that his spiritual presence would still be among humankind.*

*July 2*

## Jesus tells the parable of the unforgiving debtor

*MATTHEW 18:21-22 (Harmony 120a)*

hen Peter came to him and asked, "Sir, how often should I forgive a brother who sins against me? Seven times?"

"No!" Jesus replied, "seventy times seven!"

When Jesus explained that we should forgive others "seventy times seven" times, he meant that we shouldn't even keep track of how many times we forgive someone. We should always forgive those who are truly repentant, no matter how many times they ask. As Christians, we should forgive as we have been forgiven. True forgiveness means we treat the one we've forgiven as we would want to be treated. As we understand God's mercy, we will want to be like him. Having received forgiveness, we will pass it on to others. Is there someone you say you have forgiven, but who still needs your kindness?

*The rabbis taught that people should forgive those who offend them—but only three times. Peter, trying to be especially generous, asked Jesus if seven (the "perfect" number) was enough times to forgive someone.*

*July 3*

## Jesus tells the parable of the unforgiving debtor

### MATTHEW 18:23-35 *(Harmony 120b)*

The Kingdom of Heaven can be compared to a king who decided to bring his accounts up to date. In the process, one of his debtors was brought in who owed him $10 million! He couldn't pay, so the king ordered him sold for the debt, also his wife and children and everything he had.

"But the man fell down before the king, his face in the dust, and said, 'Oh, sir, be patient with me and I will pay it all.'

"Then the king was filled with pity for him and released him and forgave his debt.

"But when the man left the king, he went to a man who owed him $2,000 and grabbed him by the throat and demanded instant payment.

"The man fell down before him and begged him to give him a little time. 'Be patient and I will pay it,' he pled.

*In Bible times, serious consequences came to those who could not pay their debts. A person lending money could seize the borrower who couldn't pay and force him or his family to work until the debt was paid. The debtor could also be thrown into prison, or his family could be sold into slavery to help pay off the debt.*

"But his creditor wouldn't wait. He had the man arrested and jailed until the debt would be paid in full.

"Then the man's friends went to the king and told him what had happened. And the king called before him the man he had forgiven and said, 'You evil-hearted wretch! Here I forgave you all that tremendous debt, just because you asked me to—shouldn't you have mercy on others, just as I had mercy on you?'

"Then the angry king sent the man to the torture chamber until he had paid every last penny due. So shall my heavenly Father do to you if you refuse to truly forgive your brothers."

### HARD TO FORGIVE

If we love someone the way Christ loves us, we will be willing to forgive. If we have experienced God's grace, we will want to pass it on to others. Forgiveness involves both attitudes and actions. If you find it difficult to *feel* forgiving of someone who has hurt you, try *acting* forgiving. Many times right actions can lead to right feelings. Because God has forgiven all our sins, we should not withhold forgiveness from others. Realizing how completely Christ has forgiven us should produce a free and generous attitude of forgiveness toward others. When we don't forgive others, we are setting ourselves outside and above Christ's law of love. Those who are unwilling to forgive have not become one with Christ.

*July 4*

## Jesus' brothers ridicule him

### JOHN 7:1-9 *(Harmony 121)*

After this, Jesus went to Galilee, going from village to village, for he wanted to stay out of Judea where the Jewish leaders were plotting his death. But soon it was time for the Tabernacle Ceremonies, one of the annual Jewish holidays, and Jesus' brothers urged him to go to Judea for the celebration.

"Go where more people can see your miracles!" they scoffed. "You can't be famous when you hide like this! If you're so great, prove it to the world!" For even his brothers didn't believe in him.

Jesus replied, "It is not the right time for me to go now. But you can go anytime and it will make no difference, for the world can't hate you; but it does hate me,

*The Tabernacle Ceremonies, also called the Feast of Tabernacles, are described in Leviticus 23:33ff. This event occurred in October, about six months after the Passover celebration. The feast commemorated the days when the Israelites wandered in the wilderness and lived in tents (Leviticus 23:43).*

because I accuse it of sin and evil. You go on, and I'll come later when it is the right time." So he remained in Galilee.

### THE EVIDENCE

Jesus' brothers had a difficult time believing in him. Some of these brothers would eventually become leaders in the church (James, for example), but for several years they were embarrassed by Jesus. After Jesus died and rose again, they finally believed. Today we have every reason to believe because we have the full record of Jesus' miracles, death, and resurrection. We also have the evidence of what the gospel has done in people's lives through the centuries. We have no excuses.

*July 5*

---

## Jesus teaches about the cost of following him

### LUKE 9:51-56 *(Harmony 122a)*

As the time drew near for his return to heaven, he moved steadily onward toward Jerusalem with an iron will.

One day he sent messengers ahead to reserve rooms for them in a Samaritan village. But they were turned away! The people of the village refused to have anything to do with them because they were headed for Jerusalem.

When word came back of what had happened, James and John said to Jesus, "Master, shall we order fire down from heaven to burn them up?" But Jesus turned and rebuked them, and they went on to another village.

*After Assyria invaded Israel, the Northern Kingdom, and resettled it with its own people (2 Kings 17:24-41), the mixed race that developed became known as the Samaritans. "Purebred" Jews hated these "half-breeds"; the Samaritans, in turn, hated the Jews.*

### REVENGE

When James and John were rejected by the Samaritan village, they didn't want to stop at shaking the dust from their feet (9:5). They wanted to retaliate by calling down fire from heaven on the people as Elijah had done on the servants of a wicked king of Israel (2 Kings 1). When others reject or scorn us, we too may feel like retaliating. We must remember that judgment belongs to God, and we must not expect him to use his power to carry out our personal vendettas.

## Jesus teaches about the cost of following him

*LUKE 9:57-62 (also in MATTHEW 8:18-22)*
*(Harmony 122b)*

As they were walking along someone said to Jesus, "I will always follow you no matter where you go."

But Jesus replied, "Remember, I don't even own a place to lay my head. Foxes have dens to live in, and birds have nests, but I, the Messiah, have no earthly home at all."

Another time, when he invited a man to come with him and to be his disciple, the man agreed—but wanted to wait until his father's death.

Jesus replied, "Let those without eternal life concern themselves with things like that. Your duty is to come and preach the coming of the Kingdom of God to all the world."

*Jesus was always direct with those who wanted to follow him. He made sure they counted the cost and set aside any conditions they might have for following him. As God's Son, Jesus did not hesitate to demand complete loyalty. Even family loyalty was not to take priority over the demands of obedience.*

Another said, "Yes, Lord, I will come, but first let me ask permission of those at home."

But Jesus told him, "Anyone who lets himself be distracted from the work I plan for him is not fit for the Kingdom of God.

### CROSS AND CROWN

What does Jesus want from us? Total dedication, not halfhearted commitment. Following Jesus is not always easy or comfortable. Often it means great cost and sacrifice, with no earthly rewards or security. Jesus didn't have a place to call home. You may find that following Christ costs you popularity, friendships, leisure time, or treasured habits. But while the cost of following Christ is high, the value of being Christ's disciple is even higher. Discipleship is an investment that lasts for eternity and yields incredible rewards. We can't pick and choose among Jesus' ideas and follow him selectively; we have to accept the cross along with the crown, judgment as well as mercy. We must count the cost and be willing to abandon everything else that has given us security. Focusing on Jesus, we should allow nothing to distract us from the manner of living that he calls good and true.

## Jesus teaches openly at the Temple

### JOHN 7:10-13 *(Harmony 123a)*

*B*ut after his brothers had left for the celebration, then he went too, though secretly, staying out of the public eye. The Jewish leaders tried to find him at the celebration and kept asking if anyone had seen him. There was a lot of discussion about him among the crowds. Some said, "He's a wonderful man," while others said, "No, he's duping the public." But no one had the courage to speak out for him in public for fear of reprisals from the Jewish leaders.

*The religious leaders had a great deal of power over the common people. Apparently these leaders couldn't do much to Jesus at this time, but they threatened anyone who might publicly support him. Excommunication from the synagogue was one of the reprisals for believing in Jesus (9:22). To a Jew, this was a severe punishment.*

**SPEAK UP**

Jesus came with the greatest gift ever offered, so why did he often act secretly? The religious leaders hated him, and many would refuse his gift of salvation, no matter what he said or did. The more Jesus taught and worked publicly, the more these leaders would cause trouble for him and his followers. So it was necessary for Jesus to teach and work as quietly as possible. Many people today have the privilege of teaching, preaching, and worshiping publicly with little persecution. These believers should be grateful and make the most of their opportunities to proclaim the gospel. Although many people talk about Christ in church, when it comes to making a public statement about their faith, they are often embarrassed. Jesus says that he will acknowledge us before God if we acknowledge him before others (Matthew 10:32). Be courageous! Speak up for Christ!

## Jesus teaches openly at the Temple

### JOHN 7:14-24 *(Harmony 123b)*

*T*hen, midway through the festival, Jesus went up to the Temple and preached openly. The Jewish leaders were surprised when they heard him. "How can he know so much when he's never been to our schools?" they asked.

So Jesus told them, "I'm not teaching you my own thoughts, but those of God who sent me. If any of you really determines to do God's will, then you will certainly know whether my teaching is from God or is merely my own. Anyone presenting his own ideas is looking for praise for himself, but anyone seeking to honor the one who sent him is a good and true person. None of *you* obeys the laws of Moses! So why pick on *me* for breaking them? Why kill *me* for this?"

*Have you ever listened to religious speakers and wondered if they were telling the truth? Test them: (1) Their words should agree with, not contradict, the Bible; (2) their words should point to God and his will, not to themselves.*

The crowd replied, "You're out of your mind! Who's trying to kill you?"

Jesus replied, "I worked on the Sabbath by healing a man, and you were surprised. But you work on the Sabbath, too, whenever you obey Moses' law of circumcision (actually, however, this tradition of circumcision is older than the Mosaic law); for if the correct time for circumcising your children falls on the Sabbath, you go ahead and do it, as you should. So why should I be condemned for making a man completely well on the Sabbath? Think this through and you will see that I am right."

### MORE THAN REQUIRED

The Pharisees spent their days trying to achieve holiness by keeping the meticulous rules that they had added to God's Laws. Jesus' accusation that they didn't keep Moses' laws stung them deeply. In spite of their pompous pride in themselves and their rules, they did not even fulfill a legalistic religion, for they were living far below what the law of Moses required. Their plot to commit murder was certainly against the Law. Jesus' followers should do *more* than the moral law requires, not by adding to its requirements, but by going beyond and beneath the mere do's and don't's of the Law to the spirit of the Law. This means being kind and forgiving, serving others, and showing love.

## Jesus teaches openly at the Temple

*JOHN 7:25-31 (Harmony 123c)*

ome of the people who lived there in Jerusalem said among themselves, "Isn't this the man they are trying to kill? But here he is preaching in public, and they say nothing to him. Can it be that our leaders have learned, after all, that he really is the Messiah? But how could he be? For we know where this man was born; when Christ comes, he will just appear and no one will know where he comes from."

So Jesus, in a sermon in the Temple, called out, "Yes, you know me and where I was born and raised, but I am the representative of one you don't know, and he is Truth. I know him because I was with him, and he sent me to you."

*There was a popular tradition that the Messiah would simply appear. But those who believed this tradition were ignoring the Scriptures that clearly predicted the Messiah's birthplace (Micah 5:2).*

Then the Jewish leaders sought to arrest him; but no hand was laid on him, for God's time had not yet come.

Many among the crowds at the Temple believed on him. "After all," they said, "what miracles do you expect the Messiah to do that this man hasn't done?"

### NO NEUTRAL GROUND

Many consider neutrality to be a sign of maturity and objectivity. Maintaining a neutral position toward Christ may be popular, but it is dangerous. People stay undecided about Jesus under the pretense of not wanting to make a hasty or wrong judgment. But Jesus never allowed indecision. He confronted men and women with the unavoidable choice of belief or unbelief. Today those who remain undecided must understand that they remain, by that choice, in opposition to Christ. You can't sit on the fence; whose side are you on?

## Religious leaders attempt to arrest Jesus

*JOHN 7:32-44 (Harmony 124a)*

When the Pharisees heard that the crowds were in this mood, they and the chief priests sent officers to arrest Jesus. But Jesus told them, "Not yet! I am to be here a little longer. Then I shall return to the one who sent me. You will search for me but not find me. And you won't be able to come where I am!"

The Jewish leaders were puzzled by this statement. "Where is he planning to go?" they asked. "Maybe he is thinking of leaving the country and going as a missionary among the Jews in other lands, or maybe even to the Gentiles! What does he mean about our looking for him and not being able to find him, and, 'You won't be able to come where I am'?"

*Although the Romans ruled Palestine, they gave the Jewish religious leaders authority over minor civil and religious affairs. The religious leaders supervised their own Temple guards and gave the officers power to arrest anyone causing a disturbance or breaking any of their ceremonial laws.*

On the last day, the climax of the holidays, Jesus shouted to the crowds, "If anyone is thirsty, let him come to me and drink. For the Scriptures declare that rivers of living water shall flow from the inmost being of anyone who believes in me." (He was speaking of the Holy Spirit, who would be given to everyone believing in him; but the Spirit had not yet been given, because Jesus had not yet returned to his glory in heaven.)

When the crowds heard him say this, some of them declared, "This man surely is the prophet who will come just before the Messiah." Others said, "He *is* the Messiah." Still others, "But he *can't* be! Will the Messiah come from *Galilee?* For the Scriptures clearly state that the Messiah will be born of the royal line of David, in *Bethlehem,* the village where David was born." So the crowd was divided about him. And some wanted him arrested, but no one touched him.

#### COME AND DRINK

Jesus used the term *living water* in 4:10 to indicate eternal life. Here he used the term to refer to the Holy Spirit. The two go together: Wherever the Holy Spirit is accepted, he brings eternal life. Jesus' words, "come to me and drink," alluded to the theme of many Bible passages that talk about the Messiah's life-giving blessings (Isaiah 12:2-3; 44:3-4; 58:11). In promising to give the Holy Spirit to all who believed, Jesus was claiming to be the Messiah, for that was something only the Messiah could do. The Holy Spirit empowered Jesus' followers at Pentecost (Acts 2) and has since been available to all who believe in Jesus as Savior. If you know Christ, you have the Holy Spirit living in you. Depend on him for power for living the Christian life.

*July 11*

---

## Religious leaders attempt to arrest Jesus

*JOHN 7:45-52 (Harmony 124b)*

The Temple police who had been sent to arrest him returned to the chief priests and Pharisees. "Why didn't you bring him in?" they demanded.

"He says such wonderful things!" they mumbled. "We've never heard anything like it."

"So you also have been led astray?" the Pharisees mocked. "Is there a single one of us Jewish rulers or Pharisees who believes he is the Messiah? These stupid crowds do, yes; but what do they know about it? A curse upon them anyway!"

Then Nicodemus spoke up. (Remember him? He was the Jewish leader who came secretly to interview Jesus.) "Is it legal to convict a man before he is even tried?" he asked.

*Nicodemus was the Pharisee who visited Jesus at night (John 3). Apparently Nicodemus had become a secret believer. Most of the Pharisees hated Jesus and wanted to kill him, so Nicodemus risked his reputation and high position when he spoke up for Jesus.*

They replied, "Are you a wretched Galilean too? Search the Scriptures and see for yourself—no prophets will come from Galilee!"

### KEEPERS OF THE TRUTH

Nicodemus confronted the Pharisees with their failure to keep their own laws. The Pharisees were losing ground—the Temple guards came back impressed by Jesus (7:46), and one of the Pharisees' own, Nicodemus, was defending him. With their hypocritical motives being exposed and their prestige slowly eroding, they began to move to protect themselves. Pride would interfere with their ability to reason, and soon they would become obsessed with getting rid of Jesus just to save face. What was good and right no longer mattered. It is easy to think that we have the truth and that those who disagree with us do not have any truth at all. But God's truth is available to everyone. Don't copy the Pharisees' self-centered and narrow attitude.

## Jesus forgives an adulterous woman

*JOHN 8:1-11 (Harmony 125)*

esus returned to the Mount of Olives, but early the next morning he was back again at the Temple. A crowd soon gathered, and he sat down and talked to them. As he was speaking, the Jewish leaders and Pharisees brought a woman caught in adultery and placed her out in front of the staring crowd.

"Teacher," they said to Jesus, "this woman was caught in the very act of adultery. Moses' law says to kill her. What about it?"

They were trying to trap him into saying something they could use against him, but Jesus stooped down and wrote in the dust with his finger. They kept demanding an answer, so he stood up again and said, "All right, hurl the stones at her until she dies. But only he who never sinned may throw the first!"

*The Jewish leaders had already disregarded the Law by arresting the woman without the man. The Law required that both parties to adultery be stoned (Leviticus 20:10; Deuteronomy 22:22). The leaders were using the woman as a trap so they could trick Jesus.*

Then he stooped down again and wrote some more in the dust. And the Jewish leaders slipped away one by one, beginning with the eldest, until only Jesus was left in front of the crowd with the woman.

Then Jesus stood up again and said to her, "Where are your accusers? Didn't even one of them condemn you?"

"No, sir," she said.

And Jesus said, "Neither do I. Go and sin no more."

### THE FIRST STONE

This is a significant statement about judging others. Because Jesus upheld the legal penalty for adultery, stoning, he could not be accused of being against the Law. But by saying that only a sinless person could throw the first stone, he highlighted the importance of compassion and forgiveness. When others are caught in sin, are you quick to pass judgment? To do so is to act as though you have never sinned. It is God's role to judge, not ours. Our role is to show forgiveness and compassion. Jesus didn't condemn the woman accused of adultery, but neither did he ignore or condone her sin. He told the woman to leave her life of sin. Jesus stands ready to forgive any sin in your life, but confession and repentance mean a change of heart. With God's help we can accept Christ's forgiveness and stop our wrongdoing.

## Jesus is the Light of the world

### JOHN 8:12 *(Harmony 126a)*

*L*ater, in one of his talks, Jesus said to the people, "I am the Light of the world. So if you follow me, you won't be stumbling through the darkness, for living light will flood your path."

*Jesus was speaking in the part of the Temple where the offerings were put, where candles burned to symbolize the pillar of fire that led the people of Israel through the wilderness (Exodus 13:21-22). In this context, Jesus called himself the Light of the world. The pillar of fire represented God's presence, protection, and guidance. Jesus brings God's presence, protection, and guidance.*

**THE LIGHT OF THE WORLD**

What does following Christ mean? As a soldier follows his captain, so we should follow Christ, our Commander. As a slave follows his master, so we should follow Christ, our Lord. As we follow the advice of a trusted counselor, so we should follow Jesus' commands to us in Scripture. As we follow the laws of our nation, so we should follow the laws of the Kingdom of Heaven. When we follow Jesus, the true Light, we can avoid walking blindly and falling into sin. He lights the path ahead of us so we can see how to live. He removes the darkness of sin from our lives. Have you allowed the light of Christ to shine into your life? Let Christ guide your life, and you'll never need to stumble in darkness. Is he the Light of *your* world?

## Jesus is the Light of the world

### JOHN 8:13-20 *(Harmony 126b)*

*T*he Pharisees replied, "You are boasting—and lying!"

Jesus told them, "These claims are true even though I make them concerning myself. For I know where I came from and where I am going, but you don't know this about me. You pass judgment on me without knowing the facts. I am not judging you now; but if I were, it would be an absolutely correct judgment in every respect, for I have with me the Father who sent me. Your laws say that if two men agree on something that has happened, their witness is accepted as fact. Well, I am one witness, and my Father who sent me is the other."

"Where is your father?" they asked.

Jesus answered, "You don't know who I am, so you don't know who my Father is. If you knew me, then you would know him too."

*The Pharisees argued that Jesus' claim was legally invalid because he had no other witnesses. Jesus responded that his confirming witness was God himself. Jesus and the Father made two witnesses, the number required by the Law (Deuteronomy 19:15).*

Jesus made these statements while in the section of the Temple known as the Treasury. But he was not arrested, for his time had not yet run out.

### THE TRUTH

The Pharisees thought Jesus was either a lunatic or a liar. Jesus provided them with a third alternative: He was telling the truth. Because most of the Pharisees refused to consider the third alternative, they never recognized him as Messiah and Lord. If you are seeking to know who Jesus is, do not close any door before looking through it honestly. Only with an open mind will you know the truth that he is Messiah and Lord.

*July 15*

## Jesus warns of coming judgment

*JOHN 8:21-29 (Harmony 127)*

Later he said to them again, "I am going away; and you will search for me, and die in your sins. And you cannot come where I am going."

The Jews asked, "Is he planning suicide? What does he mean, 'You cannot come where I am going'?"

Then he said to them, "You are from below; I am from above. You are of this world; I am not. That is why I said that you will die in your sins; for unless you believe that I am the Messiah, the Son of God, you will die in your sins."

*If the Jewish religious leaders would not believe in Jesus while he was with them, they would run the risk of not having any further opportunity. They would die in their sin because they had rejected the only one who could save them.*

"Tell us who you are," they demanded.

He replied, "I am the one I have always claimed to be. I could condemn you for much and teach you much, but I won't, for I say only what I am told to by the one who sent me; and he is Truth." But they still didn't understand that he was talking to them about God.

So Jesus said, "When you have killed the Messiah, then you will realize that I am he and that I have not been telling you my own ideas, but have spoken what the Father taught me. And he who sent me is with me—he has not deserted me—for I always do those things that are pleasing to him."

### WHAT DO YOU WANT?

Those questioning Jesus were convinced they understood God's plan. They thought they had a clear idea of exactly what kind of savior they needed, and Jesus did not fit that pattern. Are you trusting Jesus to be your Savior because he knows best, or are you reserving final judgment just in case a "better" option comes along? Are you trusting God to graciously meet your needs even when you do not fully understand them, or are you clinging to the belief that you know best what God can do for you? Are you still shopping for a better offer? Only Jesus can give forgiveness and eternal life.

*July 16*

## Jesus speaks about God's true children

**JOHN 8:30-33** *(Harmony 128a)*

 hen many of the Jewish leaders who heard him say these things began believing him to be the Messiah.

Jesus said to them, "You are truly my disciples if you live as I tell you to, and you will know the truth, and the truth will set you free."

"But we are descendants of Abraham," they said, "and have never been slaves to any man on earth! What do you mean, 'set free'?"

### SET FREE

Sin has a way of enslaving us, controlling us, dominating us, and dictating our actions. Jesus can free you from this slavery that keeps you

*To know the truth is to know God's revelation to people. That revelation is Jesus himself. Therefore, Jesus is the Truth that makes us free (8:36). He is the source of truth, the perfect standard of what is right.*

from becoming the person God created you to be. If sin is restraining, mastering, or enslaving you, Jesus can break its power over your life. He frees us from the consequences of sin, from self-deception, and from deception by Satan. He shows us clearly the way to everlasting life with God. Thus Jesus does not give us freedom to do what we want, but freedom to follow God. As we seek to serve God, Jesus' perfect truth frees us to be all that God meant us to be.

*July 17*

---

## Jesus speaks about God's true children

*JOHN 8:34-47 (Harmony 128b)*

Jesus replied, "You are slaves of sin, every one of you. And slaves don't have rights, but the Son has every right there is! So if the Son sets you free, you will indeed be free—(Yes, I realize that you are descendants of Abraham!) And yet some of you are trying to kill me because my message does not find a home within your hearts. I am telling you what I saw when I was with my Father. But you are following the advice of *your* father."

*The attitudes and actions of these leaders clearly identified them as followers of Satan. They may not have been conscious of this, but their hatred of truth, their lies, and their murderous intentions indicated how much control the devil had over them.*

"Our father is Abraham," they declared.

"No!" Jesus replied, "for if he were, you would follow his good example. But instead you are trying to kill me—and all because I told you the truth I heard from God. Abraham wouldn't do a thing like that! No, you are obeying your *real* father when you act that way."

They replied, "We were not born out of wedlock—our true Father is God himself."

Jesus told them, "If that were so, then you would love me, for I have come to you from God. I am not here on my own, but he sent me. Why can't you understand what I am saying? It is because you are prevented from doing so! For you are the children of your father the devil and you love to do the evil things he does. He was a murderer from the beginning and a hater of truth—there is not an iota of truth in him. When he lies, it is perfectly normal; for he is the father of liars. And so when I tell the truth, you just naturally don't believe it!

"Which of you can truthfully accuse me of one single sin? No one! And since I am telling you the truth, why don't you believe me? Anyone whose Father is God listens gladly to the words of God. Since you don't, it proves you aren't his children."

**WHOSE CHILD?**

Jesus made a distinction between hereditary children and *true* children. The religious leaders were hereditary children of Abraham (founder of the Jewish nation) and therefore claimed to be children of God. But their actions showed them to be true children of Satan, for they lived under Satan's guidance. True children of Abraham (faithful followers of God) would not act as they did. Your church membership and family connections will not make you a true child of God. Your true father is the one you imitate and obey.

*July 18*

## Jesus states he is eternal

*JOHN 8:48-59 (Harmony 129)*

"You Samaritan! Foreigner! Devil!" the Jewish leaders snarled. "Didn't we say all along you were possessed by a demon?"

"No," Jesus said, "I have no demon in me. For I honor my Father—and you dishonor me. And though I have no wish to make myself great, God wants this for me and judges those who reject me. With all the earnestness I have I tell you this—no one who obeys me shall ever die!"

The leaders of the Jews said, "Now we know you are possessed by a demon. Even Abraham and the mightiest prophets died, and yet you say that obeying you will keep a man from dying! So you are greater than our father Abraham, who died? And greater than the prophets, who died? Who do you think you are?" Then Jesus told them this: "If I am merely boasting about myself, it doesn't count. But it is my Father—and you claim him as your God—who is saying these glorious things about me. But you do not even know him. I do. If I said otherwise, I would be as great a liar as you! But it is true—I know him and fully obey him. Your father Abraham rejoiced to see my day. He knew I was coming and was glad."

*The Jewish leaders:* "You aren't even fifty years old—sure, you've seen Abraham!"

*Jesus:* "The absolute truth is that I was in existence before Abraham was ever born!"

*In accordance with the law in Leviticus 24:16, the religious leaders were ready to stone Jesus for claiming to be God. They well understood what Jesus was claiming, and because they didn't believe him, they charged him with blasphemy.*

At that point the Jewish leaders picked up stones to kill him. But Jesus was hidden from them, and walked past them and left the Temple.

### THE TRUE SON OF GOD

This is one of the most powerful statements uttered by Jesus. When he said that he existed before Abraham was born, he undeniably proclaimed his divinity. Not only did Jesus say that he existed before Abraham; he also applied God's holy name (*I AM*—Exodus 3:14) to himself. This claim demands a response. It cannot be ignored. The Jewish leaders tried to stone Jesus for blasphemy because he claimed equality with God. But Jesus *is* God. How have you responded to Jesus, the Son of God?

## July 19

## Jesus sends out seventy messengers

### LUKE 10:1-16 *(Harmony 130)*

he Lord now chose seventy other disciples and sent them on ahead in pairs to all the towns and villages he planned to visit later.

These were his instructions to them: "Plead with the Lord of the harvest to send out more laborers to help you, for the harvest is so plentiful and the workers so few. Go now, and remember that I am sending you out as lambs among wolves. Don't take any money with you, or a beggar's bag, or even an extra pair of shoes. And don't waste time along the way.

*Jesus gave two rules for the disciples to follow as they traveled: They were to eat what was set before them— that is, they were to accept hospitality without being picky—and they were to heal the sick. Because of the healings, people would be willing to listen to the gospel.*

"Whenever you enter a home, give it your blessing. If it is worthy of the blessing, the blessing will stand; if not, the blessing will return to you.

"When you enter a village, don't shift around from home to home, but stay in one place, eating and drinking without question whatever is set before you. And don't hesitate to accept hospitality, for the workman is worthy of his wages!

"If a town welcomes you, follow these two rules:

(1) Eat whatever is set before you.

(2) Heal the sick; and as you heal them, say, 'The Kingdom of God is very near you now.'

"But if a town refuses you, go out into its streets and say, 'We wipe the dust of your town from our feet as a public announcement of your doom. Never forget how close you were to the Kingdom of God!' Even wicked Sodom will be better off than such a city on the Judgment Day. What horrors await you, you cities of Chorazin and Bethsaida! For if the miracles I did for you had been done in the cities of Tyre and Sidon, their people would have sat in deep repentance long ago, clothed in sackcloth and throwing ashes on their heads to show their remorse. Yes, Tyre and Sidon will receive less punishment on the Judgment Day than you. And you people of Capernaum, what shall I say about you? Will you be exalted to heaven? No, you shall be brought down to hell."

Then he said to the disciples, "Those who welcome you are welcoming me. And those who reject you are rejecting me. And those who reject me are rejecting God who sent me."

### NO UNEMPLOYMENT

Far more than twelve people had been following Jesus. Here Jesus designated a group of seventy to prepare a number of towns for Jesus' later visit. Jesus was sending thirty-five teams of two to reach the multitudes. These teams were not to try to do the job without help; rather, they were to ask God for more workers. Some people, as soon as they understand the gospel, want to go to work immediately contacting unsaved people. This story suggests a different approach: Begin by mobilizing people to pray. And before praying for unsaved people, pray that other concerned disciples will join you in reaching out to them. In Christian service there is no unemployment. God has work enough for everyone. Don't just sit back and watch others work—look for ways to help with the harvest.

*July 20*

---

## The seventy messengers return

*LUKE 10:17-20 (Harmony 131a)*

*W*hen the seventy disciples returned, they joyfully reported to him, "Even the demons obey us when we use your name."

"Yes," he told them, "I saw Satan falling from heaven as a flash of lightning! And I have given you authority over all the power of the Enemy, and to walk among serpents and scorpions and to crush them.

Nothing shall injure you! However, the important thing is not that demons obey you, but that your names are registered as citizens of heaven."

### CITIZENS

The disciples had seen tremendous results as they ministered in Jesus' name and with his authority. They were elated by the victories they had witnessed, and Jesus shared their enthusiasm. He helped them get their priorities right, however, by reminding them of their most important victory—that their names were written in heaven. This honor was more important than any of their accomplishments. As we see God's wonders at work in and through us, we should not lose sight of the greatest wonder of all—our heavenly citizenship.

*Some interpreters believe this verse refers to Satan's original fall, and explain that Satan's pride led to all the evil we see on earth today. To Jesus' disciples, who were thrilled with their power over evil spirits ("serpents and scorpions"), he may have been giving this stern warning: "Yours is the kind of pride that led to Satan's downfall. Be careful!"*

*July 21*

## The seventy messengers return

### LUKE 10:21-24 *(Harmony 131b)*

hen he was filled with the joy of the Holy Spirit and said, "I praise you, O Father, Lord of heaven and earth, for hiding these things from the intellectuals and worldly wise and for revealing them to those who are as trusting as little children. Yes, thank you, Father, for that is the way you wanted it. I am the Agent of my Father in everything; and no one really knows the Son except the Father, and no one really knows the Father except the Son and those to whom the Son chooses to reveal him."

Then, turning to the twelve disciples, he said quietly, "How privileged you are to see what you have seen. Many a prophet and king of old has longed for these days, to see and hear what you have seen and heard!"

*Old Testament men of God such as David and the prophet Isaiah made many God-inspired predictions that Jesus fulfilled. As Peter later wrote, these prophets wondered what their words meant and when they would be fulfilled (1 Peter 1:10-13). In Jesus' words, they wanted "to see and hear what you have seen and heard"—the coming of God's Kingdom.*

## EQUALLY AVAILABLE

Jesus thanked God that spiritual truth was for everyone, and not just for the elite. Many of life's rewards seem to go to the intelligent, the rich, the good-looking, or the powerful, but the Kingdom of God is equally available to all, regardless of position or abilities. We come to Jesus not through strength or brains, but through childlike trust. Jesus is not opposed to engaging in scholarly pursuits; he is opposed to spiritual pride (being wise in one's own eyes). Christ's mission was to reveal God the Father to people. His words brought difficult ideas down to earth. He explained God's love through parables, teachings, and, most of all, his life. By examining Jesus' actions, principles, and attitudes, we can understand God more clearly. Join Jesus in thanking God that we all have equal access to him. Trust in God's grace, not in your personal qualifications, for your citizenship in the Kingdom.

# July 22

## Jesus tells the parable of the Good Samaritan

### LUKE 10:25-27 *(Harmony 132a)*

One day an expert on Moses' laws came to test Jesus' orthodoxy by asking him this question: "Teacher, what does a man need to do to live forever in heaven?"

Jesus replied, "What does Moses' law say about it?"

"It says," he replied, "that you must love the Lord your God with all your heart, and with all your soul, and with all your strength, and with all your mind. And you must love your neighbor just as much as you love yourself."

*This lawyer was quoting Deuteronomy 6:5 and Leviticus 19:18. He correctly understood that the Law demanded total devotion to God and love for one's neighbor.*

### NOT SO DIFFERENT

Jesus would answer the lawyer's question by telling the parable of the Good Samaritan. There was deep hatred between Jews and Samaritans. The Jews saw themselves as pure descendants of Abraham, while the Samaritans were a mixed race produced when Jews from the Northern Kingdom intermarried with other peoples after Israel's exile. To this lawyer, the person least likely to act correctly would be the Samaritan. In fact, he could not bear to say "Samaritan" in answer to Jesus' question. The lawyer's attitude betrayed his lack of the very thing that he had earlier said the Law commanded—love. In our churches today, it's our natural inclination to feel uncomfortable around people who are different from us and to gravitate toward those who are similar to us. But when we allow our differences to separate us from our fellow believers, we are disregarding clear biblical teaching. Make a point to seek out and appreciate people who are not just like you and your friends. You may find that you have a lot in common with them.

*July 23*

## Jesus tells the parable of the Good Samaritan

*LUKE 10:28-37 (Harmony 132b)*

ight!" Jesus told him. *"Do* this and *you* shall live!"

The man wanted to justify his lack of love for some kinds of people, so he asked, "Which neighbors?"

Jesus replied with an illustration: "A Jew going on a trip from Jerusalem to Jericho was attacked by bandits. They stripped him of his clothes and money, and beat him up and left him lying half dead beside the road.

"By chance a Jewish priest came along; and when he saw the man lying there, he crossed to the other side of the road and passed him by. A Jewish Temple-assistant walked over and looked at him lying there, but then went on.

"But a despised Samaritan came along, and when he saw him, he felt deep pity. Kneeling beside him the Samaritan soothed his wounds with medicine and bandaged them. Then he put the man on his donkey and walked along beside him till they came to an inn, where he nursed him through the night. The next day he handed the innkeeper two twenty-dollar bills and told him to take care of the man. 'If his bill runs higher than that,' he said, 'I'll pay the difference the next time I am here.'

*That Jesus would use an example of the road between Jerusalem and Jericho for the man to be attacked would have rung true to his audience. The road was rocky, surrounded with crags to hide bandits, and had a reputation for being dangerous to lone travelers.*

"Now which of these three would you say was a neighbor to the bandits' victim?"

The man replied, "The one who showed him some pity."

Then Jesus said, "Yes, now go and do the same."

The lawyer treated the wounded man as a topic for discussion; the thieves, as an object to exploit; the priest, as a problem to avoid; and the Levite, as an object of curiosity. Only the Samaritan treated him as a person to love. From the parable we learn three principles about loving our neighbor: (1) Lack of love is often easy to justify, even though it is never right; (2) our neighbor is anyone of any race, creed, or social background who is in need; and (3) love means acting to meet the person's need. Wherever you live, there are needy people close by. There is no good reason for refusing to help.

*July 24*

---

## Jesus visits Mary and Martha

### *LUKE 10:38-42 (Harmony 133)*

As Jesus and the disciples continued on their way to Jerusalem they came to a village where a woman named Martha welcomed them into her home. Her sister Mary sat on the floor, listening to Jesus as he talked.

But Martha was the jittery type and was worrying over the big dinner she was preparing.

She came to Jesus and said, "Sir, doesn't it seem unfair to you that my sister just sits here while I do all the work? Tell her to come and help me."

*Jesus, after returning to Jerusalem for the Tabernacle Ceremonies (John 7:2), visited his friends Mary, Martha, and Lazarus, who lived in the tiny village of Bethany, just outside Jerusalem on the Mount of Olives.*

But the Lord said to her, "Martha, dear friend, you are so upset over all these details! There is really only one thing worth being concerned about. Mary has discovered it—and I won't take it away from her!"

**SERVING WHOM?**

Mary and Martha both loved Jesus. On this occasion they were both serving him. But Martha thought Mary's style of serving was inferior to hers. She didn't realize that in her desire to serve, she was actually neglecting her guest. Jesus did not blame Martha for being concerned about household chores. He was only asking her to set priorities. It is possible for service to Christ to degenerate into mere busywork that is no longer full of devotion to God. Are you so busy doing things *for* Jesus that you're not spending any time *with* him? Don't let your service become self-serving.

## Jesus teaches his disciples about prayer

### LUKE 11:1-4 *(Harmony 134a)*

Once when Jesus had been out praying, one of his disciples came to him as he finished and said, "Lord, teach us a prayer to recite just as John taught one to his disciples."

And this is the prayer he taught them: "Father, may your name be honored for its holiness; send your Kingdom soon. Give us our food day by day. And forgive our sins—for we have forgiven those who sinned against us. And don't allow us to be tempted."

*God's provision is daily, not all at once. We cannot store it up and then cut off communication with God. And we dare not be self-satisfied. If you are running low on strength, consider how long you have been away from the Source.*

**PRAISING, FORGIVING**

Notice the order in this prayer. First Jesus praised God; then he made his requests. Praising God first puts us in the right frame of mind to tell him about our needs. Too often our prayers are more like shopping lists than conversations. When Jesus taught his disciples to pray, he made forgiveness the cornerstone of their relationship with God. God has forgiven our sins; we must now forgive those who have wronged us. To remain unforgiving shows we have not understood that we ourselves deeply need to be forgiven. Think of some people who have wronged you. Have you forgiven them? How will God deal with you if he treats you as you treat others?

## Jesus teaches his disciples about prayer

### LUKE 11:5-10 *(Harmony 134b)*

Then, teaching them more about prayer, he used this illustration: "Suppose you went to a friend's house at midnight, wanting to borrow three loaves of bread. You would shout up to him, 'A friend of mine has just arrived for a visit and I've nothing to give him to eat.' He would call down from his bedroom, 'Please don't ask me to get up. The door is locked for the night and we are all in bed. I just can't help you this time.'

"But I'll tell you this—though he won't do it as a friend, if you keep knocking long enough, he will get up and give you everything you want—just because of your persistence. And so it is with prayer—keep on asking and you will keep on getting; keep on looking and you will keep on finding; knock and the door will be opened. Everyone who asks, receives; all who seek, find; and the door is opened to everyone who knocks."

*Everyone who asks, receives, if their requests are made in faith. To ask in faith is to ask with confidence that God will align our desires with his purposes.*

### PERSISTENCE

Have you ever grown tired of praying for something or someone? Our vigilance is an expression of our faith that God answers our prayers. Faith shouldn't die if the answers come slowly, for the delay may be God's way of working his will in our lives. When you feel tired of praying, know that God is present, always listening, always answering—maybe not in ways you had hoped, but in ways that he knows are best. Persistence, or boldness, in prayer overcomes our insensitivity, not God's. To practice persistence does more to change our hearts and minds than his, and it helps us understand and express the intensity of our need. Persistence in prayer helps us recognize God's work. Are you waiting for God's timing? Trust his judgment for your best interests.

## July 27

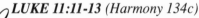

## Jesus teaches his disciples about prayer

**LUKE 11:11-13** *(Harmony 134c)*

ou men who are fathers—if your boy asks for bread, do you give him a stone? If he asks for fish, do you give him a snake? If he asks for an egg, do you give him a scorpion? Of course not!

"And if even sinful persons like yourselves give children what they need, don't you realize that your heavenly Father will do at least as much, and give the Holy Spirit to those who ask for him?"

*God is the perfect Father. Although some people's fathers may not have been very good examples, God can be depended on to always do what is best for his children.*

### GOD'S GIFT

Even though good fathers make mistakes, they treat their children well. How much better our perfect heavenly Father treats his children! The most important gift he could ever give us is the Holy Spirit (Acts 2:1-4), whom he promised to give all believers after his death, resurrection, and return to heaven (John 15:26). At Pentecost (Acts 2:4), the Holy Spirit was made available to all who believe in Jesus. We receive the Holy Spirit when we receive Jesus Christ. Pray with an attitude of positive expectancy. Your heavenly Father wants the very best for you.

*July 28*

## Jesus answers hostile accusations

### *LUKE 11:14-26 (Harmony 135a)*

*O*nce, when Jesus cast out a demon from a man who couldn't speak, his voice returned to him. The crowd was excited and enthusiastic, but some said, "No wonder he can cast them out. He gets his power from Satan, the king of demons!" Others asked for something to happen in the sky to prove his claim of being the Messiah.

He knew the thoughts of each of them, so he said, "Any kingdom filled with civil war is doomed; so is a home filled with argument and strife. Therefore, if what you say is true, that Satan is fighting against himself by empowering me to cast out his demons, how can his kingdom survive? And if I am empowered by Satan, what about your own followers? For they cast out demons! Do you think this proves they are possessed by Satan? Ask *them* if you are right! But if I am casting out demons because of power from God, it proves that the Kingdom of God has arrived.

*Regardless of how great Satan's power is, Jesus is stronger still. Satan, who had controlled the kingdom of this world for thousands of years, was now being controlled and overpowered by Jesus and the Kingdom of Heaven. He will bind Satan and dispose of him for eternity (see Revelation 20:2, 10).*

"For when Satan, strong and fully armed, guards his palace, it is safe—until someone stronger and better armed attacks and overcomes him and strips him of his weapons and carries off his belongings.

"Anyone who is not for me is against me; if he isn't helping me, he is hurting my cause.

"When a demon is cast out of a man, it goes to the deserts, searching there for rest; but finding none, it returns to the person it left, and finds that its former home is all swept and clean. Then it goes and gets seven other demons more evil than itself, and they all enter the man. And so the poor fellow is seven times worse off than he was before."

**EMPTIED, FILLED**

Jesus was illustrating an unfortunate human tendency—our desire to reform often does not last long. In Israel's history, almost as soon as a good king would pull down idols, a bad king would set them up again. It is not enough to be emptied of evil; we must then be filled with the power of the Holy Spirit to accomplish God's new purpose in our lives. If we are controlled by the Holy Spirit, we produce the kind of fruit that pleases God (as described in Galatians 5:22-23). We do not need to fear the Spirit's control. He does not possess us against our wills or treat us as robots.

## July 29

## Jesus answers hostile accusations

### LUKE 11:27-28 *(Harmony 135b)*

*A*s he was speaking, a woman in the crowd called out, "God bless your mother—the womb from which you came, and the breasts that gave you suck!"

He replied, "Yes, but even more blessed are all who hear the Word of God and put it into practice."

*This woman was complimenting Jesus by complimenting his mother. Jesus, however, implied that he wanted obedience far more than compliments.*

**OBEY FIRST**

Jesus was speaking to people who put extremely high value on family ties. Their genealogies were important guarantees that they were part of God's chosen people. A man's value came from his ancestors, and a woman's value came from the sons she bore. Jesus' response to the woman meant that a person's obedience to God is more important than his or her place on the family tree. The patient work of consistent obedience is even more important than the honor of bearing a respected son. How do you rate your obedience? God is more than willing to give you the power to obey him with all your heart.

## Jesus warns against unbelief

### LUKE 11:29-32 *(Harmony 136)*

*A*s the crowd pressed in upon him, he preached them this sermon: "These are evil times, with evil people. They keep asking for some strange happening in the skies to prove I am the Messiah, but the only proof I will give them is a miracle like that of Jonah, whose experiences proved to the people of Nineveh that God had sent him. My similar experience will prove that God has sent me to these people.

*God had asked Jonah to preach repentance to the Gentiles (non-Jews). Jesus was affirming Jonah's message. Salvation is not only for Jews, but for all people. Matthew 12:40 adds another explanation: Jesus would die and then rise after three days, just as the prophet Jonah was rescued after three days in the belly of the great fish.*

"And at the Judgment Day the queen of Sheba shall arise and point her finger at this generation, condemning it, for she went on a long, hard journey to listen to the wisdom of Solomon; but one far greater than Solomon is here and few pay any attention.

"The men of Nineveh, too, shall arise and condemn this nation, for they repented at the preaching of Jonah; and someone far greater than Jonah is here, but this nation won't listen."

#### LIABLE TO JUDGMENT

The cruel, warlike men of Nineveh, capital of Assyria, repented when Jonah preached to them—and Jonah did not even care about them. The heathen queen of Sheba praised the God of Israel when she heard Solomon's wisdom, and Solomon was full of faults. By contrast, Jesus, the perfect Son of God, had come to people that he loved dearly—but they rejected him. Thus God's chosen people made themselves more liable to judgment than either a notoriously wicked nation or a powerful heathen queen. The Ninevites and the queen of Sheba had turned to God with far less evidence than Jesus was giving his listeners—and far less than we have today. We have eyewitness reports of the risen Jesus, the continuing power of the Holy Spirit unleashed at Pentecost, easy access to the Bible, and knowledge of two thousand years of Christ's acts through his church. With the knowledge and insight available to us, our response to Christ ought to be even more complete and wholehearted. What spiritual resources do you have? How do you use them to increase your knowledge of Christ?

## Jesus teaches about the light within

*LUKE 11:33-36 (Harmony 137)*

*N*o one lights a lamp and hides it! Instead, he puts it on a lampstand to give light to all who enter the room. Your eyes light up your inward being. A pure eye lets sunshine into your soul. A lustful eye shuts out the light and plunges you into darkness. So watch out that the sunshine isn't blotted out. If you are filled with light within, with no dark corners, then your face will be radiant too, as though a floodlight is beamed upon you."

*Lust is more than inappropriate sexual desire. It can be an unnatural or greedy desire for anything (such as sports, knowledge, possessions, influence).*

### SEEING THE LIGHT

The lamp is Christ; the eye represents spiritual understanding and insight. A lustful eye is less sensitive and can blot out the light of Christ's presence. If you have a hard time seeing God at work in the world and in your life, check your vision. Are any sinful desires blinding you to Christ? If so, what can you do? Our world is filled with impurity. We can stay pure in an impure environment by reading God's Word and doing what it says (Psalm 119:9).

## Jesus criticizes the religious leaders

### *LUKE 11:37-44 (Harmony 138a)*

As he was speaking, one of the Pharisees asked him home for a meal. When Jesus arrived, he sat down to eat without first performing the ceremonial washing required by Jewish custom. This greatly surprised his host.

Then Jesus said to him, "You Pharisees wash the outside, but inside you are still dirty—full of greed and wickedness! Fools! Didn't God make the inside as well as the outside? Purity is best demonstrated by generosity.

"But woe to you Pharisees! For though you are careful to tithe even the smallest part of your income, you completely forget about justice and the love of God. You should tithe, yes, but you should not leave these other things undone.

*This washing was done not for health reasons, but as a symbol of washing away any contamination from touching anything unclean. Not only did the Pharisees make a public show of their washing, but they also commanded everyone else to follow a practice originally intended only for the priests.*

"Woe to you Pharisees! For how you love the seats of honor in the synagogues and the respectful greetings from everyone as you walk through the markets! Yes, awesome judgment is awaiting you. For you are like hidden graves in a field. Men go by you with no knowledge of the corruption they are passing."

#### GENEROSITY

The Pharisees loved to think of themselves as "clean," but their stinginess toward God and the poor proved that they were not as clean as they thought. How do you use the resources God has entrusted to you? Are you generous in meeting the needs around you? Your generosity reveals much about the purity of your heart. It is easy to rationalize not helping others because we have already given to the church, but a person who follows Jesus should share with needy neighbors. While tithing is important to the life of the church, our compassion must not stop there. Where we can help, we should help.

## Jesus criticizes the religious leaders

*LUKE 11:45-54 (Harmony 138b)*

*S*ir," said an expert in religious law who was standing there, "you have insulted my profession, too, in what you just said."

"Yes," said Jesus, "the same horrors await you! For you crush men beneath impossible religious demands—demands that you yourselves would never think of trying to keep. Woe to you! For you are exactly like your ancestors who killed the prophets long ago. Murderers! You agree with your fathers that what they did was right—you would have done the same yourselves.

*God's prophets have been persecuted and murdered throughout history. But this generation was rejecting more than a human prophet—they were rejecting God himself— the One to whom all their history and prophecy were pointing.*

"This is what God says about you: 'I will send prophets and apostles to you, and you will kill some of them and chase away the others.'

"And you of this generation will be held responsible for the murder of God's servants from the founding of the world—from the murder of Abel to the murder of Zechariah who perished between the altar and the sanctuary. Yes, it will surely be charged against you.

"Woe to you experts in religion! For you hide the truth from the people. You won't accept it for yourselves, and you prevent others from having a chance to believe it."

The Pharisees and legal experts were furious; and from that time on they plied him fiercely with a host of questions, trying to trap him into saying something for which they could have him arrested.

### TRULY CLEAN

Jesus criticized the Pharisees and the lawyers harshly because they (1) cleaned their outsides but not their insides, (2) remembered to give a tenth of even their garden herbs, but neglected justice, (3) loved praise and attention, (4) loaded people down with burdensome religious demands, (5) would not accept the truth about Jesus, and (6) prevented others from believing the truth as well. They went wrong by focusing on outward appearances and ignoring the inner condition of their hearts. We do the same when our service comes from a desire to be seen rather than from a pure heart and out of a love for others. People may sometimes be fooled, but God isn't. Don't be a Christian on the outside only. Bring your inner life under God's control, and your outer life will naturally reflect him.

## Jesus speaks against hypocrisy

### *LUKE 12:1-3 (Harmony 139a)*

*M*eanwhile the crowds grew until thousands upon thousands were milling about and crushing each other. He turned now to his disciples and warned them, "More than anything else, beware of these Pharisees and the way they pretend to be good when they aren't. But such hypocrisy cannot be hidden forever. It will become as evident as yeast in dough. Whatever they have said in the dark shall be heard in the light, and what you have whispered in the inner rooms shall be broadcast from the housetops for all to hear!"

*The Pharisees' hypocrisy was evidenced by the burdens they added to God's Law. To the commandment to remember the Sabbath (Exodus 20:8), they had added instructions regarding how far a person could walk on the Sabbath. Healing a person was considered unlawful work on the Sabbath, although rescuing a trapped animal was permitted. No wonder Jesus condemned their additions to the Law.*

**KEEPING UP APPEARANCES**

As Jesus watched the huge crowds waiting to hear him, he warned his disciples against hypocrisy—trying to appear good when one's heart is far from God. The Pharisees could not keep their attitudes hidden forever. Their selfishness would act like yeast, and soon they would expose themselves for what they really were—power-hungry impostors, not devoted religious leaders. It is easy to be angry at the blatant hypocrisy of the Pharisees, but each of us must resist the temptation to settle for the appearance of respectability when our hearts are far from God.

## Jesus speaks against hypocrisy

### *LUKE 12:4-7 (Harmony 139b)*

*D*ear friends, don't be afraid of these who want to murder you. They can only kill the body; they have no power over your souls. But I'll tell you whom to fear—fear God who has the power to kill and then cast into hell.

"What is the price of five sparrows? A couple of pennies? Not much more than that. Yet God does not forget a single one of them. And he knows the number of hairs on your head! Never fear, you are far more valuable to him than a whole flock of sparrows."

*To "fear" God means to honor and respect him as the almighty, sovereign God, the ruler of the universe. We don't have to be afraid and run from him, because he loves us. But we must submit to his authority and obey him.*

**FEAR?**

Fear of opposition or ridicule can weaken our witness for Christ. Often we cling to peace and comfort, even at the cost of our walk with God. Jesus reminds us here that we should fear God who controls eternity, not merely temporal consequences. Our true value is God's estimate of our worth, not our peers'. Other people evaluate and categorize us according to how we perform, what we achieve, and how we look. But God cares for us, as he does for all of his creatures, because we belong to him. So we can face life without fear.

*August 5*

## Jesus speaks against hypocrisy

### LUKE 12:8-12 (Harmony 139c)

And I assure you of this: I, the Messiah, will publicly honor you in the presence of God's angels if you publicly acknowledge me here on earth as your Friend. But I will deny before the angels those who deny me here among men. (Yet those who speak against me may be forgiven—while those who speak against the Holy Spirit shall never be forgiven.)

"And when you are brought to trial before these Jewish rulers and authorities in the synagogues, don't be concerned about what to say in your defense, for the Holy Spirit will give you the right words even as you are standing there."

*Jesus said that blasphemy against the Holy Spirit is unforgivable. This sin means attributing to Satan the work that the Holy Spirit accomplishes, thus it is deliberate and ongoing rejection of the Holy Spirit's work and even of God himself.*

**DENY OR CONFESS?**

We deny Jesus when we (1) hope no one will think we are Christians, (2) decide *not* to speak up for what is right, (3) are silent about our relationship with God, (4) blend into society, (5) accept our culture's non-Christian values. By contrast, we confess him when we (1) live moral, upright, Christ-honoring lives, (2) look for opportunities to share our faith with others, (3) help others in need, (4) take a stand for justice, (5) love others, (6) acknowledge our loyalty to Christ, (7) use our lives and resources to carry out his desires rather than our own.

## *August 6*

---

## Jesus tells the parable of the rich fool

### *LUKE 12:13-21 (Harmony 140)*

When someone called from the crowd, "Sir, please tell my brother to divide my father's estate with me."

But Jesus replied, "Man, who made me a judge over you to decide such things as that? Beware! Don't always be wishing for what you don't have. For real life and real living are not related to how rich we are."

Then he gave an illustration: "A rich man had a fertile farm that produced fine crops. In fact, his barns were full to overflowing—he couldn't get everything in. He thought about his problem, and finally exclaimed, 'I know—I'll tear down my barns and build bigger ones! Then I'll have room enough. And I'll sit back and say to myself, "Friend, you have enough stored away for years to come. Now take it easy! Wine, women, and song for you!"'

"But God said to him, 'Fool! Tonight you die. Then who will get it all?'

"Yes, every man is a fool who gets rich on earth but not in heaven."

*The rich man in Jesus' story died before he could begin to use what was stored in his big barns. Planning for retirement—preparing for life before death—is wise, but neglecting life after death is disastrous.*

### THE GOOD LIFE

Jesus is pointing to a higher issue—a correct attitude toward the accumulation of wealth. Life is more than material goods; far more important is our relationship with God. Jesus says that the good life has nothing to do with being wealthy, so be on guard against greed (desire for what we don't have). This is the exact opposite of what society usually says. Advertisers spend millions of dollars to entice us to think that if we buy more and more of their products, we will be happier, more fulfilled, more comfortable. How do you respond to the constant pressure to buy? Learn to tune out expensive enticements and concentrate instead on the truly good life—living in a relationship with God and doing his work.

## Jesus warns about worry

*LUKE 12:22-31 (Harmony 141a)*

hen turning to his disciples he said, "Don't worry about whether you have enough food to eat or clothes to wear. For life consists of far more than food and clothes. Look at the ravens—they don't plant or harvest or have barns to store away their food, and yet they get along all right—for God feeds them. And you are far more valuable to him than any birds!

*Worry is pointless because it can't fill any of our needs; worry is foolish because the Creator of the universe loves us and knows what we need. He promises to meet all our real needs, but not necessarily all our desires.*

"And besides, what's the use of worrying? What good does it do? Will it add a single day to your life? Of course not! And if worry can't even do such little things as that, what's the use of worrying over bigger things?

"Look at the lilies! They don't toil and spin, and yet Solomon in all his glory was not robed as well as they are. And if God provides clothing for the flowers that are here today and gone tomorrow, don't you suppose that he will provide clothing for you, you doubters? And don't worry about food— what to eat and drink; don't worry at all that God will provide it for you. All mankind scratches for its daily bread, but your heavenly Father knows your needs. He will always give you all you need from day to day if you will make the Kingdom of God your primary concern."

### AT THE CENTER

Seeking the Kingdom of God means making Jesus the Lord and King of your life. He must control every area—your work, play, plans, relationships. Is the Kingdom only one of your many concerns, or is it central to all you do? Are you holding back any areas of your life from God's control? As Lord and Creator, he wants to help provide what you need as well as guide how you use what he provides.

## Jesus warns about worry

### *LUKE 12:32-34 (Harmony 141b)*

*S*o don't be afraid, little flock. For it gives your Father great happiness to give you the Kingdom. Sell what you have and give to those in need. This will fatten your purses in heaven! And the purses of heaven have no rips or holes in them. Your treasures there will never disappear; no thief can steal them; no moth can destroy them. Wherever your treasure is, there your heart and thoughts will also be."

*God does not command all believers to sell everything they have. What he wants is believers who hold their possessions loosely, willing to sell or give away in order to help someone else.*

**TREASURE HUNT**

Money seen as an end in itself quickly traps us and cuts us off from both God and the needy. The key to using money wisely is to see how much we can use for God's purposes, not how much we can accumulate for ourselves. Does God's love touch your wallet? Does your money free you to help others? Where do you put your time, money, and energy? What do you think about most? Consider how you should change the way you use your resources in order to reflect Kingdom values more accurately.

## Jesus warns about preparing for his coming

### *LUKE 12:35-40 (Harmony 142a)*

*B*e prepared—all dressed and ready—for your Lord's return from the wedding feast. Then you will be ready to open the door and let him in the moment he arrives and knocks. There will be great joy for those who are ready and waiting for his return. He himself will seat them and put on a waiter's uniform and serve them as they sit and eat! He may come at nine o'clock at night—or even at midnight. But whenever he comes, there will be joy for his servants who are ready!

"Everyone would be ready for him if they knew the exact hour of his return—just

*Jesus repeatedly said that he would leave this world but would return at some future time (see Matthew 24; 25; John 14:1-3). He also said that a Kingdom is being prepared for his followers.*

as they would be ready for a thief if they knew when he was coming. So be ready all the time. For I, the Messiah, will come when least expected."

### GETTING READY

Christ's return at an unexpected time is not a trap, a trick by which God hopes to catch us off guard. In fact, God is delaying his return so more people will have the opportunity to follow him (see 2 Peter 3:9). Before Christ's return we have time to live out our beliefs and to reflect God's love as we relate to others.

People who are ready for their Lord's return are (1) not hypocritical, but sincere (12:1); (2) not fearful, but ready to witness (12:4-9); (3) not worried, but trusting (12:25-26); (4) not greedy, but generous (12:34); (5) not lazy, but diligent (12:37). May your life be more like Christ's so that, when he comes, you will be ready to greet him joyfully.

*August 10*

## Jesus warns about preparing for his coming

### LUKE 12:41-48 *(Harmony 142b)*

*P*eter asked, "Lord, are you talking just to us or to everyone?" And the Lord replied, "I'm talking to any faithful, sensible man whose master gives him the responsibility of feeding the other servants. If his master returns and finds that he has done a good job, there will be a reward—his master will put him in charge of all he owns.

"But if the man begins to think, 'My Lord won't be back for a long time,' and begins to whip the men and women he is supposed to protect, and to spend his time at drinking parties and in drunkenness—well, his master will return without notice and remove him from his position of trust and assign him to the place of the unfaithful. He will be severely punished, for though he knew his duty he refused to do it.

"But anyone who is not aware that he is doing wrong will be punished only lightly. Much is required from those to whom much is given, for their responsibility is greater.

*Watchful and faithful leaders will be given increased opportunities and responsibilities. The more resources, talents, and understanding we have, the more we are responsible to use them effectively. God will not hold us responsible for gifts he has not given us, but all of us have enough gifts and duties to keep us busy until Jesus comes.*

**FUTURE REWARD**

Jesus promises a reward for those who have been faithful to the Master. While we sometimes experience immediate and material rewards for our obedience to God, this is not always the case. If it were so, we would be tempted to boast about our achievements and do good only for what we get. Jesus said that if we look for rewards now, we will lose them later (see Mark 8:36). Our heavenly rewards will be the most accurate reflection of what we have done on earth, and they will be far greater than we can imagine.

## August 11

## Jesus warns about coming division

*LUKE 12:49-53 (Harmony 143)*

have come to bring fire to the earth, and, oh, that my task were completed! There is a terrible baptism ahead of me, and how I am pent up until it is accomplished!

"Do you think I have come to give peace to the earth? *No!* Rather, strife and division! From now on families will be split apart, three in favor of me, and two against—or perhaps the other way around. A father will decide one way about me; his son, the other; mother and daughter will disagree; and the decision of an honored mother-in-law will be spurned by her daughter-in-law."

*The "baptism" to which Jesus referred was his coming crucifixion. Jesus was dreading the physical pain, of course, but even worse would be the spiritual pain of complete separation from God that would accompany his death for the sins of the world.*

**TAKING A RISK**

In these strange and unsettling words, Jesus revealed that his coming often results in conflict. He demands a response, so intimate groups may be torn apart when some choose to follow him and others refuse to do so. There is no middle ground with Jesus. Loyalties must be declared and commitments made, sometimes to the point of severing other relationships. Are you willing to risk your family's disapproval in order to gain eternal life?

## Jesus warns about the future crisis

### *LUKE 12:54-59 (Harmony 144)*

hen he turned to the crowd and said, "When you see clouds beginning to form in the west, you say, 'Here comes a shower.' And you are right.

"When the south wind blows you say, 'Today will be a scorcher.' And it is. Hypocrites! You interpret the sky well enough, but you refuse to notice the warnings all around you about the crisis ahead. Why do you refuse to see for yourselves what is right?

"If you meet your accuser on the way to court, try to settle the matter before it reaches the judge, lest he sentence you to jail; for if that happens, you won't be free again until the last penny is paid in full."

*For most of recorded history, the world's principal occupation was farming. The farmer depended directly on the weather for his livelihood. He needed just the right amounts of sun and rain—not too much, not too little—to make his living, and he grew skilled at interpreting natural signs.*

**KINGDOM SIGNS**

Jesus was announcing an earthshaking event—the coming of God's Kingdom. Like a rainstorm or a sunny day, there were signs that the Kingdom would soon arrive. But Jesus' hearers, though skilled at interpreting weather signs, were intentionally ignoring the signs of the times. Jesus' question could be asked of many today, "Why do you refuse to see for yourselves what is right?" Have you taken Jesus at his word? See for yourself the truth of his words.

## Jesus calls the people to repent

### *LUKE 13:1-5 (Harmony 145a)*

bout this time he was informed that Pilate had butchered some Jews from Galilee as they were sacrificing at the Temple in Jerusalem.

"Do you think they were worse sinners than other men from Galilee?" he asked. "Is that why they suffered? Not at all! And don't you realize that you also will perish unless you leave your evil ways and turn to God?

"And what about the eighteen men who died when the Tower of Siloam fell on them? Were they the worst sinners in Jerusalem? Not at all! And you, too, will perish unless you repent."

*Whether a person is killed in a tragic accident or miraculously survives is not a measure of righteousness. Everyone has to die; that's part of being human. But people don't need to stay dead. Jesus promises that those who believe in him will not perish but have eternal life (John 3:16).*

**TOUGH QUESTIONS**

Pilate may have killed the Galileans because he thought they were rebelling against Rome; those killed by the Tower of Siloam may have been working for the Romans on an aqueduct there. The Pharisees, who were opposed to using force to deal with Rome, would have said that the Galileans deserved to die for rebelling. The Zealots, a group of anti-Roman terrorists, would have said the aqueduct workers deserved to die for cooperating. Jesus said that neither the Galileans nor the workers should be blamed for their calamity. And instead of blaming others, everyone should look to his or her own day of judgment. Death may come at any time. Being a believer doesn't shield you from death, or even from tragic death. Are you ready to die? Do you know for sure that you'll be with the Savior?

*August 14*

## Jesus calls the people to repent

### LUKE 13:6-9 *(Harmony 145b)*

hen he used this illustration: "A man planted a fig tree in his garden and came again and again to see if he could find any fruit on it, but he was always disappointed. Finally he told his gardener to cut it down. 'I've waited three years and there hasn't been a single fig!' he said. 'Why bother with it any longer? It's taking up space we can use for something else.'

" 'Give it one more chance,' the gardener answered. 'Leave it another year, and I'll give it special attention and plenty of fertilizer. If we get figs next year, fine; if not, I'll cut it down.' "

*Fig trees were plentiful in Israel. In this parable, the fig tree also represents the nation of Israel. The fruitless fig tree would be cut down; Israel would be cut off from God's blessing for refusing God's Son.*

**NO FRUIT**

In the Old Testament, a fruitful tree was often used as a symbol of godly living (see, for example, Psalm 1:3 and Jeremiah 17:7-8). Jesus pointed out what would happen to the other kind of tree—the kind that took valuable time and space and still produced nothing for the patient gardener. This was one way Jesus warned his listeners that God would not tolerate forever their lack of productivity. (Luke 3:9 records John the Baptist's version of the same message.) Have you been enjoying God's special treatment without giving anything in return? If so, respond to the Gardener's patient care, and begin to bear the fruit God has created you to produce.

## *August 15*

---

## Jesus heals the handicapped woman

### *LUKE 13:10-17 (Harmony 146)*

One Sabbath as he was teaching in a synagogue, he saw a seriously handicapped woman who had been bent double for eighteen years and was unable to straighten herself.

Calling her over to him Jesus said, "Woman, you are healed of your sickness!" He touched her, and instantly she could stand straight. How she praised and thanked God!

But the local Jewish leader in charge of the synagogue was very angry about it because Jesus had healed her on the Sabbath day. "There are six days of the week to work," he shouted to the crowd. "Those are the days to come for healing, not on the Sabbath!"

But the Lord replied, "You hypocrite! You work on the Sabbath! Don't you untie your cattle from their stalls on the Sabbath and lead them out for water? And is it wrong for me, just because it is the Sabbath day, to free this Jewish woman from the bondage in which Satan has held her for eighteen years?"

*In our fallen world, disease and disability are common. Their causes are many and often multiple—inadequate nutrition, contact with a source of infection, lowered defenses, and even direct attack by Satan. Whatever the immediate cause of our illness, we can trace its original source to Satan, the author of all the evil in our world. The good news is that Jesus is more powerful than any devil or disease.*

This shamed his enemies. And all the people rejoiced at the wonderful things he did.

#### THE LETTER OF THE LAW

Why was healing considered work? The religious leaders saw healing as part of a doctor's profession, and practicing one's profession on the Sabbath was prohibited. The synagogue ruler could not see beyond the law to Jesus' compassion in healing this handicapped woman. Jesus shamed him and the other leaders by pointing out their hypocrisy. The Pharisees hid behind their own set of laws to avoid love's obligations. We too can use the letter of the Law to rationalize away our obligation to care for others (for example, by tithing regularly and then refusing to help a needy neighbor). But people's needs are more important than rules and regulations. Take time to help others, even if doing so might compromise your public image.

## August 16

## Jesus teaches about the Kingdom of God

### LUKE 13:18-21 (Harmony 147)

Now he began teaching them again about the Kingdom of God: "What is the Kingdom like?" he asked. "How can I illustrate it? It is like a tiny mustard seed planted in a garden; soon it grows into a tall bush and the birds live among its branches.

"It is like yeast kneaded into dough, which works unseen until it has risen high and light."

*The mustard plant grows to be quite large; in fact, one of the largest plants in Palestine. And yet its seeds are the tiniest. Jesus' audience easily understood his illustration.*

**LET IT GROW**

The general expectation among Jesus' hearers was that the Messiah would come as a great king and leader, freeing the nation from Rome and restoring Israel's former glory. But Jesus said his Kingdom was beginning quietly. Like the tiny mustard seed that grows into an enormous tree, or the spoonful of yeast that makes the bread dough double in size, the Kingdom of God would eventually push outward until the whole world was changed. You are a part of that Kingdom because people have continued to spread the gospel since the days of Christ. What are you doing to continue the growth of the Kingdom?

## Jesus heals the man who was born blind

### JOHN 9:1-5 *(Harmony 148a)*

As he was walking along, he saw a man blind from birth. "Master," his disciples asked him, "why was this man born blind? Was it a result of his own sins or those of his parents?" "Neither," Jesus answered. "But to demonstrate the power of God. All of us must quickly carry out the tasks assigned us by the one who sent me, for there is little time left before the night falls and all work comes to an end. But while I am still here in the world, I give it my light."

*In chapter 9, we see four different reactions to Jesus. The neighbors revealed surprise and skepticism; the Pharisees showed disbelief and prejudice; the parents believed but kept quiet for fear of excommunication; and the healed man showed consistent, growing faith.*

**SUFFERING**

A common belief in Jewish culture was that calamity or suffering was the result of some great sin. But Christ used this man's suffering to teach about faith and to glorify God. We live in a fallen world where good behavior is not always rewarded and bad behavior not always punished. Therefore, innocent people sometimes suffer. If God took suffering away whenever we asked, we would follow him for comfort and convenience, not out of love and devotion. Regardless of the reasons for our suffering, Jesus has the power to help us deal with it. When you suffer from a disease, tragedy, or disability, try not to ask Why did this happen to me? or What did I do wrong? Instead, ask God to give you strength for the trial and a clearer perspective on what is happening.

## Jesus heals the man who was born blind

### JOHN 9:6-12 *(Harmony 148b)*

Then he spat on the ground and made mud from the spittle and smoothed the mud over the blind man's eyes, and told him, "Go and wash in the Pool of Siloam" (the word *Siloam* means "sent"). So the man went where he was sent and washed and came back seeing!

His neighbors and others who knew him as a blind beggar asked each other, "Is this the same fellow—that beggar?"

Some said yes, and some said no. "It can't be the same man," they thought, "but he surely looks like him!"

And the beggar said, "I *am* the same man!"

Then they asked him how in the world he could see. What had happened?

And he told them, "A man they call Jesus made mud and smoothed it over my eyes and told me to go to the Pool of Siloam and wash off the mud. I did, and I can see!"

"Where is he now?" they asked.

"I don't know," he replied.

*The Pool of Siloam was built by Hezekiah. His workers constructed an underground tunnel from a spring outside the city walls to carry water into the city. Thus the people could always get water without fear of being attacked. This was especially important during times of siege (see 2 Kings 20:20; 2 Chronicles 32:30).*

### STEPS OF FAITH

Jesus' miracles were meant to strengthen people's faith and lead them to believe in Jesus as the Messiah. Christ's miracles were significant, not just because of their power, but because of their purpose—to help, to heal, and to point people to God. This man's simple act of faith in going to wash, as Jesus instructed, resulted in his restored sight. Faith is a step between promise and assurance. Miracles seem so out of reach for our feeble faith. But every miracle, large or small, begins with an act of obedience. We may not see the solution until we take the first step of faith.

*August 19*

## Religious leaders question the blind man

*JOHN 9:13-23 (Harmony 149a)*

 hen they took the man to the Pharisees. Now as it happened, this all occurred on a Sabbath. Then the Pharisees asked him all about it. So he told them how Jesus had smoothed the mud over his eyes, and when it was washed away, he could see!

Some of them said, "Then this fellow Jesus is not from God because he is working on the Sabbath."

Others said, "But how could an ordinary sinner do such miracles?" So there was a deep division of opinion among them.

Then the Pharisees turned on the man who had been blind and demanded, "This man who opened your eyes—who do you say he is?"

"I think he must be a prophet sent from God," the man replied.

The Jewish leaders wouldn't believe he had been blind until they called in his parents and asked them, "Is this your son? Was he born blind? If so, how can he see?"

*While the Pharisees conducted investigations and debated about Jesus, people were being healed and lives were being changed. The Pharisees' skepticism was based not on insufficient evidence, but on jealousy of Jesus' popularity and his influence on the people.*

His parents replied, "We know this is our son and that he was born blind, but we don't know what happened to make him see, or who did it. He is old enough to speak for himself. Ask him."

They said this in fear of the Jewish leaders who had announced that anyone saying Jesus was the Messiah would be excommunicated.

**SABBATH REST**

The Jewish Sabbath, Saturday, was the weekly holy day of rest. The Pharisees had made a long list of specific do's and don'ts regarding the Sabbath. Kneading the clay and healing the man were considered work and therefore were forbidden. Jesus may have purposely made the clay in order to emphasize his teaching about the Sabbath—that it is right to care for others' needs even if it involves working on a day of rest. The Sabbath had two purposes: It was a time *to rest* and a time *to remember* what God had done. We need rest. Without time out from the bustle, life loses its meaning. In our day, as in Moses' day, taking time out is not easy. Your Sabbath rest may be different from others'; to you gardening might be restful while someone else would consider it work. Don't get bogged down in laws and judging. God created a Sabbath for you. He reminds us that without Sabbaths we will forget the purpose for all of our activity and lose the balance crucial to a faithful life. Make sure that your Sabbath provides a time of both refreshment and remembrance of God.

*August 20*

## Religious leaders question the blind man

*JOHN 9:24-34 (Harmony 149b)*

 o for the second time they called in the man who had been blind and told him, "Give the glory to God, not to Jesus, for we know Jesus is an evil person."

"I don't know whether he is good or bad," the man replied, "but I know this: *I was blind, and now I see!*"

"But what did he do?" they asked. "How did he heal you?"

"Look!" the man exclaimed. "I told you once; didn't you listen? Why do you want to hear it again? Do you want to become his disciples too?"

*The man's new faith was severely tested by some of the authorities. He was cursed and evicted from the synagogue—a horrible punishment for a Jew.*

Then they cursed him and said, "You are his disciple, but we are disciples of Moses. We know God has spoken to Moses, but as for this fellow, we don't know anything about him."

"Why, that's very strange!" the man replied. "He can heal blind men, and yet you don't know anything about him! Well, God doesn't listen to evil men, but he has open ears to those who worship him and do his will. Since the world began there has never been anyone who could open the eyes of someone born blind. If this man were not from God, he couldn't do it."

"You illegitimate bastard, you!" they shouted. "Are you trying to teach *us?*" And they threw him out.

### SPREAD THE NEWS

By now the man who had been blind had heard the same questions over and over. He did not know how or why he was healed, but he knew that his life had been miraculously changed, and he was not afraid to tell the truth. You don't need to know all the answers in order to share Christ with others. It is important to tell them how he has changed your life. Then trust that God will use your words to help others believe in him too.

*August 21*

## Jesus teaches about spiritual blindness

### *JOHN 9:35-41 (Harmony 150)*

When Jesus heard what had happened, he found the man and said, "Do you believe in the Messiah?"

The man answered, "Who is he, sir, for I want to."

"You have seen him," Jesus said, "and he is speaking to you!"

"Yes, Lord," the man said, "I believe!" And he worshiped Jesus. Then Jesus told him, "I have come into the world to give sight to those who are spiritually blind and to show those who think they see that they are blind."

The Pharisees who were standing there asked, "Are you saying we are blind?"

"If you were blind, you wouldn't be guilty," Jesus replied. "But your guilt remains because you claim to know what you are doing."

*People lose a vital ability when they can no longer see their own sinfulness. The results are broken relationships, authority out of control, blindness to the needy, and forgetfulness toward God. Spiritual blindness is a matter of life and death.*

### GETTING TO KNOW HIM

The longer this man experienced his new life through Christ, the more confident he became in the one who had healed him. He gained not only physical sight but also spiritual sight as he recognized Jesus first as a prophet (9:17), then as his Lord. When you turn to Christ, you begin to see him differently. The longer you walk with him, the better you will understand who he is. Peter tells us to "grow in spiritual strength and become better acquainted with our Lord and Savior Jesus Christ" (2 Peter 3:18). If you want to know more about Jesus, keep walking with him.

*August 22*

## Jesus is the Good Shepherd

### JOHN 10:1-10 *(Harmony 151a)*

*A*nyone refusing to walk through the gate into a sheepfold, who sneaks over the wall, must surely be a thief! For a shepherd comes through the gate. The gatekeeper opens the gate for him, and the sheep hear his voice and come to him; and he calls his own sheep by name and leads them out. He walks ahead of them; and they follow him, for they recognize his voice. They won't follow a stranger but will run from him, for they don't recognize his voice."

Those who heard Jesus use this illustration didn't understand what he meant, so he explained it to them.

"I am the Gate for the sheep," he said. "All others who came before me were thieves and robbers. But the true sheep did not listen to them. Yes, I am the Gate.

*At night, sheep were often gathered into a sheepfold to protect them from thieves, weather, and wild animals. The sheepfolds were caves, sheds, or open areas surrounded by walls made of stones or branches. The shepherd often slept in the fold to protect the sheep.*

Those who come in by way of the Gate will be saved and will go in and out and find green pastures. The thief's purpose is to steal, kill and destroy. My purpose is to give life in all its fullness."

### THE GOOD SHEPHERD

The New Testament calls Jesus the Good Shepherd (John 10:11); the great Shepherd (Hebrews 13:20); and the Head Shepherd (1 Peter 5:4). Sheep are completely dependent on the shepherd for provision, guidance, and protection. As the Lord is the Good Shepherd, so we are his sheep—not frightened, passive animals, but obedient followers, wise enough to follow one who will lead us in the right places and in right ways. When we allow the Good Shepherd to guide us, we have contentment. When we choose to sin, however, we go our own way and cannot blame God for the environment we create for ourselves. Rebelling against the Shepherd's leading is actually rebelling against our own best interests. Remember this the next time you are tempted to go your own way rather than the Shepherd's way.

*August 23*

## Jesus is the Good Shepherd

*JOHN 10:11-16 (Harmony 151b)*

I am the Good Shepherd. The Good Shepherd lays down his life for the sheep. A hired man will run when he sees a wolf coming and will leave the sheep, for they aren't his and he isn't their shepherd. And so the wolf leaps on them and scatters the flock. The hired man runs because he is hired and has no real concern for the sheep.

"I am the Good Shepherd and know my own sheep, and they know me, just as my Father knows me and I know the Father; and I lay down my life for the sheep. I have other sheep, too, in another fold. I must bring them also, and they will heed my voice; and there will be one flock with one Shepherd."

*The "other sheep" were non-Jews. Jesus came to save Gentiles as well as Jews. This is an insight into Christ's worldwide mission—to die for the sins of the world. People tend to want to restrict God's blessings to their own group, but Jesus refuses to be limited by the fences we build.*

### PAST, PRESENT, AND FUTURE

A hired man tends the sheep for money, while the shepherd does it for love. The shepherd owns the sheep and is committed to them. Jesus is not merely doing a job; he is committed to love us and even lay down his life for us. False teachers and false prophets do not have this commitment. Jesus *did* die for us. He has *once and for all* paid the penalty for our sins by his own sacrificial death, and he can be depended on to restore our broken relationship with God. We are released from sin's domination over us when we commit ourselves to Christ, trusting completely in what he has done for us. No one can add to what Jesus did to save us; our past, present, and future sins are all forgiven, and Jesus is with the Father as a sign that our sins are forgiven. If you are a Christian, remember that Christ has paid the price for your sins once and for all.

*August 24*

## Jesus is the Good Shepherd

### *JOHN 10:17-21 (Harmony 151c)*

The Father loves me because I lay down my life that I may have it back again. No one can kill me without my consent—I lay down my life voluntarily. For I have the right and power to lay it down when I want to and also the right and power to take it again. For the Father has given me this right."

When he said these things, the Jewish leaders were again divided in their opinions about him. Some of them said, "He has a demon or else is crazy. Why listen to a man like that?"

Others said, "This doesn't sound to us like a man possessed by a demon! Can a demon open the eyes of blind men?"

*If Jesus had been merely a man, his claims to be God would have proved him insane. But his miracles proved his words true—he really was God. The Jewish leaders could not see beyond their own prejudices, and they looked at Jesus only from a human perspective— Jesus confined in a human box. But Jesus was not limited by their restricted vision.*

#### LAYING IT DOWN

Jesus is God, thus he could say that he would both lay down his life *and* take it back again. Jesus' death and resurrection, as part of God's plan for the salvation of the world, were under God's full control. No one could kill Jesus without his consent. It was important that Jesus die on the cross to take the punishment for sin, but it was also important that he rise from the dead. The resurrection of Christ is the center of the Christian faith. Because Christ rose from the dead as he promised, we know that what he said is true—he is God. Because he rose, we have certainty that our sins are forgiven. Because he rose, he lives and represents us to God. Because he rose and defeated death, we know we will also be raised.

## Religious leaders surround Jesus at the Temple

*JOHN 10:22-30 (Harmony 152a)*

It was winter, and Jesus was in Jerusalem at the time of the Dedication Celebration. He was at the Temple, walking through the section known as Solomon's Hall. The Jewish leaders surrounded him and asked, "How long are you going to keep us in suspense? If you are the Messiah, tell us plainly."

"I have already told you, and you don't believe me," Jesus replied. "The proof is in the miracles I do in the name of my Father. But you don't believe me because you are not part of my flock. My sheep recognize my voice, and I know them, and they follow me. I give them eternal life and they shall never perish. No one shall snatch them away from me, for my Father has given them to me, and he is more powerful than anyone else, so no one can kidnap them from me. I and the Father are one."

*The Dedication Celebration commemorated the cleansing of the Temple under Judas Maccabeus in 165 B.C. after Antiochus Epiphanes had defiled it a few years earlier by sacrificing a pig on the altar of burnt offering. The feast was celebrated toward the end of December. This is also the present-day Feast of Lights called Hanukkah.*

### ON WHOSE TERMS?

The statement "I and the Father are one" is the clearest statement of Jesus' divinity he ever made. Jesus and his Father are not the same person, but they are one in essence and nature. Thus Jesus was not merely a good teacher—he was God. His claim to be God was unmistakable. The religious leaders wanted to kill him because their laws said that anyone claiming to be God should die. Nothing could persuade them that Jesus' claim was true. Jesus tried to correct their mistaken ideas, but they clung to the wrong idea of what kind of Messiah God would send. Such blindness still keeps people away from Jesus. They want him on their own terms; they do not want him if it means changing their whole lives. Have you accepted Jesus on his terms?

## Religious leaders surround Jesus at the Temple

*JOHN 10:31-42 (Harmony 152b)*

hen again the Jewish leaders picked up stones to kill him. Jesus said, "At God's direction I have done many a miracle to help the people. For which one are you killing me?"

They replied, "Not for any good work, but for blasphemy; you, a mere man, have declared yourself to be God."

"In your own Law it says that men are gods!" he replied. "So if the Scripture, which cannot be untrue, speaks of those as gods to whom the message of God came, do you call it blasphemy when the one sanctified and sent into the world by the Father says, 'I am the Son of God'? Don't believe me unless I do miracles of God. But if I do, believe them even if you don't believe me. Then you will become convinced that the Father is in me, and I in the Father."

*The Jewish leaders attempted to carry out the directive found in Leviticus 24:16 regarding those who blaspheme (claim to be God). They intended to stone Jesus.*

Once again they started to arrest him. But he walked away and left them, and went beyond the Jordan River to stay near the place where John was first baptizing. And many followed him.

"John didn't do miracles," they remarked to one another, "but all his predictions concerning this man have come true." And many came to the decision that he was the Messiah.

#### OUR ONLY SOURCE

"Scripture . . . cannot be untrue" is a clear statement of the truth of the Bible. If we accept Christ as Lord, we also must accept his testimony to the Bible as God's Word. The whole Bible is God's inspired Word. Because it is inspired and trustworthy, we should *read* it and *apply* it to our lives. The Bible is our standard for testing everything else that claims to be true. It is our safeguard against false teaching and our source of guidance for how we should live. It is our only source of knowledge about how we can be saved. God wants to show you what is true and equip you to live for him. How much time do you spend in God's Word? Read it regularly to discover God's truth and to become confident in your life and faith. Develop a plan for reading the whole Bible, not just the familiar passages.

## Jesus teaches about entering the Kingdom

### *LUKE 13:22-30 (Harmony 153)*

*H*e went from city to city and village to village, teaching as he went, always pressing onward toward Jerusalem.

Someone asked him, "Will only a few be saved?"

And he replied, "The door to heaven is narrow. Work hard to get in, for the truth is that many will try to enter but when the head of the house has locked the door, it will be too late. Then if you stand outside knocking, and pleading, 'Lord, open the door for us,' he will reply, 'I do not know you.'

"'But we ate with you, and you taught in our streets,' you will say.

"And he will reply, 'I tell you, I don't know you. You can't come in here, guilty as you are. Go away.'

*This is the second time Luke reminds us that Jesus was intentionally going to Jerusalem (the other time is in 9:51). Jesus knew he was on his way to die, but he continued preaching to large crowds. The prospect of death did not deter Jesus from his mission.*

"And there will be great weeping and gnashing of teeth as you stand outside and see Abraham, Isaac, Jacob, and all the prophets within the Kingdom of God—for people will come from all over the world to take their places there. And note this: some who are despised now will be greatly honored then; and some who are highly thought of now will be least important then."

#### THE FEAST

There will be many surprises in God's Kingdom. Some who are despised now will be greatly honored then; some influential people here will be left outside the gates. Many "great" people on this earth (in God's eyes) are virtually ignored by the rest of the world. What matters to God is not a person's earthly popularity, status, wealth, heritage, or power, but his or her commitment to Christ. How do your values match what the Bible tells you to value? Put God in first place, and you will join people from all over the world who will take their places at the feast in the Kingdom of Heaven.

## Jesus grieves over Jerusalem

*LUKE 13:31-35 (Harmony 154)*

A few minutes later some Pharisees said to him, "Get out of here if you want to live, for King Herod is after you!"

Jesus replied, "Go tell that fox that I will keep on casting out demons and doing miracles of healing today and tomorrow; and the third day I will reach my destination. Yes, today, tomorrow, and the next day! For it wouldn't do for a prophet of God to be killed except in Jerusalem!

"O Jerusalem, Jerusalem! The city that murders the prophets. The city that stones those sent to help her. How often I have wanted to gather your children together even as a hen protects her brood under her wings, but you wouldn't let me. And now—now your house is left desolate. And you will never again see me until you say, 'Welcome to him who comes in the name of the Lord.' "

*Jerusalem, the city of God, symbolized the entire nation. It was Israel's largest city and the nation's spiritual and political capital. Jews from around the world visited it frequently. But Jerusalem had a history of rejecting God's prophets (1 Kings 19:10; 2 Chronicles 24:19; Jeremiah 2:30; 26:20-23), and it would reject the Messiah just as it had rejected his forerunners.*

### GOD'S TIMING

The Pharisees weren't interested in protecting Jesus from danger—they were trying to trap him. The Pharisees urged Jesus to leave because they wanted to stop him from going to Jerusalem, not because they feared Herod. But Jesus' life, work, and death were not to be determined by Herod or the Pharisees. His life was planned and directed by God himself, and his mission would unfold in God's time and according to God's plan. When you are following God's will, you must do whatever he calls you to do without letting any obstacles get in your way. God will make sure that his will is accomplished.

## August 29

## Jesus heals a man with dropsy

### *LUKE 14:1-6 (Harmony 155)*

One Sabbath as he was in the home of a member of the Jewish Council, the Pharisees were watching him like hawks to see if he would heal a man who was present who was suffering from dropsy.

Jesus said to the Pharisees and legal experts standing around, "Well, is it within the Law to heal a man on the Sabbath day, or not?"

And when they refused to answer, Jesus took the sick man by the hand and healed him and sent him away.

*Luke, the physician, identified this man's disease—he was suffering from dropsy, an abnormal accumulation of fluid in bodily tissues and cavities.*

Then he turned to them: "Which of you doesn't work on the Sabbath?" he asked. "If your cow falls into a pit, don't you proceed at once to get it out?"

Again they had no answer.

#### UNAFRAID

Earlier Jesus had been invited to a Pharisee's home for discussion (7:36). This time a prominent Pharisee invited Jesus to his home specifically to trap him into saying or doing something for which he could be arrested. It may be surprising to see Jesus on the Pharisees' turf after he had denounced them so many times. But Jesus was not afraid to face the Pharisees, even though he knew that their purpose was to trick him into breaking their laws. Jesus was not afraid of confrontation; neither should his followers be. We can trust God to help us have the right words, and trust him to accomplish his will through us.

## August 30

## Jesus teaches about seeking honor

### *LUKE 14:7-14 (Harmony 156)*

When he noticed that all who came to the dinner were trying to sit near the head of the table, he gave them this advice: "If you are invited to a wedding feast, don't always head for the best seat. For if someone more respected than you shows up, the host will bring him over to where you are sitting and say, 'Let this man sit here instead.' And you, embarrassed, will have to take whatever seat is left at the foot of the table!

"Do this instead—start at the foot; and when your host sees you he will come and say, 'Friend, we have a better place than this for you!' Thus you will be honored in front of all the other guests. For everyone who tries to honor himself shall be humbled; and he who humbles himself shall be honored." Then he turned to his host. "When you put on a dinner," he said, "don't invite friends, brothers, relatives, and rich neighbors! For they will return the invitation. Instead, invite the poor, the crippled, the lame, and the blind. Then at the resurrection of the godly, God will reward you for inviting those who can't repay you."

*Jesus taught two lessons here. First, he spoke to the guests, telling them not to seek places of honor. Service is more important in God's Kingdom than status. Second, he told the host not to be exclusive about whom he invites. God opens his Kingdom to everyone.*

### REALISTIC EVALUATION

How can we humble ourselves? Some people try to give the appearance of humility in order to manipulate others. Others think that humility means putting themselves down. Truly humble people only compare themselves with Christ, realize their sinfulness, and understand their limitations. On the other hand, they also recognize their gifts and strengths and are willing to use them as Christ directs. Healthy self-esteem is important because some of us think too little of ourselves. On the other hand, some of us overestimate ourselves. The key to an honest and accurate evaluation is knowing the basis of our self-worth—our identity in Christ. Apart from him, we aren't capable of very much by eternal standards; in him, we are valuable and capable of worthy service. Evaluating yourself by the worldly standards of success and achievement can cause you to think too much about your worth in the eyes of others and thus miss your true value in God's eyes. Humility is not self-degradation; it is realistic assessment and commitment to serve.

## Jesus tells the parable of the great feast

### *LUKE 14:15-24 (Harmony 157)*

*H*earing this, a man sitting at the table with Jesus exclaimed, "What a privilege it would be to get into the Kingdom of God!"

Jesus replied with this illustration: "A man prepared a great feast and sent out many invitations. When all was ready, he sent his servant around to notify the guests that it was time for them to arrive. But they all began making excuses. One said he had just bought a field and wanted to inspect it, and asked to be excused. Another said he had just bought five pair of oxen and wanted to try them out. Another had just been married and for that reason couldn't come.

*In Israel's history, God's first invitation came from Moses and the prophets; the second came from his Son. The religious leaders accepted the first invitation. They believed that God had called them to be his people, but they insulted God by refusing to accept his Son.*

"The servant returned and reported to his master what they had said. His master was angry and told him to go quickly into the streets and alleys of the city and to invite the beggars, crippled, lame, and blind. But even then, there was still room.

"'Well, then,' said his master, 'go out into the country lanes and out behind the hedges and urge anyone you find to come, so that the house will be full. For none of those I invited first will get even the smallest taste of what I had prepared for them.'"

#### ACCEPT THE INVITATION

It was customary to send two invitations to a party—the first to announce the event; the second to tell the guests that everything was ready. The guests in Jesus' story insulted the host by making excuses when they received the second invitation. In Jesus' story, many people turned down the invitation to the banquet because the timing was inconvenient. We too can resist or delay responding to God's invitation, and our excuses may sound reasonable—work duties, family responsibilities, financial needs, and so forth. Nevertheless, God's invitation is the most important event in our lives, no matter how inconveniently it may be timed. What are your favorite excuses? Jesus reminds us that the time will come when God will pull his invitation and offer it to others—then it will be too late to get into the banquet.

## Jesus teaches about the cost of being a disciple

*LUKE 14:25-27 (Harmony 158a)*

reat crowds were following him. He turned around and addressed them as follows: "Anyone who wants to be my follower must love me far more than he does his own father, mother, wife, children, brothers, or sisters—yes, more than his own life—otherwise he cannot be my disciple. And no one can be my disciple who does not carry his own cross and follow me."

*To love Jesus far more than even one's family means that, ultimately, Jesus is the focus of one's life. Loved ones should never be allowed to pull a person away from Christ.*

**TOTAL SUBMISSION**

Jesus' audience was well aware of what it meant to carry one's own cross. When the Romans led a criminal to his execution site, he was forced to carry the cross on which he would die. This showed his submission to Rome and warned observers that they had better submit too. Jesus spoke this teaching to get the crowds to think through their enthusiasm for him. He encouraged those whose commitment was superficial either to go deeper or to turn back. Following Christ means total submission to him—perhaps even to the point of death. Jesus wants more than enthusiasm—he wants total dedication. Have you dedicated your life to Jesus?

## Jesus teaches about the cost of being a disciple

*LUKE 14:28-35 (Harmony 158b)*

ut don't begin until you count the cost. For who would begin construction of a building without first getting estimates and then checking to see if he has enough money to pay the bills? Otherwise he might complete only the foundation before running out of funds. And then how everyone would laugh!

"'See that fellow there?' they would mock. 'He started that building and ran out of money before it was finished!'

"Or what king would ever dream of going to war without first sitting down with his counselors and discussing whether his army of 10,000 is strong enough to defeat the 20,000 men who are marching against him?

"If the decision is negative, then while the enemy troops are still far away, he will send a truce team to discuss terms of peace. So no one can become my disciple unless he first sits down and counts his blessings—and then renounces them all for me.

*What are the costs of the Christian life? Christians may face loss of social status or wealth. They may have to give up control over their money, their time, or their career. They may be hated, separated from their family, and even put to death. Following Christ does not mean a trouble-free life.*

"What good is salt that has lost its saltiness? Flavorless salt is fit for nothing—not even for fertilizer. It is worthless and must be thrown out. Listen well if you would understand my meaning."

**STAY SALTY**

Salt can lose its flavor. When it gets wet and then dries, nothing is left but a tasteless residue. Many Christians blend into the world and avoid the cost of standing up for Christ. But Jesus says if Christians lose their distinctive saltiness, they become worthless. Just as salt flavors and preserves food, we are to preserve the good in the world, help keep it from spoiling, and bring new flavor to life. This requires careful planning, willing sacrifice, and unswerving commitment to Christ's Kingdom. Being "salty" is not easy, but if a Christian fails in this function, he or she fails to represent Christ in the world. How salty are you?

*September 3*

## Jesus tells the parable of the lost sheep

*LUKE 15:1-7 (Harmony 159)*

Dishonest tax collectors and other notorious sinners often came to listen to Jesus' sermons; but this caused complaints from the Jewish religious leaders and the experts on Jewish law because he was associating with such despicable people—even eating with them!

So Jesus used this illustration: "If you had a hundred sheep and one of them strayed away and was lost in the wilderness, wouldn't you leave the ninety-nine others to go and search for the lost one until you found it? And then you would joyfully carry it home on your shoulders. When you arrived you would call together your friends and neighbors to rejoice with you because your lost sheep was found.

"Well, in the same way heaven will be happier over one lost sinner who returns to God than over ninety-nine others who haven't strayed away!"

*It may seem foolish for the shepherd to leave ninety-nine sheep to go search for just one. But the shepherd knew that the ninety-nine would be safe in the sheepfold, whereas the lost sheep was in danger. God's love for each individual is so great that he seeks each one out and rejoices when he or she is "found."*

### GUILT BY ASSOCIATION

Why were the Pharisees and scribes bothered that Jesus associated with these people? The religious leaders were always careful to stay "clean" according to Old Testament Law. In fact, they went well beyond the Law in their avoidance of certain people and situations and in their ritual washings. By contrast, Jesus took their concept of "cleanness" lightly. He risked defilement by touching those who had leprosy and by neglecting to wash in the Pharisees' prescribed manner, and he showed complete disregard for their sanctions against associating with certain classes of people. He came to offer salvation to sinners, to show that God loves them. Jesus didn't worry about the accusations. Instead, he continued going to those who needed him, regardless of the effect on his reputation. What keeps you from people who need Christ? Jesus associated with sinners because he wanted to bring the lost sheep—people considered beyond hope—the gospel of God's Kingdom. Before you were a believer, God sought you; and his love is still seeking those who are yet lost.

*September 4*

## Jesus tells the parable of the lost coin

### LUKE 15:8-10 *(Harmony 160)*

*O*r take another illustration: A woman has ten valuable silver coins and loses one. Won't she light a lamp and look in every corner of the house and sweep every nook and cranny until she finds it? And then won't she call in her friends and neighbors to rejoice with her? In the same way there is joy in the presence of the angels of God when one sinner repents."

**EXTRAORDINARY LOVE**

We may be able to understand a God who would forgive sinners who come to him for mercy. But a God who tenderly searches for sinners and then joyfully forgives them must possess an extraordinary love! That is what prompted Jesus to come to earth to search for lost people and save them. God has extraordinary love for you. If you feel far from God, don't despair. He is searching for you. Each individual is precious to God. He grieves over every loss and rejoices whenever one of his children is found and brought into the Kingdom.

*Palestinian women received ten silver coins as a wedding gift. Besides their monetary value, these coins held sentimental value like that of a wedding ring, and to lose one would be extremely distressing. Just as a woman would rejoice at finding her lost coin or ring, so the angels would rejoice over a repentant sinner.*

*September 5*

## Jesus tells the parable of the lost son

### LUKE 15:11-24 *(Harmony 161a)*

o further illustrate the point, he told them this story: "A man had two sons. When the younger told his father, 'I want my share of your estate now, instead of waiting until you die!' his father agreed to divide his wealth between his sons.

"A few days later this younger son packed all his belongings and took a trip to a distant land, and there wasted all his money on parties and prostitutes. About the time his money was gone a great famine swept over the land, and he began to starve. He persuaded a local farmer to hire him to feed his pigs. The boy became so hungry that even the pods he was feeding the swine looked good to him. And no one gave him anything.

"When he finally came to his senses, he said to himself, 'At home even the hired men have food enough and to spare, and here I am, dying of hunger! I will go home to my father

*In the two preceding stories, the seeker actively looked for the coin and the sheep, which could not return by themselves. In this story, the father watched and waited. He was dealing with a human being with a will of his own, but he was ready to greet his son if he returned. In the same way, God's love is constant and patient and welcoming.*

and say, "Father, I have sinned against both heaven and you, and am no longer worthy of being called your son. Please take me on as a hired man.'"

"So he returned home to his father. And while he was still a long distance away, his father saw him coming, and was filled with loving pity and ran and embraced him and kissed him.

"His son said to him, 'Father, I have sinned against heaven and you, and am not worthy of being called your son—'

"But his father said to the slaves, 'Quick! Bring the finest robe in the house and put it on him. And a jeweled ring for his finger; and shoes! And kill the calf we have in the fattening pen. We must celebrate with a feast, for this son of mine was dead and has returned to life. He was lost and is found.' So the party began."

### BREAKING AWAY

The younger son, like many who are rebellious and immature, wanted to be free to live as he pleased, and he had to hit bottom before he came to his senses. It often takes great sorrow and tragedy to cause people to look to the only One who can help them. Are you trying to live life your own way, selfishly pushing aside any responsibility or commitment that gets in your way? Stop and look before you hit bottom. You will save yourself and your family much grief.

*September 6*

## Jesus tells the parable of the lost son

### *LUKE 15:25-32 (Harmony 161b)*

*M*eanwhile, the older son was in the fields working; when he returned home, he heard dance music coming from the house, and he asked one of the servants what was going on.

"'Your brother is back,' he was told, 'and your father has killed the calf we were fattening and has prepared a great feast to celebrate his coming home again unharmed.'

"The older brother was angry and wouldn't go in. His father came out and begged him, but he replied, 'All these years I've worked hard for you and never once refused to do a single thing you told me to; and in all that time you never gave

*In Jesus' story the older brother represented the Pharisees, who were angry and resentful that sinners were being welcomed into God's Kingdom. How easy it is to resent God's gracious forgiveness of others whom we consider to be far worse sinners than ourselves.*

me even one young goat for a feast with my friends. Yet when this son of yours comes back after spending your money on prostitutes, you celebrate by killing the finest calf we have on the place.'

"'Look, dear son,' his father said to him, 'you and I are very close, and everything I have is yours. But it is right to celebrate. For he is your brother; and he was dead and has come back to life! He was lost and is found!'"

### JOY IN FORGIVING

In the story of the lost son, the father's response is contrasted with the older brother's. The father forgave because he was filled with love. The son refused to forgive because he was bitter about the injustice of the situation. His resentment rendered him just as lost to the father's love as his younger brother had been. Don't let anything keep you from forgiving others. If you are refusing to forgive people, you are missing a wonderful opportunity to experience joy and share it with others. Make your joy grow: Forgive somebody who has hurt you.

*September 7*

## Jesus tells the parable of the shrewd accountant

**LUKE 16:1-12** *(Harmony 162a)*

Jesus now told this story to his disciples: "A rich man hired an accountant to handle his affairs, but soon a rumor went around that the accountant was thoroughly dishonest.

"So his employer called him in and said, 'What's this I hear about your stealing from me? Get your report in order, for you are to be dismissed.'

"The accountant thought to himself, 'Now what? I'm through here, and I haven't the strength to go out and dig ditches, and I'm too proud to beg. I know just the thing! And then I'll have plenty of friends to take care of me when I leave!'

*If we use our money to help those in need or to help others find Christ, our earthly investment will bring eternal benefit. When we obey God, the unselfish use of possessions will follow.*

"So he invited each one who owed money to his employer to come and discuss the situation. He asked the first one, 'How much do you owe him?' 'My debt is 850 gallons of olive oil,' the man replied. 'Yes, here is the contract you signed,' the accountant told him. 'Tear it up and write another one for half that much!'

"'And how much do you owe him?' he asked the next man. 'A thousand bushels of wheat,' was the reply. 'Here,' the accountant said, 'take your note and replace it with one for only 800 bushels!'

"The rich man had to admire the rascal for being so shrewd. And it is true that the citizens of this world are more clever [in dishonesty!] than the godly are. But shall I tell *you* to act that way, to buy friendship through cheating? Will this ensure your entry into an everlasting home in heaven? *No!* For unless you are honest in small matters, you won't be in large ones. If you cheat even a little, you won't be honest with greater responsibilities. And if you are untrustworthy about worldly wealth, who will trust you with the true riches of heaven? And if you are not faithful with other people's money, why should you be entrusted with money of your own?"

### MONEY MATTERS MATTER

Our use of money is a good test of the lordship of Christ in our lives. (1) Let us use our resources wisely because they belong to God, and not to us. (2) Money can be used for good or evil; let us use ours for good. (3) Money has a lot of power, so we must use it carefully and thoughtfully. (4) We must use our material goods in a way that will foster faith and obedience (see 12:33-34). Our integrity often meets its match in money matters. God calls us to be honest even in small details that we could easily rationalize away. Heaven's riches are far more valuable than earthly wealth. But if we are not trustworthy with our money here (no matter how much or little we have), we will be unfit to handle the vast riches of God's Kingdom. Don't let your integrity slip in small matters, and it will not fail you in crucial decisions either.

*September 8*

## Jesus tells the parable of the shrewd accountant

### LUKE 16:13-18 (Harmony 162b)

or neither you nor anyone else can serve two masters. You will hate one and show loyalty to the other, or else the other way around—you will be enthusiastic about one and despise the other. You cannot serve both God and money."

The Pharisees, who dearly loved their money, naturally scoffed at all this.

Then he said to them, "You wear a noble, pious expression in public, but God knows your evil hearts. Your pretense brings you honor from the people, but it is an abomination in the sight of God. Until John the Baptist began to preach, the laws of Moses and the messages of the prophets were your guides. But John introduced the Good News that the Kingdom of God would come soon. And now eager multitudes are pressing in. But that doesn't mean that the Law has lost its force in even the smallest point. It is as strong and unshakable as heaven and earth.

"So anyone who divorces his wife and marries someone else commits adultery, and anyone who marries a divorced woman commits adultery."

*John the Baptist's ministry was the dividing line between the Old and New Testaments (John 1:15-18). With the arrival of Jesus came the realization of all the prophets' hopes. Jesus emphasized that his Kingdom fulfilled the Law (the Old Testament); it did not cancel it (Matthew 5:17). His was not a new system but the culmination of the old.*

### MASTER MONEY

Money has the power to take God's place in your life. It can become your master. How can you tell if you are a slave to money? (1) Do you think and worry about it frequently? (2) Do you give up doing what you should do or would like to do in order to make more money? (3) Do you spend a great deal of time caring for your possessions? (4) Is it difficult for you to give money away? (5) Are you in debt?

Money is a hard master and a deceptive one. Wealth promises power and control, but often it cannot deliver. Great fortunes can be made—and lost—overnight, and no amount of money can provide health, happiness, or eternal life. How much better it is to let God be your Master. His servants have peace of mind and security, both now and forever. Heaven's riches are far more valuable than earthly wealth.

## September 9

## Jesus tells about the rich man and the beggar

### LUKE 16:19-31 *(Harmony 163)*

here was a certain rich man," Jesus said, "who was splendidly clothed and lived each day in mirth and luxury. One day Lazarus, a diseased beggar, was laid at his door. As he lay there longing for scraps from the rich man's table, the dogs would come and lick his open sores. Finally the beggar died and was carried by the angels to be with Abraham in the place of the righteous dead. The rich man also died and was buried, and his soul went into hell. There, in torment, he saw Lazarus in the far distance with Abraham.

"'Father Abraham,' he shouted, 'have some pity! Send Lazarus over here if only to dip the tip of his finger in water and cool my tongue, for I am in anguish in these flames.'

"But Abraham said to him, 'Son, remember that during your lifetime you had everything you wanted, and Lazarus had nothing. So now he is here being comforted and you are in anguish. And besides, there is a great chasm separating us, and anyone wanting to come to you from here is stopped at its edge; and no one over there can cross to us.'

"Then the rich man said, 'O Father Abraham, then please send him to my father's home—for I have five brothers—to warn them about this place of torment lest they come here when they die.'

"But Abraham said, 'The Scriptures have warned them again and again. Your brothers can read them anytime they want to.'

"The rich man replied, 'No, Father Abraham, they won't bother to read them. But if someone is sent to them from the dead, then they will turn from their sins.'

"But Abraham said, 'If they won't listen to Moses and the prophets, they won't listen even though someone rises from the dead.'"

*The rich man thought that his five brothers would surely believe a messenger who had been raised from the dead. But Jesus said that if they did not believe Moses and the prophets, who spoke constantly of the duty to care for the poor, not even a resurrection would convince them.*

### HOARD OR HELP?

The Pharisees considered wealth to be a proof of a person's righteousness. Jesus startled them with this story where a diseased beggar is rewarded and a rich man is punished. The rich man did not go to hell because of his wealth but because he was self-centered. He refused to feed Lazarus, take him in, or care for him. He was hard-hearted in spite of his great blessings. The amount of money we have is not as important as the way we use it. What is your attitude toward your money and possessions? Do you hoard them selfishly, or do you use them to help others?

## Jesus tells about forgiveness and faith

### LUKE 17:1-4 *(Harmony 164a)*

*T*here will always be temptations to sin," Jesus said one day to his disciples, "but woe to the man who does the tempting. If he were thrown into the sea with a huge rock tied to his neck, he would be far better off than facing the punishment in store for those who harm these little children's souls. I am warning you!

"Rebuke your brother if he sins, and forgive him if he is sorry. Even if he wrongs you seven times a day and each time turns again and asks forgiveness, forgive him."

*Jesus may have been directing this warning at the religious leaders who taught their converts their own hypocritical ways (see Matthew 23:15). They were perpetuating an evil system. A person who teaches others has a solemn responsibility (James 3:1).*

**POINTING OUT SIN**

To rebuke does not mean to point out every sin we see; it means to bring sin to a person's attention with the purpose of restoring him or her to God and to fellow humans. When you feel you must rebuke another Christian for a sin, check your attitudes before you speak. Do you love the person? Are you willing to forgive? Unless rebuke is tied to forgiveness, it will not help the sinning person. It's too easy to point out someone else's faults or sins. If we feel we must admonish someone, we should be sure we are confronting that person in love and forgiveness, not because we are annoyed, inconvenienced, or seeking to blame him or her.

## Jesus tells about forgiveness and faith

### LUKE 17:5-10 *(Harmony 164b)*

*O*ne day the apostles said to the Lord, "We need more faith; tell us how to get it."

"If your faith were only the size of a mustard seed," Jesus answered, "it would be large enough to uproot that mulberry tree over there and send it hurtling into the sea! Your command would bring immediate results! When a servant comes in from plowing or taking care of sheep, he doesn't just sit down and eat, but first prepares his master's meal and serves him his supper before he eats his own. And he is not even thanked, for he is merely doing what he is supposed to do. Just so, if you merely obey me, you should not consider yourselves worthy of praise. For you have simply done your duty!"

*If we have obeyed God, we have only done our duty and should regard it as a privilege. Obedience is not something extra we do; it is our duty. However, Jesus is not rendering our service as meaningless or useless, nor is he doing away with rewards. He is attacking unwarranted self-esteem and spiritual pride.*

**SEED FAITH**

The disciples' request was genuine; they wanted the faith necessary for such radical forgiveness. But Jesus didn't directly answer their question because the amount of faith is not as important as its genuineness. Faith is total dependence on God and a willingness to do his will. Faith is not something we use to put on a show for others; it is complete and humble obedience to God's will, readiness to do whatever he calls us to do. A mustard seed is small, but it is alive and growing. Like a tiny seed, a small amount of genuine faith in God will take root and grow. Almost invisible at first, it will begin to spread, first under the ground and then visibly. Although each change will be gradual and imperceptible, soon this faith will have produced major results that will uproot and destroy competing loyalties. We don't need more faith; a tiny seed of faith is enough, if it is alive and growing. The amount of faith isn't as important as the right kind of faith—faith in our all-powerful God. Ask God to increase your faith and to give you the strength to act on the faith you have.

*September 12*

## Lazarus becomes ill and dies

### JOHN 11:1-16 *(Harmony 165)*

*D*o you remember Mary, who poured the costly perfume on Jesus' feet and wiped them with her hair? Well, her brother Lazarus, who lived in Bethany with Mary and her sister Martha, was sick. So the two sisters sent a message to Jesus telling him, "Sir, your good friend is very, very sick."

But when Jesus heard about it he said, "The purpose of his illness is not death, but for the glory of God. I, the Son of God, will receive glory from this situation."

Although Jesus was very fond of Martha, Mary, and Lazarus, he stayed where he was for the next two days and made no move to go to them. Finally, after the two days, he said to his disciples, "Let's go to Judea."

But his disciples objected. "Master," they said, "only a few days ago the Jewish leaders in Judea were trying to kill you. Are you going there again?"

*The raising of Lazarus was an essential display of Jesus' power, and the resurrection from the dead is a crucial belief of Christian faith. Jesus not only raised himself from the dead (10:18), but he has the power to raise others.*

Jesus replied, "There are twelve hours of daylight every day, and during every hour of it a man can walk safely and not stumble. Only at night is there danger of a wrong step, because of the dark." Then he said, "Our friend Lazarus has gone to sleep, but now I will go and waken him!"

The disciples, thinking Jesus meant Lazarus was having a good night's rest, said, "That means he is getting better!" But Jesus meant Lazarus had died.

Then he told them plainly, "Lazarus is dead. And for your sake, I am glad I wasn't there, for this will give you another opportunity to believe in me. Come, let's go to him."

Thomas, nicknamed "The Twin," said to his fellow disciples, "Let's go too—and die with him."

### WAITING ON GOD

Jesus loved this family and often stayed with them. He knew their pain but did not respond immediately. His delay had a specific purpose. God's timing, especially his delays, may make us think he is not answering or is not answering the way we want. But he will meet all our needs according to his perfect schedule and purpose (Philippians 4:19). If Jesus had been with Lazarus during the final moments of Lazarus's sickness, Jesus might have healed Lazarus rather than let him die. But Lazarus died so that Jesus' power over death could be shown to his disciples and others. Any trial a believer faces can ultimately bring glory to God because God can bring good out of any bad situation (Genesis 50:20; Romans 8:28). When trouble comes, do you grumble, complain, and blame God, or do you see your problems as opportunities to honor him?

## Jesus comforts Mary and Martha

*JOHN 11:17-26 (Harmony 166a)*

*W*hen they arrived at Bethany, they were told that Lazarus had already been in his tomb for four days. Bethany was only a couple of miles down the road from Jerusalem, and many of the Jewish leaders had come to pay their respects and to console Martha and Mary on their loss. When Martha got word that Jesus was coming, she went to meet him. But Mary stayed at home.

*The village of Bethany is located about two miles east of Jerusalem on the road to Jericho. It was near enough to Jerusalem for Jesus and the disciples to be in danger, but far enough away so as not to attract attention prematurely.*

Martha said to Jesus, "Sir, if you had been here, my brother wouldn't have died. And even now it's not too late, for I know that God will bring my brother back to life again, if you will only ask him to."

Jesus told her, "Your brother will come back to life again."

"Yes," Martha said, "when everyone else does, on Resurrection Day."

Jesus told her, "I am the one who raises the dead and gives them life again. Anyone who believes in me, even though he dies like anyone else, shall live again. He is given eternal life for believing in me and shall never perish. Do you believe this, Martha?"

### HIS AWESOME POWER

Their brother was growing very sick, so Mary and Martha called for Jesus to help. They believed in his ability to help because they had seen his miracles. We too know of Jesus' miracles, both from Scripture and through changed lives we have seen. When we need extraordinary help, Jesus offers extraordinary resources. We should not hesitate to ask him for assistance. Jesus has power over life and death as well as power to forgive sins because he is the Creator of life (see 14:6). He who *is* life can surely restore life. Whoever believes in Christ has a spiritual life that death cannot conquer or diminish in any way. When we realize Christ's power and how wonderful his offer to us really is, how can we help but commit our lives to him! To those of us who believe, what wonderful assurance and certainty we have: "I will live again—and you will too" (14:19).

## Jesus comforts Mary and Martha

*JOHN 11:27-36 (Harmony 166b)*

es, Master," she told him. "I believe you are the Messiah, the Son of God, the one we have so long awaited."

Then she left him and returned to Mary and, calling her aside from the mourners, told her, "He is here and wants to see you." So Mary went to him at once.

Now Jesus had stayed outside the village, at the place where Martha met him. When the Jewish leaders who were at the house trying to console Mary saw her leave so hastily, they assumed she was going to Lazarus's tomb to weep; so they followed her.

*Martha is best known for being too busy to sit down and talk with Jesus (Luke 10:38-42). But here we see her as a woman of deep faith. Her statement of faith is exactly the response that Jesus wants from us.*

When Mary arrived where Jesus was, she fell down at his feet, saying, "Sir, if you had been here, my brother would still be alive."

When Jesus saw her weeping and the Jewish leaders wailing with her, he was moved with indignation and deeply troubled. "Where is he buried?" he asked them.

They told him, "Come and see." Tears came to Jesus' eyes.

"They were close friends," the Jewish leaders said. "See how much he loved him."

### JESUS CARES

When Jesus saw the weeping and wailing, he too wept openly. Perhaps he empathized with their grief, or perhaps he was troubled at their unbelief. In either case, Jesus showed that he cares enough for us to weep with us in our sorrow. John stresses that we have a God who cares. This portrait contrasts with the popular Greek concept that God had no emotions and no messy involvement with humans. Here we see many of Jesus' emotions—compassion, indignation, sorrow, even frustration. He often expressed deep emotion, and we must never be afraid to reveal our true feelings to him. He understands them, for he experienced them. Be honest, and don't try to hide anything from your Savior. He cares.

## Jesus raises Lazarus from the dead

### *JOHN 11:37-44 (Harmony 167)*

*B*ut some said, "This fellow healed a blind man—why couldn't he keep Lazarus from dying?"

And again Jesus was moved with deep anger. Then they came to the tomb. It was a cave with a heavy stone rolled across its door.

"Roll the stone aside," Jesus told them.

But Martha, the dead man's sister, said, "By now the smell will be terrible, for he has been dead four days."

"But didn't I tell you that you will see a wonderful miracle from God if you believe?" Jesus asked her.

So they rolled the stone aside. Then Jesus looked up to heaven and said, "Father, thank you for hearing me. (You always hear me, of course, but I said it because of all these people standing here, so that they will believe you sent me.)" Then he shouted, "Lazarus, come out!"

And Lazarus came—bound up in the gravecloth, his face muffled in a head swath. Jesus told them, "Unwrap him and let him go!"

*Tombs at this time were usually caves carved in the limestone rock of a hillside. A tomb was often large enough for people to walk inside. Several bodies would be placed in one tomb. After burial, a large stone would be rolled across the entrance to the tomb.*

#### TRAGEDIES INTO TRIUMPHS

Lazarus came back to life, but he would die again physically. Yet, because he believed in Jesus, he would be raised again to eternal life. We know this because Jesus Christ came back to life. All Christians, including those living when Christ returns, will live with Christ forever. Therefore, we need not despair when loved ones die or world events take a tragic turn. God will turn our tragedies to triumphs, our poverty to riches, our pain to glory, and our defeat to victory. All believers throughout history will stand reunited in God's very presence, safe and secure. Comfort and reassure each other with this great hope.

## Religious leaders plot to kill Jesus

*JOHN 11:45-53 (Harmony 168a)*

And so at last many of the Jewish leaders who were with Mary and saw it happen, finally believed on him. But some went away to the Pharisees and reported it to them. Then the chief priests and Pharisees convened a council to discuss the situation.

"What are we going to do?" they asked each other. "For this man certainly does miracles. If we let him alone the whole nation will follow him—and then the Roman army will come and kill us and take over the Jewish government."

And one of them, Caiaphas, who was high priest that year, said, "You stupid idiots—let this one man die for the people— why should the whole nation perish?"

This prophecy that Jesus should die for the entire nation came from Caiaphas in his position as high priest—he didn't think of it by himself, but was inspired to say it. It was a prediction that Jesus' death would not be for Israel only, but for all the children of God scattered around the world. So from that time on the Jewish leaders began plotting Jesus' death.

*The Jewish leaders knew that if they didn't stop Jesus, the Romans would discipline them. Rome gave partial freedom to the Jews as long as they were quiet and obedient. Jesus' miracles often caused a disturbance. The leaders feared that Rome's displeasure would bring additional hardship to their nation.*

### HARD HEARTS

Even when confronted point-blank with the power of Jesus' deity, some refused to believe. These eyewitnesses not only rejected Jesus; they also plotted his murder. They were so hardened that they preferred to reject God's Son rather than admit that they were wrong. When we judge others, we automatically consider ourselves to be better. Beware of pride. If allowed to grow, it can lead to enormous sin.

## Religious leaders plot to kill Jesus

### JOHN 11:54-57 (Harmony 168b)

*J*esus now stopped his public ministry and left Jerusalem; he went to the edge of the desert, to the village of Ephraim, and stayed there with his disciples.

The Passover, a Jewish holy day, was near, and many country people arrived in Jerusalem several days early so that they could go through the cleansing ceremony before the Passover began. They wanted to see Jesus, and as they gossiped in the Temple, they asked each other, "What do you think? Will he come for the Passover?" Meanwhile the chief priests and Pharisees had publicly announced that anyone seeing Jesus must report him immediately so that they could arrest him.

*Passover was a holiday designed to celebrate Israel's deliverance from Egypt and to remind the people what God had done. Many Jews came to Jerusalem to celebrate this holy day.*

### QUIET TIME

Lazarus's return to life became the last straw for the religious leaders who were bent on killing Jesus. So Jesus stopped his public ministry and took his disciples away from Jerusalem to Ephraim, a town several miles to the north. Jesus needed time to talk to his disciples and teach them many things before he died. He wanted to get away from the conflict in Jerusalem so the disciples could rest and concentrate on his words for them. At times all of us need to get away from the busyness of our daily routines, resting and listening to God. Set aside a certain time each day when you can quietly listen and talk to God.

## Jesus heals ten lepers

### LUKE 17:11-19 (Harmony 169)

*A*s they continued onward toward Jerusalem, they reached the border between Galilee and Samaria, and as they entered a village there, ten lepers stood at a distance, crying out, "Jesus, sir, have mercy on us!"

He looked at them and said, "Go to the Jewish priest and show him that you are healed!" And as they were going, their leprosy disappeared.

*Not only was this man a leper, he was also a Samaritan—a race despised by the Jews as idolatrous half-breeds. Once again Luke is pointing out that God's grace is for everybody.*

One of them came back to Jesus, shouting, "Glory to God, I'm healed!" He fell flat on the ground in front of Jesus, face downward in the dust, thanking him for what he had done. This man was a despised Samaritan.

Jesus asked, "Didn't I heal ten men? Where are the nine? Does only this foreigner return to give glory to God?"

And Jesus said to the man, "Stand up and go; your faith has made you well."

### GRATEFUL BELIEVERS

Jesus healed all ten lepers, but only one returned to thank him. It is possible to receive God's great gifts with an ungrateful spirit—nine of the ten men did so. Only the thankful man, however, learned that his faith had played a role in his healing; and only grateful Christians grow in understanding God's grace. God does not demand that we thank him, but he is pleased when we do so. And he uses our responsiveness to teach us more about himself.

*September 19*

## Jesus teaches about the coming of the Kingdom of God

### LUKE 17:20-21 *(Harmony 170a)*

One day the Pharisees asked Jesus, "When will the Kingdom of God begin?" Jesus replied, "The Kingdom of God isn't ushered in with visible signs. You won't be able to say, 'It has begun here in this place or there in that part of the country.' For the Kingdom of God is within you.

*Some versions say, "the Kingdom of God is among you." The Kingdom within them emphasized that it would begin with spiritual change within. The Kingdom among them emphasized that he, the King, was in their midst.*

### THE KINGDOM WITHIN

The Pharisees asked when God's Kingdom would come, not knowing that it had already arrived. The Kingdom of God is not like an earthly kingdom with geographical boundaries. Instead, it begins with the work of God's Spirit in people's lives and in relationships. When Jesus ascended into heaven, God's Kingdom would remain in the hearts of all believers through the presence of the Holy Spirit. Still today we must resist looking to institutions or programs for evidence of the progress of God's Kingdom. Instead, we should look for what God is doing in people's hearts.

*September 20*

---

## Jesus teaches about the coming of the Kingdom of God

*LUKE 17:22-37 (Harmony 170b)*

*L*ater he talked again about this with his disciples. "The time is coming when you will long for me to be with you even for a single day, but I won't be here," he said. "Reports will reach you that I have returned and that I am in this place or that; don't believe it or go out to look for me. For when I return, you will know it beyond all doubt. It will be as evident as the lightning that flashes across the skies. But first I must suffer terribly and be rejected by this whole nation.

*Many will claim to be the Messiah, and many will claim that Jesus has returned—and people will believe them. Jesus warns us never to take such reports seriously, no matter how convincing they may sound. When Jesus returns, his power and presence will be evident to everyone.*

"When I return the world will be as indifferent to the things of God as the people were in Noah's day. They ate and drank and married—everything just as usual right up to the day when Noah went into the ark and the Flood came and destroyed them all.

"And the world will be as it was in the days of Lot: people went about their daily business—eating and drinking, buying and selling, farming and building—until the morning Lot left Sodom. Then fire and brimstone rained down from heaven and destroyed them all. Yes, it will be 'business as usual' right up to the hour of my return.

"Those away from home that day must not return to pack; those in the fields must not return to town—remember what happened to Lot's wife! Whoever clings to his life shall lose it, and whoever loses his life shall save it. That night two men will be asleep in the same room, and one will be taken away, the other left. Two women will be working together at household tasks; one will be taken, the other left; and so it will be with men working side by side in the fields."

"Lord, where will they be taken?" the disciples asked.

Jesus replied, "Where the body is, the vultures gather!"

Life will be going on as usual on the day Christ returns. There will be no warning. Most people will be going about their everyday tasks, indifferent to the demands of God. They will be as surprised by Christ's return as the people in Noah's day were by the Flood (Genesis 6–8) or the people in Lot's day by the destruction of Sodom (Genesis 19). We don't know the time of Christ's return, but we do know that he is coming. He may come today, tomorrow, or centuries in the future. Whenever Christ returns, we must be morally and spiritually ready. Live as if Jesus were returning today.

*September 21*

---

## Jesus tells the parable of the persistent widow

*LUKE 18:1-8 (Harmony 171)*

One day Jesus told his disciples a story to illustrate their need for constant prayer and to show them that they must keep praying until the answer comes.

"There was a city judge," he said, "a very godless man who had great contempt for everyone. A widow of that city came to him frequently to appeal for justice against a man who had harmed her. The judge ignored her for a while, but eventually she got on his nerves.

"'I fear neither God nor man,' he said to himself, 'but this woman bothers me. I'm going to see that she gets justice, for she is wearing me out with her constant coming!'"

*Widows and orphans were among the most vulnerable of all God's people, and both Old Testament prophets and New Testament apostles insisted that these needy people be properly cared for. See, for example, Exodus 22:22-24; Isaiah 1:17; 1 Timothy 5:3; James 1:27.*

Then the Lord said, "If even an evil judge can be worn down like that, don't you think that God will surely give justice to his people who plead with him day and night? Yes! He will answer them quickly! But the question is: When I, the Messiah, return, how many will I find who have faith and are praying?"

### CONSTANT PRAYER

To repeat our prayers until the answer comes does not mean endless repetition or painfully long prayer sessions. Constant prayer means keeping our requests constantly before God as we live for him day by day, believing he will answer. When we live by faith, we are not to give up. God may delay answering, but his delays always have good reasons. As we persist in prayer we grow in character, faith, and hope.

*September 22*

## Jesus tells the parable of two men who prayed

### LUKE 18:9-14 *(Harmony 172)*

hen he told this story to some who boasted of their virtue and scorned everyone else:

"Two men went to the Temple to pray. One was a proud, self-righteous Pharisee, and the other a cheating tax collector. The proud Pharisee 'prayed' this prayer: 'Thank God, I am not a sinner like everyone else, especially like that tax collector over there! For I never cheat, I don't commit adultery, I go without food twice a week, and I give to God a tenth of everything I earn.' *The people who lived near Jerusalem often went to the Temple to pray. The Temple was the center of their worship.*

"But the corrupt tax collector stood at a distance and dared not even lift his eyes to heaven as he prayed, but beat upon his chest in sorrow, exclaiming, 'God, be merciful to me, a sinner.' I tell you, this sinner, not the Pharisee, returned home forgiven! For the proud shall be humbled, but the humble shall be honored."

#### PRIDE'S TRAP

The Pharisee did not go to the Temple to pray to God, but to announce to all within earshot how good he was. The tax collector went recognizing his sin and begging for mercy. Self-righteousness is dangerous. It leads to pride, causes a person to despise others, and prevents him or her from learning anything from God. The tax collector's prayer should be our prayer because we all need God's mercy every day. Don't let pride in your achievements cut you off from God.

*September 23*

## Jesus teaches about marriage and divorce

### MATTHEW 19:1-12 *(also in MARK 10:1-12)* *(Harmony 173)*

fter Jesus had finished this address, he left Galilee and circled back to Judea from across the Jordan River. Vast crowds followed him, and he healed their sick. Some

Pharisees came to interview him and tried to trap him into saying something that would ruin him.

"Do you permit divorce?" they asked.

"Don't you read the Scriptures?" he replied. "In them it is written that at the beginning God created man and woman, and that a man should leave his father and mother, and be forever united to his wife. The two shall become one—no longer two, but one! And no man may divorce what God has joined together."

*Women were often treated as property. Marriage and divorce were regarded as transactions similar to buying and selling land. But Jesus condemned this attitude, clarifying God's original intention—that marriage bring oneness (Genesis 2:24).*

"Then, why," they asked, "did Moses say a man may divorce his wife by merely writing her a letter of dismissal?"

Jesus replied, "Moses did that in recognition of your hard and evil hearts, but it was not what God had originally intended. And I tell you this, that anyone who divorces his wife, except for fornication, and marries another, commits adultery."

Jesus' disciples then said to him, "If that is how it is, it is better not to marry!"

"Not everyone can accept this statement," Jesus said. "Only those whom God helps. Some are born without the ability to marry, and some are disabled by men, and some refuse to marry for the sake of the Kingdom of Heaven. Let anyone who can, accept my statement."

### COMMITTED TO PERMANENCE

God allowed divorce as a concession to people's sinfulness. Divorce was not approved, but it was instituted to protect the injured party in a bad situation. Unfortunately, the Pharisees used Deuteronomy 24:1 as a proof text for divorce. Jesus explained that this was not God's intent; instead, God wants married people to consider their marriage permanent. Don't enter marriage with the option of getting out. Your marriage is more likely to be happy if from the outset you are committed to permanence. Don't be hard-hearted like these Pharisees, but be hardheaded in your determination, with God's help, to stay together.

## Jesus blesses little children

### MARK 10:13-16 (also in MATTHEW 19:13-15; LUKE 18:15-17) (Harmony 174)

*O*nce when some mothers were bringing their children to Jesus to bless them, the disciples shooed them away, telling them not to bother him.

But when Jesus saw what was happening he was very much displeased with his disciples and said to them, "Let the children come to me, for the Kingdom of God belongs to such as they. Don't send them away! I tell you as seriously as I know how that anyone who refuses to come to God as a little child will never be allowed into his Kingdom."

Then he took the children into his arms and placed his hands on their heads and he blessed them.

*Jesus didn't mean that heaven is only for children but that people need child-like attitudes of trust in God. The receptiveness of little children was a great contrast to the stubbornness of the religious leaders who let their education and sophistication stand in the way of the simple faith needed to believe in Jesus.*

**WELCOME THE CHILDREN**

It was customary for a mother to bring her children to a rabbi for a blessing, and that is why these mothers gathered around Jesus. The disciples, however, thought the children were unworthy of the Master's time—less important than whatever else he was doing. But Jesus welcomed them because little children have the kind of faith and trust needed to enter God's Kingdom. It is important that we introduce our children to Jesus and that we ourselves approach him with childlike attitudes of acceptance, faith, and trust.

## Jesus speaks to the rich young man

### MARK 10:17-31 (also in MATTHEW 19:16-30; LUKE 18:18-30) (Harmony 175)

*A*s he was starting out on a trip, a man came running to him and knelt down and asked, "Good Teacher, what must I do to get to heaven?"

"Why do you call me good?" Jesus asked. "Only God is truly good! But as for your question—you know the commandments: don't kill, don't commit adultery, don't steal, don't lie, don't cheat, respect your father and mother."

"Teacher," the man replied, "I've never once broken a single one of those laws."

Jesus felt genuine love for this man as he looked at him. "You lack only one thing," he told him; "go and sell all you have and give the money to the poor—and you shall have treasure in heaven—and come, follow me."

*Jesus does not ask that all believers sell everything they have. However, because money represents power, authority, and success, often it is difficult for wealthy people to realize their need and their powerlessness to save themselves. The rich in talent or intelligence suffer the same difficulty. The person who has everything on earth can still lack what is most important— eternal life.*

Then the man's face fell, and he went sadly away, for he was very rich.

Jesus watched him go, then turned around and said to his disciples, "It's almost impossible for the rich to get into the Kingdom of God!"

This amazed them. So Jesus said it again: "Dear children, how hard it is for those who trust in riches to enter the Kingdom of God. It is easier for a camel to go through the eye of a needle than for a rich man to enter the Kingdom of God."

The disciples were incredulous! "Then who in the world can be saved, if not a rich man?" they asked.

Jesus looked at them intently, then said, "Without God, it is utterly impossible. But with God everything is possible."

Then Peter began to mention all that he and the other disciples had left behind. "We've given up everything to follow you," he said.

And Jesus replied, "Let me assure you that no one has ever given up anything—home, brothers, sisters, mother, father, children, or property—for love of me and to tell others the Good News, who won't be given back, a hundred times over, homes, brothers, sisters, mothers, children, and land—with persecutions!

"All these will be his here on earth, and in the world to come he shall have eternal life. But many people who seem to be important now will be the least important then; and many who are considered least here shall be greatest there."

### GIVING, GAINING

Peter and the other disciples had paid a high price—leaving their homes and jobs—to follow Jesus. But Jesus reminded Peter that following him has its benefits as well as its sacrifices. Any believer who has had to give up something to follow Christ will be paid back in this life as well as in the next. For example, if you must give up a secure job, you will find that God offers a secure relationship with himself now and forever. If you must give up your family's approval, you will gain the love of the family of God. The disciples had begun to pay the price of following Jesus, and Jesus said they would be rewarded. Don't dwell on what you have given up; think about what you have gained, and give thanks for it. You can never outgive God.

## September 26

## Jesus tells the parable of the workers paid equally

### MATTHEW 20:1-16 *(Harmony 176)*

*H*ere is another illustration of the Kingdom of Heaven. The owner of an estate went out early one morning to hire workers for his harvest field. He agreed to pay them $20 a day and sent them out to work.

"A couple of hours later he was passing a hiring hall and saw some men standing around waiting for jobs, so he sent them also into his fields, telling them he would pay them whatever was right at the end of the day. At noon and again around three o'clock in the afternoon he did the same thing.

*Jesus further clarified the membership rules of the Kingdom of Heaven— entrance is by God's grace alone. In this parable, God is the landowner, and believers are the laborers.*

"At five o'clock that evening he was in town again and saw some more men standing around and asked them, 'Why haven't you been working today?'

"'Because no one hired us,' they replied.

"'Then go on out and join the others in my fields,' he told them.

"That evening he told the paymaster to call the men in and pay them, beginning with the last men first. When the men hired at five o'clock were paid, each received $20. So when the men hired earlier came to get theirs, they assumed they would receive much more. But they, too, were paid $20.

"They protested, 'Those fellows worked only one hour, and yet you've paid them just as much as those of us who worked all day in the scorching heat.'

"'Friend,' he answered one of them, 'I did you no wrong! Didn't you agree to work all day for $20? Take it and go. It is my desire to pay all the same; is it against the law to give away my money if I want to? Should you be angry because I am kind?' And so it is that the last shall be first, and the first, last."

### WHO DESERVES IT?

This parable is not about rewards but about salvation. It is a strong teaching about *grace,* God's generosity. We shouldn't begrudge those who turn to God in the last moments of life because, in reality, *no one* deserves eternal life.

Many people we don't expect to see in the Kingdom will be there. The criminal who repented as he was dying (Luke 23:40-43) will be there along with people who have believed and served God for many years. Do you resent God's gracious acceptance of the despised, the outcast, and the sinners who have turned to him for forgiveness? Are you ever jealous of what God has given to another person? Instead, focus on God's gracious benefits to you, and be thankful for what you have.

## September 27

# Jesus predicts his death the third time

*LUKE 18:31-34 (also in MATTHEW 20:17-19; MARK 10:32-34) (Harmony 177)*

Gathering the Twelve around him he told them, "As you know, we are going to Jerusalem. And when we get there, all the predictions of the ancient prophets concerning me will come true. I will be handed over to the Gentiles to be mocked and treated shamefully and spat upon, and lashed and killed. And the third day I will rise again."

But they didn't understand a thing he said. He seemed to be talking in riddles.

### NO ACCIDENT

Jesus' death and resurrection should have come as no surprise to the disciples. Here he clearly explained to them what would happen to him. Unfortunately, they didn't really hear what he was saying. Jesus said he was the Messiah, but they thought the Messiah would be a conquering king. He spoke to

*Some predictions about what would happen to Jesus are found in Psalm 41:9 (betrayal); Psalm 22:16-18 and Isaiah 53:4-7 (crucifixion); Psalm 16:10 (resurrection). Even though Jesus spoke plainly, the disciples would not grasp the significance of his words until they saw the risen Christ face to face.*

them of resurrection, but they heard only his words about death. Because Jesus often spoke in parables, the disciples may have thought that his words on death and resurrection were another parable that they weren't astute enough to understand. The Gospels include Jesus' predictions of his death and resurrection to show that these events were God's plan from the beginning and not accidents. We can trust that all the other predictions about the future for all believers will also come true.

## September 28

### Jesus teaches about serving others

*MARK 10:35-45 (also in MATTHEW 20:20-28)*
*(Harmony 178)*

hen James and John, the sons of Zebedee, came over and spoke to him in a low voice. "Master," they said, "we want you to do us a favor."

"What is it?" he asked.

"We want to sit on the thrones next to yours in your Kingdom," they said, "one at your right and the other at your left!"

But Jesus answered, "You don't know what you are asking! Are you able to drink from the bitter cup of sorrow I must drink from? Or to be baptized with the baptism of suffering I must be baptized with?"

"Oh, yes," they said, "we are!"

And Jesus said, "You shall indeed drink from my cup and be baptized with my baptism, but I do not have the right to place you on thrones next to mine. Those appointments have already been made."

*A ransom was the price paid to release a slave from bondage. Jesus often told his disciples that he must die, but here he told them why—to redeem all people from the bondage of sin and death. The disciples thought that as long as Jesus was alive, he could save them. But Jesus revealed that only his death would save them and the world.*

When the other disciples discovered what James and John had asked, they were very indignant. So Jesus called them to him and said, "As you know, the kings and great men of the earth lord it over the people; but among you it is different. Whoever wants to be great among you must be your servant. And whoever wants to be greatest of all must be the slave of all. For even I, the Messiah, am not here to be served, but to help others, and to give my life as a ransom for many."

### TRUE LEADERS

James and John wanted the highest positions in Jesus' Kingdom, but Jesus told them that true greatness comes in serving others. Jesus described leadership from a new perspective. Instead of using people, we are to serve them. Jesus' mission was to serve others and to give his life away. A real leader has a servant's heart. Most businesses, organizations, and institutions measure greatness by high personal achievement. In Christ's Kingdom, however, service is the way to get ahead. The desire to be on top will hinder, not help. Rather than seeking to have your needs met, look for ways that you can minister to the needs of others. Servant leaders appreciate others' worth and realize that they're not above any job. If you see something that needs to be done, don't wait to be asked. Take the initiative, and do it like a faithful servant.

## September 29

## Jesus heals a blind beggar

### MARK 10:46-52 (also in MATTHEW 20:29-34; LUKE 18:35-43) (Harmony 179)

*A*nd so they reached Jericho. Later, as they left town, a great crowd was following. Now it happened that a blind beggar named Bartimaeus (the son of Timaeus) was sitting beside the road as Jesus was going by.

When Bartimaeus heard that Jesus from Nazareth was near, he began to shout out, "Jesus, Son of David, have mercy on me!"

"Shut up!" some of the people yelled at him.

But he only shouted the louder, again and again, "O Son of David, have mercy on me!"

When Jesus heard him, he stopped there in the road and said, "Tell him to come here."

So they called the blind man. "You lucky fellow," they said, "come on, he's calling you!" Bartimaeus yanked off his old coat and flung it aside, jumped up and came to Jesus.

*The blind man called Jesus "Son of David," a title for the Messiah (Isaiah 11:1-3). This means that he understood Jesus to be the long-awaited Messiah. A poor and blind beggar could see that Jesus was the Messiah, while the religious leaders who saw his miracles were blinded to his identity and refused to recognize him as the Messiah.*

"What do you want me to do for you?" Jesus asked.

"O Teacher," the blind man said, "I want to see!"

And Jesus said to him, "All right, it's done. Your faith has healed you."

Beggars often waited along the roads near cities, because that was where they were able to contact the most people. Usually disabled in some way, beggars were unable to earn a living. Medical help was not available for their problems, and people tended to ignore their obligation to care for the needy (Leviticus 25:35-38). Thus beggars had little hope of escaping their degrading way of life. But this blind beggar took hope in the Messiah. He shamelessly cried out for Jesus' attention, and Jesus said that his faith allowed him to see. No matter how desperate your situation may seem, if you call out to Jesus in faith, he will help you.

## September 30

---

## Jesus brings salvation to Zacchaeus's home

### LUKE 19:1-7 *(Harmony 180a)*

As Jesus was passing through Jericho, a man named Zacchaeus, one of the most influential Jews in the Roman tax-collecting business (and, of course, a very rich man), tried to get a look at Jesus, but he was too short to see over the crowds. So he ran ahead and climbed into a sycamore tree beside the road, to watch from there.

When Jesus came by, he looked up at Zacchaeus and called him by name! "Zacchaeus!" he said. "Quick! Come down! For I am going to be a guest in your home today!"

Zacchaeus hurriedly climbed down and took Jesus to his house in great excitement and joy.

*To finance their great world empire, the Romans levied heavy taxes on all nations under their control. The Jews opposed these taxes because they supported a secular government and its heathen gods, but they were still forced to pay.*

But the crowds were displeased. "He has gone to be the guest of a notorious sinner," they grumbled.

Tax collectors were among the most unpopular people in Israel. Jews by birth, they chose to work for Rome and were considered traitors. Besides, it was common knowledge that tax collectors were making themselves rich by gouging their fellow Jews. No wonder the people muttered when Jesus went home with the tax collector Zacchaeus. But despite the fact that Zacchaeus was both a cheater and a turncoat,

Jesus loved him; and in response, the little tax collector was converted. In every society certain groups of people are considered "untouchable" because of their political views, their immoral behavior, or their lifestyle. We should not give in to social pressure to avoid these people. Jesus loves them, and they need to hear his Good News.

## Jesus brings salvation to Zacchaeus's home

### *LUKE 19:8-10 (Harmony 180b)*

eanwhile, Zacchaeus stood before the Lord and said, "Sir, from now on I will give half my wealth to the poor, and if I find I have overcharged anyone on his taxes, I will penalize myself by giving him back four times as much!"

Jesus told him, "This shows that salvation has come to this home today. This man was one of the lost sons of Abraham, and I, the Messiah, have come to search for and to save such souls as his."

*When Jesus said Zacchaeus was a son of Abraham and yet was lost, he must have shocked his hearers in at least two ways. They would not have liked to acknowledge that this unpopular tax collector was a fellow son of Abraham, and they would not have wished to admit that sons of Abraham could be lost. But a person is not saved by a good heritage or condemned by a bad one; faith is more important than genealogy.*

**A CHANGED LIFE**

Judging from the crowd's reaction to him, Zacchaeus must have been a very crooked tax collector. But after he met Jesus, he realized that his life needed straightening out. By giving to the poor and making restitution—with generous interest—to those he had cheated, Zacchaeus demonstrated inward change by outward action. It is not enough to follow Jesus in your head or heart alone. Intellectual assent—agreement with a set of Christian teachings—is incomplete faith. True faith transforms our lives. If our lives remain unchanged, we don't truly believe the truths we claim to believe. You must show your faith by changed behavior. Has your faith resulted in action? What changes do you need to make?

## Jesus tells the parable of the king's ten servants

*LUKE 19:11-27 (Harmony 181)*

*A*nd because Jesus was nearing Jerusalem, he told a story to correct the impression that the Kingdom of God would begin right away.

"A nobleman living in a certain province was called away to the distant capital of the empire to be crowned king of his province. Before he left he called together ten assistants and gave them each $2,000 to invest while he was gone. But some of his people hated him and sent him their declaration of independence, stating that they had rebelled and would not acknowledge him as their king.

"Upon his return he called in the men to whom he had given the money, to find out what they had done with it, and what their profits were.

"The first man reported a tremendous gain—ten times as much as the original amount!

*The king punished the one man because (1) he didn't share his master's interest in the kingdom; (2) he didn't trust his master's intentions; (3) his only concern was for himself, and (4) he did nothing to use the money. Some people on earth are loyal to God while others refuse to acknowledge his lordship. Each will receive rewards or punishment.*

"'Fine!' the king exclaimed. 'You are a good man. You have been faithful with the little I entrusted to you, and as your reward, you shall be governor of ten cities.'

"The next man also reported a splendid gain—five times the original amount.

"'All right!' his master said. 'You can be governor over five cities.'

"But the third man brought back only the money he had started with. 'I've kept it safe,' he said, 'because I was afraid you would demand my profits, for you are a hard man to deal with, taking what isn't yours and even confiscating the crops that others plant.' 'You vile and wicked slave,' the king roared. 'Hard, am I? That's exactly how I'll be toward you! If you knew so much about me and how tough I am, then why didn't you deposit the money in the bank so that I could at least get some interest on it?'

"Then turning to the others standing by he ordered, 'Take the money away from him and give it to the man who earned the most.'

"'But, sir,' they said, 'he has enough already!'

" 'Yes,' the king replied, 'but it is always true that those who have, get more, and those who have little, soon lose even that. And now about these enemies of mine who revolted—bring them in and execute them before me.'"

### UNTIL HE COMES

This story showed Jesus' followers what they were to do during the time between Jesus' departure and his second coming. Because we live in that time period, it applies directly to us. We have been given excellent resources to build and expand God's Kingdom. Jesus expects us to use these talents so that they multiply and the Kingdom grows. He asks each of us to account for what we do with his gifts. While awaiting the coming of the Kingdom of God in glory, we must do Christ's work. Like the king in this story, God has given you gifts to use for the benefit of his Kingdom. Do you want the Kingdom to grow? Do you trust God to govern it fairly? Are you as concerned for others' welfare as you are for your own? Are you willing to use faithfully what he has entrusted to you?

*October 3*

---

## A woman anoints Jesus with perfume

### *MARK 14:3-9 (also in MATTHEW 26:6-13; JOHN 12:1-11) (Harmony 182)*

eanwhile Jesus was in Bethany, at the home of Simon the leper; during supper a woman came in with a beautiful flask of expensive perfume. Then, breaking the seal, she poured it over his head.

Some of those at the table were indignant among themselves about this "waste," as they called it.

"Why, she could have sold that perfume for a fortune and given the money to the poor!" they snarled.

But Jesus said, "Leave her alone; why berate her for doing a good thing? You always have the poor among you, and they badly need your help, and you can aid them whenever you want to; but I won't be here much longer.

*Where Mark says "some," John specifically mentions Judas (John 12:4-5). Judas's indignation over Mary's act of worship was based not on concern for the poor but on greed. Because Judas was the treasurer of Jesus' ministry and had embezzled funds (John 12:6), he no doubt wanted the perfume sold so that the proceeds could be put into his care.*

"She has done what she could and has anointed my body ahead of time for burial. And I tell you this in solemn truth, that wherever the Good News is preached throughout the world, this woman's deed will be remembered and praised."

### TRUE WORSHIP

Nard was a fragrant ointment imported from the mountains of India. Thus it was very expensive. The amount Mary used was worth a year's wages. This act and Jesus' response to it do not teach us to ignore the poor so we can spend money extravagantly for Christ. This was a unique act for a specific occasion—an anointing that anticipated Jesus' burial and a public declaration of faith in him as Messiah. Jesus was praising Mary for her unselfish act of worship. The essence of worshiping Christ is to regard him with the utmost love, respect, and devotion, and to be willing to sacrifice to him what is most precious.

*October 4*

---

## Jesus rides into Jerusalem on a donkey

*LUKE 19:28-35 (also in MATTHEW 21:1-7;*
*MARK 11:1-7; JOHN 12:12-19) (Harmony 183a)*

After telling this story, Jesus went on toward Jerusalem, walking along ahead of his disciples. As they came to the towns of Bethphage and Bethany, on the Mount of Olives, he sent two disciples ahead, with instructions to go to the next village, and as they entered they were to look for a donkey tied beside the road. It would be a colt, not yet broken for riding.

"Untie him," Jesus said, "and bring him here. And if anyone asks you what you are doing, just say, 'The Lord needs him.'"

They found the colt as Jesus said, and sure enough, as they were untying it, the owners demanded an explanation.

"What are you doing?" they asked. "Why are you untying our colt?"

And the disciples simply replied, "The Lord needs him!" So they brought the colt to Jesus and threw some of their clothing across its back for Jesus to sit on.

*Jesus began his last week on earth by riding into Jerusalem on a donkey under a canopy of palm branches, with crowds hailing him as their king. The great Passover festival was about to begin, and Jews had come to Jerusalem from all over the Roman world during this weeklong celebration. On Palm Sunday we celebrate Jesus' triumphal entry into Jerusalem.*

Jesus came, not as a warring king on a horse or in a chariot, but as a gentle and peaceable king on a donkey's colt, just as Zechariah 9:9 had predicted. After Jesus' resurrection, the disciples would understand for the first time many of the prophecies that they had missed along the way. Jesus' words and actions would take on new meaning and make more sense. In retrospect, the disciples saw how Jesus had led them into a deeper and better understanding of his truth. Reflect on the events leading up to where you are now spiritually. How has God led you to this point? As you grow older you will look back and see God's involvement more clearly than you do now. Stop right now and thank God for what he has done for you and how he led you to himself.

*October 5*

## Jesus rides into Jerusalem on a donkey

### *MATTHEW 21:8-11 (also in MARK 11:8-11; LUKE 19:36-44) (Harmony 183b)*

*A*nd some in the crowd threw down their coats along the road ahead of him, and others cut branches from the trees and spread them out before him.

Then the crowds surged on ahead and pressed along behind, shouting, "God bless King David's Son!" . . . "God's Man is here!" . . . "Bless him, Lord!" . . . "Praise God in highest heaven!"

The entire city of Jerusalem was stirred as he entered. "Who is this?" they asked.

And the crowds replied, "It's Jesus, the prophet from Nazareth up in Galilee."

**THE WRONG IDEA**

The people who were praising God for giving them a king had the wrong idea about Jesus. They expected him to be a national leader who would restore their nation to its former glory, and thus they were deaf to the words of their prophets and blind to Jesus' real mission. When it became apparent that Jesus was not going to fulfill their

*Upon approaching Jerusalem, Jesus wept and prophesied the city's destruction due to its rejection of him (see Luke 19:41-44). About forty years after Jesus made this prediction, his words came true. In A.D. 66, the Jews revolted against Roman control. Three years later Titus, son of the Emperor Vespasian, was sent to crush the rebellion. Roman soldiers laid siege to Jerusalem, and in A.D. 70 they entered the city and burned it. Six hundred thousand Jews were killed during Titus's onslaught.*

hopes, many people would turn against him. The Jewish leaders had rejected their King (Luke 19:47). They had gone too far. They had rejected God's offer of salvation in Jesus Christ when they were visited by God himself, and soon their nation would suffer. God did not turn away from the Jewish people who obeyed him, however, and he continues to offer salvation to the people he loves, both Jews and Gentiles. Eternal life is within your reach—accept it while the opportunity is still offered.

*October 6*

## Jesus clears the Temple again

### MARK 11:12-19 (also in MATTHEW 21:12-17; LUKE 19:45-48) (Harmony 184)

*T*he next morning as they left Bethany, he felt hungry. A little way off he noticed a fig tree in full leaf, so he went over to see if he could find any figs on it. But no, there were only leaves, for it was too early in the season for fruit.

Then Jesus said to the tree, "You shall never bear fruit again!" And the disciples heard him say it.

When they arrived back in Jerusalem, he went to the Temple and began to drive out the merchants and their customers, and knocked over the tables of the money changers and the stalls of those selling doves, and stopped everyone from bringing in loads of merchandise.

*The leaders had several reasons for wanting to get rid of Jesus, mostly the fact that he had damaged their business in the Temple by driving the merchants out, preaching against injustice, and favoring the poor over the rich. Also, his great popularity was in danger of attracting Rome's attention.*

He told them, "It is written in the Scriptures, 'My Temple is to be a place of prayer for all nations,' but you have turned it into a den of robbers."

When the chief priests and other Jewish leaders heard what he had done, they began planning how best to get rid of him. Their problem was their fear of riots because the people were so enthusiastic about Jesus' teaching.

That evening as usual they left the city.

#### WHEN TO GET ANGRY

This is the second time Jesus cleared the Temple (see John 2:13-17). Merchants and money changers had set up their booths in the court of the Gentiles in the Temple, crowding out the Gentiles who had come from all over the civilized world to worship

God. The merchants sold sacrificial animals at high prices, taking advantage of those who had come long distances. The money changers exchanged all international currency for the special Temple coins—the only money the merchants would accept. They often deceived foreigners who didn't know the exchange rates. Their commercialism in God's house frustrated people's attempts at worship. This, of course, greatly angered Jesus, but he did not sin in his anger. Christians should be upset about sin and injustice and should take a stand against them. Unfortunately, believers are often passive about these important issues and get angry instead over personal insults and petty irritations.

## October 7

### Jesus explains why he must die

#### JOHN 12:20-25 (Harmony 185a)

*S*ome Greeks who had come to Jerusalem to attend the Passover paid a visit to Philip, who was from Bethsaida, and said, "Sir, we want to meet Jesus." Philip told Andrew about it, and they went together to ask Jesus.

Jesus replied that the time had come for him to return to his glory in heaven, and that "I must fall and die like a kernel of wheat that falls into the furrows of the earth. Unless I die I will be alone—a single seed. But my death will produce many new wheat kernels—a plentiful harvest of new lives. If you love your life down here—you will lose it. If you despise your life down here—you will exchange it for eternal glory."

*These Greeks probably were converts to the Jewish faith. They may have gone to Philip because, though he was a Jew, he had a Greek name.*

#### LOVE AND HATE

This is a beautiful picture of the necessary sacrifice of Jesus. Unless a grain of wheat is buried in the ground, it will not become a blade of wheat producing many more seeds. Jesus had to die to pay the penalty for our sin, but also to show his power over death. Jesus calls us to be so committed to living for Christ that we "hate" our lives by comparison. This does not mean that we long to die or that we are careless or destructive with the life God has given but that we are willing to die if doing so will glorify Christ. We must disown the tyrannical rule of our own self-centeredness. By laying aside our striving for advantage, security, and pleasure, we can serve God lovingly and freely. Releasing control of our lives and transferring that control to Christ bring eternal life and genuine joy.

## Jesus explains why he must die

### *JOHN 12:26-36 (Harmony 185b)*

If these Greeks want to be my disciples, tell them to come and follow me, for my servants must be where I am. And if they follow me, the Father will honor them. Now my soul is deeply troubled. Shall I pray, 'Father, save me from what lies ahead'? But that is the very reason why I came! Father, bring glory and honor to your name."

Then a voice spoke from heaven saying, "I have already done this, and I will do it again." When the crowd heard the voice, some of them thought it was thunder, while others declared an angel had spoken to him.

Then Jesus told them, "The voice was for your benefit, not mine. The time of judgment for the world has come—and the time when Satan, the prince of this world, shall be cast out. And when I am lifted up on the cross, I will draw everyone to me." He said this to indicate how he was going to die.

*The ruler of this world is Satan, an angel who rebelled against God. Satan is real, not symbolic, and is constantly working against God and those who obey him. Satan has great power, but people can be delivered from his reign of spiritual darkness because of Christ's victory on the cross. Satan is powerful, but Jesus is much more powerful.*

"Die?" asked the crowd. "We understood that the Messiah would live forever and never die. Why are you saying he will die? What Messiah are you talking about?"

Jesus replied, "My light will shine out for you just a little while longer. Walk in it while you can, and go where you want to go before the darkness falls, for then it will be too late for you to find your way. Make use of the Light while there is still time; then you will become light bearers."

After saying these things, Jesus went away and was hidden from them.

#### WHOM DO YOU SEEK?

The crowd could not believe what Jesus was saying about the Messiah. They were waving palm branches for a victorious leader who would set up a political, earthly kingdom that would never end. From their reading of certain Scriptures, they thought the Messiah would never die (Psalms 89:35-36; 110:4; Isaiah 9:7). Other passages, however, showed that he would (Isaiah 53:5-9). Jesus' words did not mesh with the crowd's concept of the Messiah! First he had to suffer and die—then he would one day set up his eternal Kingdom. What kind of Messiah, or Savior, are you seeking? Beware of trying to force Jesus into your own mold—he won't fit.

## Most of the people do not believe in Jesus

### *JOHN 12:37-43 (Harmony 186)*

*B*ut despite all the miracles he had done, most of the people would not believe he was the Messiah. This is exactly what Isaiah the prophet had predicted: "Lord, who will believe us? Who will accept God's mighty miracles as proof?" But they couldn't believe, for as Isaiah also said: "God has blinded their eyes and hardened their hearts so that they can neither see nor understand nor turn to me to heal them." Isaiah was referring to Jesus when he made this prediction, for he had seen a vision of the Messiah's glory.

However, even many of the Jewish leaders believed him to be the Messiah but wouldn't admit it to anyone because of their fear that the Pharisees would excommunicate them from the synagogue; for they loved the praise of men more than the praise of God.

*People in Jesus' time, like those in the time of Isaiah, would not believe despite the evidence (12:37). As a result, God hardened their hearts. Does that mean God intentionally prevented these people from believing in him? No, he simply confirmed their own choices. For such people, it is virtually impossible to come to God.*

### TEMPORARY PRAISE

Along with those who refused to believe, many believed but refused to admit it. This is just as bad, and Jesus had strong words for such people (see Matthew 10:32-33). People who will not take a stand for Jesus are afraid of rejection or ridicule. Many Jewish leaders wouldn't admit to faith in Jesus because they feared excommunication from the synagogue (which was their livelihood) and loss of their prestigious place in the community. But the praise of others is fickle and short-lived. We should be much more concerned about God's eternal acceptance than about the temporary approval of other people.

## Jesus summarizes his message

*JOHN 12:44-50 (Harmony 187)*

esus shouted to the crowds, "If you trust me, you are really trusting God. For when you see me, you are seeing the one who sent me. I have come as a Light to shine in this dark world, so that all who put their trust in me will no longer wander in the darkness. If anyone hears me and doesn't obey me, I am not his judge—for I have come to save the world and not to judge it. But all who reject me and my message will be judged at the Day of Judgment by the truths I have spoken. For these are not my own ideas, but I have told you what the Father said to tell you. And I know his instructions lead to eternal life; so whatever he tells me to say, I say!"

*We often wonder what God is like. How can we know the Creator when he doesn't make himself visible? Jesus said plainly that those who see him see God because he is God. If you want to know what God is like, study the person and words of Jesus Christ.*

### DECISION TIME

The purpose of Jesus' first mission on earth was not to judge people, but to show them the way to find salvation and eternal life. When he comes again, one of his main purposes will be to judge people for how they lived on earth. Christ's words that we would *not* accept and obey will condemn us. On the Day of Judgment, those who have accepted Jesus and have lived his way will be raised to eternal life (1 Corinthians 15:51-57; 1 Thessalonians 4:15-18; Revelation 21:1-7), and those who have rejected Jesus and have lived any way they pleased will face eternal punishment (Revelation 21:8). Decide now which side you'll be on, for the consequences of your decision last forever.

## Jesus says the disciples can pray for anything

### *MARK 11:20-25 (also in MATTHEW 21:18-22)*
### *(Harmony 188)*

*N*ext morning, as the disciples passed the fig tree he had cursed, they saw that it was withered from the roots! Then Peter remembered what Jesus had said to the tree on the previous day and exclaimed, "Look, Teacher! The fig tree you cursed has withered!"

In reply Jesus said to the disciples, "If you only have faith in God—this is the absolute truth—you can say to this Mount of Olives, 'Rise up and fall into the Mediterranean,' and your command will be obeyed. All that's required is that you really believe and have no doubt! Listen to me! You can pray for *anything,* and *if you believe, you have it;* it's yours! But when you are praying, first forgive anyone you are holding a grudge against, so that your Father in heaven will forgive you your sins too."

*Jesus' judgment on the fig tree occurred early in the spring fig season when the leaves usually would begin to bud. The figs normally grow as the leaves fill out, but this tree, though full of leaves, had no fruit. The tree looked promising but offered no figs. Jesus' harsh words to the fig tree could be applied to the nation of Israel. Fruitful in appearance only, Israel was spiritually barren.*

#### THE PRAYER OF FAITH

The kind of prayer that moves mountains is prayer for the fruitfulness of God's Kingdom. It would seem impossible to move a mountain into the sea, so Jesus used that picture to say that God can do anything. God will answer your prayers, but not as a result of your positive mental attitude. Other conditions must be met: (1) You must be a believer; (2) you must not hold a grudge against another person; (3) you must not pray with selfish motives; (4) your request must be for the good of God's Kingdom. To pray effectively, you need faith in *God,* not faith in the object of your request. If you focus only on your request, you will be left with nothing when your request is refused. Be a person of prayer, and watch God move mountains.

## Religious leaders challenge Jesus' authority

### MARK 11:26-33 (also in MATTHEW 21:23-27; LUKE 20:1-8) (Harmony 189)

By this time they had arrived in Jerusalem again, and as he was walking through the Temple area, the chief priests and other Jewish leaders came up to him demanding, "What's going on here? Who gave you the authority to drive out the merchants?"

Jesus replied, "I'll tell you if you answer one question! What about John the Baptist? Was he sent by God, or not? Answer me!"

They talked it over among themselves. "If we reply that God sent him, then he will say, 'All right, why didn't you accept him?' But if we say God didn't send him, then the people will start a riot." (For the people all believed strongly that John was a prophet.)

*Jesus took the Jewish leaders' trap and turned it back on them. How exasperated they must have been that they were unable to get Jesus to say anything that they could use against him!*

So they said, "We can't answer. We don't know."

To which Jesus replied, "Then I won't answer your question either!"

#### TRUE MOTIVES

The religious leaders asked Jesus who had given him the authority to chase away the merchants and money changers. Their question was a trap. If Jesus said his authority was from God, they would accuse him of blasphemy; if he said his authority was his own, they would dismiss him as a fanatic. To expose their real motives, Jesus countered their question with a question about John the Baptist. The leaders' silence proved that they were not interested in the truth. They simply wanted to get rid of Jesus because he was undermining their authority. Sometimes people will ask questions about your faith to try to trip you up or make fun of you. Others will ask questions, sincerely looking for answers. Spend your time with those who really want answers.

## Jesus tells the parable of the two sons

### MATTHEW 21:28-32 *(Harmony 190)*

*B*ut what do you think about this? A man with two sons told the older boy, 'Son, go out and work on the farm today.' 'I won't,' he answered, but later he changed his mind and went. Then the father told the youngest, 'You go!' and he said, 'Yes, sir, I will.' But he didn't. Which of the two was obeying his father?"

*This indictment surely made the Jewish leaders furious. That such people as evil men and prostitutes could be in heaven and not the pious leaders was absurd. But Jesus turns the world's values upside down.*

They replied, "The first, of course."

Then Jesus explained his meaning: "Surely evil men and prostitutes will get into the Kingdom before you do. For John the Baptist told you to repent and turn to God, and you wouldn't, while very evil men and prostitutes did. And even when you saw this happening, you refused to repent, and so you couldn't believe."

**PHONIES**

The son who said he would obey and then didn't represented the nation of Israel in Jesus' day. They said they wanted to do God's will, but they constantly disobeyed. They were phony, just going through the motions. It is dangerous to pretend to obey God when our hearts are far from him because God knows our true intentions. Our actions must match our words. *Knowing* God's will is not the same as *doing* it. Don't just go through the motions.

## Jesus tells the parable of the wicked farmers

### MATTHEW 21:33-46 *(also in MARK 12:1-12; LUKE 20:9-19) (Harmony 191)*

*N*ow listen to this story: A certain landowner planted a vine-yard with a hedge around it, and built a platform for the watchman, then leased the vineyard to some farmers on a sharecrop basis, and went away to live in another country.

"At the time of the grape harvest he sent his agents to the farmers to collect his share. But the farmers attacked his men, beat one, killed one, and stoned another.

"Then he sent a larger group of his men to collect for him, but the results were the same. Finally the owner sent his son, thinking they would surely respect him.

"But when these farmers saw the son coming, they said among themselves, 'Here comes the heir to this estate; come on, let's kill him and get it for ourselves!' So they dragged him out of the vineyard and killed him.

*Jesus referred to himself as the stone rejected by the builders. Although he would be rejected by most of the Jewish leaders, he would become the cornerstone of a new "building," the church (Acts 4:11-12). Likewise, Jesus' life and teaching would be the church's foundation.*

"When the owner returns, what do you think he will do to those farmers?"

The Jewish leaders replied, "He will put the wicked men to a horrible death and lease the vineyard to others who will pay him promptly."

Then Jesus asked them, "Didn't you ever read in the Scriptures: 'The stone rejected by the builders has been made the honored cornerstone; how remarkable! what an amazing thing the Lord has done'?

"What I mean is that the Kingdom of God shall be taken away from you, and given to a nation that will give God his share of the crop. All who stumble on this rock of truth shall be broken, but those it falls on will be scattered as dust."

When the chief priests and other Jewish leaders realized that Jesus was talking about them—that they were the farmers in his story—they wanted to get rid of him but were afraid to try because of the crowds, for they accepted Jesus as a prophet.

### STUMBLING STONE

The characters in this story are easily identified. Even the religious leaders got the point. The owner of the vineyard is God; the vineyard is Israel; the vinedressers are the religious leaders; the servants are the prophets and priests God sent to Israel; the son is the Messiah, Jesus; and the others are the Gentiles. Jesus' parable indirectly answered the religious leaders' question about his authority; it also showed them that he knew about their plan to kill him. There is no difference between those who ignore Christ and those who refuse to believe. All who stumble over Jesus, the Cornerstone, will be judged in the end. When sharing your faith, keep the focus on Christ. He's the only one who really matters.

## Jesus tells the parable of the wedding feast

*MATTHEW 22:1-14 (Harmony 192)*

*J*esus told several other stories to show what the Kingdom of Heaven is like.

"For instance," he said, "it can be illustrated by the story of a king who prepared a great wedding dinner for his son. Many guests were invited, and when the banquet was ready, he sent messengers to notify everyone that it was time to come. But all refused! So he sent other servants to tell them, 'Everything is ready and the roast is in the oven. Hurry!'

"But the guests he had invited merely laughed and went on about their business, one to his farm, another to his store; others beat up his messengers and treated them shamefully, even killing some of them.

"Then the angry king sent out his army and destroyed the murderers and burned their city. And he said to his servants, 'The wedding feast is ready, and the guests I invited aren't worthy of the honor. Now go out to the street corners and invite everyone you see.'

*It was customary for wedding guests to be given garments to wear to the dinner. It was unthinkable to refuse to wear these garments. That would insult the host, who could only assume that the guest was arrogant and thought he didn't need these garments, or that he or she did not want to take part in the wedding celebration. The wedding garments picture the righteousness needed to enter God's Kingdom.*

"So the servants did, and brought in all they could find, good and bad alike; and the banquet hall was filled with guests. But when the king came in to meet the guests, he noticed a man who wasn't wearing the wedding robe provided for him.

"'Friend,' he asked, 'how does it happen that you are here without a wedding robe?' And the man had no reply.

"Then the king said to his aides, 'Bind him hand and foot and throw him out into the outer darkness where there is weeping and gnashing of teeth.' For many are called, but few are chosen."

### R.S.V.P.

In this culture, two invitations were expected when wedding dinners were given. The first invitation asked the guests to attend; the second one announced that all was ready. In this story the king invited his guests three times, and each time they rejected his invitation. God wants us to join him at his table, which will last for eternity. That's why he sends us invitations again and again. What should you do to accept his invitation?

## Religious leaders question Jesus about taxes

*MARK 12:13-17 (also in MATTHEW 22:15-22;*
*LUKE 20:20-26) (Harmony 193)*

*B*ut they sent other religious and political leaders to talk with him and try to trap him into saying something he could be arrested for.

"Teacher," these spies said, "we know you tell the truth no matter what! You aren't influenced by the opinions and desires of men, but sincerely teach the ways of God. Now tell us, is it right to pay taxes to Rome, or not?"

Jesus saw their trick and said, "Show me a coin and I'll tell you."

When they handed it to him he asked, "Whose picture and title is this on the coin?" They replied, "The emperor's."

*The Pharisees were primarily a religious group concerned for ritual purity; the Herodians were a Jewish political group that approved of Herod's compromises with Rome. Normally the two groups totally avoided each other.*

"All right," he said, "if it is his, give it to him. But everything that belongs to God must be given to God!" And they scratched their heads in bafflement at his reply.

### WHOSE IMAGE?

Anyone who avoided paying taxes faced harsh penalties. The Jews hated to pay taxes to Rome because the money supported their oppressors and symbolized their subjection. Much of the tax money also went to maintain the heathen Temples and luxurious lifestyles of Rome's upper class. The Pharisees and Herodians hoped to trap Jesus with this tax question. A yes would mean that he supported Rome—this would turn the people against him. A no would bring accusations of treason and rebellion against Rome and could lead to civil penalties. But Jesus answered wisely, saying that the coin bearing the emperor's image should be given to the emperor. But human lives, which bear God's image, belong to God. Are you giving God all that is rightfully his? Give your life to God—you bear his image.

# Religious leaders question Jesus about the resurrection

*MARK 12:18-27 (also in MATTHEW 22:23-32;*
*LUKE 20:27-40) (Harmony 194)*

hen the Sadducees stepped forward—a group of men who say there is no resurrection. Here was their question:

"Teacher, Moses gave us a law that when a man dies without children, the man's brother should marry his widow and have children in his brother's name. Well, there were seven brothers and the oldest married and died, and left no children. So the second brother married the widow, but soon he died too and left no children. Then the next brother married her and died without children, and so on until all were dead, and still there were no children; and last of all, the woman died too.

*The Sadducees' real question was not about marriage but about the doctrine of resurrection. Because the Sadducees followed only the Pentateuch (Genesis through Deuteronomy), Jesus quoted from Exodus 3:6 to prove that there is life after death. God spoke of Abraham, Isaac, and Jacob years after their deaths as if they still lived. God's covenant with all people exists beyond death.*

"What we want to know is this: In the resurrection, whose wife will she be, for she had been the wife of each of them?"

Jesus replied, "Your trouble is that you don't know the Scriptures and don't know the power of God. For when these seven brothers and the woman rise from the dead, they won't be married—they will be like the angels.

"But now as to whether there will be a resurrection—have you never read in the book of Exodus about Moses and the burning bush? God said to Moses, 'I *am* the God of Abraham, and I *am* the God of Isaac, and I *am* the God of Jacob.'

"God was telling Moses that these men, though dead for hundreds of years, were still very much alive, for he would not have said, 'I *am* the God' of those who don't exist! You have made a serious error."

### FUTURE LIFE

What life will be like after the resurrection is far beyond our ability to understand or imagine (Isaiah 64:4; 1 Corinthians 2:9). We need not be afraid of eternal life because of the unknowns, however. Jesus' statement does not mean that people won't recognize their partners in the coming Kingdom. It simply means that God's new order will not be an extension of this life and that the same physical and natural rules won't apply. Instead of wondering what God's coming Kingdom will be like, we should concentrate on our relationship with Christ right now, because in the new Kingdom we will be with him. If we learn to love and trust Christ *now*, we will not be afraid of what he has in store for us then.

## October 18

### Religious leaders question Jesus about the greatest commandment

*MARK 12:28-34 (also in MATTHEW 22:33-40) (Harmony 195)*

One of the teachers of religion who was standing there listening to the discussion realized that Jesus had answered well. So he asked, "Of all the commandments, which is the most important?"

Jesus replied, "The one that says, 'Hear, O Israel! The Lord our God is the one and only God. And you must love him with all your heart and soul and mind and strength.'

"The second is: 'You must love others as much as yourself.' No other commandments are greater than these."

The teacher of religion replied, "Sir, you have spoken a true word in saying that there is only one God and no other. And I know it is far more important to love him with all my heart and understanding and strength, and to love others as myself, than to offer all kinds of sacrifices on the altar of the Temple."

Realizing this man's understanding, Jesus said to him, "You are not far from the Kingdom of God." And after that, no one dared ask him any more questions.

*The Pharisees, who had classified over six hundred laws, often tried to distinguish the more important from the less important. But they failed to see that all the commands in the Old Testament lead to Christ.*

#### LAW OF LOVE

God's laws are not burdensome. They can be reduced to two simple principles: 1 Love God and 2) love others. These commands are from the Old Testament (Deuteronomy 6:5; Leviticus 19:18). When you love God completely and care for others as you care for yourself, then you have fulfilled the intent of the Ten Commandments and the other Old Testament laws. According to Jesus, these two commandments summarize all God's laws. Let them rule your thoughts, decisions, and actions. When you are uncertain about what to do, ask yourself which course of action best demonstrates love for God and love for others.

## Religious leaders cannot answer Jesus' question

*MATTHEW 22:41-46 (also in MARK 12:35-37;*
*LUKE 20:41-44) (Harmony 196)*

hen, surrounded by the Pharisees, he asked them a question: "What about the Messiah? Whose son is he?"

"The son of David," they replied.

"Then why does David, speaking under the inspiration of the Holy Spirit, call him 'Lord'?" Jesus asked. "For David said,

'God said to my Lord, Sit at my right hand until I put your enemies beneath your feet.'

"Since David called him 'Lord,' how can he be merely his son?"

They had no answer. And after that no one dared ask him any more questions.

*The Jewish religious leaders should have been the first to recognize Jesus as the promised Messiah, rejoice over his arrival, and lead the nation to follow him. Instead, they refused to believe.*

### THE MOST IMPORTANT QUESTION

The Pharisees and Sadducees had asked their questions. Then Jesus turned the tables and asked them a question that went right to the heart of the matter—what they thought about the Messiah's identity. The Pharisees knew that the Messiah would be a descendant of David, but they did not understand that he would be more than a human descendant—he would be God in the flesh. Jesus quoted from Psalm 110:1 to show that David had known that the Messiah would be both human and divine. The Pharisees expected only a human ruler to restore Israel's greatness as in the days of David and Solomon.

The central issue of life is what we believe about Jesus. Other spiritual questions are irrelevant unless we first decide to believe that Jesus is who he said.

## Jesus warns against the religious leaders

*MATTHEW 23:1-12 (also in MARK 12:38-40;*
*LUKE 20:45-47) (Harmony 197)*

When Jesus said to the crowds, and to his disciples, "You would think these Jewish leaders and these Pharisees were Moses, the way they keep making up so many laws! And of course you should obey their every whim! It may be all right to do what they say, but above anything else, *don't follow their example.* For they don't do what they tell you to do. They load you with impossible demands that they themselves don't even try to keep.

*The little prayer boxes, called phylacteries, contained Scripture verses. Very religious people wore these boxes on their forehead and arms in order to obey Deuteronomy 6:8 and Exodus 13:9, 16. But the prayer boxes had become more important for the status they gave than for the truth they contained.*

"Everything they do is done for show. They act holy by wearing on their arms little prayer boxes with Scripture verses inside, and by lengthening the memorial fringes of their robes. And how they love to sit at the head table at banquets and in the reserved pews in the synagogue! How they enjoy the deference paid them on the streets and to be called 'Rabbi' and 'Master'! Don't ever let anyone call you that. For only God is your Rabbi and all of you are on the same level, as brothers. And don't address anyone here on earth as 'Father,' for only God in heaven should be addressed like that. And don't be called 'Master,' for only one is your master, even the Messiah.

"The more lowly your service to others, the greater you are. To be the greatest, be a servant. But those who think themselves great shall be disappointed and humbled; and those who humble themselves shall be exalted."

### MAKE SURE THEY MATCH

Jesus again exposed the hypocritical attitudes of the religious leaders who knew the Scriptures but did not live by them. The Pharisees' traditions and their interpretations and applications of the laws had become as important to them as God's Law itself. Their laws were not all bad—some were beneficial. Usually Jesus did not condemn what the Pharisees taught but what they *were*—hypocrites. They didn't care about *being* holy—just *looking* holy in order to receive the people's admiration and praise. Today, like the Pharisees, many people who know the Bible do not let it change their lives. They say they follow Jesus, but they don't live by his standards of love. Make sure that your actions match your beliefs.

## Jesus condemns the religious leaders

### MATTHEW 23:13-36 *(Harmony 198)*

*W*oe to you, Pharisees, and you other religious leaders. Hypocrites! For you won't let others enter the Kingdom of Heaven and won't go in yourselves. And you pretend to be holy, with all your long, public prayers in the streets, while you are evicting widows from their homes. Hypocrites! Yes, woe upon you hypocrites. For you go to all lengths to make one convert, and then turn him into twice the son of hell you are yourselves. Blind guides! Woe upon you! For your rule is that to swear 'By God's Temple' means nothing—you can break that oath, but to swear 'By the gold in the Temple' is binding! Blind fools! Which is greater, the gold, or the Temple that sanctifies the gold? And you say that to take an oath 'By the altar' can be broken, but to swear 'By the gifts on the altar' is binding! Blind! For which is greater, the gift on the altar, or the altar itself that sanctifies the gift? When you swear 'By the altar,' you are swearing by it and everything on it, and when you swear 'By the Temple,' you are swearing by it and by God who lives in it. And when you swear 'By heavens,' you are swearing by the Throne of God and by God himself.

*Being a religious leader in Jerusalem was very different from being a pastor in a secular society today. Israel's history, culture, and daily life centered around its relationship with God. The religious leaders were the best known, most powerful, and most respected of all leaders. Jesus made these stinging accusations because the leaders' hunger for more power, money, and status had made them lose sight of God, and their blindness was spreading to the whole nation.*

"Yes, woe upon you, Pharisees, and you other religious leaders—hypocrites! For you tithe down to the last mint leaf in your garden, but ignore the important things—justice and mercy and faith. Yes, you should tithe, but you shouldn't leave the more important things undone. Blind guides! You strain out a gnat and swallow a camel.

"Woe to you, Pharisees, and you religious leaders—hypocrites! You are so careful to polish the outside of the cup, but the inside is foul with extortion and greed. Blind Pharisees! First cleanse the inside of the cup, and then the whole cup will be clean.

"Woe to you, Pharisees, and you religious leaders! You are like beautiful mausoleums—full of dead men's bones, and of foulness and corruption. You try to look like saintly men, but underneath those pious robes of yours are hearts besmirched with every sort of hypocrisy and sin.

"Yes, woe to you, Pharisees, and you religious leaders—hypocrites! For you build monuments to the prophets killed by your fathers and lay flowers on the graves of the godly men they destroyed, and say, 'We certainly would never have acted as our fathers did.'

"In saying that, you are accusing yourselves of being the sons of wicked men. And you are following in their steps, filling up the full measure of their evil. Snakes! Sons of vipers! How shall you escape the judgment of hell?

"I will send you prophets, and wise men, and inspired writers, and you will kill some by crucifixion, and rip open the backs of others with whips in your synagogues, and hound them from city to city, so that you will become guilty of all the blood of murdered godly men from righteous Abel to Zechariah (son of Barachiah), slain by you in the Temple between the altar and the sanctuary. Yes, all the accumulated judgment of the centuries shall break upon the heads of this very generation."

### DON'T SWALLOW A CAMEL!

The Pharisees strained their water so they wouldn't accidentally swallow a gnat—an unclean insect according to the Law. Meticulous about the details of ceremonial cleanliness, they nevertheless had lost their perspective on inner purity. Ceremonially clean on the outside, they had corrupt hearts. It's possible to obey the details of the laws but still be disobedient in our general behavior. Jesus condemned the Pharisees and religious leaders for outwardly appearing saintly and holy but inwardly remaining full of corruption and greed. Living our Christianity merely as a show for others is like washing a cup on the outside only. When we are clean on the inside, our cleanliness on the outside won't be a sham.

*October 22*

## Jesus grieves over Jerusalem again

### MATTHEW 23:37-39 *(Harmony 199)*

 Jerusalem, Jerusalem, the city that kills the prophets and stones all those God sends to her! How often I have wanted to gather your children together as a hen gathers her chicks beneath her wings, but you wouldn't let me. And now your house is left to you, desolate. For I tell you this, you will never see me again until you are ready to welcome the one sent to you from God."

### PROTECTION

Here we see the depth of Jesus' feelings for lost people and for his beloved city, which would soon be destroyed. Jesus wanted to gather his people together as a hen protects her chicks under her wings, but they wouldn't let him. Jesus also wants to protect us if we will just come to him. Many times we hurt and don't know where to turn. We reject Christ's help because we don't think he can give us what we need. But who knows our needs better than our Creator? Those who turn to Jesus will find that he helps and comforts as no one else can.

*Jerusalem was the capital city of God's chosen people, the home of David, Israel's greatest king, and the location of the Temple, the earthly dwelling place of God. It was intended to be the center of worship of the true God and a symbol of justice to all people. But Jerusalem had become blind to God and insensitive to human need.*

*October 23*

## A poor widow gives all she has

***MARK 12:41-44 (also in LUKE 21:1-4) (Harmony 200)***

hen he went over to the collection boxes in the Temple and sat and watched as the crowds dropped in their money. Some who were rich put in large amounts. Then a poor widow came and dropped in two pennies.

He called his disciples to him and remarked, "That poor widow has given more than all those rich men put together! For they gave a little of their extra fat, while she gave up her last penny."

### GIFTS THAT COUNT

In the Lord's eyes, this poor widow had given more than all the others put together, although her gift was by far the smallest. She had given all she had to live on, in contrast to the way most of us handle our money. When we consider giving a certain percentage of our income a great accomplishment, we resemble those who had given "what they didn't

*Jesus was in the area of the Temple called the Court of Women. The treasury was located there or in an adjoining walkway. In this area were seven boxes in which worshipers could deposit their Temple tax and six boxes for freewill offerings like the one given by this woman.*

need." Here, Jesus was admiring generous and sacrificial giving. Not only was she poor; as a widow she had few resources for making money. Her small gift was a sacrifice, but she gave it willingly. As believers, we should consider increasing our giving—whether of money, time, or talents—to a point beyond convenience or safety.

*October 24*

---

## Jesus tells about the future

### *MARK 13:1-4 (also in MATTHEW 24:1-3; LUKE 21:5-7) (Harmony 201a)*

As he was leaving the Temple that day, one of his disciples said, "Teacher, what beautiful buildings these are! Look at the decorated stonework on the walls."

Jesus replied, "Yes, look! For not one stone will be left upon another, except as ruins."

And as he sat on the slopes of the Mount of Olives across the valley from Jerusalem, Peter, James, John, and Andrew got alone with him and asked him, "Just when is all this going to happen to the Temple? Will there be some warning ahead of time?"

*The Mount of Olives rises above Jerusalem to the east. From its slopes a person can look down into the city and see the Temple. Zechariah 14:1-4 predicts that the Messiah will stand on this very mountain when he returns to set up his eternal Kingdom.*

**BE READY**

The disciples wanted to know when the Temple would be destroyed. Jesus gave them a prophetic picture of that time, including events leading up to it. He also talked about future events connected with his return to earth to judge all people. Jesus predicted both near and distant events without putting them in chronological order. Some of the disciples lived to see the destruction of Jerusalem in A.D. 70. This event would assure them that everything else Jesus predicted would also happen.

Jesus warned his followers about the future so that they could learn how to live in the present. Many predictions Jesus made in this passage have not yet been fulfilled. He did not make them so that we would guess when they might be fulfilled, but to help us remain spiritually alert and prepared at all times as we wait for his return. What changes would you make if you knew that Jesus would return one of these days? Be ready for his second coming.

## Jesus tells about the future

### MARK 13:5-13 (also in MATTHEW 24:4-14; LUKE 21:8-19) (Harmony 201b)

So Jesus launched into an extended reply. "Don't let anyone mislead you," he said, "for many will come declaring themselves to be your Messiah and will lead many astray. And wars will break out near and far, but this is not the signal of the end-time.

"For nations and kingdoms will proclaim war against each other, and there will be earthquakes in many lands, and famines. These herald only the early stages of the anguish ahead. But when these things begin to happen, watch out! For you will be in great danger. You will be dragged before the courts, and beaten in the synagogues, and accused before governors and kings of being my followers. This is your opportunity to tell them the Good News. And the Good News must first be made known in every nation before the end-time finally comes. But when you are arrested and stand trial, don't worry about what to say in your defense. Just say what God tells you to. Then you will not be speaking, but the Holy Spirit will.

*Jesus predicted that his followers would be severely persecuted by those who hated what he stood for. In the midst of terrible persecutions, however, they could have hope, knowing that salvation was theirs.*

"Brothers will betray each other to death, fathers will betray their own children, and children will betray their parents to be killed. And everyone will hate you because you are mine. But all who endure to the end without renouncing me shall be saved."

#### END SIGNS

What are the signs of the end times? There have been people in every generation since Christ's resurrection claiming to know exactly when Jesus will return. No one has been right yet, however, because Christ will return on God's timetable, not ours. Jesus predicted that before his return, many believers would be misled by false teachers claiming to have revelations from God.

According to Scripture, the one clear sign of Christ's return will be his unmistakable appearance in the clouds which will be seen by all people (13:26; Revelation 1:7). In other words, you do not have to wonder whether a certain person is the Messiah or whether these are the "end times." When Jesus returns, *you will know* beyond a doubt because it will be evident to all true believers. Beware of groups who claim special knowledge of the last days, because no one knows when that time will be (13:32). Be cautious about saying, "This is it!" but be bold in your total commitment to have your heart and life ready for Christ's return.

*October 26*

---

## Jesus tells about the future

### MATTHEW 24:15-22 (also in MARK 13:14-20; LUKE 21:20-24) (Harmony 201c)

So, when you see the horrible thing (told about by Daniel the prophet) standing in a holy place (Note to the reader: You know what is meant!), then those in Judea must flee into the Judean hills. Those on their porches must not even go inside to pack before they flee. Those in the fields should not return to their homes for their clothes.

"And woe to pregnant women and to those with babies in those days. And pray that your flight will not be in winter, or on the Sabbath. For there will be persecution such as the world has never before seen in all its history and will never see again.

*While the "horrible thing" has specific applications in history, it also can be seen as any deliberate attempt to mock and deny the reality of God's presence.*

"In fact, unless those days are shortened, all mankind will perish. But they will be shortened for the sake of God's chosen people."

#### NEEDED KNOWLEDGE

The "horrible thing" is the desecration of the Temple by God's enemies. This has happened repeatedly in Israel's history: in 597 B.C. when Nebuchadnezzar looted the Temple and took Judean captives to Babylon (2 Chronicles 36); in 168 B.C. when Antiochus Epiphanes sacrificed a pig to Zeus on the sacred Temple altar (Daniel 9:27; 11:30-31); in A.D. 70 when the Roman general Titus placed an idol on the site of the burned-out Temple after the destruction of Jerusalem. Just a few years after Jesus gave this warning the emperor Caligula made plans to put a statue of himself in the Temple, but he died before this could be carried out. Talking about the end times, Jesus telescoped near future and far future events, as did the Old Testament prophets. Many of these persecutions have already occurred; more are yet to come. But God is in control of even the length of each persecution. He will not forget his people. This is all we need to know about the future to motivate us to live rightly now.

## Jesus tells about his return

### MATTHEW 24:23-28 (also in MARK 13:21-23)
### (Harmony 202a)

*T*hen if anyone tells you, 'The Messiah has arrived at such and such a place, or has appeared here or there,' don't believe it. For false Christs shall arise, and false prophets, and will do wonderful miracles so that if it were possible, even God's chosen ones would be deceived. See, I have warned you.

"So if someone tells you the Messiah has returned and is out in the desert, don't bother to go and look. Or, that he is hiding at a certain place, don't believe it! For as the lightning flashes across the sky from east to west, so shall my coming be, when I, the Messiah, return. And wherever the carcass is, there the vultures will gather."

*Jesus' warnings about false teachers still hold true. Upon close examination we can see that many nice-sounding messages don't agree with God's message in the Bible. Only a solid foundation in God's Word can equip believers to perceive the errors and distortions in false teaching.*

**DECEPTIONS**

Is it possible for Christians to be deceived? Yes. So convincing will be the arguments and proofs from deceivers in the end times that it will be difficult *not* to fall away from Christ. If we are prepared, Jesus says, we can remain faithful. But if we are not prepared, we will turn away. To penetrate the disguises of false teachers we can ask: (1) Have their predictions come true, or do they have to revise them to fit what's already happened? (2) Does any teaching utilize a small section of the Bible to the neglect of the whole? (3) Does the teaching contradict what the Bible says about God? (4) Are the practices meant to glorify the teacher or Christ? (5) Do the teachings promote hostility toward other Christians?

# Jesus tells about his return

*MATTHEW 24:29-35 (also in MARK 13:24-31;*
*LUKE 21:25-33) (Harmony 202b)*

mmediately after the persecution of those days the sun will be darkened, and the moon will not give light, and the stars will seem to fall from the heavens, and the powers overshadowing the earth will be convulsed.

"And then at last the signal of my coming will appear in the heavens, and there will be deep mourning all around the earth. And the nations of the world will see me arrive in the clouds of heaven, with power and great glory. And I shall send forth my angels with the sound of a mighty trumpet blast, and they shall gather my chosen ones from the farthest ends of the earth and heaven.

*The nations of the earth will mourn because unbelievers will suddenly realize that they have chosen the wrong side. Everything they have mocked will be happening, and it will be too late for them.*

"Now learn a lesson from the fig tree. When her branch is tender and the leaves begin to sprout, you know that summer is almost here. Just so, when you see all these things beginning to happen, you can know that my return is near, even at the doors. Then at last this age will come to its close.

"Heaven and earth will disappear, but my words remain forever. But no one knows the date and hour when the end will be—not even the angels. No, nor even God's Son. Only the Father knows."

### ETERNAL TRUTH

In Jesus' day the world seemed concrete, dependable, and permanent. These days many people fear its destruction by nuclear war. Jesus tells us, however, that even if the earth should pass away, the truth of his words will never be changed or abolished. God and his Word provide the only stability in our unstable world. How shortsighted people are who spend their time learning about this temporary world and accumulating its possessions, while neglecting the Bible and its eternal truths!

## Jesus tells about remaining watchful

*MATTHEW 24:36-51 (also in MARK 13:32-37;*
*LUKE 21:34-38) (Harmony 203)*

*T*he world will be at ease—banquets and parties and weddings—just as it was in Noah's time before the sudden coming of the Flood; people wouldn't believe what was going to happen until the Flood actually arrived and took them all away. So shall my coming be.

"Two men will be working together in the fields, and one will be taken, the other left. Two women will be going about their household tasks; one will be taken, the other left.

"So be prepared, for you don't know what day your Lord is coming.

"Just as a man can prevent trouble from thieves by keeping watch for them, so you can avoid trouble by always being ready for my unannounced return.

"Are you a wise and faithful servant of the Lord? Have I given you the task of managing my household, to feed my children day by day? Blessings on you if I return and find you faithfully doing your work. I will put such faithful ones in charge of everything I own!

*When Jesus said that even he did not know the time of the end, he was affirming his humanity. Of course God the Father knows the time, and Jesus and the Father are one. But when Jesus became a man, he voluntarily gave up the unlimited use of his divine attributes. The emphasis of this verse is not on Jesus' lack of knowledge, but rather on the fact that no one knows. It is God the Father's secret to be revealed when he wills.*

"But if you are evil and say to yourself, 'My Lord won't be coming for a while,' and begin oppressing your fellow servants, partying and getting drunk, your Lord will arrive unannounced and unexpected, and severely whip you and send you off to the judgment of the hypocrites; there will be weeping and gnashing of teeth."

#### WHILE WAITING . . .

Jesus' words here tell us how to live while we wait for his return: (1) We are not to be misled by confusing claims or speculative interpretations of what will happen. (2) We should not be afraid to tell people about Christ, despite what they might say or do to us. (3) We must stand firm by faith and not be surprised by persecutions. (4) We must be morally alert, obedient to the commands for living found in God's Word. Jesus didn't want to promote discussions on prophetic timetables. We're not supposed to "figure out" when he's coming back. Instead, it is good that we *don't* know exactly when Christ will return. If we knew the precise date, we might be tempted to be lazy in our work for Christ. Worse yet, we might plan to keep sinning and then turn to God right at the end. Heaven is not our only goal; we have work to do here. And we must keep on doing it until death or until we see the unmistakable return of our Savior.

*October 30*

## Jesus tells the parable of the ten bridesmaids

### MATTHEW 25:1-13 *(Harmony 204)*

The Kingdom of Heaven can be illustrated by the story of ten bridesmaids who took their lamps and went to meet the bridegroom. But only five of them were wise enough to fill their lamps with oil, while the other five were foolish and forgot.

"So, when the bridegroom was delayed, they lay down to rest until midnight, when they were roused by the shout, 'The bridegroom is coming! Come out and welcome him!'

"All the girls jumped up and trimmed their lamps. Then the five who hadn't any oil begged the others to share with them, for their lamps were going out.

*This parable is about a wedding. On the wedding day the bridegroom went to the bride's house for the ceremony; then the bride and groom, along with a great procession, would return to the groom's house for a great feast, often lasting a week.*

"But the others replied, 'We haven't enough. Go instead to the shops and buy some for yourselves.'

"But while they were gone, the bridegroom came, and those who were ready went in with him to the marriage feast, and the door was locked.

"Later, when the other five returned, they stood outside, calling, 'Sir, open the door for us!'

"But he called back, 'Go away! It is too late!'

"So stay awake and be prepared, for you do not know the date or moment of my return."

#### DON'T BE OUT SHOPPING

These ten virgins were waiting to join the bride and groom in their wedding procession, and they hoped to take part in the wedding banquet. But when the groom didn't come at the expected time, five of them were out of lamp oil. By the time they had purchased extra oil, it was too late to join the feast. When Jesus returns to take his people to heaven, we must be ready. Spiritual preparation cannot be bought or borrowed at the last minute. Our relationship with God must be our own. Christ's second coming will be swift and sudden. There will be no opportunity for last-minute repentance or bargaining. The choice we have already made will determine our eternal destiny.

*October 31*

## Jesus tells the parable of the loaned money

*MATTHEW 25:14-30 (Harmony 205)*

Again, the Kingdom of Heaven can be illustrated by the story of a man going into another country, who called together his servants and loaned them money to invest for him while he was gone.

"He gave $5,000 to one, $2,000 to another, and $1,000 to the last—dividing it in proportion to their abilities—and then left on his trip. The man who received the $5,000 began immediately to buy and sell with it and soon earned another $5,000. The man with $2,000 went right to work, too, and earned another $2,000.

*This last man was thinking only of himself. He hoped to play it safe and protect himself from his hard master; thus he was judged for his self-centeredness. We must not make excuses to avoid doing what God calls us to do.*

"But the man who received the $1,000 dug a hole in the ground and hid the money for safekeeping.

"After a long time their master returned from his trip and called them to him to account for his money. The man to whom he had entrusted the $5,000 brought him $10,000.

"His master praised him for good work. 'You have been faithful in handling this small amount,' he told him, 'so now I will give you many more responsibilities. Begin the joyous tasks I have assigned to you.'

"Next came the man who had received the $2,000, with the report, 'Sir, you gave me $2,000 to use, and I have doubled it.'

"'Good work,' his master said. 'You are a good and faithful servant. You have been faithful over this small amount, so now I will give you much more.'

"Then the man with the $1,000 came and said, 'Sir, I knew you were a hard man, and I was afraid you would rob me of what I earned, so I hid your money in the earth and here it is!'

"But his master replied, 'Wicked man! Lazy slave! Since you knew I would demand your profit, you should at least have put my money into the bank so I could have some interest. Take the money from this man and give it to the man with the $10,000. For the man who uses well what he is given shall be given more, and he shall have abundance. But from the man who is unfaithful, even what little responsibility he has shall be taken from him. And throw the useless servant out into outer darkness: there shall be weeping and gnashing of teeth.'"

### A GOOD INVESTMENT

The master divided the money among his servants according to their abilities. No one received more or less than he could handle. If he failed in his assignment, his excuse could not be that he was overwhelmed. Failure could come only from laziness or hatred toward the master. The talents represent any kind of resource we are given. God gives us time, gifts, and other resources according to our abilities, and he expects us to invest them wisely until he returns. Our time, abilities, and money aren't ours in the first place—we are caretakers, not owners. We are responsible to use well what God has given us. The issue is not how much we have, but how well we use what we have.

## Jesus tells about the final judgment

### *MATTHEW 25:31-46 (Harmony 206)*

*B*ut when I, the Messiah, shall come in my glory, and all the angels with me, then I shall sit upon my throne of glory. And all the nations shall be gathered before me. And I will separate the people as a shepherd separates the sheep from the goats, and place the sheep at my right hand, and the goats at my left.

"Then I, the King, shall say to those at my right, 'Come, blessed of my Father, into the Kingdom prepared for you from the founding of the world. For I was hungry and you fed me; I was thirsty and you gave me water; I was a stranger and you invited me into your homes; naked and you clothed me; sick and in prison, and you visited me.'

*Jesus used sheep and goats to picture the division between believers and unbelievers. Sheep and goats often grazed together but were separated when it came time to shear the sheep. Ezekiel 34:17-24 also refers to the separation of sheep and goats.*

"Then these righteous ones will reply, 'Sir, when did we ever see you hungry and feed you? Or thirsty and give you anything to drink? Or a stranger, and help you? Or naked, and clothe you? When did we ever see you sick or in prison, and visit you?'

"And I, the King, will tell them, 'When you did it to these my brothers, you were doing it to me!' Then I will turn to those on my left and say, 'Away with you, you cursed ones, into the eternal fire prepared for the devil and his demons. For I was hungry and you wouldn't feed me; thirsty, and you wouldn't give me anything to drink; a stranger, and you refused me hospitality; naked, and you wouldn't clothe me; sick, and in prison, and you didn't visit me.'

"Then they will reply, 'Lord, when did we ever see you hungry or thirsty or a stranger or naked or sick or in prison, and not help you?'

"And I will answer, 'When you refused to help the least of these my brothers, you were refusing help to me.'

"And they shall go away into eternal punishment; but the righteous into everlasting life."

#### THE GREAT PRETENDERS

God will separate his obedient followers from pretenders and unbelievers. The real evidence of our belief is the way we act. To treat all persons we encounter as if they were

Jesus is no easy task. What we do for others demonstrates what we really think about Jesus' words to us—feed the hungry, give the homeless a place to stay, look after the sick. These acts do not depend on wealth, ability, or intelligence; they are simple acts freely given and freely received. We have no excuse to neglect those who have deep needs, and we cannot hand over this responsibility to the church or government. Jesus demands our personal involvement in caring for others' needs (Isaiah 58:7). How well do your actions separate you from pretenders and unbelievers?

*November 2*

---

## Religious leaders plot to kill Jesus

### *MATTHEW 26:1-5 (also in MARK 14:1-2; LUKE 22:1-2) (Harmony 207)*

*W*hen Jesus had finished this talk with his disciples, he told them,
"As you know, the Passover celebration begins in two days, and I shall be betrayed and crucified."

At that very moment the chief priests and other Jewish officials were meeting at the residence of Caiaphas the high priest, to discuss ways of capturing Jesus quietly and killing him. "But not during the Passover celebration," they agreed, "for there would be a riot."

*All Jewish males over the age of twelve were required to go to Jerusalem for the Passover feast, followed by a seven-day festival called the Festival of Unleavened Bread. For these feasts, Jews from all over the Roman Empire converged on Jerusalem to celebrate one of the most important events in their history.*

**EASY TO JUSTIFY**

Caiaphas was the ruling high priest during Jesus' ministry. He was the son-in-law of Annas, the previous high priest. The Roman government had taken over the process of appointing all political and religious leaders. Caiaphas served for eighteen years, longer than most high priests, suggesting that he was gifted at cooperating with the Romans. He was the first to recommend Jesus' death in order to "save" the nation (John 11:49-50). This was a deliberate plot to kill Jesus. Without this plot there would have been no groundswell of popular opinion against him. In fact, because of Jesus' popularity, the religious leaders were afraid to arrest him during the Passover; they did not want their actions to incite a riot. So these religious leaders, so pious in their self-righteousness and law-keeping, were at the high priest's house planning murder. We can criticize these leaders (and rightfully so), but we should admit that it is easy to justify our sinful actions! Be honest about sin—don't rationalize.

## Judas agrees to betray Jesus

**LUKE 22:3-6 (also in MATTHEW 26:14-16;**
**MARK 14:10-11)** *(Harmony 208)*

hen Satan entered into Judas Iscariot, who was one of the twelve disciples, and he went over to the chief priests and captains of the Temple guards to discuss the best way to betray Jesus to them. They were, of course, delighted to know that he was ready to help them and promised him a reward. So he began to look for an opportunity for them to arrest Jesus quietly when the crowds weren't around.

*Satan's part in the betrayal of Jesus does not remove any of the responsibility from Judas. Disillusioned because Jesus had been talking about dying rather than about setting up his Kingdom, Judas may have been trying to force Jesus' hand and make him use his power to prove he was the Messiah.*

**WEAK SPOTS**

Why would Judas want to betray Jesus? Judas, like the other disciples, expected Jesus to start a political rebellion and overthrow Rome. As treasurer, Judas certainly assumed that he would be given an important position in Jesus' new government. However, Judas soon realized that Jesus' Kingdom was not physical or political, but spiritual. Judas's greedy desire for money and status could not be realized if he followed Jesus, so he betrayed Jesus in exchange for money and favor from the religious leaders. Judas allowed his desires to put him in a position where Satan could manipulate him. Satan is good at finding our weak spots and trying to use them for his purposes. That's why it's so important to yield every part of your life to Christ. Recognize your weak spots and yield them to Jesus' power.

## Disciples prepare for the Passover

**LUKE 22:7-13 (also in MATTHEW 26:17-19;**
**MARK 14:12-16)** *(Harmony 209)*

ow the day of the Passover celebration arrived, when the Passover lamb was killed and eaten with the unleavened bread. Jesus sent Peter and John ahead to find a place to prepare their Passover meal.

"Where do you want us to go?" they asked.

And he replied, "As soon as you enter Jerusalem, you will see a man walking along carrying a pitcher of water. Follow him into the house he enters, and say to the man who lives there, 'Our Teacher says for you to show us the guest room where he can eat the Passover meal with his disciples.' He will take you upstairs to a large room all ready for us. That is the place. Go ahead and prepare the meal there."

They went off to the city and found everything just as Jesus had said, and prepared the Passover supper.

*The Passover meal included the sacrifice of a lamb because of the association with the Exodus from Egypt. When the Jews were getting ready to leave, God told them to kill a lamb and paint its blood on the doorposts of their houses. They then were to prepare the meat for food. Peter and John had to buy and prepare the lamb as well as the unleavened bread, herbs, wine, and other ceremonial food.*

#### REMEMBERING

Passover became an annual remembrance of how God delivered the Hebrews from Egypt. Each year the people would pause to remember the day when the destroyer (God's angel of death) had passed over their homes. They would give thanks to God for saving them from death and bringing them out of a land of slavery and sin. Believers today have experienced a day of deliverance as well—the day we were delivered from spiritual death and slavery to sin. The Lord's Supper is our Passover remembrance of our new life and freedom from sin. The next time struggles and trials come, remember how God has delivered you in the past and focus on his promise of new life with him.

*November 5*

## Jesus washes the disciples' feet

### JOHN 13:1-11 (Harmony 210a)

Jesus knew on the evening of Passover Day that it would be his last night on earth before returning to his Father. During supper the devil had already suggested to Judas Iscariot, Simon's son, that this was the night to carry out his plan to betray Jesus. Jesus knew that the Father had given him everything and that he had come from God and would return to God. And how he loved his disciples! So he got up from the supper table, took off his robe, wrapped a towel around his loins, poured water into a basin, and began to wash the disciples' feet and to wipe them with the towel he had around him.

When he came to Simon Peter, Peter said to him, "Master, you shouldn't be washing our feet like this!"

Jesus replied, "You don't understand now why I am doing it; some day you will."

"No," Peter protested, "you shall never wash my feet!"

"But if I don't, you can't be my partner," Jesus replied.

Simon Peter exclaimed, "Then wash my hands and head as well—not just my feet!"

*John 13–17 tells us what Jesus said to his disciples on the night before his death. These words were all spoken in one evening. With only the disciples as his audience, Jesus gave final instructions to prepare them for his death and resurrection, events that would change their lives forever.*

Jesus replied, "One who has bathed all over needs only to have his feet washed to be entirely clean. Now you are clean—but that isn't true of everyone here." For Jesus knew who would betray him. That is what he meant when he said, "Not all of you are clean."

### TRUE LEADERS

Imagine being Peter and watching Jesus wash the others' feet, all the while moving closer to you. Seeing his Master behave like a slave must have confused Peter. He still did not understand Jesus' teaching that to be a leader, a person must be a servant. This is not a comfortable passage for leaders who find it difficult to serve those beneath them. The world's system of leadership is very different from leadership in God's Kingdom. Worldly leaders are often selfish and arrogant as they claw their way to the top. (Some kings in the ancient world gave themselves the title "Benefactor.") But among Christians, the leader is to be the one who *serves* best. There are different styles of leadership—some lead through public speaking, some through administering, some through relationships—but every Christian leader needs a servant's heart. How do you treat those who work under you (whether children, employees, or volunteers)? Ask the people you lead how you can serve them better.

*November 6*

---

## Jesus washes the disciples' feet

### *JOHN 13:12-20 (Harmony 210b)*

After washing their feet he put on his robe again and sat down and asked, "Do you understand what I was doing? You call me 'Master' and 'Lord,' and you do well to say it, for it is true. And since I, the Lord and Teacher, have washed your feet, you ought to wash each other's feet. I have given you an example to follow: do as I have done to you. How true it is that a servant is not greater than his master. Nor is the messenger more important than the one who sends him. You know these things—now do them! That is the path of blessing.

*Jesus did not wash his disciples' feet just to get them to be nice to each other. His far greater goal for them was to extend his mission on earth after he had left them. These men were to move into the world, serving God, each other, and all people to whom they took the message of salvation.*

"I am not saying these things to all of you; I know so well each one of you I chose. The Scripture declares, 'One who eats supper with me will betray me,' and this will soon come true. I tell you this now so that when it happens, you will believe on me.

"Truly, anyone welcoming my messenger is welcoming me. And to welcome me is to welcome the Father who sent me."

### FOLLOW THROUGH

Jesus was the model servant, and he showed his servant attitude to his disciples. Washing guests' feet was a job for a household servant to carry out when guests arrived. But Jesus wrapped a towel around his waist, as the lowliest slave would do, and washed and dried his disciples' feet. If even he, God in the flesh, is willing to serve, we his followers must also be servants, willing to serve in any way that glorifies God. Are you willing to follow Christ's example of serving? Whom can you serve today? There is a special blessing for those who not only agree that humble service is Christ's way but who also follow through and do it (13:17).

## November 7

## Jesus and his disciples have the Last Supper

*JOHN 13:21-30 (also in MATTHEW 26:20-29; MARK 14:17-25; LUKE 22:14-30 (Harmony 211)*

Now Jesus was in great anguish of spirit and exclaimed, "Yes, it is true—one of you will betray me." The disciples looked at each other, wondering whom he could mean. Since I was sitting next to Jesus at the table, being his closest friend, Simon Peter motioned to me to ask him who it was who would do this terrible deed.

So I turned and asked him, "Lord, who is it?"

*The honored guest at a meal would be singled out by the host by giving him or her a piece of bread dipped in sauce.*

He told me, "It is the one I honor by giving the bread dipped in the sauce."

And when he had dipped it, he gave it to Judas, son of Simon Iscariot. As soon as Judas had eaten it, Satan entered into him. Then Jesus told him, "Hurry—do it now."

None of the others at the table knew what Jesus meant. Some thought that since Judas was their treasurer, Jesus was telling him to go and pay for the food or to give some money to the poor. Judas left at once, going out into the night.

### MATCHING WORDS AND ACTIONS

Judas, the very man who would betray Jesus, was at the table with the others. Judas had already determined to betray Jesus, but in cold-blooded hypocrisy he shared the fellowship of this meal. It is easy to become enraged or shocked by what Judas did; yet professing commitment to Christ and then denying him with one's life is also betraying him. It is denying Christ's love to disobey him; it is denying his truth to distrust him; it is denying his deity to reject his authority. Do your words and actions match? If not, consider a change of mind and heart that will protect you from making a terrible mistake.

## November 8

## Jesus predicts Peter's denial

*JOHN 13:31-38 (also in LUKE 22:31-38) (Harmony 212)*

As soon as Judas left the room, Jesus said, "My time has come; the glory of God will soon surround me—and God shall receive great praise because of all that happens to me. And God shall give me his own glory, and this so very soon. Dear, dear children, how brief are these moments before I must go away and leave you! Then, though you search for me, you cannot come to me—just as I told the Jewish leaders.

"And so I am giving a new commandment to you now—love each other just as much as I love you. Your strong love for each other will prove to the world that you are my disciples."

Simon Peter said, "Master, where are you going?"

And Jesus replied, "You can't go with me now; but you will follow me later."

*Peter proudly told Jesus that he was ready to die for him. But Jesus corrected him. Jesus knew Peter would deny that he knew Jesus that very night to protect himself (18:25-27).*

"But why can't I come now?" he asked, "for I am ready to die for you."
Jesus answered, "Die for me? No—three times before the cock
crows tomorrow morning, you will deny that you even know me!"

### LOVING AS CHRIST LOVED

Love is more than simply warm feelings; it is an attitude that reveals itself in action. To love others was not a new commandment (see Leviticus 19:18), but to love others as much as Christ loved others was revolutionary. Now we are to love others based on Jesus' sacrificial love for us. Such love will not only bring unbelievers to Christ; it will also keep believers strong and united in a world hostile to God. Jesus was a living example of God's love as we are to be living examples of Jesus' love. How can we love others as Jesus loves us? By helping when it's not convenient, by giving when it hurts, by devoting energy to others' welfare rather than our own, by absorbing hurts from others without complaining or fighting back. This kind of loving is difficult to do. That is why people notice when you do it and know you are empowered by a supernatural source.

## November 9

## Jesus is the way to the Father

*JOHN 14:1-7 (Harmony 213a)*

*L*et not your heart be troubled. You are trusting God, now trust in me. There are many homes up there where my Father lives, and I am going to prepare them for your coming. When everything is ready, then I will come and get you, so that you can always be with me where I am. If this weren't so, I would tell you plainly. And you know where I am going and how to get there."

"No, we don't," Thomas said. "We haven't any idea where you are going, so how can we know the way?"

Jesus told him, "I am the Way—yes, and the Truth and the Life. No one can get to the Father except by means of me. If you had known who I am, then you would have known who my Father is. From now on you know him—and have seen him!"

*As the Way, Jesus is our path to the Father. As the Truth, he is the reality of all God's promises. As the Life, he joins his divine life to ours, both now and eternally.*

### ONE WAY

Jesus says he is the *only* way to God the Father. This is one of the most basic and important passages in Scripture. How can we know the way to God? Only through

Jesus. Some people may argue that this way is too narrow. In reality, it is wide enough for the whole world, if the world chooses to accept it. Instead of worrying about how limited it sounds to have only one way, we should be saying, "Thank you, God, for providing a sure way to get to you!" Jesus is the Way because he is both God and man. By uniting our lives with his, we are united with God. Trust Jesus to take you to the Father, and all the benefits of being God's child will be yours.

## *November 10*

## Jesus is the way to the Father

### *JOHN 14:8-14 (Harmony 213b)*

Philip said, "Sir, show us the Father and we will be satisfied."

Jesus replied, "Don't you even yet know who I am, Philip, even after all this time I have been with you? Anyone who has seen me has seen the Father! So why are you asking to see him? Don't you believe that I am in the Father and the Father is in me? The words I say are not my own but are from my Father who lives in me. And he does his work through me. Just believe it—that I am in the Father and the Father is in me. Or else believe it because of the mighty miracles you have seen me do.

*Jesus is the visible, tangible image of the invisible God. He is the complete revelation of what God is like. Jesus explained to Philip, who wanted to see the Father, that to know Jesus is to know God. The search for God, for truth and reality, ends in Christ.*

"In solemn truth I tell you, anyone believing in me shall do the same miracles I have done, and even greater ones, because I am going to be with the Father. You can ask him for *anything,* using my name, and I will do it, for this will bring praise to the Father because of what I, the Son, will do for you. Yes, ask *anything,* using my name, and I will do it!"

#### ASKING IN FAITH

When Jesus says we can ask for anything, we must remember that our asking must be in his name—that is, according to God's character and will. God will not grant requests contrary to his nature or his will, and we cannot use his name as a magic formula to fulfill our selfish desires. If we are sincerely following God and seeking to do his will, then our requests will be in line with what he wants, and he will grant them.

## Jesus promises the Holy Spirit

*JOHN 14:15-21 (Harmony 214a)*

f you love me, obey me; and I will ask the Father and he will give you another Comforter, and he will never leave you. He is the Holy Spirit, the Spirit who leads into all truth. The world at large cannot receive him, for it isn't looking for him and doesn't recognize him. But you do, for he lives with you now and some day shall be in you. No, I will not abandon you or leave you as orphans in the storm—I will come to you. In just a little while I will be gone from the world, but I will still be present with you. For I will live again—and you will too. When I come back to life again, you will know that I am in my Father, and you in me, and I in you. The one who obeys me is the one who loves me; and because he loves me, my Father will love him; and I will too, and I will reveal myself to him."

*Jesus was soon going to leave the disciples, but he would remain with them. How could this be? The Helper—the Spirit of God himself—would come after Jesus was gone to care for and guide the disciples. The Holy Spirit is the very presence of God within us and all believers, helping us live as God wants and building Christ's church on earth.*

### GOD KNOWS THE FUTURE

Sometimes people wish they knew the future so they could prepare for it. God has chosen not to give us this knowledge. He alone knows what will happen, but he tells us all we need to know to *prepare* for the future. When we live by his standards, he will not leave us; he will come to us, he will be in us, and he will show himself to us. God knows what will happen, and, because he will be with us through it all, we need not fear. We don't have to know the future to have faith in God; we have to have faith in God to be secure about the future.

## Jesus promises the Holy Spirit

*JOHN 14:22-26 (Harmony 214b)*

Judas (not Judas Iscariot, but his other disciple with that name) said to him, "Sir, why are you going to reveal yourself only to us disciples and not to the world at large?"

Jesus replied, "Because I will only reveal myself to those who love me and obey me. The Father will love them too, and we will come to them and live with them. Anyone who doesn't obey me doesn't love me. And remember, I am not making up this answer to your question! It is the answer given by the Father who sent me.

*Because the disciples were still expecting Jesus to establish an earthly kingdom and overthrow Rome, they found it hard to understand why he did not tell the world at large that he was the Messiah. Ever since Pentecost, the gospel of the Kingdom has been proclaimed in the whole world.*

"I am telling you these things now while I am still with you. But when the Father sends the Comforter instead of me—and by the Comforter I mean the Holy Spirit—he will teach you much, as well as remind you of everything I myself have told you."

#### CONFIDENT IN THE WORD

Jesus promised the disciples that the Holy Spirit would help them remember what he had been teaching them. This promise ensures the validity of the New Testament. The disciples were eyewitnesses of Jesus' life and teachings, and the Holy Spirit helped them remember what they had seen and heard without taking away their individual perspectives. We can be confident that the Gospels are accurate records of what Jesus taught and did (see 1 Corinthians 2:10-14). The Holy Spirit can also help us. As we study the Bible, we can trust him to plant truth in our minds, convince us of God's will, and remind us when we stray from it.

## Jesus promises the Holy Spirit

### JOHN 14:27-31 *(Harmony 214c)*

I am leaving you with a gift—peace of mind and heart! And the peace I give isn't fragile like the peace the world gives. So don't be troubled or afraid. Remember what I told you—I am going away, but I will come back to you again. If you really love me, you will be very happy for me, for now I can go to the Father, who is greater than I am. I have told you these things before they happen so that when they do, you will believe in me.

*As God the Son, Jesus willingly submits to God the Father. On earth, Jesus also submitted to many of the physical limitations of his humanity (Philippians 2:6-7). (See verse 31)*

"I don't have much more time to talk to you, for the evil prince of this world approaches. He has no power over me, but I will freely do what the Father requires of me so that the world will know that I love the Father. Come, let's be going."

**THE PEACE OF GOD**

Sin, fear, uncertainty, doubt, and numerous other forces are at war within us. The peace of God comes into our hearts, helping to restrain these hostile forces and offering comfort in place of conflict. Jesus says he will give us that peace if we are willing to accept it from him.

The end result of the Holy Spirit's work in our lives is deep and lasting peace. Unlike worldly peace, which is usually defined as the absence of conflict, this peace is confident assurance in any circumstance; with Christ's peace, we have no need to fear the present or the future. If your life is full of stress, allow the Holy Spirit to fill you with Christ's peace.

## Jesus teaches about the Vine and the branches

### JOHN 15:1-4 *(Harmony 215a)*

I am the true Vine, and my Father is the Gardener. He lops off every branch that doesn't produce. And he prunes those branches that bear fruit for even larger crops. He has already tended you by pruning you back for greater strength and usefulness by means of the commands I gave you. Take care to live in me, and let me live in you. For a branch can't produce fruit when severed from the vine. Nor can you be fruitful apart from me."

*The grapevine is a prolific plant; a single vine bears many grapes. In the Old Testament, grapes symbolized Israel's fruitfulness in doing God's work on the earth (Psalm 80:8; Isaiah 5:1-7; Ezekiel 19:10-14). In the Passover meal, the fruit of the vine symbolized God's goodness to his people.*

**VINE BRANCHES**

Christ is the Vine, and God is the Gardener who cares for the branches to make them fruitful. The branches are all those who claim to be followers of Christ. The fruitful branches are true believers who by their living union with Christ produce much fruit. But those who become unproductive—those who turn back from following Christ after making a superficial commitment—will be separated from the vine. Unproductive followers are as good as dead and will be cut off and tossed aside. Those who won't bear fruit for God or who try to block the efforts of God's followers will be cut off from the divine flow of life. Keep your focus on Christ, the Vine—that is your only source of strength and life.

*November 15*

## Jesus teaches about the Vine and the branches

*JOHN 15:5-8 (Harmony 215b)*

Yes, I am the Vine; you are the branches. Whoever lives in me and I in him shall produce a large crop of fruit. For apart from me you can't do a thing. If anyone separates from me, he is thrown away like a useless branch, withers, and is gathered into a pile with all the others and burned. But if you stay in me and obey my commands, you may ask any request you like, and it will be granted! My true disciples produce bountiful harvests. This brings great glory to my Father."

*Fruit is not limited to soul winning. In this chapter, answered prayer, joy, and love are mentioned as fruit (15:7, 11-12). Galatians 5:22-24 and 2 Peter 1:5-8 describe additional fruit: qualities of Christian character.*

**LIFE IN CHRIST**

Many people try to be good, honest people who do what is right. But Jesus says that the only way to live a truly good life is to stay close to him, like a branch attached to the vine.

Apart from Christ our efforts are unfruitful. Living in Christ means (1) believing that he is God's Son (1 John 4:15), (2) receiving him as Savior and Lord (1:12), (3) doing what God says (1 John 3:24), (4) continuing to believe the gospel (1 John 2:24), and (5) relating in love to the community of believers, Christ's body (15:12). Are you receiving the nourishment and life offered by Christ, the Vine? If not, you are missing a special gift he has for you.

## *November 16*

## Jesus teaches about the Vine and the branches

### *JOHN 15:9-16 (Harmony 215c)*

have loved you even as the Father has loved me. Live within my love. When you obey me you are living in my love, just as I obey my Father and live in his love. I have told you this so that you will be filled with my joy. Yes, your cup of joy will overflow! I demand that you love each other as much as I love you. And here is how to measure it—the greatest love is shown when a person lays down his life for his friends; and you are my friends if you obey me. I no longer call you slaves, for a master doesn't confide in his slaves; now you are my friends, proved by the fact that I have told you everything the Father told me.

*Jesus made the first choice— to live and to die for us, to invite us to live with him forever. We make the next choice—to accept or reject his offer. Without his choice, we would have no choice to make.*

"You didn't choose me! I chose you! I appointed you to go and produce lovely fruit always, so that no matter what you ask for from the Father, using my name, he will give it to you."

#### HIGHS AND LOWS

When things are going well, we feel elated. When hardships come, we can sink into depression. But true joy transcends the rolling waves of circumstance. Joy comes from a consistent relationship with Jesus Christ. When our lives are intertwined with his, he will help us to walk through adversity without sinking into debilitating lows and to manage prosperity without moving into deceptive highs. The joy of living with Jesus Christ daily will keep us levelheaded, no matter how high or low our circumstances.

## Jesus warns about the world's hatred

### *JOHN 15:17-25 (Harmony 216a)*

*Q* demand that you love each other, for you get enough hate from the world! But then, it hated me before it hated you. The world would love you if you belonged to it; but you don't—for I chose you to come out of the world, and so it hates you. Do you remember what I told you? 'A slave isn't greater than his master!' So since they persecuted me, naturally they will persecute you. And if they had listened to me, they would listen to you! The people of the world will persecute you because you belong to me, for they don't know God who sent me.

*Because Jesus Christ is Lord and Master, he should call us servants; instead, he calls us friends. How comforting and reassuring to be chosen as Christ's friends. Because he is Lord and Master, we owe him our unqualified obedience. But most important, Jesus asks us to obey him because we love him.*

"They would not be guilty if I had not come and spoken to them. But now they have no excuse for their sin. Anyone hating me is also hating my Father. If I hadn't done such mighty miracles among them they would not be counted guilty. But as it is, they saw these miracles and yet they hated both of us—me and my Father. This has fulfilled what the prophets said concerning the Messiah, 'They hated me without reason.'"

#### COMMANDED TO LOVE

Jesus offers hope. The Holy Spirit gives strength to endure the unreasonable hatred and evil in our world and the hostility many have toward Christ. This is especially comforting for those facing persecution. But all Christians should expect to get plenty of hatred from the world. Thus, it's important to give one another love and support. Do you allow small problems to get in the way of loving other believers? Jesus commands that you love them, and he will give you the strength to do it.

## Jesus warns about the world's hatred

### JOHN 15:26–16:4 *(Harmony 216b)*

*B*ut I will send you the Comforter—the Holy Spirit, the source of all truth. He will come to you from the Father and will tell you all about me. And you also must tell everyone about me because you have been with me from the beginning.

"I have told you these things so that you won't be staggered by all that lies ahead. For you will be excommunicated from the synagogues, and indeed the time is coming when those who kill you will think they are doing God a service. This is because they have never known the Father or me. Yes, I'm telling you these things now so that when they happen you will remember I warned you. I didn't tell you earlier because I was going to be with you for a while longer."

*Jesus uses two names for the Holy Spirit—Comforter and the source of all truth. The word Comforter conveys the helping, encouraging, and strengthening work of the Spirit. Source of all truth points to the teaching, illuminating, and reminding work of the Spirit.*

**NEVER ALONE**

In his last moments with his disciples, Jesus (1) warned them about further persecution, (2) told them where, when, and why he was going, and (3) assured them that they would not be left alone, but that the Spirit would come. Jesus knew what lay ahead, and he did not want the disciples' faith shaken or destroyed. God wants you to know that you are not alone. You have the Holy Spirit to comfort you, teach you truth, and help you.

## Jesus teaches about the Holy Spirit

### JOHN 16:5-11 *(Harmony 217a)*

*B*ut now I am going away to the one who sent me; and none of you seems interested in the purpose of my going; none wonders why. Instead you are only filled with sorrow. But the fact of the matter is that it is best for you that I go away, for if I don't, the Comforter won't come. If I do, he will—for I will send him to you.

"And when he has come he will convince the world of its sin, and of the availability of God's goodness, and of deliverance from judgment. The world's sin is unbelief in me; there is righteousness available because I go to the Father and you shall see me no more; there is deliverance from judgment because the prince of this world has already been judged."

*Three important tasks of the Holy Spirit are (1) convicting the world of its sin and calling it to repentance; (2) revealing the standard of God's righteousness to anyone who believes, because Christ would no longer be physically present on earth; and (3) demonstrating Christ's judgment over Satan.*

### THE SPIRIT

Unless Jesus had done what he had come to do, there would be no gospel. If he had not died, he could not have removed our sins; he could not have risen again and defeated death. If he had not gone back to the Father, the Holy Spirit would not have come. Christ's presence on earth was limited to one place at a time. His leaving meant that he could be present to the whole world through the Holy Spirit. God wants you to know you are not alone.

*November 20*

---

## Jesus teaches about the Holy Spirit

### *JOHN 16:12-16 (Harmony 217b)*

*O*h, there is so much more I want to tell you, but you can't understand it now. When the Holy Spirit, who is truth, comes, he shall guide you into all truth, for he will not be presenting his own ideas, but will be passing on to you what he has heard. He will tell you about the future. He shall praise me and bring me great honor by showing you my glory. All the Father's glory is mine; this is what I mean when I say that he will show you my glory.

"In just a little while I will be gone, and you will see me no more; but just a little while after that, and you will see me again!"

*When Jesus said he would be "gone" in just a little while, he was referring to his death, now only a few hours away. But they would see him again after his resurrection three days later.*

### THE PATHFINDER

The Holy Spirit is our guide, navigator, and pathfinder. Jesus gave us a reliable map when he gave us his life and his words. These essential resources assist us to find our way as his disciples. Jesus has also given us time. The original disciples could not absorb all Jesus had to teach them at once. Jesus said the Holy Spirit would tell them "about the future"—the nature of their mission, the opposition they would face, and the final outcome of their efforts. They didn't fully understand these promises until the Holy Spirit had come after Jesus' death and resurrection. Some steps of discipleship cannot even be comprehended until we have taken previous steps of obedience. We must never resent the limitations we have. Our knowledge of the way and the future will always be limited. Instead, we must trust and follow the pathfinder Christ has given us.

## November 21

## Jesus teaches about using his name in prayer

*JOHN 16:17-28 (Harmony 218a)*

*W*hatever is he saying?" some of his disciples asked. "What is this about 'going to the Father'? We don't know what he means."

Jesus realized they wanted to ask him so he said, "Are you asking yourselves what I mean? The world will greatly rejoice over what is going to happen to me, and you will weep. But your weeping shall suddenly be turned to wonderful joy when you see me again. It will be the same joy as that of a woman in labor when her child is born—her anguish gives place to rapturous joy and the pain is forgotten. You have sorrow now, but I will see you again and then you will rejoice; and no one can rob you of that joy. At that time you won't need to ask me for anything, for you can go directly to the Father and ask him, and he will give you what you ask for because you use my name. You haven't tried this before, but begin now. Ask, using my name, and you will receive, and your cup of joy will overflow.

*What a contrast between the disciples and the world! The world rejoiced as the disciples wept, but the disciples would see him again (in three days) and rejoice. The world's values are often the opposite of God's values.*

"I have spoken of these matters very guardedly, but the time will come when this will not be necessary and I will tell you plainly all about the Father. Then you will present your petitions over my signature! And I won't need to ask the Father to grant you these requests, for the Father himself loves you dearly because you love me and believe that I came from the Father. Yes, I came from the Father into the world and will leave the world and return to the Father."

**A NEW DAY**

Jesus is talking about a new relationship between the believer and God. Previously, people had approached God through priests. After Jesus' resurrection, any believer could approach God directly. A new day has dawned and now all believers are priests, talking with God personally and directly (see Hebrews 10:19-23). We approach God, not because of our own merit, but because Jesus, our great High Priest, has made us acceptable to God.

*November 22*

## Jesus teaches about using his name in prayer

### *JOHN 16:29-33 (Harmony 218b)*

*A*t last you are speaking plainly," his disciples said, "and not in riddles. Now we understand that you know everything and don't need anyone to tell you anything. From this we believe that you came from God."

"Do you finally believe this?" Jesus asked. "But the time is coming—in fact, it is here—when you will be scattered, each one returning to his own home, leaving me alone. Yet I will not be alone, for the Father is with me. I have told you all this so that you will have peace of heart and mind. Here on earth you will have many trials and sorrows; but cheer up, for I have overcome the world."

*The disciples believed Jesus' words because they were convinced that he knew everything. But their belief was only a first step toward the great faith they would receive when the Holy Spirit would come to live in them.*

**THE OVERCOMER**

With these words, Jesus told his disciples to take courage. In spite of the inevitable struggles they would face, they could take courage that Jesus had "overcome the world." In the book of Revelation, Jesus is called "the A and the Z, the Beginning and the Ending of all things" (Revelation 1:8). Jesus is the eternal Lord and Ruler of the past, present, and future (see also Revelation 4:8; Isaiah 44:6; 48:12-15). Without him you have nothing that is eternal, nothing that can change your life, nothing that can save you from sin. Is the Lord your reason for living, the "A and the Z" of your life? Honor the One who is the beginning and the end of all existence, wisdom, and power.

## Jesus prays for himself

### JOHN 17:1-5 *(Harmony 219)*

*W*hen Jesus had finished saying all these things he looked up to heaven and said, "Father, the time has come. Reveal the glory of your Son so that he can give the glory back to you. For you have given him authority over every man and woman in all the earth. He gives eternal life to each one you have given him. And this is the way to have eternal life—by knowing you, the only true God, and Jesus Christ, the one you sent to earth! I brought glory to you here on earth by doing everything you told me to. And now, Father, reveal my glory as I stand in your presence, the glory we shared before the world began."

*Before Jesus came to earth, he was one with God. At this point, when his mission on earth was almost finished, Jesus was asking his Father to restore him to his original place of honor and authority. Jesus' resurrection and ascension—and Stephen's dying exclamation (Acts 7:56)—attest that Jesus did return to his exalted position at the right hand of God.*

#### KNOWING GOD

Jesus explained knowing God as the essence of having eternal life. Eternal life is a gift we receive when we enter into a personal relationship with God in Jesus Christ. We cannot know God unless we have eternal life, and at the core of eternal life is intimate knowledge of God.

Eternal life gives us the capacity for intimacy with others who have eternal life. Jesus is the source of eternal life. Our first step toward eternal life includes realizing that we don't have it. That sense of separation, rebellion, lostness, or inadequacy before God is defined as "sin" in the Bible. When we admit our sin, turn away from it and then to Christ, Christ's love lives in us through the Holy Spirit. Eternal life is not just being around forever; for believers it means eternity with God, their loving Father.

## Jesus prays for his disciples

### JOHN 17:6-12 *(Harmony 220a)*

I have told these men all about you. They were in the world, but then you gave them to me. Actually, they were always yours, and you gave them to me; and they have obeyed you. Now they know that everything I have is a gift from you, for I have passed on to them the commands you gave me; and they accepted them and know of a certainty that I came down to earth from you, and they believe you sent me.

*Judas was "the son of hell," who was lost because he betrayed Jesus (see Psalm 41:9).*

"My plea is not for the world but for those you have given me because they belong to you. And all of them, since they are mine, belong to you; and you have given them back to me with everything else of yours, and so *they are my glory!* Now I am leaving the world, and leaving them behind, and coming to you. Holy Father, keep them in your own care—all those you have given me—so that they will be united just as we are, with none missing. During my time here I have kept safe within your family all of these you gave me. I guarded them so that not one perished, except the son of hell, as the Scriptures foretold."

#### IN THE WORLD

Like Jesus' original disciples, we still live in the world. "The world" is a system of values typified by Satan himself, centered on power, deceit, and self-will. While we're in the world, Satan wants to neutralize or destroy us. As Jesus' disciples today, we are on a collision course with the world's values; therefore, we need God's protection. The fact that we are *in* the world does not grant us license to become *of* the world. We must not betray Jesus by loving the world. We must be sure that we allow Christ—not the media and the world around us—to define who we are.

## Jesus prays for his disciples

### JOHN 17:13-19 *(Harmony 220b)*

*A*nd now I am coming to you. I have told them many things while I was with them so that they would be filled with my joy. I have given them your commands. And the world hates them because they don't fit in with it, just as I don't. I'm not asking you to take them out of the world, but to keep them safe from Satan's power. They are not part of this world any more than I am. Make them pure and holy through teaching them your words of truth. As you sent me into the world, I am sending them into the world, and I consecrate myself to meet their need for growth in truth and holiness."

*A follower of Christ becomes pure and holy through believing and obeying the Word of God (Hebrews 4:12). He or she has already accepted forgiveness through Christ's sacrificial death (Hebrews 7:26-27). But daily application of God's Word has a purifying effect on our minds and hearts.*

**SENT ONES**

The world hates Christians because Christians' values differ from the world's. Because Christ's followers don't cooperate with the world by joining in their sin, they are living accusations against the world's immorality. The world follows Satan's agenda, and Satan is the avowed enemy of Jesus and his people. Yet Jesus didn't ask God to take believers *out* of the world but instead to use them *in* the world. Because Jesus sends us into the world, we should not try to escape from the world, nor should we avoid all relationships with non-Christians. We are called to be salt and light (Matthew 5:13-16), and we are to do the work that God sent us to do.

## Jesus prays for future believers

### JOHN 17:20-21 *(Harmony 221a)*

*I* am not praying for these alone but also for the future believers who will come to me because of the testimony of these. My prayer for all of them is that they will be of one heart and mind, just as you and I are, Father—that just as you are in me and I am in you, so they will be in us, and the world will believe you sent me."

When Jesus prayed for all who would believe through the apostles' testimony, he was praying for every future believer. In a sense, everyone who has become a Christian has done so through the apostles' message because they wrote the New Testament and

*The pattern of Jesus' prayer provides a helpful outline for us. He prayed for himself, for those close to him, and for those beyond his immediate sphere who would be affected by the ministry of his friends.*

were the founders of the Christian church. Jesus prayed for you and others you know, that you would have unity (17:11), protection from Satan (17:15), and holiness (17:17). Realizing that Jesus was praying for you should give you great comfort during times of discouragement and confidence as you work for his Kingdom. Jesus had you in mind as he prepared for the cross.

*November 27*

---

## Jesus prays for future believers

*JOHN 17:22-26 (Harmony 221b)*

have given them the glory you gave me—the glorious unity of being one, as we are—I in them and you in me, all being perfected into one—so that the world will know you sent me and will understand that you love them as much as you love me. Father, I want them with me—these you've given me—so that they can see my glory. You gave me the glory because you loved me before the world began!

*Jesus asked that the Father's love would be in believers and that he himself (Jesus) would be in them. This expresses the Father's desire, and because it is his desire, he will make sure it is accomplished.*

"O righteous Father, the world doesn't know you, but I do; and these disciples know you sent me. And I have revealed you to them and will keep on revealing you so that the mighty love you have for me may be in them, and I in them."

Jesus' great desire for his disciples was that they would become one. He wanted them unified as a powerful witness to the reality of God's love. Christian unity provides an environment for the gospel message to make its clearest impact; lack of unity among Christians frequently drives people away. Are you helping to unify the body of Christ, the church? You can pray for other Christians, avoid gossip, build others up, work together in humility, give your time and money, exalt Christ, and refuse to get side-tracked arguing over divisive matters.

---

## Jesus again predicts Peter's denial

### MARK 14:26-31 (also in MATTHEW 26:30-35) (Harmony 222)

*T*hen they sang a hymn and went out to the Mount of Olives.

"All of you will desert me," Jesus told them, "for God has declared through the prophets, 'I will kill the Shepherd, and the sheep will scatter.' But after I am raised to life again, I will go to Galilee and meet you there."

Peter said to him, "I will never desert you no matter what the others do!"

"Peter," Jesus said, "before the cock crows a second time tomorrow morning you will deny me three times."

"No!" Peter exploded. "Not even if I have to die with you! I'll *never* deny you!" And all the others vowed the same.

*It's easy to think that Satan temporarily gained the upper hand in this drama about Jesus' death. But we see later that God was in control, even in the death of his Son. Satan gained no victory—everything occurred exactly as God had planned.*

**FAITH IN A CRUCIBLE**

This was the second time that evening that Jesus predicted that his disciples would desert him (see Luke 22:31-34; John 13:31-38 for the first prediction). And for a second time, all the disciples declared that they would die before deserting Jesus. A few hours later, however, they all would scatter. Talk is cheap. It is easy to say we are devoted to Christ, but our claims are meaningful only when they are tested in the crucible of persecution. How strong is your faith? Is it strong enough to stand up under intense trial?

---

## Jesus agonizes in the garden

### MARK 14:32-42 (also in MATTHEW 26:36-46; LUKE 22:39-46) (Harmony 223)

*A*nd now they came to an olive grove called the Garden of Gethsemane, and he instructed his disciples, "Sit here, while I go and pray."

He took Peter, James, and John with him and began to be filled with horror and deepest distress. And he said to them, "My soul is crushed by sorrow to the point of death; stay here and watch with me."

He went on a little farther and fell to the ground and prayed that if it were possible the awful hour awaiting him might never come.

"Father, Father," he said, "everything is possible for you. Take away this cup from me. Yet I want your will, not mine."

*Jesus was in great sorrow and distress over his approaching physical pain, separation from the Father, and death for the sins of the world. The divine course was set, but he, in his human nature, still struggled (Hebrews 5:7-9). Because of the anguish Jesus experienced, he can relate to our suffering.*

Then he returned to the three disciples and found them asleep.

"Simon!" he said. "Asleep? Couldn't you watch with me even one hour? Watch with me and pray lest the Tempter overpower you. For though the spirit is willing enough, the body is weak."

And he went away again and prayed, repeating his pleadings. Again he returned to them and found them sleeping, for they were very tired. And they didn't know what to say.

The third time when he returned to them he said, "Sleep on; get your rest! But no! The time for sleep has ended! Look! I am betrayed into the hands of wicked men. Come! Get up! We must go! Look! My betrayer is here!"

### WANTING GOD'S WILL

Was Jesus trying to get out of his task? Jesus expressed his true feelings, but he did not deny or rebel against God's will. He reaffirmed his desire to do what God wanted. Jesus' prayer highlights the terrible suffering he had to endure—an agony so much more magnified because he had to take on the sins of the whole world. This "cup" was the agony of alienation from God, his Father, at the cross (Hebrews 5:7-9). The sinless Son of God took on our sins and was separated for a while from God so that we could be eternally saved. While praying, Jesus was aware of what doing the Father's will would cost him. He understood the suffering he was about to encounter, and he did not want to have to endure the horrible experience. But Jesus prayed, "I want your will not mine." Anything worth having costs something. What does your commitment to God cost you? Be willing to pay the price to gain something worthwhile in the end.

## Jesus is betrayed and arrested

### JOHN 18:1-9 (also in MATTHEW 26:47; MARK 14:43; LUKE 22:47) (Harmony 224a)

*A*fter saying these things Jesus crossed the Kidron ravine with his disciples and entered a grove of olive trees. Judas, the betrayer, knew this place, for Jesus had gone there many times with his disciples.

The chief priests and Pharisees had given Judas a squad of soldiers and police to accompany him. Now with blazing torches, lanterns, and weapons they arrived at the olive grove.

Jesus fully realized all that was going to happen to him. Stepping forward to meet them he asked, "Whom are you looking for?"

*Judas was given a contingent of police and soldiers in order to seize Jesus and bring him before the religious court for trial. The religious leaders had issued the warrant for Jesus' arrest, and Judas was acting as Jesus' official accuser.*

"Jesus of Nazareth," they replied.

"I am he," Jesus said. And as he said it, they all fell backwards to the ground!

Once more he asked them, "Whom are you searching for?"

And again they replied, "Jesus of Nazareth."

"I told you I am he," Jesus said; "and since I am the one you are after, let these others go." He did this to carry out the prophecy he had just made, "I have not lost a single one of those you gave me."

#### DON'T RUN AWAY

John does not record Judas's kiss of greeting (Matthew 26:49; Mark 14:45; Luke 22:47-48), but Judas's kiss marked a turning point for the disciples. With Jesus' arrest, each one's life would be radically different. For the first time, Judas openly betrayed Jesus before the other disciples. For the first time, Jesus' loyal disciples ran away from him (Matthew 26:56). The band of disciples would undergo severe testing before they were transformed from hesitant followers to dynamic leaders. You may have made big mistakes in your life, committed sins you're ashamed to remember. Yet nothing is beyond Jesus' forgiveness. He can help you become the person he wants you to become, but you must allow him to forgive you and work in your life. He did it for these disciples—and they changed the world!

## Jesus is betrayed and arrested

*MATTHEW 26:48-56 (also in MARK 14:44-52; LUKE 22:48-53; JOHN 18:10-11) (Harmony 224b)*

*J*udas had told them to arrest the man he greeted, for that would be the one they were after. So now Judas came straight to Jesus and said, "Hello, Master!" and embraced him in friendly fashion.

Jesus said, "My friend, go ahead and do what you have come for." Then the others grabbed him.

One of the men with Jesus pulled out a sword and slashed off the ear of the high priest's servant.

"Put away your sword," Jesus told him. "Those using swords will get killed. Don't you realize that I could ask my Father for thousands of angels to protect us, and he would send them instantly? But if I did, how would the Scriptures be fulfilled that describe what is happening now?" Then Jesus spoke to the crowd. "Am I some dangerous criminal," he asked, "that you had to arm yourselves with swords and clubs before you could arrest me? I was with you teaching daily in the Temple and you didn't stop me then. But this is all happening to fulfill the words of the prophets as recorded in the Scriptures."

At that point, all the disciples deserted him and fled.

> *Judas had told the crowd to arrest the man he kissed. This was not an arrest by Roman soldiers under Roman law, but an arrest by the religious leaders. Judas pointed Jesus out not because Jesus was hard to recognize, but because Judas had agreed to be the formal accuser in case a trial was called.*

### FORCING THE ISSUE

The religious leaders had not arrested Jesus in the Temple for fear of a riot. Instead, they came secretly at night, under the influence of the prince of darkness, Satan himself. Although it had looked as though Satan were getting the upper hand, everything was proceeding according to God's plan. It was time for Jesus to die. Still not understanding this and wanting to protect Jesus, one of the disciples (Peter, see John 18:10) pulled a sword and wounded the high priest's servant. But Jesus told Peter to put away his sword and allow God's plan to unfold. At times it is tempting to take matters into our own hands, to force the issue. Usually such moves lead to sin. Instead, we must trust God to work out his plan.

## Annas questions Jesus

### JOHN 18:12-24 *(Harmony 225)*

*S*o the Jewish police, with the soldiers and their lieutenant, arrested Jesus and tied him. First they took him to Annas, the father-in-law of Caiaphas, the high priest that year. Caiaphas was the one who told the other Jewish leaders, "Better that one should die for all."

Simon Peter followed along behind, as did another of the disciples who was acquainted with the high priest. So that other disciple was permitted into the courtyard along with Jesus, while Peter stood outside the gate. Then the other disciple spoke to the girl watching at the gate, and she let Peter in. The girl asked Peter, "Aren't you one of Jesus' disciples?"

"No," he said, "I am not!"

The police and the household servants were standing around a fire they had made, for it was cold. And Peter stood there with them, warming himself.

Inside, the high priest began asking Jesus about his followers and what he had been teaching them.

*Both Annas and Caiaphas had been high priests. Annas was Israel's high priest from A.D. 6 to 15, when he was deposed by Roman rulers. Caiaphas, Annas's son-in-law, was appointed high priest from A.D. 18 to 36 or 37. According to Jewish law, the office of high priest was held for life. Many Jews therefore still considered Annas the high priest and continue to call him by that title. But although Annas retained much authority among the Jews, Caiaphas made the final decisions.*

Jesus replied, "What I teach is widely known, for I have preached regularly in the synagogue and Temple; I have been heard by all the Jewish leaders and teach nothing in private that I have not said in public. Why are you asking me this question? Ask those who heard me. You have some of them here. They know what I said."

One of the soldiers standing there struck Jesus with his fist. "Is that the way to answer the high priest?" he demanded.

"If I lied, prove it," Jesus replied. "Should you hit a man for telling the truth?"

Then Annas sent Jesus, bound, to Caiaphas the high priest.

#### POINTING FINGERS

We can easily get angry at the Council for their injustice in condemning Jesus, but we must remember that Peter and the rest of the disciples also contributed to Jesus' pain by deserting and denying him (Matthew 26:56, 75). Only hours earlier, these disciples had vowed never to leave Jesus (Matthew 26:35). While most of us are not like the religious leaders, we are all like the disciples, for all of us have been guilty of denying that Christ is Lord in vital areas of our lives or of keeping secret our identity as believers in times of pressure. Don't excuse yourself by pointing at others whose sins seem worse than yours. Instead, admit your guilt and come to Jesus for forgiveness and healing.

## December 3

## Caiaphas questions Jesus

### MARK 14:53-65 (also in MATTHEW 26:57-68)
(Harmony 226)

*J*esus was led to the high priest's home where all of the chief priests and other Jewish leaders soon gathered. Peter followed far behind and then slipped inside the gates of the high priest's residence and crouched beside a fire among the servants.

Inside, the chief priests and the whole Jewish Supreme Court were trying to find something against Jesus that would be sufficient to condemn him to death. But their efforts were in vain. Many false witnesses volunteered, but they contradicted each other.

Finally some men stood up to lie about him and said, "We heard him say, 'I will destroy this Temple made with human hands and in three days I will build another, made without human hands!'" But even then they didn't get their stories straight!

Then the high priest stood up before the Court and asked Jesus, "Do you refuse to answer this charge? What do you have to say for yourself?"

*The Romans controlled Israel, but the Jews were given some authority over religious and minor civil disputes. The Jewish ruling body, the Sanhedrin, was made up of seventy-one of Israel's religious leaders. This trial by the Sanhedrin (the Jewish council of religious leaders) had two phases. A small group met at night (John 18:12-24), and then the full Sanhedrin met at daybreak (Luke 22:66-71).*

To this Jesus made no reply.

Then the high priest asked him. "Are you the Messiah, the Son of God?"

Jesus said, "I am, and you will see me sitting at the right hand of God, and returning to earth in the clouds of heaven."

Then the high priest tore at his clothes and said, "What more do we need? Why wait for witnesses? You have heard his blasphemy. What is your verdict?" And the vote for the death sentence was unanimous.

Then some of them began to spit at him, and they blindfolded him and began to hammer his face with their fists.

"Who hit you that time, you prophet?" they jeered. And even the bailiffs were using their fists on him as they led him away.

### YOU MUST DECIDE

Jesus made no reply to the first question because it was based on confusing and erroneous evidence. Not answering was wiser than trying to clarify the fabricated accusations. But if Jesus had refused to answer the second question, it could have been taken as a denial of his mission. Jesus declared, in no uncertain terms, that he was the Messiah. The high priest accused Jesus of blasphemy—calling himself God. To the Jews, this was a great crime, punishable by death (Leviticus 24:16). The religious leaders refused even to consider that Jesus' words might be true. They had decided against Jesus, and in so doing, had sealed their own fate as well as his. Like the members of the Council, you must decide whether Jesus' words are blasphemy or truth. Your decision has eternal implications.

*December 4*

---

## Peter denies knowing Jesus

### *MARK 14:66-72 (also in MATTHEW 26:69-75; LUKE 22:54-65; JOHN 18:25-27) (Harmony 227)*

eanwhile Peter was below in the courtyard. One of the maids who worked for the high priest noticed Peter warming himself at the fire.

She looked at him closely and then announced, *"You* were with Jesus, the Nazarene."

Peter denied it. "I don't know what you're talking about!" he said, and walked over to the edge of the courtyard.

Just then, a rooster crowed.

The maid saw him standing there and began telling the others, "There he is! There's that disciple of Jesus!"

Peter denied it again.

*Peter's curse was more than just a common swear word. He was making the strongest denial he could think of by denying with an oath that he knew Jesus. He was saying, in effect, "May God strike me dead if I'm lying."*

A little later others standing around the fire began saying to Peter, "You are, too, one of them, for you are from Galilee!"

He began to curse and swear. "I don't even know this fellow you are talking about," he said.

And immediately the rooster crowed the second time. Suddenly Jesus' words flashed through Peter's mind: "Before the cock crows twice, you will deny me three times." And he began to cry.

### STAGES OF DENIAL

There were three stages to Peter's denial. First he acted confused and tried to divert attention from himself by changing the subject. Second, using an oath, he denied that he knew Jesus. Third, he began to curse and swear. Believers who deny Christ often begin doing so subtly by pretending not to know him. When opportunities to discuss religious issues come up, they walk away or pretend they don't know the answers. With only a little more pressure, they can be induced to deny flatly their relationship with Christ. If you find yourself subtly diverting conversation so you don't have to talk about Christ, watch out. You may be on the road to denying him.

*December 5*

---

## The council of religious leaders condemns Jesus

*LUKE 22:66-71 (also in MATTHEW 27:1-2; MARK 15:1)*
*(Harmony 228)*

Early the next morning at daybreak the Jewish Supreme Court assembled, including the chief priests and all the top religious authorities of the nation. Jesus was led before this Council and instructed to state whether or not he claimed to be the Messiah.

But he replied, "If I tell you, you won't believe me or let me present my case. But the time is soon coming when I, the Messiah, shall be enthroned beside Almighty God."

They all shouted, "Then you claim you are the Son of God?"

And he replied, "Yes, I am."

"What need do we have for other witnesses?" they shouted. "For we ourselves have heard him say it."

*These leaders tried Jesus for religious offenses such as calling himself the Son of God, which, according to law, was blasphemy. The trial was fixed: These religious leaders had already decided to kill Jesus (Luke 22:2).*

Jesus, in effect, agreed with the high priest's words that Jesus was the Son of God by saying, "Yes, I am." Jesus identified himself with God by using a familiar title for God found in the Old Testament: "I AM" (Exodus 3:14). The high priest recognized Jesus' claim and accused him of blasphemy. For any other human this claim would have been blasphemy, but in this case it was true. Blasphemy, the sin of claiming to be God or of attacking God's authority and majesty in any way, was punishable by death. The Jewish leaders had the evidence they wanted. The one man in all of history for whom they had been looking and waiting stood in their midst, and told them who he was, and they chose to kill him. Jesus is standing with us today; he is the answer to what all humanity needs and desires. Unfortunately, many decide to crucify him rather than fall to their knees in worship. Have you taken Jesus at his word? Have you believed in him as your Messiah?

## December 6

---

## Judas kills himself

### MATTHEW 27:3-10 *(Harmony 229)*

*A*bout that time Judas, who betrayed him, when he saw that Jesus had been condemned to die, changed his mind and deeply regretted what he had done, and brought back the money to the chief priests and other Jewish leaders.

"I have sinned," he declared, "for I have betrayed an innocent man."

"That's your problem," they retorted.

Then he threw the money onto the floor of the Temple and went out and hanged himself. The chief priests picked the money up. "We can't put it in the collection," they said, "since it's against our laws to accept money paid for murder."

*These chief priests felt no guilt in giving Judas money to betray an innocent man, but when Judas returned the money, the priests couldn't accept it because it was wrong to accept money paid for murder! Their hatred for Jesus had caused them to lose all sense of justice.*

They talked it over and finally decided to buy a certain field where the clay was used by potters, and to make it into a cemetery for foreigners who died in Jerusalem. That is why the cemetery is still called "The Field of Blood."

This fulfilled the prophecy of Jeremiah which says,

> "They took the thirty pieces of silver—the price at which he was valued by the people of Israel—and purchased a field from the potters as the Lord directed me."

## TOO LATE

Jesus' formal accuser wanted to drop his charges, but the religious leaders refused to halt the trial. When he betrayed Jesus, perhaps Judas was trying to force Jesus' hand to get him to lead a revolt against Rome. This did not work, of course. Whatever his reason, Judas changed his mind, but it was too late. Many of the plans we set into motion cannot be reversed. It is best to think of the potential consequences before we launch into an action we may later regret.

# December 7

## Jesus stands trial before Pilate

*JOHN 18:28-38 (also in MATTHEW 27:11-14; MARK 15:2-5; LUKE 23:1-5) (Harmony 230)*

Jesus' trial before Caiaphas ended in the early hours of the morning. Next he was taken to the palace of the Roman governor. His accusers wouldn't go in themselves for that would "defile" them, they said, and they wouldn't be allowed to eat the Passover lamb. So Pilate, the governor, went out to them and asked, "What is your charge against this man? What are you accusing him of doing?"

*Pilate knew what was going on; he knew that the religious leaders hated Jesus, and he did not want to act as their executioner. They could not sentence Jesus to death themselves—permission had to come from a Roman leader. But Pilate initially refused to sentence Jesus without sufficient evidence.*

"We wouldn't have arrested him if he weren't a criminal!" they retorted.

"Then take him away and judge him yourselves by your own laws," Pilate told them.

"But we want him crucified," they demanded, "and your approval is required." This fulfilled Jesus' prediction concerning the method of his execution.

Then Pilate went back into the palace and called for Jesus to be brought to him. "Are you the King of the Jews?" he asked him.

"'King' as *you* use the word or as the *Jews* use it?" Jesus asked.

"Am I a Jew?" Pilate retorted. "Your own people and their chief priests brought you here. Why? What have you done?"

Then Jesus answered, "I am not an earthly king. If I were, my followers would have fought when I was arrested by the Jewish leaders. But my Kingdom is not of the world."

Pilate replied, "But you are a king then?"

"Yes," Jesus said. "I was born for that purpose. And I came to bring truth to the world. All who love the truth are my followers."

"What is truth?" Pilate exclaimed. Then he went out again to the people and told them, "He is not guilty of any crime."

### THE TRUTH

Some people today try to say that if only they could talk to Jesus, question him, and spend time with him personally, they would believe. Pilate had that chance. Pilate asked Jesus a straightforward question, and Jesus answered clearly. Jesus is a king, but one whose Kingdom is not of this world. There seems to have been no question in Pilate's mind that Jesus spoke the truth and was innocent of any crime. It also seems apparent that while recognizing the truth, Pilate chose to reject it. It is a tragedy when we fail to recognize the truth. It is a greater tragedy when we recognize the truth but fail to heed it.

*December 8*

## Jesus stands trial before Herod

*LUKE 23:6-12 (Harmony 231)*

s he then a Galilean?" Pilate asked.

When they told him yes, Pilate said to take him to King Herod, for Galilee was under Herod's jurisdiction; and Herod happened to be in Jerusalem at the time. Herod was delighted at the opportunity to see Jesus, for he had heard a lot about him and had been hoping to see him perform a miracle.

He asked Jesus question after question, but there was no reply. Meanwhile, the chief priests and the other religious leaders stood there shouting their accusations.

Now Herod and his soldiers began mocking and ridiculing Jesus; and putting a kingly robe on him, they sent him back to Pilate. That day Herod and Pilate—enemies before—became fast friends.

### "NOT GUILTY"

Herod, also called Herod Antipas, was in Jerusalem that weekend for the Passover celebration. (This was the Herod who had killed John the Baptist.) Pilate hoped to pass Jesus

*Herod was the part-Jewish ruler of Galilee and Perea. Pilate was the Roman governor of Judea and Samaria. Those four provinces had been united under Herod the Great. But when Herod died in 4 B.C., the kingdom was divided among his sons. Archelaus, the son who had received Judea and Samaria, was removed from office within ten years, and his provinces were then ruled by a succession of Roman governors, of whom Pilate was the fifth.*

off on Herod because he knew that Jesus had lived and worked in Galilee. Herod Antipas had two advantages over Pilate: He came from a hereditary, part-Jewish monarchy, and he had held his position much longer. But Pilate had two advantages over Herod: He was a Roman citizen and an envoy of the emperor, and his position had been created to replace Herod's ineffective half brother. It is not surprising that the two men were uneasy around each other. Jesus' trial, however, brought them together. Because Pilate had recognized Herod's authority over Galilee, Herod had stopped feeling threatened by the Roman politician. And because neither man knew what to do in this predicament, their common problem united them. When Herod sent Jesus back to Pilate, it was with the verdict of "not guilty." How unfortunate that these two leaders were unable to save an innocent man! If you had been in their position, how would you have decided? When you face a tough decision, you can take the easy way out, or you can stand for what is right, regardless of the cost. If we know to do right and don't do it, it is sin (James 4:17).

*December 9*

---

## Pilate hands Jesus over to be crucified

### *JOHN 18:39–19:16 (also in MATTHEW 27:15-26; MARK 15:6-15; LUKE 23:13-25) (Harmony 232)*

$\mathcal{B}$ut you have a custom of asking me to release someone from prison each year at Passover. So if you want me to, I'll release the 'King of the Jews.'"

But they screamed back. "No! Not this man, but Barabbas!" Barabbas was a robber.

Then Pilate laid open Jesus' back with a leaded whip, and the soldiers made a crown of thorns and placed it on his head and robed him in royal purple. "Hail, 'King of the Jews!'" they mocked, and struck him with their fists.

Pilate went outside again and said to the Jews, "I am going to bring him out to you now, but understand clearly that I find him *not guilty.*"

*Scourging could have killed Jesus. The usual procedure was to bare the upper half of the victim's body and tie his hands to a pillar before whipping him with a three-pronged whip. The number of lashes was determined by the severity of the crime; up to forty were permitted under Jewish law (Deuteronomy 25:3).*

Then Jesus came out wearing the crown of thorns and the purple robe. And Pilate said, "Behold the man!"

At sight of him the chief priests and Jewish officials began yelling, "Crucify! Crucify!"

"*You* crucify him," Pilate said. "I find him *not guilty.*"

They replied, "By our laws he ought to die because he called himself the Son of God."

When Pilate heard this, he was more frightened than ever. He took Jesus back into the palace again and asked him, "Where are you from?" but Jesus gave no answer.

"You won't talk to me?" Pilate demanded. "Don't you realize that I have the power to release you or to crucify you?"

Then Jesus said, "You would have no power at all over me unless it were given to you from above. So those who brought me to you have the greater sin."

Then Pilate tried to release him, but the Jewish leaders told him, "If you release this man, you are no friend of Caesar's. Anyone who declares himself a king is a rebel against Caesar."

At these words Pilate brought Jesus out to them again and sat down at the judgment bench on the stone-paved platform. It was now about noon of the day before Passover.

And Pilate said to the Jews, "Here is your king!"

"Away with him," they yelled. "Away with him—crucify him!"

"What? Crucify your king?" Pilate asked.

"We have no king but Caesar," the chief priests shouted back.

Then Pilate gave Jesus to them to be crucified.

### WHO'S IN CONTROL?

Throughout the trial we see that Jesus was in control, not Pilate or the religious leaders. Pilate vacillated, the Jewish leaders reacted out of hatred and anger, but Jesus remained composed. He knew the truth, he knew God's plan, and he knew the reason for his trial. Despite the pressure and persecution, Jesus remained unmoved. It was really Pilate and the religious leaders who were on trial, not Jesus. When you are questioned or ridiculed because of your faith, remember that while you may be on trial before your accusers, they are on trial before God.

## Roman soldiers mock Jesus

### MARK 15:16-20 (also in MATTHEW 27:27-31)
### (Harmony 233)

 hen the Roman soldiers took him into the barracks of the palace, called out the entire palace guard, dressed him in a purple robe, and made a crown of long, sharp thorns and put it on his head. Then they saluted, yelling, "Yea! King of the Jews!" And they beat him on the head with a cane, and spat on him, and went down on their knees to "worship" him.

When they finally tired of their sport, they took off the purple robe and put his own clothes on him again, and led him away to be crucified.

*Crucifixion was the Roman penalty for rebellion. Only slaves or those who were not Roman citizens could be crucified. If Jesus died by crucifixion, he would die the death of a rebel and slave. Crucifixion also put the responsibility for killing Jesus on the Romans, and thus the crowds could not blame the religious leaders.*

**ALONE BUT UNAFRAID**

These Roman soldiers were merciless in their torture of Jesus. Yet Jesus had already been deserted by all his disciples when they ran from the garden in terror. One of his closest friends, Peter, denied that he ever knew Jesus. Another disciple, Judas, betrayed him. The crowds who had followed Jesus stood by and did nothing. Two influential leaders, Pilate and Herod, refused to do anything. The religious leaders, who should have been the first to recognize the Messiah, actively promoted Jesus' death. Jesus took all of this for our sakes so that he could go to the cross and carry out the plan of salvation. When people don't understand your faith, or they make fun of it, remember what Jesus went through for you and remain strong.

## Jesus is led away to be crucified

### *LUKE 23:26-31 (also in MATTHEW 27:32-34; MARK 15:21-24; JOHN 19:17) (Harmony 234)*

*A*s the crowd led Jesus away to his death, Simon of Cyrene, who was just coming into Jerusalem from the country, was forced to follow, carrying Jesus' cross. Great crowds trailed along behind, and many grief-stricken women.

But Jesus turned and said to them, "Daughters of Jerusalem, don't weep for me, but for yourselves and for your children. For the days are coming when the women who have no children will be counted fortunate indeed. Mankind will beg the mountains to fall on them and crush them, and the hills to bury them. For if such things as this are done to me, the Living Tree, what will they do to you?"

*Luke alone mentions the tears of the Jewish women while Jesus was being led through the streets to his execution. Jesus told them not to weep for him but for themselves. He knew that in only about forty years, Jerusalem and the Temple would be destroyed by the Romans.*

#### SIMON'S SERVICE

Colonies of Jews existed outside Judea. Simon had made a Passover pilgrimage to Jerusalem all the way from Cyrene in North Africa. Simon certainly never expected to carry a condemned man's cross to the execution site, yet the Roman soldiers forced him to do so. Simon alone is remembered for this particular act of service—carrying the crossbeam after Jesus, in his beaten humanity, was unable to do so. Small acts can have big effects. Simon could not have saved Jesus' life, but he did help carry the cross. At some point, it seems that Simon also came to believe in this condemned man as his Savior, for the Bible records that his sons, Alexander and Rufus, became well known later in the early church (Romans 16:13). Never discount the long-reaching effects of small acts of help and service.

## Jesus is placed on the cross

### MATTHEW 27:35-44 (also in MARK 15:25-32; LUKE 23:32-43; JOHN 19:18-27) (Harmony 235)

*A*fter the crucifixion, the soldiers threw dice to divide up his clothes among themselves. Then they sat around and watched him as he hung there. And they put a sign above his head, "This is Jesus, the King of the Jews."

Two robbers were also crucified there that morning, one on either side of him. And the people passing by hurled abuse, shaking their heads at him and saying, "So! You can destroy the Temple and build it again in three days, can you? Well, then, come on down from the cross if you are the Son of God!"

*The wine was offered to Jesus to help deaden his pain. But Jesus refused—he would suffer fully conscious and with a clear mind.*

And the chief priests and Jewish leaders also mocked him. "He saved others," they scoffed, "but he can't save himself! So you are the King of Israel, are you? Come down from the cross and we'll believe you! He trusted God—let God show his approval by delivering him! Didn't he say, 'I am God's Son'?"

And the robbers also threw the same in his teeth.

#### THE WAY OF THE CROSS

When James and John asked Jesus for the places of honor next to him in his Kingdom, he told them they didn't know what they were asking (Mark 10:35-39). Here, as Jesus was preparing to inaugurate his Kingdom through his death, the places on his right and on his left were taken by dying men—criminals. As Jesus explained to his two position-conscious disciples, a person who wants to be close to Jesus must be prepared to suffer and die. The way to the Kingdom is the way of the cross. Taking a stand for Christ may invite suffering and pain, but Jesus will be there with you, through it all.

---

## Jesus dies on the cross

### MATTHEW 27:45-50 (also in MARK 15:33-37; LUKE 23:44-46; JOHN 19:28-30) (Harmony 236a)

*T*hat afternoon, the whole earth was covered with darkness for three hours, from noon until three o'clock.

About three o'clock, Jesus shouted, "Eli, Eli, lama sabach-thani?" which means, "My God, my God, why have you forsaken me?"

Some of the bystanders misunderstood and thought he was calling for Elijah. One of them ran and filled a sponge with sour wine and put it on a stick and held it up to him to drink. But the rest said, "Leave him alone. Let's see whether Elijah will come and save him."

Then Jesus shouted out again, dismissed his spirit, and died.

*We do not know how this darkness occurred, but it is clear that God caused it. Nature testified to the gravity of Jesus' death, while Jesus' friends and enemies alike fell silent in the encircling gloom. The darkness on that Friday afternoon was both physical and spiritual.*

**THE CUP**

Jesus was not questioning God; he was quoting the first line of Psalm 22—a deep expression of the anguish he was feeling as he was taking on the sins of the world, which caused him to be separated from his Father. *This* was what Jesus had dreaded as he had prayed to God in the garden to take the cup from him (26:39). The physical agony was horrible; even worse was the period of spiritual separation from his Father. Jesus suffered this double death so that we would never have to experience eternal separation from God. Jesus has gone through so much for you. What can you do for him?

---

## Jesus dies on the cross

### MATTHEW 27:51-56 (also in MARK 15:38-41; LUKE 23:47-49; JOHN 19:31-37) (Harmony 236b)

*A*nd look! The curtain secluding the Holiest Place in the Temple was split apart from top to bottom; and the earth shook, and rocks broke, and tombs opened, and many godly men and women who had died came back to life again. After Jesus' resurrection, they left the cemetery and went into Jerusalem, and appeared to many people there.

*Christ's death was accompanied by at least four miraculous events: darkness, the tearing in two of the veil in the Temple, an earthquake, and dead people rising from their tombs. Jesus' death, therefore, could not have gone unnoticed. Everyone knew something significant had happened.*

The soldiers at the crucifixion and their sergeant were terribly frightened by the earthquake and all that happened. They exclaimed, "Surely this was God's Son."

And many women who had come down from Galilee with Jesus to care for him were watching from a distance. Among them were Mary Magdalene and Mary the mother of James and Joseph, and the mother of James and John (the sons of Zebedee).

### DIRECT ACCESS

The tearing of the Temple curtain symbolized Christ's work on the cross. The Temple had three parts: the courts for all the people; the Holy Place, where only priests could enter; and the Most Holy Place, where the high priest alone could enter once a year to atone for the sins of the people. It was in the Most Holy Place that the Ark of the Covenant, and God's presence with it, rested. The curtain that was torn had closed off the Most Holy Place from view. At Christ's death, the barrier between God and man was split in two. Now all people can approach God directly through Christ (Hebrews 9:1-14; 10:19-22). Because of Christ's ultimate sacrifice, we have direct access to God. You can talk to God about anything, at any time. Stay close to him.

*December 15*

## Jesus is laid in the tomb

### JOHN 19:38-42 (also in MATTHEW 27:57-61; MARK 15:42-47; LUKE 23:50-56) (Harmony 237)

*A*fterwards Joseph of Arimathea, who had been a secret disciple of Jesus for fear of the Jewish leaders, boldly asked Pilate for permission to take Jesus' body down; and Pilate told him to go ahead. So he came and took it away. Nicodemus, the man who had come to Jesus at night, came too, bringing a hundred pounds of embalming ointment made from myrrh and aloes. Together they wrapped Jesus' body in a long linen cloth saturated with the spices, as is the Jewish custom of burial. The place of crucifixion was near a grove of trees, where there was a new tomb, never used before. And so, because of the need for haste before the Sabbath, and because the tomb was close at hand, they laid him there.

**CHANGED LIVES**

The Gospel writers described four particular people who were changed in the process of Jesus' death. The criminal, dying on the cross beside Jesus, asked Jesus to include him in his Kingdom (Luke 23:39-43). The Roman centurion proclaimed that surely Jesus was the Son of God (Mark 15:39). Joseph and Nicodemus, members of the Council and secret followers of Jesus (7:50-52), came out of hiding. These men were changed more by Jesus' death than by his life. They realized who Jesus was, and that realization brought out their belief, proclamation, and action. When confronted with Jesus and his death, we should be changed—to believe, proclaim, and act.

*Joseph of Arimathea and Nicodemus were secret followers of Jesus. Joseph was a leader and honored member of the Jewish Council (the Sanhedrin). Nicodemus, also a member of the Council, had come to Jesus by night (3:1) and later tried to defend him before the other religious leaders (7:50-52). They risked their reputations to provide for Jesus' burial.*

*December 16*

## Guards are posted at the tomb

### MATTHEW 27:62-66 *(Harmony 238)*

The next day—at the close of the first day of the Passover ceremonies—the chief priests and Pharisees went to Pilate, and told him, "Sir, that liar once said, 'After three days I will come back to life again.' So we request an order from you sealing the tomb until the third day, to prevent his disciples from coming and stealing his body and then telling everyone he came back to life! If that happens, we'll be worse off than we were at first."

*The tomb where Jesus was laid was probably a man-made cave cut out of one of the many limestone hills in the area. These caves were often large enough to walk into.*

"Use your own Temple police," Pilate told them. "They can guard it safely enough."

So they sealed the stone and posted guards to protect it from intrusion.

**NOTHING CAN STOP IT**

The religious leaders took Jesus' resurrection claims more seriously than the disciples did. The disciples didn't remember Jesus' teaching about his resurrection

(20:17-19), but the religious leaders did. Because of his claims, they were almost as afraid of Jesus after his death as when he was alive. They tried to take every precaution that his body would remain in the tomb. The tomb was sealed by stringing a cord across the stone that had been rolled over the entrance. The cord was sealed at each end with clay. But the religious leaders took a further precaution, asking that guards be placed at the tomb's entrance. With such precautions, the only way the tomb could be empty would be for Jesus to rise from the dead. The Pharisees failed to understand that no rock, seal, guard, or army could prevent the Son of God from rising again. Because Jesus came back to life, we know that nothing that happens to us can prevent us from rising again and enjoying eternity with our Lord.

*December 17*

## Jesus rises from the dead

### *MARK 16:1-8 (also in MATTHEW 28:1-7; LUKE 24:1-8; JOHN 20:1) (Harmony 239a)*

he next evening, when the Sabbath ended, Mary Magdalene and Salome and Mary the mother of James went out and purchased embalming spices.

Early the following morning, just at sunrise, they carried them out to the tomb. On the way they were discussing how they could ever roll aside the huge stone from the entrance.

But when they arrived they looked up and saw that the stone—a *very* heavy one—was already moved away and the entrance was open! So they entered the tomb—and there on the right sat a young man clothed in white. The women were startled, but the angel said, "Don't be so surprised. Aren't you looking for Jesus, the Nazarene who was crucified? He isn't here! He has come back to life! Look, that's where his body was lying. Now go and give this message to his disciples including Peter:

"'Jesus is going ahead of you to Galilee. You will see him there, just as he told you before he died!'"

The women fled from the tomb, trembling and bewildered, too frightened to talk.

*The women purchased the spices on Saturday evening after the Sabbath had ended so they could go to the tomb early the next morning and anoint Jesus' body as a sign of love, devotion, and respect. Bringing spices to the tomb was like bringing flowers to a grave today.*

## RESURRECTION REALITY

The Resurrection is vitally important for many reasons: (1) Jesus kept his promise to rise from the dead, so we can believe that he will keep all his other promises. (2) The Resurrection ensures that the ruler of God's eternal Kingdom will be the living Christ, not just an idea, hope, or dream. (3) Christ's resurrection gives us the assurance that we also will be resurrected (1 Corinthians 15:12-19). (4) The power of God that brought Christ's body back from the dead is available to us to bring our morally and spiritually dead selves back to life so that we can change and grow. (5) The Resurrection provides the substance of the church's witness to the world. We do not merely tell lessons from the life of a good teacher; we proclaim the reality of the resurrection of Jesus Christ.

*December 18*

---

# Jesus rises from the dead

### JOHN 20:2-9 (also in LUKE 24:9-12) (Harmony 239b)

*S*he ran and found Simon Peter and me and said, "They have taken the Lord's body out of the tomb, and I don't know where they have put him!"

We ran to the tomb to see; I outran Peter and got there first, and stooped and looked in and saw the linen cloth lying there, but I didn't go in. Then Simon Peter arrived and went on inside. He also noticed the cloth lying there, while the swath that had covered Jesus' head was rolled up in a bundle and was lying at the side. Then I went in too, and saw, and believed that he had risen—for until then we hadn't realized that the Scriptures said he would come to life again!

*The linen cloths that had been wrapped around Jesus' body were left as if Jesus had passed right through them. The handkerchief was still rolled up in the shape of a head, and it was at about the right distance from the wrappings that had enveloped Jesus' body. A grave robber couldn't possibly have made off with Jesus' body and left the linens as if they were still shaped around it.*

### STAGES OF BELIEF

People who hear about the Resurrection for the first time may need time before they can comprehend this amazing story. Like Mary and the disciples, they may pass through four stages of belief. (1) At first, they may think the story is a fabrication, impossible to believe (20:2). (2) Like Peter, they may check out the facts and still be puzzled about what happened (20:6). (3) Only when they encounter Jesus personally will they be able to accept the fact of the Resurrection

(20:16). (4) Then, as they commit themselves to the risen Lord and devote their lives to serving him, they will begin to understand fully the reality of his presence with them (20:28). If people don't understand when you tell them about Jesus' resurrection, give them time. Even the disciples didn't believe it at first!

## December 19

## Jesus appears to Mary Magdalene

### JOHN 20:10-18 (also in MARK 16:9-11) (Harmony 240)

*W*e went on home, and by that time Mary had returned to the tomb and was standing outside crying. And as she wept, she stooped and looked in and saw two white-robed angels sitting at the head and foot of the place where the body of Jesus had been lying.

"Why are you crying?" the angels asked her.

"Because they have taken away my Lord," she replied, "and I don't know where they have put him."

*Jesus did not want to be detained at the tomb. If he did not ascend to heaven, the Holy Spirit could not come. Both he and Mary had important work to do.*

She glanced over her shoulder and saw someone standing behind her. It was Jesus, but she didn't recognize him!

"Why are you crying?" he asked her. "Whom are you looking for?"

She thought he was the gardener. "Sir," she said, "if you have taken him away, tell me where you have put him, and I will go and get him."

"Mary!" Jesus said. She turned toward him.

"Master!" she exclaimed.

"Don't touch me," he cautioned, "for I haven't yet ascended to the Father. But go find my brothers and tell them that I ascend to my Father and your Father, my God and your God."

Mary Magdalene found the disciples and told them, "I have seen the Lord!" Then she gave them his message.

#### HE IS NEAR

Mary didn't recognize Jesus at first. Her grief had blinded her; she couldn't see him because she didn't expect to see him. Then Jesus spoke her name, and immediately she recognized him. Imagine the love that flooded her heart when she heard her Savior saying her name. Jesus is near you, and he is calling your name. Can you, like Mary, regard him as your Lord? Are you filled with joy by this good news, and do you share it with others?

## Jesus appears to the women

### MATTHEW 28:8-10 *(Harmony 241)*

he women ran from the tomb, badly frightened, but also filled with joy, and rushed to find the disciples to give them the angel's message. And as they were running, suddenly Jesus was there in front of them!

"Good morning!" he said. And they fell to the ground before him, holding his feet and worshiping him.

Then Jesus said to them, "Don't be frightened! Go tell my brothers to leave at once for Galilee, to meet me there."

*By "my brothers," Jesus meant his disciples. This showed that he had forgiven them, even after they had deserted him. Their relationship would now be even stronger than before.*

**HE WON'T GIVE UP**

Jesus told the women to pass a message on to the disciples—that he would meet them in Galilee, as he had previously told them (Mark 14:28). But the disciples, afraid of the religious leaders, stayed hidden behind locked doors in Jerusalem (John 20:19). The disciples had already run away from Jesus at the time of his greatest need; one of them had betrayed Jesus to his death and another had denied ever knowing him. Imagine the sorry group they must have been as they sat hidden and locked away. But Jesus did not give up on them. He met them first right in their secret room in Jerusalem (Luke 24:36) and then later in Galilee (John 21). Jesus gives second chances—and more! No matter how bad your sin, he is ready to forgive. He has great work for you to do!

## Religious leaders bribe the guards

### MATTHEW 28:11-15 *(Harmony 242)*

As the women were on the way into the city, some of the Temple police who had been guarding the tomb went to the chief priests and told them what had happened. A meeting of all the Jewish leaders was called, and it was decided to bribe the police to say they had all been asleep when Jesus' disciples came during the night and stole his body.

"If the governor hears about it," the Council promised, "we'll stand up for you and everything will be all right."

So the police accepted the bribe and said what they were told to. Their story spread widely among the Jews and is still believed by them to this very day.

*The problem with the Council's story that the disciples stole the body is that these same disciples later suffered greatly; some were even martyred for their faith in the risen Christ. If they knew that they had stolen a dead body in order to keep up a hoax, it is highly doubtful that they would willingly die for that hoax.*

**AMAZING NEWS**

Jesus' resurrection was already causing a great stir in Jerusalem. A group of women was moving quickly through the streets, looking for the disciples to tell them the amazing news that Jesus was alive. At the same time, a group of religious leaders was plotting how to cover up the Resurrection. Today there is still a great stir over the Resurrection, and there are still only two choices—to believe that Jesus rose from the dead, or to be closed to the truth—denying it, ignoring it, or trying to explain it away. Which choice have you made?

## *December 22*

---

## Jesus appears to two believers traveling on the road

### *LUKE 24:13-35 (also in MARK 16:12-13) (Harmony 243)*

hat same day, Sunday, two of Jesus' followers were walking to the village of Emmaus, seven miles out of Jerusalem. As they walked along they were talking of Jesus' death, when suddenly Jesus himself came along and joined them and began walking beside them. But they didn't recognize him, for God kept them from it.

"You seem to be in a deep discussion about something," he said. "What are you so concerned about?" They stopped short, sadness written across their faces. And one of them, Cleopas, replied, "You must be the only person in Jerusalem who hasn't heard about the terrible things that happened there last week."

"What things?" Jesus asked.

"The things that happened to Jesus, the Man from Nazareth," they said. "He was a Prophet who did incredible miracles and was a mighty Teacher, highly regarded by both God and man. But the chief priests and our religious leaders arrested him and handed him over to the Roman government to be condemned to death, and they crucified him. We had thought he was the glorious Messiah and that he had come to rescue Israel.

"And now, besides all this—which happened three days ago—some women from our group of his followers were at his tomb early this morning and came back with an amazing report that his body was missing, and that they had seen some angels there who told them Jesus is alive! Some of our men ran out to see, and sure enough, Jesus' body was gone, just as the women had said."

Then Jesus said to them, "You are such foolish, foolish people! You find it so hard to believe all that the prophets wrote in the Scriptures! Wasn't it clearly predicted by the prophets that the Messiah would have to suffer all these things before entering his time of glory?"

*The disciples from Emmaus were counting on Jesus to redeem Israel—that is, to rescue the nation from its enemies. Most Jews believed that the Old Testament prophecies pointed to a military and political Messiah; they didn't realize that the Messiah had come to redeem people from slavery to sin. When Jesus died, therefore, they lost all hope. They didn't understand that Jesus' death offered the greatest hope possible.*

Then Jesus quoted them passage after passage from the writings of the prophets, beginning with the book of Genesis and going right on through the Scriptures, explaining what the passages meant and what they said about himself.

By this time they were nearing Emmaus and the end of their journey. Jesus would have gone on, but they begged him to stay the night with them, as it was getting late. So he went home with them. As they sat down to eat, he asked God's blessing on the food and then took a small loaf of bread and broke it and was passing it over to them, when suddenly—it was as though their eyes were opened—they recognized him! And at that moment he disappeared!

They began telling each other how their hearts had felt strangely warm as he talked with them and explained the Scriptures during the walk down the road. Within the hour they were on their way back to Jerusalem, where the eleven disciples and the other followers of Jesus greeted them with these words, "The Lord has really risen! He appeared to Peter!"

Then the two from Emmaus told their story of how Jesus had appeared to them as they were walking along the road and how they had recognized him as he was breaking the bread.

### STEP OF FAITH

Why did Jesus call these disciples foolish? Even though they well knew the biblical prophecies, they failed to understand that Christ's suffering was his path to glory. They could not understand why God did not intervene to save Jesus from the cross. The world has not changed its values: A suffering servant is no more popular today than two thousand years ago. But we have not only the witness of the Old Testament prophets, but also the witness of the New Testament apostles and the history of the Christian church all pointing to Jesus' victory over death. Will we step outside the values of our culture and put our faith in Jesus? Or will we foolishly continue to be baffled by his Good News?

## December 23

## Jesus appears to the disciples behind locked doors

### LUKE 24:36-43 (also in JOHN 20:19-23) (Harmony 244)

*A*nd just as they were telling about it, Jesus himself was suddenly standing there among them, and greeted them. But the whole group was terribly frightened, thinking they were seeing a ghost!

"Why are you frightened?" he asked. "Why do you doubt that it is really I? Look at my hands! Look at my feet! You can see that it is I, myself! Touch me and make sure that I am not a ghost! For ghosts don't have bodies, as you see that I do!" As he spoke, he held out his hands for them to see the marks of the nails, and showed them the wounds in his feet.

Still they stood there undecided, filled with joy and doubt.

Then he asked them, "Do you have anything here to eat?"

They gave him a piece of broiled fish, and he ate it as they watched!

*Jesus' body wasn't just a figment of the imagination or the appearance of a ghost—the disciples touched him, and he ate food. On the other hand, his body wasn't merely a restored human body like Lazarus's (John 11)—he was able to appear and disappear. Jesus' resurrected body was immortal. This is the kind of body we will be given at the resurrection of the dead (see 1 Corinthians 15:42-50).*

#### HIS REPRESENTATIVES

The disciples knew that the tomb was empty but didn't understand that Jesus had risen, and they were filled with fear—even when Jesus appeared to them. Despite the women's witness and the biblical prophecies of this very event, they still didn't believe. Today the Resurrection still catches people by surprise, and many refuse to believe. What more will it take? For these disciples it took the living, breathing Jesus in their midst. For many people today, it takes the presence of living, breathing Christians. As part of Christ's body on earth, you have the responsibility to be his representative to a lost world. What do people think of Christ when they think of you?

## Jesus appears to the disciples, including Thomas

*JOHN 20:24-31 (also in MARK 16:14) (Harmony 245)*

One of the disciples, Thomas, "The Twin," was not there at the time with the others. When they kept telling him, "We have seen the Lord," he replied, "I won't believe it unless I see the nail wounds in his hands—and put my fingers into them—and place my hand into his side."

Eight days later the disciples were together again, and this time Thomas was with them. The doors were locked; but suddenly, as before, Jesus was standing among them and greeting them.

Then he said to Thomas, "Put your finger into my hands. Put your hand into my side. Don't be faithless any longer. Believe!"

"My Lord and my God!" Thomas said.

Then Jesus told him, "You believe because you have seen me. But blessed are those who haven't seen me and believe anyway."

*To understand the life and mission of Jesus more fully, all we need to do is study the Gospels. John tells us that his Gospel records only a few of the many events in Jesus' life on earth. But the gospel includes everything we need to know to believe that Jesus is the Christ, the Son of God, through whom we receive eternal life.*

Jesus' disciples saw him do many other miracles besides the ones told about in this book, but these are recorded so that you will believe that he is the Messiah, the Son of God, and that believing in him you will have life.

### GOOD DOUBTS

Jesus wasn't hard on Thomas for his doubts. Despite his skepticism, Thomas was still loyal to the believers and to Jesus himself. Some people need to doubt before they believe. If doubt leads to questions, questions lead to answers, and the answers are accepted, then doubt has done good work. It is when doubt becomes stubbornness and stubbornness becomes a lifestyle that doubt harms faith. When you doubt, don't stop there. Let your doubt deepen your faith as you continue to search for the answer.

## Jesus appears to the disciples while fishing

*JOHN 21:1-6 (Harmony 246a)*

Later Jesus appeared again to the disciples beside the Lake of Galilee. This is how it happened:

A group of us were there—Simon Peter, Thomas, "The Twin," Nathanael from Cana in Galilee, my brother James and I and two other disciples.

Simon Peter said, "I'm going fishing."

"We'll come too," we all said. We did, but caught nothing all night. At dawn we saw a man standing on the beach but couldn't see who he was.

*In this passage Jesus recommissioned Peter. Perhaps Peter needed special encouragement after his denial.*

He called, "Any fish, boys?"

"No," we replied.

Then he said, "Throw out your net on the right-hand side of the boat, and you'll get plenty of them!" So we did, and couldn't draw in the net because of the weight of the fish, there were so many!

### A CALL FROM THE BEACH

Jesus had performed a similar miracle for the disciples before. Luke 5:1-11 records how the disciples had experienced an unsuccessful night of fishing, only to have a record-breaking catch on Jesus' instructions. At the time, the disciples had been amazed to see that not only did Jesus teach, heal, and cast out demons, but he also cared about their day-to-day routine. Here the disciples had gone back to what they knew best—fishing. And Jesus came to them right where they were, performing another miracle to demonstrate his great love for them. Jesus meets us where we are, gently showing us where he wants us to be. Is he standing on the beach calling to you? Pull in your boat and listen!

## Jesus appears to the disciples while fishing

### JOHN 21:7-14 *(Harmony 246b)*

hen I said to Peter, "It is the Lord!" At that, Simon Peter put on his tunic (for he was stripped to the waist) and jumped into the water and swam ashore. The rest of us stayed in the boat and pulled the loaded net to the beach, about 300 feet away. When we got there, we saw that a fire was kindled and fish were frying over it, and there was bread.

"Bring some of the fish you've just caught," Jesus said. So Simon Peter went out and dragged the net ashore. By his count there were 153 large fish; and yet the net hadn't torn.

*Impetuous Peter jumped out of the boat and swam to the shore when he realized that it was Jesus on the beach. Clearly he wanted to talk to Jesus and to experience Jesus' forgiveness.*

"Now come and have some breakfast!" Jesus said; and none of us dared ask him if he really was the Lord, for we were quite sure of it. Then Jesus went around serving us the bread and fish.

This was the third time Jesus had appeared to us since his return from the dead.

#### WILLINGNESS TO SERVE

In this beach scene, Jesus would lead Peter through an experience that would remove the cloud of his denial. Peter had denied Jesus three times. Three times Jesus asked Peter if he loved him. Peter had repented, and here Jesus was asking him to commit his life. Peter's life changed when he finally realized who Jesus was. His occupation changed from fisherman to evangelist; his identity changed from impetuous to "rock"; and his relationship to Jesus changed—he was forgiven, and he finally understood the significance of Jesus' words about his death and resurrection. It is one thing to say you love Jesus, but the real test is willingness to serve him.

## Jesus talks with Peter

*JOHN 21:15-19* *(Harmony 247a)*

After breakfast Jesus said to Simon Peter, "Simon, son of John, do you love me more than these others?"

"Yes," Peter replied, "you know I am your friend."

"Then feed my lambs," Jesus told him.

Jesus repeated the question: "Simon, son of John, do you *really* love me?"

"Yes, Lord," Peter said, "you know I am your friend."

"Then take care of my sheep," Jesus said.

Once more he asked him, "Simon, son of John, are you even my friend?"

*This was a prediction of Peter's death by crucifixion. Tradition indicates that Peter was crucified for his faith—upside down because he did not feel worthy of dying as his Lord had died. Despite the future, Jesus told Peter to follow him.*

Peter was grieved at the way Jesus asked the question this third time. "Lord, you know my heart; you know I am," he said.

Jesus said, "Then feed my little sheep. When you were young, you were able to do as you liked and go wherever you wanted to; but when you are old, you will stretch out your hands and others will direct you and take you where you don't want to go." Jesus said this to let him know what kind of death he would die to glorify God. Then Jesus told him, "Follow me."

### DO YOU TRULY LOVE HIM?

Jesus asked Peter three times if he loved him. The first time Jesus said, "Do you love (Greek *agape*: volitional, self-sacrificial love) me more than these others?" The second time, Jesus focused on Peter alone and still used the Greek word *agape*. The third time, Jesus used the Greek word *phileo* (signifying affection, affinity, or brotherly love) and asked, in effect, "Are you even my friend?" Each time Peter responded with the Greek word *phileo*. Jesus doesn't settle for quick, superficial answers. He has a way of getting to the heart of the matter. Peter had to face his true feelings and motives when Jesus confronted him. How would you respond if Jesus asked you, "Do you love me?" Do you really love Jesus? Are you even his friend?

## Jesus talks with Peter

***JOHN 21:20-25*** *(Harmony 247b)*

eter turned around and saw the disciple Jesus loved following, the one who had leaned around at supper that time to ask Jesus, "Master, which of us will betray you?" Peter asked Jesus, "What about him, Lord? What sort of death will he die?"

Jesus replied, "If I want him to live until I return, what is that to you? *You* follow me."

So the rumor spread among the brotherhood that that disciple wouldn't die! But that isn't what Jesus said at all! He only said, "If I want him to live until I come, what is that to you?"

*Early church history reports that after John spent several years as an exile on the island of Patmos, he returned to Ephesus where he died as an old man, near the end of the first century.*

*I am that disciple!* I saw these events and have recorded them here. And we all know that my account of these things is accurate.

And I suppose that if all the other events in Jesus' life were written, the whole world could hardly contain the books!

#### DON'T COMPARE

Peter asked Jesus how John would die. Jesus replied that Peter should not concern himself with that. We tend to compare our lives to others, whether to rationalize our own level of devotion to Christ or to question God's justice. Jesus responds to us as he did to Peter: "What is that to you? *You* follow me." When you follow Christ and live as he wants you to, there is no need to compare yourself with others. People make comparisons for many reasons. Some point out others' flaws in order to feel better about themselves. Others simply want reassurance that they are doing well. When you are tempted to compare, look at Jesus Christ. His example will inspire you to do your very best, and his loving acceptance will comfort you when you fall short of your expectations.

## Jesus gives the great commission

### MATTHEW 28:16-20 (also in MARK 16:15-18)
### (Harmony 248)

hen the eleven disciples left for Galilee, going to the mountain where Jesus had said they would find him. There they met him and worshiped him—but some of them weren't sure it really was Jesus!

He told his disciples, "I have been given all authority in heaven and earth. Therefore go and make disciples in all the nations, baptizing them into the name of the Father and of the Son and of the Holy Spirit, and then teach these new disciples to obey all the commands I have given you; and be sure of this—that I am with you always, even to the end of the world."

*Jesus' words affirm the reality of the Trinity. He did not say baptize them into the names, but into the name of the Father, Son, and Holy Spirit. The word Trinity does not occur in Scripture, but it well describes the three-in-one nature of the Father, Son, and Holy Spirit.*

**GO AND TELL**

God gave Jesus authority over heaven and earth. On the basis of that authority, Jesus told his disciples to make more disciples as they preached, baptized, and taught. With this same authority, Jesus still commands us to tell others the Good News and make them disciples for the Kingdom. We are to go—whether it is next door or to another country—and make disciples. It is not an option, but a command to all who call Jesus "Lord." We are not all evangelists in the formal sense, but we have all received gifts that we can use to help fulfill the great commission. As we obey, we have comfort in the knowledge that Jesus is always with us.

## Jesus appears to the disciples in Jerusalem

### LUKE 24:44-49 (Harmony 249)

hen he said, "When I was with you before, don't you remember my telling you that everything written about me by Moses and the prophets and in the Psalms must all come true?" Then he opened their minds to understand at last these many Scriptures! And he said, "Yes, it was written long ago that the Messiah must suffer and die and rise again from the dead on the third day; and that this message of salvation should be taken from Jerusalem to all the nations: *There is forgiveness of sins for all who turn to me.* You have seen these prophecies come true.

*Luke wrote to the Greek-speaking world. He wanted them to know that Christ's message of God's love and forgiveness should go to all the world. We must never ignore the worldwide scope of Christ's gospel. God wants all the world to hear the Good News of salvation.*

"And now I will send the Holy Spirit upon you, just as my Father promised. Don't begin telling others yet—stay here in the city until the Holy Spirit comes and fills you with power from heaven.

### STUDY GOD'S WORD

The phrase "Moses, the prophets, and the Psalms" is a way to describe the entire Old Testament. In other words, the entire Old Testament points to the Messiah. For example, Jesus' role as prophet was foretold in Deuteronomy 18:15-20; his sufferings were prophesied in Psalm 22 and Isaiah 53; his resurrection was predicted in Psalm 16:9-11 and Isaiah 53:10-11. Jesus opened these people's minds to understand the Scriptures. The Holy Spirit does this in our lives today when we study the Bible. Have you ever wondered how to understand a difficult Bible passage? Besides reading surrounding passages, asking other people, and consulting reference works, pray that the Holy Spirit will open your mind to understand, giving you the needed insight to put God's Word into action in your life.

*December 31*

## Jesus ascends into heaven

### *LUKE 24:50-53 (also in MARK 16:19-20; ACTS 1:1-11)*
### *(Harmony 250)*

Then Jesus led them out along the road to Bethany, and lifting his hands to heaven, he blessed them, and then began rising into the sky, and went on to heaven. And they worshiped him, and returned to Jerusalem filled with mighty joy, and were continually in the Temple, praising God.

*Jesus' physical presence left the disciples when he returned to heaven (Acts 1:9), but the Holy Spirit soon came to comfort them and empower them to spread the gospel of salvation (Acts 2:1-4).*

**WITH YOU ALWAYS**

As the disciples stood and watched, Jesus began rising into the air, and soon he disappeared into heaven. Seeing Jesus leave must have been frightening, but the disciples knew that Jesus would keep his promise to be with them through the Holy Spirit. This same Jesus, who lived with the disciples, who died and was buried, and who rose from the dead, loves us and promises to be with us always. We can get to know him better through studying the Scriptures, praying, and allowing the Holy Spirit to make us more like Jesus.

## 250 EVENTS IN THE LIFE OF CHRIST:
## A Harmony of the Gospels

All four books in the Bible that tell the story of Jesus Christ—Matthew, Mark, Luke, and John—stand alone, emphasizing a unique aspect of Jesus' life. But when these are blended into one complete account, or harmonized, we gain new insights about the life of Christ.

This harmony combines the four Gospels into a single chronological account of Christ's life on earth. It includes every chapter and verse of each Gospel, leaving nothing out.

The harmony is divided into 250 events. The title of each event is identical to the title found in the corresponding Gospel. Parallel passages found in more than one Gospel have identical titles, helping you to identify them quickly.

Each of the 250 events in the harmony is numbered. The number of the event corresponds to the number next to the title in the Bible text. When reading one of the Gospel accounts, you will notice, at times, that some numbers are missing or out of sequence. The easiest way to locate these events is to refer to the harmony.

In addition, if you are looking for a particular event in the life of Christ, the harmony can help you locate it more rapidly than paging through all four Gospels. Each of the 250 events has a distinctive title keyed to the main emphasis of the passage to help you locate and remember the events.

This harmony will help you to better visualize the travels of Jesus, study the four Gospels comparatively, and appreciate the unity of their message.

### I. BIRTH AND PREPARATION OF JESUS CHRIST

| | MATTHEW | MARK | LUKE | JOHN |
|---|---|---|---|---|
| 1. Luke's purpose in writing | | | 1:1-4 | |
| 2. God became a human being | | | | 1:1-18 |
| 3. The ancestors of Jesus | 1:1-17 | | 3:23-38 | |
| 4. An angel promises the birth of John to Zacharias | | | 1:5-25 | |
| 5. An angel promises the birth of Jesus to Mary | | | 1:26-38 | |

|  |  | MATTHEW | MARK | LUKE | JOHN |
|---|---|---|---|---|---|
| 6. | Mary visits Elizabeth | | | 1:39-56 | |
| 7. | John the Baptist is born | | | 1:57-80 | |
| 8. | An angel appears to Joseph | 1:18-25 | | | |
| 9. | Jesus is born in Bethlehem | | | 2:1-7 | |
| 10. | Shepherds visit Jesus | | | 2:8-20 | |
| 11. | Mary and Joseph bring Jesus to the Temple | | | 2:21-40 | |
| 12. | Visitors arrive from eastern lands | 2:1-12 | | | |
| 13. | The escape to Egypt | 2:13-18 | | | |
| 14. | The return to Nazareth | 2:19-23 | | | |
| 15. | Jesus speaks with the religious teachers | | | 2:41-52 | |
| 16. | John the Baptist prepares the way for Jesus | 3:1-12 | 1:1-8 | 3:1-18 | |
| 17. | John baptizes Jesus | 3:13-17 | 1:9-11 | 3:21-22 | |
| 18. | Satan tempts Jesus in the wilderness | 4:1-11 | 1:12-13 | 4:1-13 | |
| 19. | John the Baptist declares his mission | | | | 1:19-28 |
| 20. | John the Baptist proclaims Jesus as the Messiah | | | | 1:29-34 |
| 21. | The first disciples follow Jesus | | | | 1:35-51 |
| 22. | Jesus turns water into wine | | | | 2:1-12 |

## II. MESSAGE AND MINISTRY OF JESUS CHRIST

|  |  | MATTHEW | MARK | LUKE | JOHN |
|---|---|---|---|---|---|
| 23. | Jesus clears the Temple | | | | 2:13-25 |
| 24. | Nicodemus visits Jesus at night | | | | 3:1-21 |
| 25. | John the Baptist tells more about Jesus | | | | 3:22-36 |
| 26. | Herod puts John in prison | | | 3:19-20 | |
| 27. | Jesus talks to a woman at the well | | | | 4:1-26 |
| 28. | Jesus tells about the spiritual harvest | | | | 4:27-38 |
| 29. | Many Samaritans believe in Jesus | | | | 4:39-42 |
| 30. | Jesus preaches in Galilee | 4:12-17 | 1:14-15 | 4:14-15 | 4:43-45 |
| 31. | Jesus heals a government official's son | | | | 4:46-54 |
| 32. | Jesus is rejected at Nazareth | | | 4:16-30 | |
| 33. | Four fishermen follow Jesus | 4:18-22 | 1:16-20 | | |
| 34. | Jesus teaches with great authority | | 1:21-28 | 4:31-37 | |
| 35. | Jesus heals Peter's mother-in-law and many others | 8:14-17 | 1:29-34 | 4:38-41 | |
| 36. | Jesus preaches throughout Galilee | 4:23-25 | 1:35-39 | 4:42-44 | |
| 37. | Jesus provides a miraculous catch of fish | | | 5:1-11 | |
| 38. | Jesus heals a man with leprosy | 8:1-4 | 1:40-45 | 5:12-16 | |
| 39. | Jesus heals a paralyzed man | 9:1-8 | 2:1-12 | 5:17-26 | |
| 40. | Jesus eats with sinners at Matthew's house | 9:9-13 | 2:13-17 | 5:27-32 | |
| 41. | Religious leaders ask Jesus about fasting | 9:14-17 | 2:18-22 | 5:33-39 | |
| 42. | Jesus heals a lame man by the pool | | | | 5:1-15 |
| 43. | Jesus claims to be God's Son | | | | 5:16-30 |
| 44. | Jesus supports his claim | | | | 5:31-47 |

|  |  | MATTHEW | MARK | LUKE | JOHN |
|---|---|---|---|---|---|
| 45. | The disciples pick wheat on the Sabbath | 12:1-8 | 2:23-28 | 6:1-5 | |
| 46. | Jesus heals a man's hand on the Sabbath | 12:9-14 | 3:1-6 | 6:6-11 | |
| 47. | Large crowds follow Jesus | 12:15-21 | 3:7-12 | | |
| 48. | Jesus selects the twelve disciples | | 3:13-19 | 6:12-16 | |
| 49. | Jesus gives the Beatitudes | 5:1-12 | | 6:17-26 | |
| 50. | Jesus teaches about salt and light | 5:13-16 | | | |
| 51. | Jesus teaches about the Law | 5:17-20 | | | |
| 52. | Jesus teaches about anger | 5:21-26 | | | |
| 53. | Jesus teaches about lust | 5:27-30 | | | |
| 54. | Jesus teaches about divorce | 5:31-32 | | | |
| 55. | Jesus teaches about vows | 5:33-37 | | | |
| 56. | Jesus teaches about retaliation | 5:38-42 | | | |
| 57. | Jesus teaches about loving enemies | 5:43-48 | | 6:27-36 | |
| 58. | Jesus teaches about giving to the needy | 6:1-4 | | | |
| 59. | Jesus teaches about prayer | 6:5-15 | | | |
| 60. | Jesus teaches about fasting | 6:16-18 | | | |
| 61. | Jesus teaches about money | 6:19-24 | | | |
| 62. | Jesus teaches about worry | 6:25-34 | | | |
| 63. | Jesus teaches about criticizing others | 7:1-6 | | 6:37-42 | |
| 64. | Jesus teaches about asking, seeking, knocking | 7:7-12 | | | |
| 65. | Jesus teaches about the way to heaven | 7:13-14 | | | |
| 66. | Jesus teaches about fruit in people's lives | 7:15-20 | | 6:43-45 | |
| 67. | Jesus teaches about those who build houses on rock and sand | 7:21-29 | | 6:46-49 | |
| 68. | A Roman soldier demonstrates faith | 8:5-13 | | 7:1-10 | |
| 69. | Jesus raises a widow's son from the dead | | | 7:11-17 | |
| 70. | Jesus eases John's doubt | 11:1-19 | | 7:18-35 | |
| 71. | Jesus promises rest for the soul | 11:20-30 | | | |
| 72. | A sinful woman anoints Jesus' feet | | | 7:36-50 | |
| 73. | Women accompany Jesus and the disciples | | | 8:1-3 | |
| 74. | Religious leaders accuse Jesus of being Satan | 12:22-37 | 3:20-30 | | |
| 75. | Religious leaders ask Jesus for a miracle | 12:38-45 | | | |
| 76. | Jesus describes his true family | 12:46-50 | 3:31-35 | 8:19-21 | |
| 77. | Jesus tells the parable of the four soils | 13:1-9 | 4:1-9 | 8:4-8 | |
| 78. | Jesus explains the parable of the four soils | 13:10-23 | 4:10-25 | 8:9-18 | |
| 79. | Jesus tells the parable of the growing seed | | 4:26-29 | | |
| 80. | Jesus tells the parable of the weeds | 13:24-30 | | | |
| 81. | Jesus tells the parable of the mustard seed | 13:31-32 | 4:30-34 | | |
| 82. | Jesus tells the parable of the yeast | 13:33-35 | | | |
| 83. | Jesus explains the parable of the weeds | 13:36-43 | | | |
| 84. | Jesus tells the parable of hidden treasure | 13:44 | | | |
| 85. | Jesus tells the parable of the pearl merchant | 13:45-46 | | | |

| | MATTHEW | MARK | LUKE | JOHN |
|---|---|---|---|---|
| 86. Jesus tells the parable of the fishing net | 13:47-52 | | | |
| 87. Jesus calms the storm | 8:23-27 | 4:35-41 | 8:22-25 | |
| 88. Jesus sends the demons into a herd of pigs | 8:28-34 | 5:1-20 | 8:26-39 | |
| 89. Jesus heals a bleeding woman and restores a girl to life | 9:18-26 | 5:21-43 | 8:40-56 | |
| 90. Jesus heals the blind and mute | 9:27-34 | | | |
| 91. The people of Nazareth refuse to believe | 13:53-58 | 6:1-6 | | |
| 92. Jesus urges the disciples to pray for workers | 9:35-38 | | | |
| 93. Jesus sends out the twelve disciples | 10:1-15 | 6:7-13 | 9:1-6 | |
| 94. Jesus prepares the disciples for persecution | 10:16-42 | | | |
| 95. Herod kills John the Baptist | 14:1-12 | 6:14-29 | 9:7-9 | |
| 96. Jesus feeds five thousand | 14:13-21 | 6:30-44 | 9:10-17 | 6:1-15 |
| 97. Jesus walks on water | 14:22-33 | 6:45-52 | | 6:16-21 |
| 98. Jesus heals all who touch him | 14:34-36 | 6:53-56 | | |
| 99. Jesus is the true Bread from heaven | | | | 6:22-40 |
| 100. The Jews disagree that Jesus is from heaven | | | | 6:41-59 |
| 101. Many disciples desert Jesus | | | | 6:60-71 |
| 102. Jesus teaches about inner purity | 15:1-20 | 7:1-23 | | |
| 103. Jesus sends a demon out of a girl | 15:21-28 | 7:24-30 | | |
| 104. The crowd marvels at Jesus' healings | 15:29-31 | 7:31-37 | | |
| 105. Jesus feeds four thousand | 15:32-39 | 8:1-9 | | |
| 106. Religious leaders ask for a sign in the sky | 16:1-4 | 8:10-12 | | |
| 107. Jesus warns against wrong teaching | 16:5-12 | 8:13-21 | | |
| 108. Jesus restores sight to a blind man | | 8:22-26 | | |
| 109. Peter says Jesus is the Messiah | 16:13-20 | 8:27-30 | 9:18-20 | |
| 110. Jesus predicts his death the first time | 16:21-28 | 8:31–9:1 | 9:21-27 | |
| 111. Jesus is transfigured on the mountain | 17:1-13 | 9:2-13 | 9:28-36 | |
| 112. Jesus heals a demon-possessed boy | 17:14-21 | 9:14-29 | 9:37-43 | |
| 113. Jesus predicts his death the second time | 17:22-23 | 9:30-32 | 9:44-45 | |
| 114. Peter finds the coin in the fish's mouth | 17:24-27 | | | |
| 115. The disciples argue about who would be the greatest | 18:1-6 | 9:33-37 | 9:46-48 | |
| 116. The disciples forbid another to use Jesus' name | | 9:38-42 | 9:49-50 | |
| 117. Jesus warns against temptation | 18:7-9 | 9:43-50 | | |
| 118. Jesus warns against looking down on others | 18:10-14 | | | |
| 119. Jesus teaches how to treat a believer who sins | 18:15-20 | | | |
| 120. Jesus tells the parable of the unforgiving debtor | 18:21-35 | | | |
| 121. Jesus' brothers ridicule him | | | | 7:1-9 |
| 122. Jesus teaches about the cost of following him | 8:18-22 | | 9:51-62 | |

|  |  | MATTHEW | MARK | LUKE | JOHN |
|---|---|---|---|---|---|
| 123. | Jesus teaches openly at the Temple | | | | 7:10-31 |
| 124. | Religious leaders attempt to arrest Jesus | | | | 7:32-52 |
| 125. | Jesus forgives an adulterous woman | | | | 8:1-11 |
| 126. | Jesus is the Light of the world | | | | 8:12-20 |
| 127. | Jesus warns of coming judgment | | | | 8:21-29 |
| 128. | Jesus speaks about God's true children | | | | 8:30-47 |
| 129. | Jesus states he is eternal | | | | 8:48-59 |
| 130. | Jesus sends out seventy messengers | | | 10:1-16 | |
| 131. | The seventy messengers return | | | 10:17-24 | |
| 132. | Jesus tells the parable of the Good Samaritan | | | 10:25-37 | |
| 133. | Jesus visits Mary and Martha | | | 10:38-42 | |
| 134. | Jesus teaches his disciples about prayer | | | 11:1-13 | |
| 135. | Jesus answers hostile accusations | | | 11:14-28 | |
| 136. | Jesus warns against unbelief | | | 11:29-32 | |
| 137. | Jesus teaches about the light within | | | 11:33-36 | |
| 138. | Jesus criticizes the religious leaders | | | 11:37-54 | |
| 139. | Jesus speaks against hypocrisy | | | 12:1-12 | |
| 140. | Jesus tells the parable of the rich fool | | | 12:13-21 | |
| 141. | Jesus warns about worry | | | 12:22-34 | |
| 142. | Jesus warns about preparing for his coming | | | 12:35-48 | |
| 143. | Jesus warns about coming division | | | 12:49-53 | |
| 144. | Jesus warns about the future crisis | | | 12:54-59 | |
| 145. | Jesus calls the people to repent | | | 13:1-9 | |
| 146. | Jesus heals the handicapped woman | | | 13:10-17 | |
| 147. | Jesus teaches about the Kingdom of God | | | 13:18-21 | |
| 148. | Jesus heals the man who was born blind | | | | 9:1-12 |
| 149. | Religious leaders question the blind man | | | | 9:13-34 |
| 150. | Jesus teaches about spiritual blindness | | | | 9:35-41 |
| 151. | Jesus is the Good Shepherd | | | | 10:1-21 |
| 152. | Religious leaders surround Jesus at the Temple | | | | 10:22-42 |
| 153. | Jesus teaches about entering the Kingdom | | | 13:22-30 | |
| 154. | Jesus grieves over Jerusalem | | | 13:31-35 | |
| 155. | Jesus heals a man with dropsy | | | 14:1-6 | |
| 156. | Jesus teaches about seeking honor | | | 14:7-14 | |
| 157. | Jesus tells the parable of the great feast | | | 14:15-24 | |
| 158. | Jesus teaches about the cost of being a disciple | | | | 14:25-35 |
| 159. | Jesus tells the parable of the lost sheep | | | 15:1-7 | |
| 160. | Jesus tells the parable of the lost coin | | | 15:8-10 | |
| 161. | Jesus tells the parable of the lost son | | | 15:11-32 | |
| 162. | Jesus tells the parable of the shrewd accountant | | | | 16:1-18 |
| 163. | Jesus tells about the rich man and the beggar | | | 16:19-31 | |
| 164. | Jesus tells about forgiveness and faith | | | 17:1-10 | |
| 165. | Lazarus becomes ill and dies | | | | 11:1-16 |
| 166. | Jesus comforts Mary and Martha | | | | 11:17-37 |

|  | MATTHEW | MARK | LUKE | JOHN |
|---|---|---|---|---|
| 167. Jesus raises Lazarus from the dead | | | | 11:37-44 |
| 168. Religious leaders plot to kill Jesus | | | | 11:45-57 |
| 169. Jesus heals ten men with leprosy | | | 17:11-19 | |
| 170. Jesus teaches about the coming of the Kingdom of God | | | 17:20-37 | |
| 171. Jesus tells the parable of the persistent widow | | | 18:1-8 | |
| 172. Jesus tells the parable of two men who prayed | | | 18:9-14 | |
| 173. Jesus teaches about marriage and divorce | 19:1-12 | 10:1-12 | | |
| 174. Jesus blesses little children | 19:13-15 | 10:13-16 | 18:15-17 | |
| 175. Jesus speaks to the rich young man | 19:16-30 | 10:17-31 | 18:18-30 | |
| 176. Jesus tells the parable of the workers paid equally | 20:1-16 | | | |
| 177. Jesus predicts his death the third time | 20:17-19 | 10:32-34 | 18:31-34 | |
| 178. Jesus teaches about serving others | 20:20-28 | 10:35-45 | | |
| 179. Jesus heals a blind beggar | 20:29-34 | 10:46-52 | 18:35-43 | |
| 180. Jesus brings salvation to Zacchaeus's home | | | 19:1-10 | |
| 181. Jesus tells the parable of the king's ten servants | | | 19:11-27 | |
| 182. A woman anoints Jesus with perfume | 26:6-13 | 14:3-9 | | 12:1-11 |
| 183. Jesus rides into Jerusalem on a donkey | 21:1-11 | 11:1-11 | 19:28-44 | 12:12-19 |
| 184. Jesus clears the Temple again | 21:12-17 | 11:12-19 | 19:45-48 | |
| 185. Jesus explains why he must die | | | | 12:20-36 |
| 186. Most of the people do not believe in Jesus | | | | 12:37-43 |
| 187. Jesus summarizes his message | | | | 12:44-50 |
| 188. Jesus says the disciples can pray for anything | 21:18-22 | 11:20-25 | | |
| 189. Religious leaders challenge Jesus' authority | 21:23-27 | 11:27-33 | 20:1-8 | |
| 190. Jesus tells the parable of the two sons | 21:28-32 | | | |
| 191. Jesus tells the parable of the wicked farmers | 21:33-46 | 12:1-12 | 20:9-19 | |
| 192. Jesus tells the parable of the wedding feast | 22:1-14 | | | |
| 193. Religious leaders question Jesus about paying taxes | 22:15-22 | 12:13-17 | 20:20-26 | |
| 194. Religious leaders question Jesus about the resurrection | 22:23-32 | 12:18-27 | 20:27-40 | |
| 195. Religious leaders question Jesus about the greatest commandment | 22:33-40 | 12:28-34 | | |
| 196. Religious leaders cannot answer Jesus' question | 22:41-46 | 12:35-37 | 20:41-44 | |
| 197. Jesus warns against the religious leaders | 23:1-12 | 12:38-40 | 20:45-47 | |
| 198. Jesus condemns the religious leaders | 23:13-36 | | | |
| 199. Jesus grieves over Jerusalem again | 23:37-39 | | | |

|  | MATTHEW | MARK | LUKE | JOHN |
|---|---|---|---|---|
| 200. A poor widow gives all she has | | 12:41-44 | 21:1-4 | |
| 201. Jesus tells about the future | 24:1-22 | 13:1-20 | 21:5-24 | |
| 202. Jesus tells about his return | 24:23-35 | 13:21-31 | 21:25-33 | |
| 203. Jesus tells about remaining watchful | 24:36-51 | 13:32-37 | 21:34-38 | |
| 204. Jesus tells the parable of the ten bridesmaids | 25:1-13 | | | |
| 205. Jesus tells the parable of the loaned money | 25:14-30 | | | |
| 206. Jesus tells about the final judgment | 25:31-46 | | | |

## III. DEATH AND RESURRECTION OF JESUS CHRIST

|  | MATTHEW | MARK | LUKE | JOHN |
|---|---|---|---|---|
| 207. Religious leaders plot to kill Jesus | 26:1-5 | 14:1-2 | 22:1-2 | |
| 208. Judas agrees to betray Jesus | 26:14-16 | 14:10-11 | 22:3-6 | |
| 209. Disciples prepare for the Passover | 26:17-19 | 14:12-16 | 22:7-13 | |
| 210. Jesus washes the disciples' feet | | | | 13:1-20 |
| 211. Jesus and the disciples have the Last Supper | 26:20-29 | 14:17-25 | 22:14-30 | 13:21-30 |
| 212. Jesus predicts Peter's denial | | | 22:31-38 | 13:31-38 |
| 213. Jesus is the way to the Father | | | | 14:1-14 |
| 214. Jesus promises the Holy Spirit | | | | 14:15-31 |
| 215. Jesus teaches about the Vine and the branches | | | | 15:1-16 |
| 216. Jesus warns about the world's hatred | | | | 15:17-16:4 |
| 217. Jesus teaches about the Holy Spirit | | | | 16:5-16 |
| 218. Jesus teaches about using his name in prayer | | | | 16:17-33 |
| 219. Jesus prays for himself | | | | 17:1-5 |
| 220. Jesus prays for his disciples | | | | 17:6-19 |
| 221. Jesus prays for future believers | | | | 17:20-26 |
| 222. Jesus again predicts Peter's denial | 26:30-35 | 14:26-31 | | |
| 223. Jesus agonizes in the garden | 26:36-46 | 14:32-42 | 22:39-46 | |
| 224. Jesus is betrayed and arrested | 26:47-56 | 14:43-52 | 22:47-53 | 18:1-11 |
| 225. Annas questions Jesus | | | | 18:12-24 |
| 226. Caiaphas questions Jesus | 26:57-68 | 14:53-65 | | |
| 227. Peter denies knowing Jesus | 26:69-75 | 14:66-72 | 22:54-65 | 18:25-27 |
| 228. The council of religious leaders condemns Jesus | 27:1-2 | 15:1 | 22:66-71 | |
| 229. Judas kills himself | 27:3-10 | | | |
| 230. Jesus stands trial before Pilate | 27:11-14 | 15:2-5 | 23:1-5 | 18:28-38 |
| 231. Jesus stands trial before Herod | | | 23:6-12 | |
| 232. Pilate hands Jesus over to be crucified | 27:15-26 | 15:6-15 | 23:13-25 | 18:39-19:16 |
| 233. Roman soldiers mock Jesus | 27:27-31 | 15:16-20 | | |
| 234. Jesus is led away to be crucified | 27:32-34 | 15:21-24 | 23:26-31 | 19:17 |
| 235. Jesus is placed on the cross | 27:35-44 | 15:25-32 | 23:32-43 | 19:18-27 |

| | | MATTHEW | MARK | LUKE | JOHN |
|---|---|---|---|---|---|
| 236. | Jesus dies on the cross | 27:45-56 | 15:33-41 | 23:44-49 | 19:28-37 |
| 237. | Jesus is laid in the tomb | 27:57-61 | 15:42-47 | 23:50-56 | 19:38-42 |
| 238. | Guards are posted at the tomb | 27:62-66 | | | |
| 239. | Jesus rises from the dead | 28:1-7 | 16:1-8 | 24:1-12 | 20:1-9 |
| 240. | Jesus appears to Mary Magdalene | | 16:9-11 | | 20:10-18 |
| 241. | Jesus appears to the women | 28:8-10 | | | |
| 242. | Religious leaders bribe the guards | 28:11-15 | | | |
| 243. | Jesus appears to two believers traveling on the road | | 16:12-13 | 24:13-35 | |
| 244. | Jesus appears to the disciples behind locked doors | | | 24:36-43 | 20:19-23 |
| 245. | Jesus appears to the disciples, including Thomas | | 16:14 | | 20:24-31 |
| 246. | Jesus appears to the disciples while fishing | | | | 21:1-14 |
| 247. | Jesus talks with Peter | | | | 21:15-25 |
| 248. | Jesus gives the great commission | 28:16-20 | 16:15-18 | | |
| 249. | Jesus appears to the disciples in Jerusalem | | | 24:44-49 | |
| 250. | Jesus ascends into heaven | | 16:19-20 | 24:50-53 | |